Beginning
C# 2005 Databases

Beginning
C# 2005 Databases

Karli Watson

WILEY

Wiley Publishing, Inc.

Beginning C# 2005 Databases

Published by
Wiley Publishing, Inc.
10475 Crosspoint Boulevard
Indianapolis, IN 46256
www.wiley.com

Copyright © 2006 by Wiley Publishing, Inc., Indianapolis, Indiana

Published simultaneously in Canada

ISBN-13: 978-0-470-04406-3
ISBN-10: 0-470-04406-3

Manufactured in the United States of America

10 9 8 7 6 5 4 3 2 1

Library of Congress Cataloging-in-Publication Data:

for donna

About the Author

Karli Watson is a freelance writer, developer, and editor and also the technical director of 3form Ltd. (www.3form.net). He started out with the intention of becoming a world-famous nanotechnologist, so perhaps one day you might recognize his name as he receives a Nobel Prize. For now, however, Karli's main academic interest is the .NET Framework and all the boxes of tricks it contains. Karli is also a snowboarding enthusiast, loves cooking, spends far too much time playing Anarchy Online, and wishes he had a cat. As yet, nobody has seen fit to publish Karli's first novel, but the rejection letters make an attractive pile. If he ever puts anything up there, you can visit Karli online at www.karliwatson.com.

Credits

Acquisitions Editor
Katie Mohr

Development Editor
Maryann Steinhart

Technical Editor
Todd Meister

Additional Material
Donna Watson

Production Editor
Angela Smith

Copy Editor
Nancy Rapoport

Editorial Manager
Mary Beth Wakefield

Production Manager
Tim Tate

Vice President and Executive Group Publisher
Richard Swadley

Vice President and Executive Publisher
Joseph B. Wikert

Compositor
Maureen Forys, Happenstance Type-o-Rama

Proofreading
James Brook
Jennifer Larsen
Word One

Indexing
Johnna VanHoose Dinse

Acknowledgments

Thanks to all at Wiley for helping me through this project and reining in my strange British stylings, to 3form for giving me the time to write, to donna for keeping me sane, Funcom for providing a much-needed retreat, and to friends and family for being patient with my deadline-laden lifestyle.

Contents

Contents

Contents

Contents

Introduction

Welcome to *Beginning C# 2005 Databases*! In this book you learn everything you need to know about developing C# applications that access databases. If you are wondering why this is such an important topic, just consider how many applications use the functionality. At first glance, you might notice a few specialized ones such as Windows applications to view and edit human resources data or Web applications that display recent sport results. Look a bit deeper, however, and you quickly find that the vast majority of applications use database data in one form or another, even if it isn't immediately obvious. Because you can store pretty much anything in a database, from simple program settings or tables of related data, through to Web site content, the possibilities are endless. Of course, you might use an alternative method for storing data, such as text files, but in almost all cases you get better performance and more robust applications from a database.

This book is the perfect starting point to learn about databases, and particularly about using Microsoft SQL Server from .NET 2.0 applications written in C#. Over the course of the book, you learn the fundamentals of database technology, how the .NET Framework can be used to access databases, and how to get the most out of your code. Along the way you are presented with numerous helpful, easy-to-follow examples that demonstrate the techniques you need. Each example increases your understanding of a particular subject, and often provides you with tips and tricks that you can adapt to different contexts in the future. Each chapter also includes exercises to reinforce key concepts, the answers to which are found at the back of the book. Taken as a whole, there is enough example code for you to see how to perform a multitude of tasks — from the most simple such as reading data from a database table, to the more advanced such as writing managed code to run inside SQL Server.

The main idea behind the book is to present you with a solid understanding of the basics of database access in C#. You'll also be exposed to many possibilities for future development. You will often learn about quite complicated techniques, but they are broken into simple steps and carefully explained. These explanations provide an appreciation for what is possible, and prepare you for handling additional resources about these subjects when you've finished the book. And you'll be able to do that without facing instant despair at attempting to learn about a completely new subject because you'll already know the basics of what you are doing.

Whom This Book Is For

This book is aimed at people who already have at least a basic understanding of .NET development with C# and who want to learn about databases and database access. The C# code used in the examples in this book is described in detail only in cases where it is quite advanced, or where it's an area you might not have looked at before. However, no experience with databases is assumed, so the database code you write (using ADO.NET) is explained from first principles. Databases themselves are explained, as well as the SQL language used to access them. This book is perfect for you if the word "database" is one that you've heard only in passing.

This book is also appropriate for those who know the basics of database access and already have experience using SQL and/or ADO.NET. After looking at the basics, you progress to some relatively advanced programming techniques, so it's likely that somewhere in this book there's a topic or two that you haven't already learned about. It's possible that you may require the first few chapters only as a refresher — if at all — but that isn't a problem, and should you find out that you're not quite as comfortable with the fundamentals as you thought you were, you have the earlier chapters available as reference material.

Also, you don't have to be an employee of a wealthy company or someone who can afford the latest development tools to get the most out of this book. All of the tools used here are available for free, including the Microsoft Express developer applications. All you need is a relatively up-to-date computer and an Internet connection and you can get everything you need. This book is as useful to students as to full-time developers.

What Does This Book Cover?

This book is divided into four main parts as described in the following sections.

The Fundamentals

Chapters 1 and 2 cover the fundamentals — everything you need to be aware of before you start. In Chapter 1 you learn exactly what the definition of a database is, the types of database that are available, and the features that databases provide. Finally, you see how to access databases using the SQL language, and take a look at how XML fits into the picture.

In Chapter 2 you move on to learn about ADO.NET, and how it can used to access databases from C# applications. You'll also see the Express tools that you'll be using in this book, and try out a few basic examples to prepare you for what is to come. This chapter also introduces the sample database used in this book, `FolktaleDB`.

Visual Database Access and Data Binding

Chapters 3–5 provide a look at data-binding techniques you can use to present and modify data in Windows and Web applications. Using data binding, you can get excellent results while writing little or no additional code — instead, you use visual tools and declarative techniques to get the behavior you want. The first two chapters concentrate on Windows applications, starting with a look at reading database data in Chapter 3 and moving on to database modifications in Chapter 4.

Chapter 5 takes what you have learned about database access with ADO.NET and applies it to Web applications. You'll see that the details are a little different — particularly with the user interface of Web applications — but that much of what you've learned is, with minor modifications, just as applicable to Web applications.

Programmatic Database Access

In Chapters 6–8, you start to look at things in a little more depth. You will already know that data binding is fantastic, but that it doesn't necessarily cater to everything you might want to do. Sometimes the only option you have is to write database access code with ADO.NET by hand. In Chapter 6 you see how to do this, learn about what is possible, and discover how to prevent common problems.

In Chapter 7 you explore views and stored procedures in databases and see how you can use them to simplify the code you need to write in client applications. By performing some of your data manipulation in SQL Server, you won't have to do it in C# code. However, there are additional things to consider when you're working with views and stored procedures, and some tasks require a little more care to implement correctly. You are provided with plenty of hands-on examples, as well as information about avoiding trouble.

Chapter 8 looks at writing code to fit into n-tier design principles, particularly how you can abstract data into custom object families. That gives you greater flexibility in dealing with data, and you will see that even when you do this, you can still make use of data binding to create database applications quickly and easily. You'll also learn how putting a bit more work in at the design phase of application development can make your life a lot easier, especially if you work as part of a development team.

Advanced Topics

Chapters 9–11 look at some advanced topics to help you streamline your applications and perform more complex tasks. You also see how to elude some pitfalls. Chapter 9 examines transactions and concurrency, which are critical in multi-user applications because difficulties can arise when more than one person accesses your data simultaneously. You learn how to deal with these situations both by detecting problems as they arise, and by ensuring that users of your applications are informed about what's happening and are permitted to take appropriate action.

In Chapter 10 you look at the more advanced world of distributed application design, focusing on remote database access across the Internet. You see how to provide Web Services to give you access to remote data, and how database data can be cached to avoid having too much traffic between Web servers and database servers.

Finally, in Chapter 11 you'll look at a topic that's new to .NET 2.0 and SQL Server 2005: writing managed code in C# that you can load into and execute inside SQL Server. This enables you to create functions, stored procedures, and more without resorting to SQL code. You'll learn how this can give you great benefits both in ease of development and advanced functionality.

Appendixes

There are three appendixes in this book. Appendix A details the installation procedure required for the .NET Framework and Express tools used in this book. Appendix B explains how to install the sample database provided for this book. Appendix C provides the answers for the exercises that are given at the end of each chapter.

What You Need to Use This Book

You need the following products to use this book:

- ❑   Microsoft .NET Framework 2.0
- ❑   Microsoft Visual C# 2005 Express Edition
- ❑   Microsoft SQL Server 2005 Express Edition

❑ Microsoft SQL Server Management Studio Express

❑ Microsoft Visual Web Developer 2005 Express Edition

You can find instructions for downloading and installing these products in Appendix A.

Conventions

To help you get the most from the text, a number of conventions are used throughout the book.

Asides to the current discussion are offset and placed in italics like this.

> **Information of importance outside of the regular text looks like this.**

As for styles used in the text:

❑ Important words are *highlighted* when introduced.

❑ Keyboard combination strokes are presented like this: Ctrl+A.

❑ Filenames, URLs, and code within the text appear in a special monofont typeface, like this: `System.capabilities`.

Code blocks and examples appear in two different ways:

```
In code examples, new code has a gray background.
The gray background is not used for code that is less important in the present
context or that has been shown before.
```

And in some instances, parts of a code example may be boldface to make it easier for you to spot a change from earlier code.

Occasionally a code line won't fit on one line in the book. In those instances, a code continuation character (↵) at the end of a line indicates that the next line is actually a continuation of it.

In text, things you should type into your computer are often shown in bold: Enter the password **M3s8halL**.

Source Code

As you work through the examples in this book, you may choose either to type in all the code manually, or use the source code files that accompany this book. All of the source code used in this book is available for download at `www.wrox.com`. Once at the site, simply locate the book's title (either by using the Search box or by using one of the title lists) and click the Download Code link on the book's detail page to obtain all the source code for the book.

Because many books have similar titles, you may find it easiest to search by ISBN; for this book, the ISBN is 0-470-04406-3.

After you download the code, just decompress it with your favorite decompression tool.

Errata

Every effort is made to ensure that there are no errors in the text or in the code. However, no one is perfect and mistakes do occur. If you find an error in one of our books, like a spelling mistake or a faulty piece of code, we would be very grateful for your feedback. By sending in errata you may save another reader hours of frustration; at the same time, you are helping us provide higher quality information.

To find the errata page for this book, go to www.wrox.com, and locate the title using the Search box or one of the title lists. Then, on the Book Search Results page, click the Errata link in the About This Book bar. On this page, you can view all errata that has been submitted for this book and posted by Wrox editors. If you don't spot "your" error on the book's Errata page, click the Errata Form link and complete the form there to send us the error you have found. We'll check the information and, if appropriate, post a message to the book's errata page and fix the problem in subsequent editions of the book.

Database Fundamentals

Before you start to look at accessing databases from C# code, there are a few basics that you need to know. It is necessary to have a formal definition of what is meant by the term database, and that's the first thing you examine in this chapter. Once you have this definition, you look in more depth at the features that databases (and, more specifically, database management systems) offer, and see the difference between relational and object-oriented database management systems. Next, you investigate many of the commonly used database management systems. Finally, you are introduced to the language used to manipulate databases, Structured Query Language (SQL). Along the way you learn the terminology used by databases, see how databases may be represented graphically, and get your first look at the database management system used in this book — SQL Server 2005 Express Edition.

If you've had any previous experience with databases, you may find that you are already familiar with much of the material in this chapter. However, this information has been included so you can avoid any ambiguities and common misconceptions that might cause problems later. Whatever your level of experience, it is well worth recapping the basics to ensure a strong foundation of knowledge for later chapters, and this chapter will also serve as a reference for you later on. Remember, get a firm grasp of the basics and the rest will come easily.

In this chapter, you learn:

- ❏ What databases are
- ❏ The terminology used for databases
- ❏ The features are offered by database management systems
- ❏ What database management systems are available
- ❏ How to manipulate data in a database

What Is a Database?

It's fair to say that most computing applications make use of data in one form or another, whether in an obvious way or with more subtlety. In most cases this data is *persistent*, which means that it is stored externally to the application and doesn't disappear when the application isn't running. For example, the following applications obviously store and manipulate data, in small or large quantities:

❑ An application used by a shop to keep records of products, sales, and stock

❑ An application used to access human resources information in a large enterprise

❑ A web page that allows the retrieval of historical currency conversion rates

It is a little less obvious whether the following applications use stored data, but it is likely that they do:

❑ Any web page you care to examine — many store some if not all the information they display in external locations.

❑ Web pages that don't display stored data, but that track user activity.

❑ Online games with persistent worlds where player and character information is stored in a centralized online location.

Of course, it's also difficult to say exactly how these applications store their data. It is possible that the software developers store data in text files on a hard disk somewhere, in computer RAM, or even on stone tablets that are manually transcribed to a computer terminal when requested by a user. It is far more likely, however, that they store data in a database.

The *Oxford English Dictionary* defines the word "database" as follows:

> *1. A structured collection of data held in computer storage; esp. one that incorporates software to make it accessible in a variety of ways; transf., any large collection of information.*

This definition alone goes some way to describing why a database is better than, for example, storing text files. A key word here is *structured*. Simply storing large amounts of data in an unstructured way, such as text files, is usually referred to as *flat-file storage*. This has many disadvantages, including the problem of compatibility when proprietary storage formats are used, the inability to locate specific information stored somewhere in the middle of the data, and the general lack of speed in reading, editing, and retrieving information.

Databases provide a standardized way to store information, and do so in a manner that promotes extremely fast access by hundreds, even thousands, of users, often simultaneously.

A phone book, for example, contains the names of individuals (or organizations), phone numbers, and possibly addresses. Flat-file storage might involve no ordering whatsoever — perhaps a bucket containing each name/phone number/address combination on a separate piece of paper (which would make retrieval of any specific one an interesting challenge at best). More likely, there would be some organization, typically by the first letter of people's last names, which is a step up from a bucket of data, but still lacking finesse. This data might make up the basis of a flat-file storage format (each record in order, encoded in some machine-readable or human-readable way), but can more accurately be called a *directory*. Directories are data stores that are organized in a way to optimize data retrieval in one specific mode of use. In this example it is easy to find the phone number of someone as long as you have his name, but the inverse scenario does not apply. If you have a phone number and want to know to whom it belongs, you won't find a phone book particularly useful. While it is technically possible, it's not something you'd want to do unless you have a lot of time on your hands. And it would be a lot easier to simply dial the number and ask to whom you were speaking. Even in flat-file storage, searching for a specific entry still means starting at the beginning and working your way through to the end in some systematic (and arbitrary) way.

Databases store data in a highly structured way, enabling multiple modes of retrieval and editing. With phone book data in a database, any of a number of tasks would be possible in a relatively simple way, including the following:

❑ Retrieve a list of phone numbers for people whose first name starts with the letters "Jo."

❑ Find all the people whose phone numbers contain numbers whose sum is less than 40.

❑ Find all the people whose address contains the phrase "Primrose" and who are listed with full names rather than initials.

Some of these operations might require a little more effort to set up than others, but they can all be done. In most cases they can be achieved by querying the database in certain ways, which means asking for the data in the right way, rather than manipulating data after it has been obtained using, say, C#.

Structure and efficiency aren't the only benefits offered by a database. With a centralized, persistent data store you have many more options, including simple data backup, mirroring data in multiple locations, and exposing data to remote applications via the Internet. You look at these and other possibilities later in this chapter.

Before I continue, one thing must be made abundantly clear from the outset. The word "database" does not — repeat, not — refer to the *application* that stores data. SQL Server, for example, is not a database. SQL Server is a database management system (DBMS). A DBMS is responsible for storing databases, and also contains all the tools necessary to access those databases. A good DBMS shields all of the technical details from you so that it doesn't matter at all where the data is actually stored. Instead, you just need to interact with whatever interfaces the DBMS supplies to manipulate the data. This might be through DBMS-supplied management tools, or programmatically using an application program interface (API) with C# or another programming language.

In fact, there are different types of DBMS to consider. The two most important and well known are:

❑ Relational database management systems (RDBMSes)

❑ Object-oriented database management systems (OODBMSes)

In the next sections you explore the differences between these types and the key features of both.

Relational Database Management Systems

Relational database management systems (RDBMSes) are what you would typically think of as a DBMS, and these are the most commonly found and often used systems. SQL Server, for example, is an RDBMS. Two things are essential for an RDBMS:

❑ Separate tables containing data

❑ Relationships between tables

The following sections examine tables; relationships; an important property of relational databases that emerges from these constraints — normalization; and one of the underlying mechanisms by which all this is achieved: keys.

Tables

Characteristically, an RDBMS splits the data stored in a database into multiple locations, each of which contains a specific set of data. These locations are called *tables*. A table contains multiple *rows*, each of which is defined in multiple *columns* (also known as *records* and *fields*).

Phone book data, for example, could be stored in a single table, where each row is a single entry containing columns for name, phone number, and address. Tables are defined such that every row they contain includes exactly the same columns — you can't include additional columns for a given row just because you feel like it. Columns are also assigned specific data types to restrict the data that they can contain. In this example all the data types are strings, although more space might be allocated to address fields because addresses typically consist of more data than names. You might decide to include an additional Boolean column in a phone book table, however, which would say whether the record was an individual or an organization. Other tables might include numeric columns, columns for binary data such as images or audio data, and so on. In addition, a table can specify whether individual columns must contain data, or whether they can contain null values (that is, not contain values).

Each table in a database has a name to describe what it contains. There are many conventions used for naming tables, but the one used in this book is to use singular names, so for a phone book table you'd use `PhoneBookEntry` for the name rather than `PhoneBookEntries`.

The name and structure of tables within a database, along with the specification of other objects that databases may contain and the relationships between these objects, are known as the *schema* of the database.

> *The word "object" is used here with caution — but correctly. Relational databases can contain many types of objects (including tables), as you will see throughout this book, but that doesn't make them object-oriented. This distinction will be made clearer in the section on OODBMSes shortly.*

Figure 1-1 shows the supposed `PhoneBookEntry` table graphically, by listing column names and data types, and whether null values are permitted.

PhoneBookEntry		
Column Name	Data Type	Allow Nulls
EntryName	varchar(250)	☐
PhoneNumber	varchar(50)	☐
Address	text	☐
IsIndividual	bit	☐
		☐

Figure 1-1: The PhoneBookEntry table

The diagram for the `PhoneBookEntry` table shows data types as used in SQL Server, where some data types also include lengths. Here, the `EntryName` field is a string of up to 250 characters, `PhoneNumber` is a string of up to 50 characters, `Address` is a string with no defined maximum size, and `IsIndividual` is a `bit` (0 or 1), which is the SQL Server type used for Boolean data.

Keys

Within database tables it is often important to uniquely identify rows, especially when defining relationships. The position of a row isn't enough here, because rows may be inserted or deleted, so any row's position might change. The order of rows is also an ambiguous concept because rows may be ordered by one or more columns in a way that varies depending on how you are using the data in the table — this is not a fixed definition. Also, the data in a single column of a table may not be enough to uniquely identify a row. At first glance, you might think that the EntryName column in the PhoneBookEntry table example could uniquely identify a row, but there is no guarantee that the values in this column will be unique. I'm sure there are plenty of Karli Watsons out there, but only one of them is writing this book. Similarly, PhoneNumber may not be unique because people in families or student housing often share one phone. And a combination of these fields is no good, either. While it is probably quite unlikely that two people with the same name share a phone, it is certainly not unheard of.

Without being able to identify a row by either its contents or its position, you are left with only one option — to add an additional column of data. By guaranteeing that every row includes a unique value in this column, you'll always be able to find a particular row when you need to. The row that you would add here is called a *primary key*, and is often referred to as the PK or ID of the row. Again, naming conventions vary, but in this book all primary keys end with the suffix Id.

Graphically, the primary key of a table is shown with a key symbol. Figure 1-2 shows a modified version of PhoneBookEntry containing a primary key.

PhoneBookEntry		
Column Name	Data Type	Allow Nulls
PhoneBookEntryId	uniqueidentifier	☐
EntryName	varchar(250)	☐
PhoneNumber	varchar(50)	☐
Address	text	☐
IsIndividual	bit	☐
		☐

Figure 1-2: The PhoneBookEntry table with a primary key

The data type used here is uniqueidentifier, which is in fact a GUID (Globally Unique IDentifier). It is not mandatory to use this data type, but it is a good thing to use. There are many reasons for this, including the fact that GUIDs are guaranteed to be unique (in all normal circumstances). Other typically seen types for primary keys include integer values and strings.

It is not always absolutely necessary to define a new column for primary key data. Sometimes the table contains a column that is unique by definition — a person's Social Security number for example. In some situations, combining two columns will give a unique value, in which case it is possible to use them to define a compound primary key. One example of this would be the combination of postal code and house number in a table of U.K. addresses. However, it is good practice to add a separate primary key anyway, and in this book most tables use uniqueidentifier primary keys.

Relationships

RDBMSes are capable of defining relationships between tables, whereby records in one table are associated (linked) with records in other tables. When storing large quantities of data, this relational aspect is both important and extremely useful. For example, in a sales database you might want to record both the products on sale and the orders placed for products. You can envisage a single table containing all this information, but it is far easier to use multiple tables — one for products, and one for orders. Each row in the orders table would be associated with one or more rows in the products table. An RDBMS would then allow you to retrieve data in a way that takes this relationship into account — for example, using the query "Fetch all the products that are associated with this order."

Relationships between items in different tables can take the following forms:

❑ One-to-one relationship: One row in one table is associated with a row in a separate table, which in turn is associated with the first row. In practice, this relationship is rare because if a one-to-one relationship is identified, it usually means that the data can be combined into a single table.

❑ One-to-many and many-to-one relationships: One row in one table is associated with multiple rows in a separate table. For example, if a list of products were divided into categories (where each product was associated with a single category), then there would be a one-to-many relationship between categories and products. Looking from the other direction, the relationship between products and categories is *many-to-one*. In practice, one-to-many and many-to-one relationships are the same thing, depending on which end of the relationship you are looking at.

❑ Many-to-many relationship: Rows in one table are freely associated with rows in another table. This is the relationship you have in the products and orders example because an order can contain multiple products, and products can be part of multiple orders.

When considering relationships, the importance of keys is immediately obvious. Without being able to uniquely identify rows it would be impossible to define a meaningful relationship. This is because associating a row in one table with a row in another table might actually associate other rows with each other by implication.

One-to-many relationships are implemented by including a foreign key field in the table at the many end of the relationship. For example, to link products with categories you add a field to the product table that acts as a foreign key to link product rows with category rows. The value of a foreign key in a row in one table typically matches the value of a primary key in another table — in fact, the columns used for primary and foreign keys are often given the same name.

The implementation of many-to-many relationships typically involves using a third, linking table. In the products/orders example, a single row in the product table may be associated with multiple records in the linking table, each of which is associated with a single order. Conversely, each row in the order table may be associated with multiple rows in the linking table, each of which is associated with a single row in the product table. In this situation, the linking table must contain two foreign keys, one for each of the tables it is linking together. Unless required for other reasons, such as when the linking table contains additional columns relating to the linkage, or represents real data in its own right, there is often no need for you to include a primary key in the linking table.

Figure 1-3 shows four tables illustrating these relationships. Depending on how you look at it, this diagram shows three one-to-many relationships (ProductCategory to Product, Product to OrderProduct, and Order to OrderProduct), or one one-to-many relationship and one many-to-many relationship (Product to Order). To simplify things, the tables don't show column data types or whether columns are nullable.

Figure 1-3: The PhoneBookEntry table with a primary key

Showing one-to-many links as a line with a key at one end and linked circles at the other (the "infinity" symbol) is just one way to display this information. You may also see lines with a 1 at one end and an ellipsis at the other. In this book, however, you'll see the format shown here throughout.

In this scheme it is typically a good idea to include a further column in the `OrderProduct` table — `Quantity`. This enables a product that appeared multiple times in a single order to be represented using a single row in `OrderProduct`, rather than several, where the number of rows would be the quantity. Without the `Quantity` column, things could quickly get out of hand for large orders!

One last thing to note here is the concept of referential integrity. Because these relationships are defined as part of the database schema, the DBMS is capable of enforcing them. This means, for example, that you can choose for the DBMS to prevent the deletion of a row that is referred to by another row. Alternatively, you could choose to have the DBMS delete any referenced rows when a row is deleted (known as a *cascaded delete*).

Normalization

Normalization is a fairly advanced topic, but one you need to be aware of from the outset. It refers to the process of ensuring that little or no data in a database is duplicated. Another way of looking at this is that it is the process of organizing the structure of data and data tables so that the most efficient method of storage is used. What happens, for example, when a single customer places more than one order? With just an order table you'd end up in a situation where customer details were duplicated because they'd need to be included in each and every order made by the customer. It would be far better to add an additional table for customers, which could be linked to multiple orders.

To extend the example: how about customers with multiple addresses? This might happen if a customer wants to send an item directly to a friend. Here, a further table containing addresses is required. But hold on — if an order is associated with a customer, and a customer has multiple addresses, how do you tell which address the order is supposed to be sent to? Clearly, even simple databases can become much more complicated quickly — and often there are multiple solutions to problems. The subject of database organization and normalization is one that you will return to many times in later chapters.

In some circumstances *redundancy*, that is, the duplication of information, can be beneficial. This is particularly true when speed is crucial because there is an overhead associated with finding a row in one table based on a foreign key in another. This may be negligible, but in large-scale, ultra-high performance applications, it can become an issue.

Object Oriented Database Management Systems

There are some situations where the integration between applications and databases must be far stronger than is possible when using RDBMSes, again mostly in high-performance applications. One approach that's been quite successful is for databases to store objects directly so that OOP applications can store and retrieve objects directly, without resorting to serialization techniques.

Because object oriented database management systems (OODBMSes) store objects directly, it is possible to manipulate data via the methods and properties of databases, and to associate objects with each other via pointers rather than the sort of relationships discussed earlier. This leads to a more navigational style of data access — getting one object can lead you to another, then another, and so on using these pointers.

Another feature of OODBMSes is that they can make use of polymorphism in much the same way as OOP programming languages — some object types inherit characteristics from a single base object type. However, other OOP features, such as encapsulation, do not mesh particularly well with the traditional view of databases, so many people dismiss OODBMSes out of hand. Nevertheless, these DBMSes have found a place in, for example, scientific areas such as high-energy physics and molecular biology.

Owing to the niche usage of these systems, and the fact that they are few and far between as well as being highly specialized, they aren't covered further in this book.

Additional Features of RDBMSes

As mentioned earlier, RDBMSes offer a lot more than the storage of data in related tables. In particular, you can rely on most to provide:

❑   Joins

❑   Functions

❑   Views

❑   Stored procedures

❑   Triggers

❑   E-mail

❑   Indexes

❑   Security

❑   Concurrency control

❑   Transactions

❑   Remote access

❑   Backups

❑   Mirroring and partitioning

❑   Management tools

In this section you look at each of these, getting a flavor for them but without going into too much depth at this stage.

Joins

In the earlier relationship discussion, it may have seemed like accessing related data from multiple tables might involve a convoluted procedure. In actual fact — luckily for us — that isn't the case. It is possible to fetch data from multiple tables simultaneously, and end up with a single set of results. The mechanism for doing this involves *joins*, of which there are several types. A join is a way to specify a relationship between two tables to obtain related data from both. A join between a product table and a category table, for example, enables you to obtain all the products belonging to a single category in one operation. This is something that you'll see in action after you've learned a bit more about the language used to execute database queries — Structured Query Language (SQL).

Functions

Any good DBMS supplies you with an extensive set of functions to use to view and manipulate data. You are likely to find mathematical functions, conversion functions, string manipulation functions, date and time manipulation functions, and so on. These enable you to perform much of your data processing inside the DBMS, reducing the amount of data that needs to be transferred to and from your applications, and improving efficiency.

DBMS functions can take several forms. There are scalar functions that return single values, table valued functions that can return multiple rows of data, and aggregate functions that work with entire data sets rather than individual values. Aggregate functions include those with capabilities to obtain the maximum value in a given column of a table, perform statistical analysis, and so on.

Another type of function that you will probably find yourself using at some point is the user-defined function. As its name suggests, you can create your own function to perform whatever task you like. User-defined functions may be scalar, table valued, or aggregate.

There is one more important feature of functions as used in SQL Server 2005 — it is possible to write them in C# code that runs (managed) inside the database. This is something you'll see in action later in this book.

Views

There are some database operations that you might want to repeat often within your applications, such as those involving joins, as detailed earlier. Rather than forcing the DBMS to combine data from multiple sources, often transforming the data along the way, it is possible to store a *view* of the data in the DBMS. A view is a stored query that obtains data from one or more tables in the database. For example, a view might be a query that obtains a list of products that include all product columns and the name of the category in an additional column. The client applications don't have to make more complicated queries involving joins to obtain this information, because it is already combined in the view. The view looks and behaves identically to a table in every way except that it doesn't actually *contain* any data; instead, it provides an indirect way to access data stored elsewhere in the database.

Apart from the obvious advantage of a view — that querying the underlying data is simplified for client applications — there is another important point to note. By telling the DBMS how the data is to be used in this way, the DBMS is capable of optimizing things further for you. It might, for example, cache view data so that retrieving its compound information becomes much faster than querying individual tables might be.

In addition, views can be defined in some quite complicated ways using functions, including user-defined functions, such that your applications can retrieve highly processed data with ease.

Stored Procedures

Stored procedures (often called *sprocs*) are an extremely important part of database programming — despite the fact that you could use a fully functioning database without ever using a sproc. Stored procedures enable you to write code that runs inside the database, capable of advanced manipulation and statistical analysis of data. Perhaps more important, their operation is optimized by the DBMS, meaning they can complete their tasks quickly. In addition, long-running stored procedures can carry on unattended inside the database while your applications are doing other things. You can even schedule them to run at regular intervals in some DBMSes.

Stored procedures don't do anything that you couldn't do by other means — for example, in C# code. However, for some operations that work with large quantities of data, it might mean transferring the data into application memory and then processing it to get a result. With stored procedures the data never has to leave the database, and only the result needs transferring to your application. With remote databases this can provide a significant performance boost.

Some DBMSes — such as SQL Server — provide you with a rich set of operations that you can use when programming stored procedures. These include cursors that you can position within sets of data to process rows sequentially, branching and looping logic, variables, and parameters. And as with functions, SQL Server lets you write stored procedures in managed C# code.

Triggers

A trigger is a specialized form of stored procedure that is executed automatically by the DBMS when certain events happen, rather than being called manually by client applications. In practice, this means defining an event that will occur at some later date ("when a new row is added to table X," for example), and then telling the DBMS to execute a certain stored procedure when that event occurs.

Triggers aren't as commonly used as some other features of DBMSes, but when they are, it's because they are the only solution to a problem, so it's good to have them. They are typically used to log or audit database access.

E-mail

Some DBMSes are capable of sending e-mails independently of other applications. This can be useful, especially when combined with triggers. It enables you to keep tabs on data in a database, as well as permitting more advanced scenarios. When orders are placed, for example, you could generate and send e-mails to customers directly from the DBMS with no external coding required. The only limitation here is that a mail server such as a simple mail transfer protocol (SMTP) server is likely to be required.

Indexes

Indexes are another way of optimizing performance by letting the DBMS know how you intend to make use of data. An index is an internally maintained table in the database that enables quick access to a row (or rows) containing specific data, such as a particular column value, a column value that contains a certain word, and so on. The exact implementation of an index is specific to the DBMS you are using so you can't make any assumptions about exactly how they are stored or how they work. However, you don't need to understand how an index is implemented to use it.

Conceptually you can think of an index as a look-up table, where you find rows in the index with a specific piece of data in one column, and the index then tells you the rows in the indexed table that match that data. To return to the phone book example, an index could be used to search for records via the phone number column instead of the name column. You would need to tell the DBMS to create an index for values in the phone number column because, by default, no indexes are created for a table other than for primary key values. By building an index based on the phone number column, the DBMS can use a much faster searching algorithm to locate rows — it no longer has to look at the phone number column of every row in the address book; instead it looks in the index (which has, effectively, already looked at every row in the address book) and finds the relevant rows.

The only downside to using indexes is that they need to be stored, so the database size increases. Indexes also need to be periodically refreshed as data in the table they are indexing changes.

The creation of indexes can be a bit of an art form. In many DBMSes it is possible to tailor indexes to closely match the queries with which they will be dealing. For example, looking for strings that end with a certain substring works well with an index built around the last 100 characters of a text column, but might not even be possible in an index built on the first 100 characters of the same column.

One commonly used type of index is the full-text index. It's useful when large quantities of text are stored in columns because the index examines the text in-depth and stores its results. This enables you to perform searches within text data much faster than would otherwise be possible because you only have to look at a word in the index rather than looking through all the text in all the columns of the original data. However, full-text indexes can require large amounts of storage.

Security

Security means a couple of things when talking about databases. For a start, it means not letting other people get access to your data. For most professional DBMSes, this isn't something you have to worry about too much. If your DBMS costs lots of money (and it probably does), you get what you pay for, and your data is secure.

The other aspect of security in databases is authorizing different users to perform different tasks. In some cases, such as in SQL Server 2005, you can approach this in a granular way. You can, for example, assign a user the rights to view data in one table but not to edit that data. You can also restrict access to individual stored procedures and control access to all manner of more esoteric functionality. Users can also be authorized to perform tasks at the DBMS level if required — such as being able to create new databases or manage existing databases.

Most DBMSes also enable you to integrate with existing forms of authentication, such as Windows account authentication. This allows for single-login applications, where users log on to a network with their usual account details, and this login is then forwarded on to the database by any applications that are used. An advantage here is that at no point does the application need to be aware of the security details entered by the user — it simply forwards them on from its context.

Alternatively, you can use DBMS-specific forms of authentication, which typically involve passing a username and password combination to the DBMS over a secure connection.

Concurrency Control

With multiple users accessing the same database at the same time, situations can arrive where the data being used by one user is out of date, or where two users attempt to edit data simultaneously. Many DBMSes include methods to deal with these circumstances, although they can be somewhat tricky to implement.

In general, there are three approaches to concurrency control that you can use, which you'll look at shortly. To understand them, you must consider an update to be an operation that involves three steps:

1. User reads the data from a row.
2. User decides what changes to make to the row data.
3. User makes changes to the row.

In all cases sequential edits are fine: that is, where one user performs steps 1–3, then another user performs steps 1–3, and so on. Problems arise when more that one user performs steps 1 and 2 based on the original state of the row, and then one user performs step 3.

The three approaches to concurrency control are as follows:

❑ **"Last in wins":** Rows (records) are unavailable only while changes are actually being made to them (during step 3). Attempts to read row data during that time (which is very short) are delayed until the row data is written. If two users make changes to a row, the last edit made applies, and earlier changes are overwritten. The important thing here is that both users might have read the data for the row (steps 1 and 2) before either of them makes a change, so the user making the second change is not aware that the row data has already been altered before making his change.

❑ **Optimistic concurrency control:** As with "last in wins," rows are unavailable only while they are being updated. However, with optimistic concurrency control, changes to row data that occur after a user reads the row (step 1) are detected. If a user attempts to update a row that has been updated since he read its data, his update will fail, and an error may occur, depending on the implementation of this scheme. If that happens, you can either discard your changes or read the new value of the row and make changes to that before committing the second change. Effectively, this could be called "first in wins."

❑ **Pessimistic concurrency control:** Rows are locked from the moment they are retrieved until the moment they are updated, that is, through steps 1–3. This may adversely affect performance, because while one user is editing a row, no other users can read data from it, but the protection of data is guaranteed. This scheme enforces sequential data access.

Most of the time, concurrency control is jointly handled by the DBMS and the client application. In this book, you will be using C# and ADO.NET, and data is handled in a *disconnected* way. This means that

that the DBMS is unaware of whether rows are "checked out" at any given time, which makes it impossible to implement pessimistic concurrency control. There are, however, ways in which optimistic concurrency control can be implemented, as you will see later in the book.

Transactions

It is often essential to perform multiple database operations together, in particular where it is vital that all operations succeed. In these cases, it is necessary to use a transaction, which comprises a set of operations. If any individual operation in the transaction fails, all operations in the transaction fail. In transaction terminology, the transaction is committed if, and only if, every operation succeeds. If any operations fail, the transaction is rolled back — which also means that the result of any operation that has already succeeded is rolled back.

For example, imagine you have a database with a table representing a list of bank accounts and balances. Transferring an amount from one account to another involves subtracting an amount from one account and adding it to another (with perhaps a three-day delay if you are a bank). These two operations must be part of a transaction because if one succeeds and one fails, then money is either lost or appears from nowhere. Using a transaction guarantees that the total of the money in the accounts remains unchanged.

There are four tenets of transactions that must be adhered for them to perform successfully; they can be remembered with the acronym ACID:

❑ **Atomicity:** This refers to the preceding description of a transaction: that either every operation in a transaction is committed, or none of them are.

❑ **Consistency:** The database must be in a legal state both before the transaction begins and after it completes. A legal state is one in which all the rules enforced by the database are adhered to correctly. For example, if the database is configured not to allow foreign key references to non-existent rows, then the transaction cannot result in a situation where this would be the case.

❑ **Isolation:** During the processing of a transaction, no other queries can be allowed to see the transient data. Only after the transaction is committed should the changes be visible.

❑ **Durability:** After a transaction is committed, the database should not be allowed to revert to the state it was in before the transaction started. For example, any data added should not subsequently be removed, and any data removed should not suddenly reappear.

For the most part, you are unlikely to come across a DBMS that violates these rules, so it isn't something that you need to worry about. Transaction support in the .NET Framework is also good, and this is something you'll be looking at later in the book.

Remote Access

A good DBMS allows remote access across an intranet and, if required, the Internet. Again, this is something that most databases permit, although some configuration (of both the DBMS and firewalls) may be necessary. It is not, however, always the best option, especially when communicating with a database across the Internet.

Later in the book you'll see how an intermediary (specifically, a web service) can be used to control remote access.

Backups

After the key tasks of being able to add, edit, and delete data in a database, perhaps the most important function of a DBMS is to enable you to back that data up. However good computers are, and however good the software you use, there are some things that are impossible to predict. Hardware failure happens — it's a fact of life, albeit an unpleasant one.

You may not be able to predict a hardware or software failure, but backing up your data regularly can make things easier to cope with when the inevitable happens. Today's DBMSes put a wealth of tools at your disposal for backing up data to disk, networked storage, tape drives, and other devices. Not only that, but backups can be scheduled at regular intervals, and the retrieval of backed-up data is made as simple as it can be. This isn't a subject that is discussed in this book, because it's more of a management subject — but that's not to say that it isn't important!

Mirroring and Partitioning

Mirroring and partitioning features are similar enough to merit being covered in the same section. They both involve sharing data across multiple logical and/or physical locations.

Mirroring means configuring multiple databases to hold the same information. The databases needn't be on the same DBMS, or even on the same computer. This has important implications for backing up because it means that if one computer goes down, you have a mirrored copy of the data ready to go. Of course, this isn't a replacement for backing up — after all, it's possible that both computers could fail at the same time. However, it does provide a fail-safe option for when things go wrong and can enable you to keep client applications running while you fix the problem. Another way that mirroring databases can be useful is where extremely large numbers of clients are using the data, or where a huge amount of data is routinely transferred to and from clients. Here, mirroring databases can provide load balancing by scaling out (adding additional computers) where database queries can be distributed among computers.

Partitioning is similar to mirroring in that multiple DBMS computers may be used. Partitioning is where data that would otherwise exist in a single table is distributed among various locations. The benefits of this are not immediately obvious, but they are important nonetheless. Consider a situation in which a large enterprise with offices worldwide wants to share data across locations. Some data may well be location-specific — local customers, for example. In that case the customer data could be divided between local DBMSes in such a way that the actual implementation is totally transparent. Each location is capable of accessing all the data in the customers table as and when required, but can make speedier queries for local customer data because that is stored on its own DBMS.

Management Tools

Most DBMSes come equipped with tools to use to manipulate data and databases via a graphical user interface (GUI). However, in some cases you will have to look hard to find them. Sometimes, only third-party applications are available, and many of them aren't free. Without the luxury of a GUI administration or management tool, you have to resort to command-line tools, which often means struggling with obscure commands and tricky syntax to get even the simplest things working. Of course, expert users sometimes prefer to use command-line tools, but we mere mortals generally find it much easier to point and click to perform tasks.

A good management tool does far more than let you look at and edit data in tables. It enables you to create and manage databases, configure backups, handle mirroring and partitioning, add stored procedures and views, create database diagrams, and administer security. In this book you use the free management studio tool that is available with SQL Server 2005 Express Edition, and you'll learn how to use its features as and when you need them.

What RDBMSes Are Available?

There are dozens of RDBMSes available, each with its own horde of loyal users and each with its own take on databases. In this section, you examine a few of the more commonly used ones and learn a little about their usage.

MySQL and PostgreSQL

MySQL (www.mysql.com) is an extremely popular RDBMS for web site creators — in part this is because it's an open source system, and therefore effectively free to use (although you have the option of paying for a commercial license if you want). This makes it the ideal partner to use with other open source software. It's common, for example, to see web sites implemented using a combination of the Apache web server, PHP, and MySQL.

However, as with all things free there are limitations. For a start, you'll find it a real help to be familiar with an array of command-line techniques, and you can't expect installation to be as easy as running an installer application. Also, there are a lot of things that MySQL has been able to do only recently. Up until the latest release at the time of writing (version 5.0, released October 2005) views, stored procedures, and triggers weren't supported, among other things. The current release does include these, although with slightly fewer features than in other implementations. There are also lower limits on many properties of databases — such as the length of table names and such. And, more important, for large amounts of data (100GB or more) MySQL is unlikely to be happy.

MySQL is a good RDBMS to use when learning about databases, or for the small-scale hobbyist, but if security, scalability, performance, and reliability are issues, there are far better options. One other thing to be aware of is that finding a GUI to use to administer MySQL can be a complex task. There are an awful lot around, and finding one to suit you that contains all the functionality you want to use isn't easy.

PostgreSQL (www.postgresql.org) is another open source RDBMS, but is aimed more at the professional user. It uses a slightly different licensing model, but is still available for free.

PostgreSQL has a slightly richer feature set when compared to MySQL, although with the release of MySQL 5.0 there isn't a lot of difference. There are a few relatively minor things, such as PostgreSQL being able to partition tables. Frankly, though, if data partitioning is something you want to make use of then an open source RDBMS probably isn't the best option.

However, as with MySQL, cost-free availability is definitely an advantage, and many people find that this is all they need. It is important to be aware, however, that like MySQL, PostgreSQL won't deal with large databases well.

DB2, Oracle, and SQL Server

DB2, Oracle, and SQL Server are the three RDBMS heavy-hitters of the database world. DB2 (www-306.ibm.com/software/data/db2) is made by IBM — in fact, there's a whole family of DB2 products — and SQL Server (www.microsoft.com/sql) is made by Microsoft, which gives you as much an idea of the intended audience as anything else. Oracle (www.oracle.com/database) is produced by Oracle Corporation, a multinational company that's primarily known for DBMSes. All three of these RDBMSes are aimed at large-scale organizations and are optimized for large amounts of data and users.

It's actually difficult to choose among them. Apart from the platforms that they run on (SQL Server is restricted to Windows operating systems, for instance), they all contain similar capabilities. They can all, for example, contain databases whose size extends into the terabyte range. They all include sophisticated tools for backing up and for other administration. And, perhaps most important, they all include their own proprietary features — yes, some things you can do in SQL Server, you can't do in DB2, and vice versa.

Each of these DBMSes has its devotees, so the choice among them is likely to come down to whichever you were first exposed to, what you learned how to use first, or personal recommendation. (I prefer SQL Server, but that's just me.)

The important thing is that when it comes to high-end applications requiring the best security and performance, these applications can't be beat. Well, not yet in any case.

Oh, one more thing. Each of these RDBMSes costs a *lot* of money, which is why in this book you'll be using....

SQL Server 2005 Express Edition

SQL Server 2005 Express Edition is a slimmed-down version of SQL Server 2005. It's available, for free, from Microsoft. In terms of usage, it can be difficult to tell it apart from the full version of SQL Server. This is by design. It is possible — indeed easy — to develop applications on the Express Edition and then migrate to the full version in a production environment. This is good news for a huge number of developers who might not otherwise have access to a SQL Server installation. It also makes the Express Edition a great way to learn about SQL Server.

This is not to say, of course, that there is no reason to use the full version of SQL Server 2005. The Express Edition is great for developing, and even (arguably) suitable for small web sites that don't get a lot of traffic and small applications with only a few users, but it is not nearly enough for enterprise-level applications. When it comes to an application that might have many thousands of users and terabytes of data storage, the Express Edition is simply not robust enough. For a full comparison of the features of the various editions of SQL Server 2005, see www.microsoft.com/sql/prodinfo/features/compare-features.mspx.

There are many other reasons for choosing SQL Server instead of another RDBMS, in particular with .NET applications. As has been noted several times, it is possible to write managed C# code that will run inside SQL Server 2005 — including SQL Server 2005 Express Edition. This is known as Common Language Runtime (CLR) integration. The .NET library also includes classes for natively accessing SQL Server data, rather than having to use a less streamlined intermediate standard such as Open Database Connectivity (ODBC). ODBC is a useful technology that provides a way to access RDBMSes with code that doesn't depend on the exact RDBMS you are using. However, in being standardized it suffers by not giving access to proprietary features, and it is slower because its instructions must be translated into native instructions.

In this book, you learn specifically about SQL Server 2005 data access with C#, using the Express Edition for simplicity (and because it's free to download and use). Please don't assume that this prevents you from learning to use other types of RDBMSes, however. In many cases, near identical code applies to other RDBMSes — and this is noted in the book where appropriate.

> To work through the examples in this book, you need to install SQL Server 2005 Express Edition. You can find instructions for doing this in Appendix A, along with instructions for installing the other Express products that are used in this book should you not have them installed already.

How Do You Use a Database?

Databases are designed to be data stores that are independent of other factors, such as the programming language you use to access them. With a few notable exceptions — CLR integration, for instance — you can use them from any programming language, or even directly (via web requests, for example) in some circumstances.

Early in the history of databases, moves were made to standardize database access. In more recent times a standard has emerged (and undergone numerous revisions) — Structured Query Language (SQL). The roots of this standard can be traced back to the 1970s, with the first accepted standard (SQL-86, published in 1986) having now evolved into the most recent version, SQL:2003 (published, unsurprisingly enough, in 2003). SQL is now ubiquitous, although every major RDBMS vendor still insists on including its own proprietary "flavor" of the language. Having said that, the core commands and syntax are (more or less) the same whatever RDBMS you use. Perhaps the only remaining controversy concerns how to pronounce SQL — "see-quell" or "ess-que-ell"? Personally, I prefer the former, but feel free to differ.

At its heart, SQL is a human-readable language. In fact, without having any prior knowledge of it, you'll probably find it reasonably simple to understand in its basic form. For example, consider the following SQL command:

```
SELECT PhoneNumber FROM PhoneBookEntry WHERE EntryName = 'Geoffrey Chaucer'
```

So, what do the words that make up this command suggest? Well, it doesn't take a huge amount of working out to guess that this command will retrieve the contents of a `PhoneNumber` column from a database called `PhoneBookEntry` for a row with an `EntryName` column that has a value of `Geoffrey Chaucer`. Admittedly, `SELECT` doesn't appear to be the most obvious name of a command that would do this (`GET` or `RETRIEVE` might seem more appropriate), but don't worry — you'll get used to it. Later in this section, you encounter a SQL primer that covers the basics of what the SQL language can achieve.

Luckily for those of us who don't want to type in reams of SQL code to do anything with databases, most RDBMSes come equipped with graphical tools for administration purposes. This isn't the case with SQL Server 2005 Express Edition, although you can inspect and administer it through the Visual C# 2005 Express

Edition interface. In addition, there is a free tool — Microsoft SQL Server Management Studio Express — that mimics the more advanced administration tool that ships with the full version of SQL Server 2005. The installation of this tool is shown in Appendix A. In this book you'll use both of these techniques, and in most cases you'll be writing no more SQL code than is necessary.

It is perfectly possible to write SQL statements manually in your code, although it is often the case that you don't have to. Many .NET controls are capable of generating SQL commands automatically, which certainly saves wear and tear on your fingers. Of course, this may not give you exactly the behavior you require, and more advanced tasks will require custom SQL code, so it's still worth learning how SQL works. This book covers these controls, but you will also learn when and where you will need to write SQL code yourself.

One subject that has become increasingly important in recent years is XML, which stands for eXtensible Markup Language. This is a platform-independent standard for representing data in text files, and has become extremely popular. It does have its disadvantages — it is a flat-file data format, after all — but these are outweighed by what it makes possible. If you have had any experience using .NET, you've no doubt encountered XML. The most recent DBMSes (including SQL Server 2005 Express Edition) include additional capabilities to deal with XML data, both as a means of storage and as a format with which to retrieve data — even if that data isn't encoded as XML to start with. It is important that you cover the basics of XML here because you are likely to need to know about it before too long.

The remainder of this section covers two topics:

❑   A SQL Primer: The basics of the SQL language and what you can do with it.

❑   XML: A brief overview of the XML language and further information on its relevance in the context of databases.

A SQL Primer

This section is by no means a comprehensive guide to using SQL. In fact, entire books are devoted to the subject, including one co-written by yours truly: *The Programmer's Guide to SQL* (APress, 2003. ISBN: 1590592182). But it does teach you the basics.

There is a lot of code in this section, and you may find it useful to run these commands against a database yourself to see what is happening. However, at this stage I don't recommend doing so. You'll get plenty of experience doing this later in the book, and for now it is best just to get a basic understanding of the SQL language and see what is possible. Later you may want to refer back to this section, so don't worry if you don't take it all in the first time around.

Basic SQL Terminology and Syntax

Before getting into the SQL language itself, there are a few bits of basic terminology and syntax of which you should be aware. First, a chunk of SQL code is known (interchangeably) as a *statement*, *command*, or *query*. SQL statements might span several lines, and whitespace (spaces, tabs, new line characters, and so forth) is ignored. SQL statements consist of keywords (such as SELECT) and operators (+, -, and so on) combined with literal values (string constants, numbers, and so on), table and column identifiers, and often functions. SQL keywords are case-independent, but are typically written in uppercase to distinguish them from other parts of the statement. Common statements, such as those that retrieve data, are often referred to by the first keyword in the statement, so you might hear people refer to a select statement, for example. SQL statements are often made up of several parts, which are known as clauses. SQL statements may also contain embedded (nested) statements known as subqueries.

SQL statements are executed, and may return one or more results. Multiple statements can be executed as a batch, which simply means "execute statements sequentially in the order that they are written." In some SQL dialects, a semicolon (;) is used to signify the end of a statement, although that is generally not required, because the context is enough to tell where one statement ends and the next begins.

Retrieving Data from Tables

Data retrieval is, as you've already seen, the job of the SELECT keyword. There are a huge number of ways to write select statements, involving a multitude of additional keywords and techniques, and the basic result is the same in all cases — you obtain a single value (a scalar result) or zero or more rows of data. The data that's returned may not be in the same format as the data in the database, because columns may be retrieved from multiple tables, combined in some way, renamed, or processed by functions before reaching you.

Here's the simplest form that a select statement can take:

```
SELECT [Column(s)] FROM [Table]
```

In it, [Column(s)] is a comma-separated list of column names and [Table] is the table containing the columns. For example:

```
SELECT EntryName, PhoneNumber FROM PhoneBookEntry
```

This retrieves a set of rows consisting of two columns, EntryName and PhoneNumber, from a table called PhoneBookEntry. This is shown graphically in Figure 1-4.

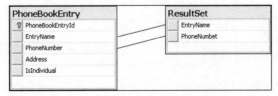

Figure 1-4: PhoneBookEntry query result set

In some circumstances, column or table names may match SQL keywords — Name, for instance, is a SQL keyword and might be used as a column name. To solve this ambiguity, SQL Server enables you to use square brackets to signify that the enclosed text should not be interpreted as a SQL keyword. You could use the text [Name] in a query to refer to a column called Name, for example. Nevertheless, it is good practice not to use SQL keywords to name columns or tables so that this is not an issue.

Often you will want to retrieve all of the data in all of the rows in a table; in that case, you can use the shorthand * to refer to all columns. For example:

```
SELECT * FROM PhoneBookEntry
```

It is worth noting that this shorthand notation can result in some (minor) overhead and reduction in performance because the RDBMS must work out what the columns are for you. That isn't something to worry too much about, and certainly not when prototyping code, but it may be something you return to when optimizing the performance of an application if you used it a lot when developing your code. The best practice is to avoid using *.

The next important thing you should know about is the capability to filter the data that you retrieve. Again, this is something you saw in an earlier example, and involves the use of the WHERE keyword to add a so-called where clause to the SELECT statement:

```
SELECT [Column(s)] FROM [Table] WHERE [Filter]
```

The filter used in a where clause may be a simple one, such as a equality between column values and a literal value:

```
SELECT EntryName, PhoneNumber FROM PhoneBookEntry
   WHERE PhoneBookEntryId = 'f4367a70-9780-11da-a72b-0800200c9a66'
```

Here data is returned for any rows that have a PhoneBookEntry column containing the value f4367a70-9780-11da-a72b-0800200c9a66. This is a GUID value, and is a unique, primary key value if this table is defined as per the example given earlier in this chapter, so the example query will return a single row of data containing the columns EntryName and PhoneNumber.

Filters can also be made up of multiple parts, combined using Boolean operators such as AND and OR, and use other comparison operators such as > for "greater than" or <= for "less than or equal to."

Another common operator in where clauses is LIKE, which you use to perform searches within text column values. When using LIKE you must supply a string literal value for comparison, which may contain wildcard symbols to widen the search criteria. In SQL Server, those symbols include % to refer to any string of zero or more characters, _ to refer to any single character, and others. For example:

```
SELECT * FROM PhoneBookEntry
   WHERE EntryName LIKE '%chaucer%' AND Address LIKE '%canterbury%'
```

This statement returns all the rows in the PhoneBookEntry table whose EntryName column contains the string chaucer and whose Address column contains the string canterbury. The query performs a case-insensitive search in SQL Server, unless the database is configured to enforce case-sensitive searching.

Combining multiple filter parts in a where clause is a flexible technique that you can use to obtain data sets that are as specific as you like. Good use of filtering can be important in the performance of your applications because minimizing the amount of data that is exchanged between your applications and your databases will lessen the time taken to make these exchanges.

Using Joins to Retrieve Data

The SELECT keyword can also be used to obtain data from multiple tables. There are alternative ways of doing this, of course, such as using complicated nested queries, but the simplest and most common way is to perform a join between pairs of tables in the query. There are several join types, each of which is useful in different circumstances. Briefly, the types of join you can perform are as follows (don't worry too much about these definitions at this stage — they will be explained in more detail shortly):

❑ Cross join: Each row in table A is joined to each row in table B.

❑ Inner join: Rows in table A and table B are joined according to the data contained in rows and the criteria you choose to compare these rows by. Rows may be excluded from the result set if no join is possible.

❑ Outer join: Similar to an inner join, but rows that would otherwise be excluded may be included in the result set depending on the exact specification of the join.

Understanding Cross Joins

The easiest of these joins to explain is the cross join, although you will probably find it the least useful. The syntax of using a cross join between, say, tables called TableA and TableB, is to specify the from clause of a query as follows:

```
FROM TableA CROSS JOIN TableB
```

Or using the simpler syntax:

```
FROM TableA, TableB
```

The full select statement includes other clauses much like queries over a single table, including column specifications and filters. For example:

```
SELECT * FROM Product, ProductCategory WHERE CategoryName = 'Things'
```

Using actual data will help you understand the query better. Let's say that the Product and ProductCategory tables contain data as shown in Figures 1-5 and 1-6.

ProductId	ProductName	ProductCost	ProductCategoryId
79360880-9790-11da-a72b-0800200c9a66	Widget	54.0000	6f237350-9790-11da-a72b-0800200c9a66
9f71efa0-9790-11da-a72b-0800200c9a66	Gadget	20.0000	914fc5a0-9790-11da-a72b-0800200c9a66
a5b04b50-9790-11da-a72b-0800200c9a66	Thingamajig	30.0000	914fc5a0-9790-11da-a72b-0800200c9a66

Figure 1-5: Product table contents

ProductCategoryId	CategoryName
6f237350-9790-11da-a72b-0800200c9a66	Things
914fc5a0-9790-11da-a72b-0800200c9a66	Stuff

Figure 1-6: ProductCategory table contents

Without considering the where clause for now, a cross join between these two tables results in the six rows shown in Figure 1-7. (Some of the GUID columns are truncated in this figure to save space.)

	ProductId	ProductName	ProductCost	ProductCategoryId	ProductCategoryId	CategoryName
1	A5B04B50-9790-...	Thingamajig	30.00	914FC5A0-9790-...	6F237350-9790-...	Things
2	79360880-9790-...	Widget	54.00	6F237350-9790-...	6F237350-9790-...	Things
3	9F71EFA0-9790-...	Gadget	20.00	914FC5A0-9790-...	6F237350-9790-...	Things
4	A5B04B50-9790-...	Thingamajig	30.00	914FC5A0-9790-...	914FC5A0-9790-...	Stuff
5	79360880-9790-...	Widget	54.00	6F237350-9790-...	914FC5A0-9790-...	Stuff
6	9F71EFA0-9790-...	Gadget	20.00	914FC5A0-9790-...	914FC5A0-9790-...	Stuff

Figure 1-7: Result of a cross join between Product and ProductCategory tables

There are six results because every row in Product (3) is combined with every row in ProductCategory (2): 3×2=6. Note that there are two ProductCategoryId columns — one from each table. This raises an important point: How do you differentiate between columns in different tables that have the same name? You do so by using an expanded reference to the columns; namely [TableName].[ColumnName]. The two columns here are therefore Product.ProductCategoryId and ProductCategory.ProductCategoryId. This is the method used by SQL Server and many other DBMSes to identify columns, and it's the syntax you would use if, say, you wanted to specify one of these columns in the column specification part of a select statement.

The addition of the where clause in the sample cross join query shown previously reduces the six-row result set to three rows — those with a CategoryName column containing the string Things (rows 1 to 3 in Figure 1-7).

At first glance this may seem useful, but the query hasn't really achieved much. Crucially, it hasn't taken into account the actual relationship between the rows of data. Each ProductCategory row is associated with a Product row in a one-to-many relationship, but that isn't reflected in the result set you get with a cross join. This relationship is achieved by the Product.ProductCategoryId column being a foreign key relating to the primary key ProductCategory.ProductCategoryId.

To obtain a more meaningful set of results, you need to use one of the other types of join. The simplest of them is the inner join.

Understanding Inner Joins

Inner joins require more information, namely a join specification, which takes a form similar to the where clause filters you saw earlier. The syntax here (omitting the column specification for now) is as follows:

```
FROM TableA INNER JOIN TableB ON [Join Specification]
```

Handily, the keywords for performing an inner join are INNER JOIN. To get the behavior discussed earlier, where the Product and ProductCategory tables are joined based on their respective ProductCategoryId columns, the query would need to be as follows:

```
SELECT * FROM Product INNER JOIN ProductCategory
    ON Product.ProductCategoryId = ProductCategory.ProductCategoryId
```

The result of this query (again with truncated GUIDs) is shown in Figure 1-8.

	ProductId	ProductName	ProductCost	ProductCategoryId	ProductCategoryId	CategoryName
1	A5B04B50-9790-...	Thingamajig	30.00	914FC5A0-9790-...	914FC5A0-9790-...	Stuff
2	79360880-9790-...	Widget	54.00	6F237350-9790-...	6F237350-9790-...	Things
3	9F71EFA0-9790-...	Gadget	20.00	914FC5A0-9790-...	914FC5A0-9790-...	Stuff

Figure 1-8: Result of an inner join between Product and ProductCategory based on ProductCategoryId columns

Adding a where clause identical to the one used earlier for the cross-join query would result in a single row being returned — row 2 in Figure 1-8.

Inner joins are powerful — even more so when you consider that they can link any number of tables together. For example:

```
SELECT [Order].OrderId, [Order].CustomerName, [Order].CustomerAddress,
       Product.ProductId, Product.ProductName, Product.ProductCost,
       ProductCategory.ProductCategoryId, ProductCategory.CategoryName,
       OrderProduct.Quantity
FROM [Order] INNER JOIN OrderProduct
ON [Order].OrderId = OrderProduct.OrderId INNER JOIN Product
ON OrderProduct.ProductId = Product.ProductId INNER JOIN ProductCategory
ON Product.ProductCategoryId = ProductCategory.ProductCategoryId
```

This may look complicated, but it really isn't. It uses lots of simple steps that look quite complex when combined. Look at the steps individually and you'll see that it's quite straightforward. Figure 1-9 illustrates the query graphically (the diamonds on the relationship lines signify inner joins — each type of join uses a different symbol).

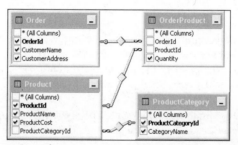

Figure 1-9: A query involving multiple inner joins

The first part of the query shows the columns to return — which are indicated by ticked boxes in Figure 1-9. Order is a SQL keyword, which is why it is enclosed in square brackets in the query.

The query contains three consecutive inner joins, each of which joins a pair of tables:

1. Order is joined to OrderProduct on the value of the OrderId columns. This results in as many rows in the result set as there are rows in the OrderProduct table, with row data from each row in the Order table being duplicated in multiple rows of the result set.

2. ProductId columns are used to add data from the Product table to the result set, and an inner join is made between OrderProduct and Product.

3. Product is joined to ProductCategory as in the previous example.

This results in a useful combination of data. The outcome gives you full order information — including what products make up an order, how many of each product are in the order, and what categories those products belong to.

You come across inner joins frequently in this book, so there are plenty more examples to get your teeth into.

You'll return to inner joins in subsequent chapters. One last note for now: It is possible to use operators other than = to join tables. For numeric fields you can, for example, use >. The results of this are more difficult to illustrate (and to explain the usefulness of), but it's something to bear in mind for later.

Understanding Outer Joins

The other types of join that you can perform are outer joins. As mentioned earlier, these are like inner joins, but are where rows that aren't joined to other rows may be included in the result set. You can see this in action if, for example, the `ProductCategory` table contains a third row, as shown in Figure 1-10.

ProductCategoryId	CategoryName
6f237350-9790-11da-a72b-0800200c9a66	Things
914fc5a0-9790-11da-a72b-0800200c9a66	Stuff
303aab40-979a-11da-a72b-0800200c9a66	Extras

Figure 1-10: ProductCategory table contents

Executing the inner join query shown earlier:

```
SELECT * FROM Product INNER JOIN ProductCategory
    ON Product.ProductCategoryId = ProductCategory.ProductCategoryId
```

gives the same results shown in Figure 1-8. The additional row in `ProductCategory` has no effect, because there is no row in `Product` with a matching `ProductCategoryId` column. This is where outer joins can come in handy. They enable you to include extra rows such as the one added to `ProductCategoryId`.

There are three types of outer join that enable you to specify which table in the join should have all of its rows included in the result set, regardless of the join specification. These are:

- ❑ **Left outer join:** Includes all rows in the first table specified in the result set.

- ❑ **Right outer join:** Includes all rows in the second table specified in the result set.

- ❑ **Full outer join:** Includes all rows in the both tables specified in the result set.

A left outer join is specified using the keywords LEFT OUTER JOIN:

```
SELECT * FROM Product LEFT OUTER JOIN ProductCategory
    ON Product.ProductCategoryId = ProductCategory.ProductCategoryId
```

This specifies that all rows in `Product` should be included. However, looking at the result set in Figure 1-8, you can see that all the `Product` rows are already in the result. This query gives the same result as an inner join in this instance. This is, in fact, enforced by the foreign key relationship between the `Product` and `ProductCategory` tables. The `Product.ProductCategoryId` column cannot be null and cannot refer to a nonexistent row in `ProductCategory`, so all the rows in `Product` are, by implication, included in the result set.

A right outer join uses the keywords RIGHT OUTER JOIN:

```
SELECT * FROM Product LEFT OUTER JOIN ProductCategory
    ON Product.ProductCategoryId = ProductCategory.ProductCategoryId
```

This time, the result set is different, as shown in Figure 1-11.

	ProductId	ProductName	ProductCost	ProductCategoryId	ProductCategoryId	CategoryName
1	79360880-9790-...	Widget	54.00	6F237350-9790-...	6F237350-9790-...	Things
2	A5B04B50-9790-...	Thingamajig	30.00	914FC5A0-9790-...	914FC5A0-9790-...	Stuff
3	9F71EFA0-9790-...	Gadget	20.00	914FC5A0-9790-...	914FC5A0-9790-...	Stuff
4	NULL	NULL	NULL	NULL	303AAB40-979A-...	Extras

Figure 1-11: The result of a right outer join between Product and ProductCategory based on ProductCategoryId columns

The additional row (row 4 in Figure 1-11) includes the data from the new column in ProductCategory combined with a bunch of null values in the columns taken from Product.

A full outer join's keywords are, predictably, FULL OUTER JOIN:

```
SELECT * FROM Product FULL OUTER JOIN ProductCategory
    ON Product.ProductCategoryId = ProductCategory.ProductCategoryId
```

This gives the same result as a right outer join. It actually includes non-joined rows from both tables, but because this applies only to ProductCategory it is the same as a right outer join in this instance. That is not always the case.

Outer joins of all kinds are less commonly used than inner joins, but can still be useful. As a simple example, only by performing an outer join can you tell that there is a product category called Extras in the preceding results. This has important ramifications in many situations and can address issues that could not be solved using, for instance, only inner joins.

Bear in mind that this discussion has barely scratched the surface of what is possible with select queries. Select statements are capable of ordering data, limiting the total number of rows returned, grouping data and performing statistical analysis on these groups, calculating columns in the result set based on column data and the results of functions, renaming columns, and much more. Again, you'll see these features in action later in the book.

Adding Data

After the section on retrieving data, it may come as somewhat of a relief to learn that adding, deleting, and updating data are typically much simpler.

Adding data is achieved using the INSERT keyword. The basic syntax of an insert query that inserts a single row into a table is as follows:

```
INSERT INTO [Table] ([Column(s)]) VALUES ([Value(s)])
```

Here, [Table] is the table to insert into, [Column(s)] is a comma-separated list of columns to insert data into, and [Value(s)] is a comma-separated list of values to insert into those columns. For example:

```
INSERT INTO ProductCategory (ProductCategoryId, CategoryName)
    VALUES ('3bd514c0-97a1-11da-a72b-0800200c9a66', 'Doodads')
```

This may be simple, but there are several points to note:

❑ The INTO keyword is optional, but it makes the query easier to read. If you want, however, you can omit it from your queries.

❑ The list of columns specified may be a subset of the columns defined in the table for several reasons:

❑ Some columns may allow null values, in which case adding data to them is optional.

❑ Some columns may be defined with default values, in which case the default will be used if the column is omitted from the insert statement.

❑ A column may be defined as an identity column, in which case the RDBMS may not allow you to insert data into it, and will generate an error if you attempt to do so. This is because identity columns are maintained by the RDBMS, and will be assigned values automatically.

❑ The columns don't have to be specified in the same order as they are defined in the table. The important thing to remember is that the column order specified in the insert statement *must* match the order of the values specified in the statement.

❑ Other rules applying to columns also apply, such as the rule that primary key values must be unique. The preceding query will execute fine once, but attempting to execute it again will result in an error because you will be attempting to insert duplicate values into ProductCategoryId.

❑ Null values can be inserted into columns using the keyword NULL.

For example, the following would be legal syntax for adding a row to the PhoneBookEntry described earlier in this chapter:

```
INSERT INTO PhoneBookEntry (EntryName, PhoneNumber, Address, IsIndividual)
VALUES ('Wayne Rooney', '555 123456', 'c/o Sven', 1)
```

The following would cause an error:

```
INSERT INTO PhoneBookEntry (EntryName, PhoneNumber, Address, IsIndividual)
VALUES ('Wayne Rooney', '555 123456', 1, 'c/o Sven')
```

In this example, the order of values supplied is wrong — it doesn't match the order specified by the column names.

This is the ideal place for a handy tip, and also the first time you will see a function in action. When using the uniqueidentifier type in SQL Server, which, as you have already seen, is a GUID value, you can use the NEWID() function to generate a GUID value. For example:

```
INSERT INTO ProductCategory (ProductCategoryId, CategoryName)
    VALUES (NEWID(), 'Doodads')
```

When this statement is executed, the NEWID() function is called and returns a GUID value that is used in the new row — meaning that you don't have to generate a GUID externally. Another practical function when adding rows is GETDATE(), which obtains the current date and time — useful when date-stamping rows. In SQL Server, you can use the datetime column data type for this purpose.

The INSERT keyword can also be used to insert multiple columns into a table at the same time. However, this cannot be achieved by specifying all of the column values as part of the statement. Instead, you must specify column values indirectly by using a SQL statement that returns a set of data — for example, a select query.

In insert statements of this form you must omit the VALUES keyword. The following is an example of a multirow insert query:

```
INSERT INTO ProductW (ProductId, ProductName, ProductCost, ProductCategoryId)
    SELECT ProductId, ProductName, ProductCost, ProductCategoryId FROM Product
    WHERE ProductName LIKE 'w%'
```

This statement copies all the products from the Product table whose ProductName column value starts with the letter w into a table called ProductW — which has exactly the same column specification as Product.

The query used to obtain data for inserting multiple rows needn't be this simple. The data could come from multiple tables, and the source columns needn't have the same names as the destination columns as long as their types match.

As with select statements, there is a lot more that you can do with insert statements, but these are the basics that you need to add data to database tables using SQL.

Deleting Data

You can delete data from databases using the DELETE keyword. But first, a word of warning — the delete statement makes it easy to accidentally delete the entire contents of a database table.

The syntax for a delete statement is as follows:

```
DELETE FROM [Table] WHERE [Filter]
```

Here, [Table] is the table from which to delete data, and [Filter] is a filter used to identify the data to delete. Delete statements operate on whole rows of data — it is not possible to delete individual columns from rows. The FROM keyword is optional (like the INTO keyword in insert statements, it can be more readable to leave it in), and the where clause is also optional.

If the where clause is omitted, *all* the rows in the table will be deleted. If you want this to happen, fine. If not, then be careful!

The following statement deletes all rows from the Product table:

```
DELETE FROM Product
```

As you can no doubt tell, this is a common mistake to make, and a serious one.

Using a filter, however, means that you can delete single records or a lot of records at once, depending on what you want to do. For example:

```
DELETE FROM ProductA WHERE ProductName NOT LIKE 'a%'
```

This query would delete all the rows from a table called `ProductA` that didn't have `ProductName` values that started with the letter `A`. Here's another example:

```
DELETE FROM ProductCategory
    WHERE ProductCategoryId = '3bd514c0-97a1-11da-a72b-0800200c9a66'
```

Because `ProductCategory.ProductCategoryId` is a primary key column that doesn't allow duplicate values, this command will delete zero or one row from the `ProductCategory` table, where the row that will be deleted has a `ProductCategoryId` column containing the GUID 3bd514c0-97a1-11da-a72b-0800200c9a66.

Updating Data

One way to update data in a database table is to delete a row and then add it again with slightly different data. However, that may be difficult or perhaps impossible to do if, for example, the table includes an identity column and you were required to keep the value of that column constant. Removing and then adding a row might also break relationships between rows, and the RDBMS may be configured to prevent you from doing this. In addition, this could cause conflicts and/or errors where multiple users access the database simultaneously.

Because of all this, the SQL specification includes another useful keyword to update data in existing rows: UPDATE. The syntax of an update statement is as follows:

```
UPDATE [Table] SET [Column Modification(s)] WHERE [Filter]
```

[Table] is the table containing the rows that you want to modify, [Column Modification(s)] is one or more comma-separated modifications to the rows in the table, and [Filter] filters the rows in the table that the update should apply to. As with previous queries, the where clause is optional.

Each column modification specification takes the following form:

```
[Column] = [Value]
```

[Column] is the name of the column to modify and [Value] is the value to replace the existing values in that column with. The value specified may be a simple literal value, or it may involve a calculation. If using a calculation, you can include the current value of a column in that calculation. For example:

```
UPDATE Product SET ProductCost = ProductCost * 1.1
```

This query would have the effect of increasing the cost of all products in the `Product` table by 10 percent, using the standard mathematical multiplication operator *.

As with delete queries, judicious use of the where clause may be required to restrict the rows where modifications should take place. Also, specifying a value for the primary key of a row in the where clause makes it possible to edit the content of individual rows.

Manipulating Databases

As well as being able to manipulate the data within databases, the SQL language includes all the commands you might need to manipulate database objects, including databases, stored procedures, tables, and so on.

For example, the following command, CREATE DATABASE, would create a new database within the DBMS:

```
CREATE DATABASE MyDatabaseOfWonders
```

Once created, you can add tables using additional SQL statements, although first you need to specify the name of the database where the statements will execute. To do so, you use the USE command:

```
USE MyDatabaseOfWonders
```

Then you can use a CREATE TABLE statement to add a table to your database:

```
CREATE TABLE [dbo].[Product]
(
    [ProductId] [uniqueidentifier] NOT NULL,
    [ProductName] [varchar](200) COLLATE Latin1_General_CI_AI NOT NULL,
    [ProductCost] [money] NOT NULL,
    [ProductCategoryId] [uniqueidentifier] NOT NULL,
    CONSTRAINT [PK_Product] PRIMARY KEY CLUSTERED
    (
        [ProductId] ASC
    ) ON [PRIMARY]
) ON [PRIMARY]
```

This command creates the Product table you've been looking at throughout this chapter. Some of the syntax used here is a little strange at first glance, but it's all easy enough to understand.

First, the table name is specified as [dbo].[Product]. This says that the Product table should belong to the dbo schema, where dbo is an abbreviation of database owner, and is a schema that exists in SQL Server 2005 databases by default. This additional specification is optional, and typically the dbo schema will be the default schema used unless additional configuration has taken place.

The next few lines specify the columns that will be contained by the table, by way of column names, data types, and whether they allow null values (the qualifier NOT NULL is used for rows that don't). Also, in the case of text fields, the collation is specified via the COLLATE keyword. The collation defines the character set to use, and therefore how the data will be stored in the database. (Different character sets require different amounts of storage for each character.)

After the column specifications, a constraint is added. Basically, constraints are additional properties that are applied to columns and define what values are allowed in columns, how the column data should be used (including key specifications), and indexing information. In this example, the ProductId column is made the primary key of the table with an ascending index and the key name PK_Product.

The final lines of code determine the partition that the table should exist in — in this case PRIMARY, which is the default installation of SQL Server.

One thing is missing here — there is no foreign key specification. Assuming that you had added the ProductCategory table, this specification would require a second command. However, before that second command runs, you need to make sure that the CREATE TABLE statement executes. To pause until previous statements have completed, use the simple SQL keyword GO:

```
GO
```

Then you would add the foreign key, in the form of another constraint:

```
ALTER TABLE [dbo].[Product] WITH CHECK ADD CONSTRAINT [FK_Product_ProductCategory]
    FOREIGN KEY ([ProductCategoryId])
    REFERENCES [dbo].[ProductCategory] ([ProductCategoryId])
GO
```

Here the `FK_Product_ProductCategory` foreign key is added, linking the `Product.ProductCategoryId` column with the `ProductCategory.ProductCategoryId` column.

There are several `CREATE` statements in the SQL vocabulary, each of which has a corresponding `ALTER` statement and also a corresponding `DROP` statement. Dropping an object means deleting it from the DBMS. This operation doesn't use the `DELETE` keyword, which is used for deleting data; mixing up these commands is potentially disastrous.

Although this chapter introduces a number of commands, you are far more likely to carry out these operations via a GUI for day-to-day use. That's fine, because making even simple mistakes with queries of this sort can cause irreparable damage.

The most useful thing about these statements so far is that they can be combined together into script files. Script files can be extremely useful for automating lengthy tasks, and the first place you will see one of these in action is in the next chapter. You will execute a SQL script file that creates the database that you will be using for examples throughout the book. The script file contains a complete database, including multiple tables, table data, and other database objects. If you were to add all of this by hand it would take a long time indeed, but executing a script takes hardly any time at all.

XML

As noted earlier, XML is a text-based format for the storage of data. It consists of two features: data and markup. Because it is "just" text, it can be read and understood on just about any computer system in existence, and its well-defined format makes it easy to process. It is also possible to define vocabularies — that is, systems of markup unique to an application or shared among many applications. As such, XML has become the universal language of choice for the interchange of information between disparate systems.

In the .NET Framework, XML is used extensively. For example, configuration files for all manner of applications are written in XML, which makes it easy to edit configurations by hand or programmatically using simple techniques. A rich set of types is defined by .NET to make it easy to manipulate XML data in various ways. XML is also the basis of SOAP (Simple Object Access Protocol), the underlying technology that makes web services both possible and platform-independent.

The rise of XML has continued unabatedly for several years, and knowledge of XML is now an essential part of pretty much any area of computing. This applies to databases, too, and many DBMSes (including SQL Server) now include tools for dealing with, consuming, and generating XML data.

The XML Format

This section cannot detail every aspect of the XML syntax, but it is a brief summary to reinforce the basic concepts of XML. After all, the chances are that you will have come across XML before, and if you haven't, there are a huge number of excellent resources, in web and print form, to get you started.

The markup in XML documents consists of data enclosed in elements, where that data may consist of nested (child) elements. Every XML document contains a single root (or document) element, and elements nested within the root element make up a hierarchy of data. Apart from the root element, XML documents may contain a single XML declaration, and zero or more processor directives. Each element, including the root element, has either a start tag and an end tag, or a single empty element tag. Start tags and empty element tags can include attributes that consist of name/value pairs.

Here's an example of an XML document:

```xml
<?xml version="1.0" encoding="utf-8" ?>
<foodStuffs>
  <foodStuff category="pizza">
    <name>Cheese and Tomato</name>
    <size>10"</size>
    <rating>4*</rating>
  </foodStuff>
  <foodStuff category="pizza">
    <name>Four Seasons</name>
    <size>8"</size>
    <rating>1*</rating>
    <isNasty />
  </foodStuff>
</foodStuffs>
```

The XML declaration on the first line of the document identifies the version of XML to which the document conforms and how it is encoded (that is, the character set used). The root element of the document is `<foodStuffs>`, which contains two `<foodStuff>` elements. Each `<foodStuff>` element has an attribute called `category`, and child elements called `<name>`, `<size>`, and `<rating>`, each of which contains text data. Each of these elements consists of a start tag (for example, `<size>`) and an end tag that includes a preceding front slash (`</size>`). The second `<foodStuff>` element also contains an empty element, `<isNasty>`, which includes a trailing front slash to indicate that the element is empty. One way of looking at this document is as an array of `foodStuff` objects, each of which has properties that are represented as attributes or child elements.

There are a few more rules concerning XML documents. For a start, they are case-sensitive. `<foodStuff>` and `<Foodstuff>`, for example, are interpreted as two completely different elements. Also, every start tag must have a matching end tag, and elements can't overlap, that is to say that the following is illegal:

```xml
<element1><element2></element1></element2>
```

Here's an example in which `<element2>` is correctly nested inside `<element1>`:

```xml
<element1><element2></element2></element1>
```

And in this example, neither element is nested in the other:

```xml
<element1></element1>
<element2></element2>
```

Storing XML Data

In the XML document shown in the previous section, it is fairly obvious how the data might map to a database table. For instance, you could have a `FoodStuff` table containing columns for `Category` (possible a foreign key field linking to a separate `Category` table), text columns for `Name`, `Size`, and `Rating`, and a `bit` type column for `IsNasty`. In the XML, the root `<foodStuffs>` element would simply be used as a placeholder containing the data, and each `<foodStuff>` element would represent a row in the table.

However, XML documents can come in other forms, too. Here's an example:

```
<?xml version="1.0" encoding="utf-8" ?>
<body>
  <h1>Funny bone results in dog days!</h1>
  Rumor has it <i>(sources unknown)</i> that a well known <br />
  comedy dog double act is due to split any day now.<br />
  <br />
  The latest information to come out of the rumor mill is that<br />
  a dispute arose about the location of a <b>buried bone</b>, and that<br />
  until it is found the dogs in question are only communicating<br />
  via their lawyers.<br />
  <br />
  More news as it happens!
</body>
```

This is, in fact, a piece of HTML. But it's a little more than that — it's actually a fragment of XHTML — an XML dialect of HTML. It's also a perfectly legal XML document, but creating a table capable of holding this information in row form would be practically impossible. Instead, storing this in a database would mean putting the whole lot in a single column of a row, in text form. SQL Server includes an `xml` datatype for storing this sort of data, or you could just use a text column. When you store data using the `xml` datatype, however, there is additional functionality that you can use, such as querying data within the document using the XQuery language.

You look at this facet of SQL Server later in the book.

Retrieving Data as XML

As well as being able to retrieve XML data stored in `xml` type columns directly as XML, SQL Server also makes it possible to retrieve data from any result set in the form of XML data. This involves an additional `FOR XML` clause, which has a number of uses and ways of customizing the format in which XML data is obtained, but can also be used simply. For example:

```
SELECT * FROM Product FOR XML AUTO
```

This query obtains data as a single string as follows:

```
<Product ProductId="A5B04B50-9790-11DA-A72B-0800200C9A66"
  ProductName="Thingamajig" ProductCost="30.0000"
  ProductCategoryId="914FC5A0-9790-11DA-A72B-0800200C9A66"/>
<Product ProductId="79360880-9790-11DA-A72B-0800200C9A66"
  ProductName="Widget" ProductCost="54.0000"
  ProductCategoryId="6F237350-9790-11DA-A72B-0800200C9A66"/>
```

```
<Product ProductId="9F71EFA0-9790-11DA-A72B-0800200C9A66"
   ProductName="Gadget" ProductCost="20.0000"
   ProductCategoryId="914FC5A0-9790-11DA-A72B-0800200C9A66"/>
```

This is not a complete, legal XML document as it stands (it has multiple root elements for one thing), but it would be easy to turn it into one.

If you are writing applications that must generate XML from data stored in a database, the FOR XML clause can speed things up dramatically — because by using the right queries it would be possible to avoid having to do any further data processing outside of SQL Server.

SQL Server also provides ways to insert rows into tables directly from XML documents and even has the capability to return XML data in response to web requests. Again, these are things that you will see later in the book, as they become pertinent.

Summary

In this chapter, you looked at the basics of databases, including how they are structured and how to access the data contained in them. You have also learned about the additional features of databases and how to use SQL to manipulate databases, and you saw a quick summary of XML and how it fits in to the database world.

Specifically, you have learned:

- ❑ What a database is
- ❑ What terminology to use when referring to databases
- ❑ How relational databases work, and what makes them useful
- ❑ What the difference is between relational and object-oriented database management systems
- ❑ What functionality databases offer above and beyond storing data
- ❑ What the differences are between many of the available DBMSes
- ❑ What SQL is
- ❑ How to retrieve, add, delete, and update data in databases using a variety of SQL queries
- ❑ What else is possible using more advanced SQL syntax
- ❑ What XML is
- ❑ How it is possible to use XML data in combination with databases

In the next chapter, you see how C# can be used to interact with SQL Server 2005 Express Edition, and you start to experiment with sample applications.

Exercises

1. Database tables must include primary keys. Is this statement true or false?

2. Which of the following are actual types of joins between tables?

    a. Inner joins

    b. Sideways joins

    c. Internal joins

    d. Left outer joins

    e. Dovetail joins

3. If you wanted to perform two update queries in which either both queries must succeed or both must fail, what technology would you use?

4. What is wrong with the following SQL statements?

    ```
    DELETE FROM MyTable
    UPDATE MyTable (Title, Amount) SET ('Oysters', 17) WHERE ItemId = 3
    ```

5. Any XML document may be inserted into a SQL database table as a set of rows. Is this statement true or false? Why?

Databases and C#

In Chapter 1 you learned a lot about databases but not a lot about how to use them with C#. That is, after all, the subject of this book — so it's about time you got started. This chapter includes quite a lot of theory to get through, but there's also a fair amount of code to sink your teeth into. From this chapter onward, you'll be looking at and using ADO.NET, the database access library used in the .NET Framework. The code in this chapter gives you a flavor for what's coming up in later chapters. You build some relatively simple example applications that will illustrate some of the key features of using ADO.NET with C#, including powerful data-binding techniques. As such, there won't be a huge amount of detail given as to how the example code works, because the specifics are covered in great depth later in the book.

Also in this chapter, you explore some of the tools that will help you use SQL Server 2005 Express Edition and, by extension, the full version of SQL Server and other databases, and you are introduced to the example database that is used in examples throughout this book.

In this chapter, you learn:

❑ What ADO.NET is and how it can be used to access databases from C# applications, both programmatically and using data binding

❑ What visual tools are available for accessing and manipulating databases

❑ How to perform a number of basic database access tasks using some simple example applications

❑ How to use this book's sample database

There are several Express products that you must install to execute the code in this and subsequent chapters. These are:

❑ Visual C# 2005 Express Edition

❑ Visual Web Developer 2005 Express Edition

❑ SQL Server 2005 Express Edition

❑ SQL Server Management Studio Express

Instructions for downloading and installing all of these can be found in Appendix A. If you haven't already done so, work through that appendix now, before continuing with this chapter.

Database Access in C#

Applications written using the .NET Framework (and therefore applications written in C#) that require database access will use ADO.NET to achieve this. This section examines what ADO.NET is and where to find it in the .NET namespaces, and provides a basic understanding of how it works.

Later, you spend some time exploring a key feature of database programming in .NET: data binding. Data binding is an extremely useful way to access databases that minimizes the amount of code you have to write. Many simple tasks can be performed using purely declarative code.

ADO.NET

ADO.NET is the latest evolution of Microsoft's data access framework and is part of the .NET Framework. Before ADO.NET, programmers used ADO (ActiveX Data Objects), a set of COM (Component Object Model) components that provide access to underlying data access code via a wrapper that is easy to use, for example, from ASP (Active Server Pages) or Visual Basic. While ADO greatly simplified database access, more advanced programmers (C++ programmers, in particular) often preferred to use more direct, quicker code, such as the OLE DB (Object Linking and Embedding for Databases) code library.

ADO.NET is much more than ADO ever hoped to be. It is the tool of choice for accessing databases from .NET code.

> *If you were to ask someone at Microsoft what ADO.NET was an abbreviation for now, you'd find that it isn't one. There is nothing "ActiveX" about it anymore. ActiveX is an older MS technology that's no longer a part of application development.*

The types contained in the ADO.NET section of the .NET Framework (all contained in the `System.Data` namespace and child namespaces thereof) include those optimized for accessing SQL Server, OLE DB, ODBC, and Oracle databases. These are all based on common classes, so accessing one DBMS using ADO.NET is much the same as accessing another.

The ADO.NET types fulfill two main functions:

❑ **Data access:** Types used to access data in databases and manipulate databases

❑ **Data representation:** Types used to contain database data, such as tables of data

These types are strongly related to each other, and you use both in database development. Strictly speaking, you could get away with using only the data access types. However, you can save yourself a lot of work if you use data access types to populate data representation types.

ADO.NET contains seven key base classes. Four of them are data access classes:

❑   DbConnection

❑   DbCommand

❑   DbDataReader

❑   DbDataAdapter

These classes, which are discussed in the following sections, are used to derive the more specific classes (such as SQL Server access classes in the System.Data.SqlClient namespace) in the more specific sections of the ADO.NET namespaces.

The other three base classes are data representation classes:

❑   DataTable

❑   DataRelation

❑   DataSet

You'll see some of the methods and properties that are important to the function of these classes, to prepare you for the code to come later in this chapter. You won't be reading about the full set of properties and methods here; instead, you see just enough to give you a flavor of things.

The DataTable class makes use of some other important classes, DataColumn, Constraint, and DataRow, which you also look at in this section.

DbConnection

The DbConnection class provides the connection to the database. When you create a DbConnection object, you supply it with all the information it needs to communicate with a DBMS, such as the location of the database, a username and password for authentication, and the database you want to access inside the DBMS.

All the other ADO.NET data access classes rely on a DbConnection object to communicate with a database. The role of the DbConnection class is illustrated in Figure 2-1.

In all derived versions of DbConnection, the connection to the database is defined by a string known as the *connection string*, which is stored in the DbConnection.ConnectionString property.

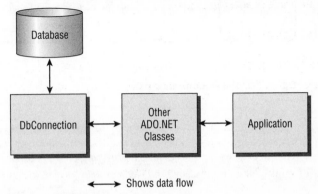

Figure 2-1: The DbConnection class

Database connections should be kept open only as long as data is being transferred, so creating an instance of `DbConnection` doesn't automatically connect to the database. Instead, the `DbConnection` class defines `Open()` and `Close()` methods to control when the connection is available for use. Many of the other ADO.NET classes are capable of controlling connection state for you — for example, some classes close the connection they are using when they finish operating.

`DbConnection` objects are also capable of participating in transactions. You can start a transaction using the `DbConnection.BeginTransaction()` method, or perform an operation as part of an existing transaction using `DbConnection.EnlistTransaction()`.

When accessing data in SQL Server or SQL Server Express databases, you will use the `SqlConnection` class, which is derived from `DbConnection`. In general, `DbConnection`, `SqlConnection`, and other derived classes are all referred to as *connection classes*.

DbCommand

The `DbCommand` class provides the primary means of interaction with a database. You can use `DbCommand` objects to execute SQL queries, run stored procedures, and so on. `DbCommand` and its derived classes are called *command classes*.

Much of the time you won't use `DbCommand` objects directly because you will be using other objects that encapsulate them. At times, however, you will want to have a greater degree of control over database communication, and `DbCommand` objects enable you to do that.

The `DbCommand` object's role is illustrated in Figure 2-2.

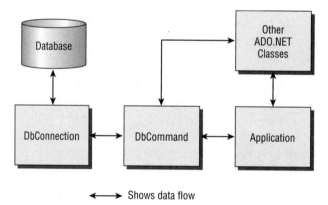

Figure 2-2: The DbCommand class

The most significant property of `DbCommand` is `DbCommand.CommandText`. To execute a SQL query, you put the text of the query into this property. You can also use `DbCommand.CommandType` to specify the type of command you want to execute, and access the underlying connection or transaction using `DbCommand.Connection` and `DbCommand.Transaction`.

It's important to note that `DbCommand` objects can be supplied with parameterized command strings, where the parameters used in the command are taken from the typed `DbCommand.Parameters` collection property. This has many advantages over simply entering parameters into the command string, as you will see in later chapters.

When you execute a command using a DbCommand object, you have three options depending on what the command does. Some commands don't return a result, in which case you can use the DbCommand.ExecuteNonQuery() method. Some commands return a single result, which can be obtained using the DbCommand.ExecuteScalar() method. Finally, many commands return multiple rows of data, so you would use the DbCommand.ExecuteReader() method, which returns a DbDataReader object (explained in the following section).

The SQL Server–specific version of DbCommand is called SqlCommand. It has a few specialized extras, such as the SqlCommand.ExecuteXmlReader() method to return results directly in XML format.

DbDataReader

The DbDataReader class enables you to read data from a result set, for example one generated by the execution of a command stored in a command object. The way that this class works is highly optimized and allows extremely fast access to database data. This optimization does have its consequences, however, such as enabling you to read data only one row at a time in a sequential manner. You can't, for example, read a row, read another row, and then go back and read the first row again. Typically, you would use a DbDataReader object (or, more specifically, a derived data reader object) to extract the row data you want to use and store it in other objects. You might, for example, read each row of a result set into a custom class stored in a custom collection or generic list object.

As with command objects, you will find that a lot of the time data reader objects are used by other classes in the ADO.NET namespaces and that you don't have to use them directly.

Figure 2-3 shows how data reader objects fit into the grand scheme of things.

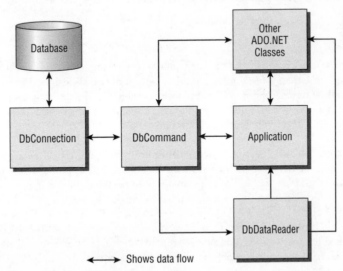

Figure 2-3: The DbDataReader class

To use a data reader object, you first call the `DbDataReader.Read()` method to select the first row in a result set. This method can be repeatedly called to move the data reader through the rows such that the data reader acts like a cursor in the result set, always referring to a single row. The `Read()` method returns `true` if a row is obtained, or `false` if not — such as when all rows have been read. You can also use the `DbDataReader.HasRows` property to see if any rows exist in the result set.

There are many properties and methods at your disposal for examining the currently selected row. You can use `DbDataReader.FieldCount` to see how many columns the current row contains, and access individual columns using the overloaded indexer of `DbDataReader`. If you know the name of the column you want to access, you can use the string-based indexer to obtain a column value, or you can use the integer-based indexer to obtain columns by position. In either case, this technique returns `object` values, which you can convert to typed data.

You can also get typed data directly using one of the many methods that `DbDataReader` exposes, such as `GetString()` and `GetInt32()`, which return `string` and `int` values respectively for the specified column, where the column is chosen by its index. To use these methods to obtain value types, it's necessary to check for null values first using the `DbDataReader.IsDBNull()` method; otherwise, null values raise exceptions. Checking for null values is necessary because database types can be null whatever their data type, unlike value types in .NET. Nullable types (such as `int?`) aren't supported in this context.

`DbDataReader` is also capable of obtaining meta-information about the data it contains, using the `DbDataReader.GetSchemaTable()` method, so that you can find out the names of columns, the data types of columns, and other information, such as whether columns can contain null values.

As with the other classes you've looked at, there is a SQL Server–specific class — `SqlDataReader` — that you'll use in this book. Among other things, that class extends `DbDataReader` by supplying methods to read data as native SQL types, which is one way around the nullable type problem. Those types, contained in the `System.Data.SqlTypes` namespace, are nullable; examples are `SqlDouble` and `SqlInt32`. They may also be operated on much like standard value types although they are, in fact, reference types.

DbDataAdapter

The `DbDataAdapter` class is the last of the core data access classes contained in ADO.NET. This is a far more sophisticated type than those you've already examined, and is designed for one purpose and one purpose only: to allow data stored in data set objects to exchange data with a database without any more intervention than is necessary. As with the previous classes, there are several derived versions of the `DbDataAdapter` class, collectively known as *data adapter classes*.

You see exactly what data set objects are shortly, but to put things simply, they are objects that you can use to represent database data in .NET object form. A data set can contain a whole table or multiple tables of data. A data adapter is used both to transfer data from a database into a table contained in a data set and to transfer data from the data set back into the database.

Under the hood, this functionality is performed by command and data reader objects, and much of the time you don't need to worry about it. However, one of the most important (and useful) features of `DbDataAdapter` is that the command objects it uses to transfer data are exposed to you, so that you can customize them to your heart's content.

Figure 2-4 shows how the `DbDataAdapter` class operates, including the command objects it contains.

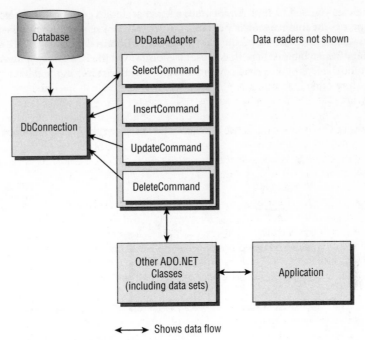

Figure 2-4: The DbDataAdapter class

The four command objects used by a data adapter are stored in the four properties: SelectCommand (for retrieving data), InsertCommand (for adding data), UpdateCommand (for editing data), and DeleteCommand (for removing data). Not all of these may be necessary for the adapter to function — for example, the adapter might be used only to retrieve data. Also, it is possible for the .NET Framework to infer values for commands based on the values of other commands — update, insert, and delete commands can be generated based on the select command, for example. The efficiency of these auto-generated commands may not be as good as commands you supply yourself, however. This is a subject you'll return to later in the book.

The two methods you will use most for data adapters are DbDataAdapter.Fill() and DbDataAdapter.Update(). The Fill() method retrieves data from the database; Update() updates the database. Both of these work in conjunction with data sets or with individual data tables. In addition, you can retrieve schema data using DbDataAdapter.FillSchema().

The SQL Server version of DbDataAdapter is SqlDataAdapter.

DataTable

DataTable is the first of the data representation classes that ADO.NET supplies. Unlike the data access classes, the data representation classes do not have any specialized derived versions for use with, for example, SQL Server. They are platform-neutral, which makes perfect sense because the data stored in databases is much the same whatever DBMS you use. In fact, the data representation classes can be used in complete isolation from databases should you want to do so — they are just a convenient way of storing data.

The `DataTable` class is used to store (here comes a shocker) tables of data. Now, before going further it is worth clearing up one thing: a table stored in a `DataTable` object need not necessarily map perfectly to a table in a database. Depending on the query you use to obtain data, a `DataTable` may contain a subset of the data from a table, where that subset is a portion of the rows in a database table, a portion of the columns in the database table, data combined from multiple tables in the database, or a combination of all of these. More often than not, a `DataTable` will match a table in the database, but this fact is still worth being aware of.

Figure 2-5 shows how you use a `DataTable` object in relation to other ADO.NET objects.

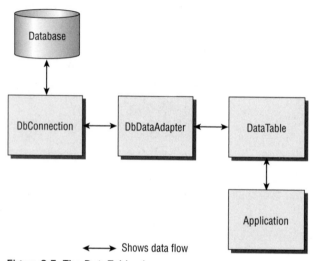

Figure 2-5: The DataTable class

To obtain a fully populated `DataTable`, you use a data adapter. Once you have a `DataTable` object containing data, you can access the rows, columns, constraints, and other information it contains. These are available through aptly named properties, including `Rows`, `Columns`, and `Constraints`.

Each of the three properties mentioned returns a collection class (`DataRowCollection`, `DataColumnCollection`, and `ConstraintCollection`). Like other collection classes, you can use them to navigate through the collection of objects they contain, add and remove items, and so on. You look at the classes that are contained in these collections in a moment.

One other extremely important aspect of the `DataTable` class concerns how data modifications are handled. For example, if you remove a row from a `DataTable` object, how does the data adapter know to remove the corresponding data from the database? The `DataTable` objects keep track of changes to the original data, not just the current state of the data. Deleting a row from a `DataTable` doesn't actually delete the data — it just results in the row being marked as deleted. For consumers of the `DataTable` object, such as your applications, it appears as though the row has been deleted, but in reality it hasn't been.

At any point you can obtain a list of the changes that have been made to a `DataTable` (in the form of another `DataTable`) using the `GetChanges()` method. You can accept the changes that have been made, overwriting the original data where appropriate, using the `AcceptChanges()` method. You might do this, for example, after changes have been committed to a database. Alternatively, you can undo all changes, perhaps when an end user hits a cancel button, using RejectChanges().

DataTable objects also expose a number of events that you can subscribe to in your applications should you want, such as RowDeleted and ColumnChanged. Using these events you can ensure that you application is responsive as well as adding additional functionality — for example, making sure that underlying database data is updated as soon as data modifications are made.

DataColumn

The DataColumn class stores all the information required to define a column in a database table. In a DataTable, the Columns property contains a DataColumnCollection, which is a collection of DataColumn objects.

DataColumn has properties that match those found in DBMSes, including ColumnName, DataType, AllowDBNull, and DefaultValue. The full set of properties may be more than exist in the specific DBMS you are using, but that quickly becomes apparent if you use a variety of DBMSes. With SQL Server, it isn't a problem.

Constraint

Constraint objects (found in the ConstraintCollection class accessible via DataTable.Constraints) are used to contain all the table metadata not included in DataColumn objects. The Constraint class is used as the base class for more specific classes: UniqueConstraint, which ensures that values in a given column or combination of columns are unique (essential for primary keys, for example), and ForeignKeyConstraint, to enforce relationships between tables.

DataRow

The DataRow class is used to store the data contained in a single row of a table. The DataTable.Rows property gives you access to a DataRowCollection object that stores multiple DataRow objects making up the data in the table. The individual columns of data within a row are accessible via an indexer, which allows access to columns by name, index, and version (if, for example, rows have been modified).

The current state of a row — that is, whether it has been modified, deleted, or changed in any way — is accessible via the DataRow.RowState property. This property is a value of type DataRowState, an enumeration that includes all possible row states. Individual DataRow objects also have methods corresponding to those found in a DataTable to accept, reject, and obtain changes. You can now infer, for example, that calling DataTable.AcceptChanges() cascades down to calling DataRow.AcceptChanges() for each row in the table.

DataRelation

When dealing with multiple DataTable objects it is often necessary to represent — and enforce — relationships between the table data. That's the job of the DataRelation class. DataRelation objects may be grouped together in a single DataRelationCollection object.

Relationships are defined using assorted properties of the DataRelation class, including ChildTable, ChildColumns, ChildKeyConstraint, ParentTable, ParentColumns, and ParentKeyConstraint. These properties are all references to appropriate objects, such as DataTable and DataColumn objects. The name of a relationship is also stored, in the DataRelation.RelationName property.

Don't worry too much about `DataRelation` objects at this stage because they encapsulate more advanced aspects of ADO.NET that you will get to later in the book.

DataSet

And so you reach perhaps the most important class that ADO.NET provides — `DataSet`. To some extent, this class is simply a collection of `DataTable` and `DataRelation` objects (as shown in Figure 2-6). The true power of `DataSet` objects, however, is how they are used in conjunction with other objects — including controls for use in web and windows applications, web services, and XML documents.

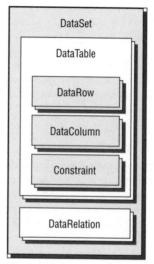

Figure 2-6: The DataSet class

`DataSet` classes contain a fair few properties and methods; many of them are similar to those found in its component parts — `GetChanges()`, `AcceptChanges()`, and `RejectChanges()`, for example. There are also important properties such as `Tables`, containing the collection of tables in the `DataSet` in the form of a `DataTableCollection` class, and `Relations`, containing a `DataRelationCollection` class with the `Relation` objects defining the relationships between tables.

The relationships between data tables and the constraints applied to data can make it awkward to manipulate the data in a `DataSet`. For example, if data exists in a one-to-many relationship between two tables, then adding a row to one table may require the existence of a row in another table. That row may not exist — for example, if both rows are to be added at the same time. Here the order in which rows are added becomes important to avoid errors; the row at the one end of the relationship must be added first. Alternatively, you can set the `DataSet.EnforceConstraints` property to `false`, in which case relationships are ignored during edit operations.

Relationship Between DataSet Objects and XML

Like the rest of ADO.NET, the `DataSet` object has been designed with XML data in mind. Data sets can be transformed into XML documents using the `DataSet.GetXml()` method, or you can extract just the schema of the data set (which includes the schema of all contained tables and other objects) as an XML document using `DataSet.GetXmlSchema()`. It is also possible to convert between a `DataSet` object and an XML document using serialization techniques because the `DataSet` class implements the `IXmlSerializable` interface.

The relationship between `DataSet` objects and XML, along with the capability to convert between these data representation formats using serialization, is used extensively in the .NET Framework. It provides an excellent way to exchange data between application tiers, as well as over the Internet. In particular, having an XML representation of a data set enables `DataSet` objects to be exchanged with web services.

Typed Data Sets

`DataSet` objects are powerful and contain a great deal of functionality, but they aren't the easiest or most logical things to use. The syntax required to access, say, a particular row of a particular table is quite obtuse. To do that, you'd have to obtain the correct table using the `DataSet.Tables` collection and the correct row using the `DataTable.Rows` collection, and then extract column data in the form of object references, or by using `DataColumn` methods — none of which is designed to make your life easy. The complete line of code required to access a particular column might look something like the following:

```
int result = (int)myDataSet.Tables["myTable"].Rows[5]["IntegerColumn"];
```

Alternatively, you can use a *typed data set*. Typed data sets are classes that derive from `DataSet`, but that include strongly typed properties and methods to make it easier to manipulate your data. If you use a typed data set, the preceding code can be simplified as follows:

```
int result = myTypedDataSet.MyTable[5].IntegerColumn;
```

While this doesn't affect the operation of the code in any way, it certainly makes it easier to type (especially with IntelliSense turned on) and easier to understand when you read it back later.

The only limitation is that you need to know at design time the structure of the data that will be contained in the data set. However, because database structure isn't likely to change much over time, this isn't usually a problem.

You can create the code for typed data sets automatically using either the `xsd.exe` tool, or through the Visual C# Express interface. The `xsd.exe` tool requires a schema, in the form of an XML schema file with the extension `.xsd`. Visual C# Express also uses schema information to create a typed data set class, but does so using information taken straight from a database, which makes it much easier to manipulate the structure of the data set.

Performance

There is a school of thought that says data sets are to be avoided if at all possible. That's because they are "heavyweight" objects and introduce an overhead that can become significant in high-performance applications. In addition, transferring data over the Web in the form of a data set can mean transferring large amounts of XML data.

To some extent, these are valid criticisms. If performance is important, it can be worth designing your own classes and populating them directly from data readers. However, data sets — and typed data sets, in particular — certainly have their place. They provide a vast array of features that are easy for you to tap into with little code, and the code you do write to manipulate them is often remarkably simple. For example, without data sets, the capability to have a representation of database data where all edits are recorded in the class, and where these edits may be transmitted back into the database with ease, could require quite a large amount of code and be rather difficult to implement.

The other great thing about using data sets is that you can use them for data binding, which you look at in the next section.

Data Binding

Data binding is a technique where data from a database is used to populate controls on a Windows or web form with little effort on the part of you, the programmer. The .NET Framework enables you to associate controls with data sources using simple code — in fact, you can achieve a great deal through the GUI, without actually writing much (if any) C# code.

Data binding requires two things: a data source and a control to bind data to. Data sources include but are not limited to database connections. You can also use objects or data taken from a web service as data sources. Using objects as data sources is a powerful technique for making use of custom collection and item classes that you design yourself, but that's a little off topic here. The key type of data source that you'll use most in this book is a database data source, which has web and Windows control versions.

When generating a data source for a database, you actually configure more than just a connection. A database data source includes information about what objects in the database you want to access. In fact, behind the scenes you will often generate a typed data set. Also behind the scenes, the ADO.NET objects you looked at earlier are all called into play. (Connections, commands, data readers, and data adapters all work together to create your data source.) You don't have to worry too much about this; all you have to do is make a data source and bind it to a control, as illustrated in Figure 2-7.

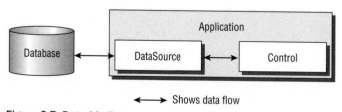

Figure 2-7: Data binding

Binding to a control means setting control properties from items in the data source (and, indirectly, items in the database). For simple controls, such as labels or text boxes, this means setting the Text property of the control to, for example, a text type column from a row in your database. You can also bind data to list controls, including drop-down lists, where each item in the list is bound to a row in a database table. More advanced controls, such as grid views, can enable you to look at complete table contents. Alternatively, you can provide custom controls and custom data-binding schemes to enable both the use and editing of data in a database.

This is all well and good at first glance, but as you can imagine, there are many issues to consider. For example, how do you enable editing of data? How do you control the look of data presented to application users? These are topics you'll examine in great detail in this book. Later in this chapter, you see some simple examples that demonstrate the raw power of data binding.

Visual Tools

Accessing a database using only a command line or script tools is possible but is rarely the best option — particularly for beginners. Luckily, you have visual tools at your disposal within Visual C# Express and Visual Web Developer Express, as well as having a stand-alone GUI for database manipulation available for use with SQL Server 2005 Express Edition: SQL Server Management Studio Express (SSMSE). The other versions of Visual Studio include similar (and more powerful) tools, and the other versions of SQL Server 2005 come with a ready-to-use GUI that is similar in function to SSMSE.

This section looks at the basic techniques of using these tools.

Express Products

In both the Visual C# (VC#) and Visual Web Developer (VWD) Express products, it's possible to view and edit databases using the Database Explorer window. In VWD, you open this window (if it doesn't already appear) by selecting View ➪ Database Explorer; in VC#, you open it by selecting View ➪ Other Windows ➪ Database Explorer menu item. The window, shown in Figure 2-8, looks the same in both cases.

Figure 2-8: The Database Explorer window

The look of this window may vary slightly depending on where it is positioned and docked in the express environment, but wherever it is, its function is the same.

The icons along the top of the Database Explorer window are for refreshing the display, stopping a refresh operation, and adding a data connection. In Figure 2-8, no connections have been added, which is the default view that you see when you look at this window for the first time. Once a connection has been added, you can expand it to see various database objects. For example, Figure 2-9 shows a Database Explorer window from VWD expanded to view a specific column of a specific table. In this case, the window is docked in the same position as the control toolbox window.

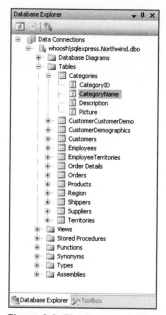

Figure 2-9: The Database Explorer window expanded

As with other items that you can select in the Visual Studio environment, selecting an item in this window allows you to view its properties in the Properties window. For the item selected in Figure 2-9, the Properties window looks like Figure 2-10.

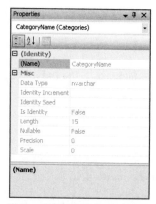

Figure 2-10: Database item properties

The properties displayed vary depending on the type of item selected.

You can edit both database structure and content through the Database Explorer window. Double-clicking on an existing table, or right-clicking the Tables folder and selecting Add New Table, takes you to the table modification screen, as shown in Figure 2-11.

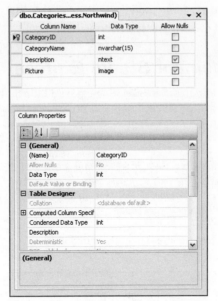

Figure 2-11: Database table modification

In Figure 2-11, an existing table is being modified. You can see the columns in the table, their data types, and additional properties relating to the selected column.

You can also view and edit table data by right-clicking on a table and selecting Show Table Data. Figure 2-12 shows the contents of a table viewed in this way.

	CategoryID	CategoryName	Description	Picture
▶	1	Beverages	Soft drinks, coff...	<Binary data>
	2	Condiments	Sweet and savo...	<Binary data>
	3	Confections	Desserts, candie...	<Binary data>
	4	Dairy Products	Cheeses	<Binary data>
	5	Grains/Cereals	Breads, crackers...	<Binary data>
	6	Meat/Poultry	Prepared meats	<Binary data>
	7	Produce	Dried fruit and b...	<Binary data>
	8	Seafood	Seaweed and fish	<Binary data>
*	NULL	NULL	NULL	NULL

Figure 2-12: Database table contents modification

Existing data can be edited here — at least for simple data types. The table shown in Figure 2-12 includes a column called Picture that contains binary data. That data would have to be edited in an alternative way — such as programmatically. The rest of the (non-primary key) data for the rows CategoryName and Description can be edited directly though this window, and new rows can be added by entering data in the bottom row, marked with an asterisk.

There are other techniques that you can use here to modify data, add database objects, and perform SQL queries, and you learn about these as you work through this book.

SQL Server Management Studio Express

SQL Server Management Studio Express (SSMSE) includes a little more functionality than the Database Explorer window in the Express products, but in essence it provides access to the same data. One difference is that there is no need to connect to specific databases in SSMSE. You connect to a DBMS, instead, and automatically have access to all the databases contained therein.

VC# Express does not permit access to databases contained in a DBMS in this way, at least not using the Database Explorer window. Instead, VC# uses local databases, which while managed by SQL Server Express, are attached only as needed and do not show up in SSMSE. VWD does not suffer from this limitation, nor do other versions of Visual Studio.

Figure 2-13 shows the preceding database displayed in SSMSE.

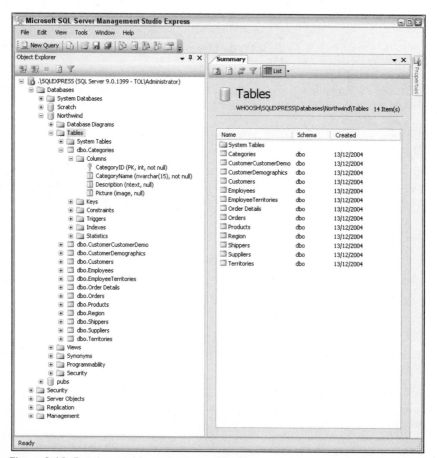

Figure 2-13: Database table contents modification

A number of basic differences are immediately apparent. First, the table names in the left pane of Figure 2-13 have a prefix of dbo, which identifies the schema to which the table belongs. The table columns include extra information in this view, so that you don't have to select them to see what type they are. The layout of folders within the database is also slightly different and provides access to database security — that is, which accounts can access the database and in what way.

Also, notice that the tree view further up the hierarchy from the expanded database includes other, non-database items. At the bottom of Figure 2-13, you can see folders for global DBMS security, replication, and more. This is because SSMSE is capable of higher-level management of SQL Server 2005 Express — not just tweaks within individual databases.

You'll return to look at these features in more depth as and when required.

Examples

You've now waded through more than enough theory. It's time to try things out for yourself. In this section, you work through a series of examples to reinforce the basic knowledge you've covered so far.

Work through these examples in the sequence that they are presented because they use the same database, which is modified as you progress.

In the first Try It Out, you create a database using Visual C# Express and add some tables and content.

Try It Out   Creating a Database

1. Open Visual C# 2005 Express Edition.

2. Click File ➪ New Project, and then select Windows Application to create a new Windows application. Name the application **Ex0201 - Create Database** and click OK. Next, select File ➪ Save All and save the project to the directory C:\BegVC#Databases\Chapter02, with the Create Directory For Solution option unchecked.

3. Select Project ➪ Add New Item.

4. Add a new SQL database called Chapter2Database.mdf to your project, as shown in Figure 2-14.

5. After you add the database, the Data Source Configuration Wizard appears. This isn't something you want to worry about for now, so click Cancel.

6. In the Solution Explorer window, double-click the Chapter2Database.mdf database item to open the Database Explorer window.

7. In the Database Explorer window, expand the Chapter2Database.mdf database item, right-click the Tables folder, and select Add New Table.

8. Add columns as shown in Figure 2-15.

9. Right-click in the row defining the FavoritePlaceId column and select Set Primary Key, as shown in Figure-2-16.

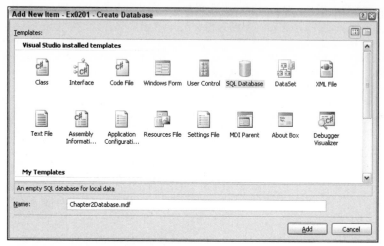

Figure 2-14: Adding a SQL database

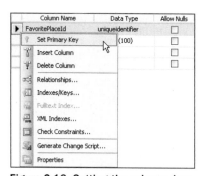

Figure 2-15: New table columns

Column Name	Data Type	Allow Nulls
FavoritePlaceId	uniqueidentifier	☐
PlaceName	varchar(100)	☐
Description	text	☐

Column Name	Data Type	Allow Nulls
FavoritePlaceId	uniqueidentifier	☐
Set Primary Key	(100)	☐
Insert Column		☐
Delete Column		☐
Relationships...		
Indexes/Keys...		
Fulltext index...		
XML Indexes...		
Check Constraints...		
Generate Change Script...		
Properties		

Figure 2-16: Setting the primary key

10. With the row defining the `FavoritePlaceId` column still selected, locate the Default Value or Binding property in the column properties below the table specification, and type the value **`NEWID()`** for this property.

11. Select File ⇨ Save Table1 and, when prompted, name the table `FavoritePlace`.

12. Add a second table in the same way, with the columns shown in Figure 2-17. Make the Id column the primary key and assign it the default value of `NEWID()`.

13. Save the new table with the name `Person`, but do not close the window showing the table structure.

Column Name	Data Type	Allow Nulls
PersonId	uniqueidentifier	☐
FullName	varchar(100)	☐
Age	int	☐
FavoritePlaceId	uniqueidentifier	☐

Figure 2-17: New table columns

14. Right-click the row for the `FavoritePlaceId` column and select Relationships.

15. The Foreign Key Relationships window opens. Click Add.

16. Select the Tables and Columns Specification property for the newly added relationship, and click the ... button at the right (see Figure 2-18) to edit the property.

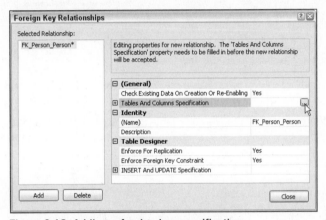

Figure 2-18: Adding a foreign key specification

17. In the Tables and Columns dialog box that appears, select `FavoritePlace` for the Primary Key Table and `FavoritePlaceId` for the column to link for both the primary and foreign key tables, as shown in Figure 2-19. Note that the Relationship Name field is automatically updated based on the tables you have chosen.

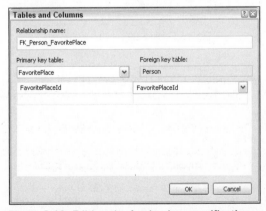

Figure 2-19: Editing the foreign key specification

18. Click OK to complete the relationship editing, and then click Close to return to the table specification. Save the table; a warning dialog appears informing you that changes to both the FavoritePlace and Person tables will be made. Click Yes to accept the changes.

19. Close the windows you have open for editing the table structures.

20. In the Database Explorer window, expand the Tables folder, right-click the FavoritePlace table, and select Show Table Data.

21. Add data to the table, as shown in Figure 2-20. Note that you shouldn't add any data to the FavoritePlaceId column — that data will be generated for you.

	FavoritePlaceId	PlaceName	Description
❶	NULL	The Seaside.	Oh I do like to be beside the seaside.
❶	NULL	My Bed.	Truly there is no place where I feel happier.
▶ ❶	NULL	On top of a mountain.	The views, and hopefully the snow.
✱	NULL	NULL	NULL

Figure 2-20: Adding favorite places

22. The data is added as you type, but to see the full row data, including the auto-generated IDs, click the Execute SQL button on the toolbar (the red exclamation mark).

23. Add the following data to the Person table (for the FavoritePlaceId field, copy the GUID value from the FavoritePlaceId column in the FavoritePlace table for the row specified):

FullName	Age	FavoritePlaceId
Oscar Wilde	30	Value for "My Bed"
Sylvia Plath	25	Value for "The Seaside"
Mary Shelley	32	Value for "On top of a mountain"
D. H. Lawrence	20	Value for "My Bed"
Edgar Allan Poe	35	Value for "On top of a mountain"

24. Close the table data windows.

25. Close the project.

How It Works

While you didn't experiment with any code in this example, you have created a Windows application and a simple, two-table database containing data and relationships between rows.

The techniques you used will be invaluable throughout this book for examining data, editing data, and modifying database structure.

In the next Try It Out, you make a simple Windows application that binds to data in the database you created, but using declarative and programmatic techniques.

Data Binding in Windows Applications

1. Create a new Windows Application in VC# called **Ex0202 - Windows Data Binding**. Save the project to the directory C:\BegVC#Databases\Chapter02, with the Create Directory For Solution option unchecked.

2. If it isn't currently visible, open the Database Explorer window (View ➪ Other Windows ➪ Database Explorer).

3. Click the Add Connection icon in Database Explorer.

4. Click Browse and locate the Chapter2Database.mdf database file created in the last example.

5. Click Open and then OK to create the connection.

6. If the data sources window isn't visible, open it (Data ➪ Show Data Sources).

7. Click Add New Data Source in the data sources window.

8. Select Database, as shown in Figure 2-21, and click Next.

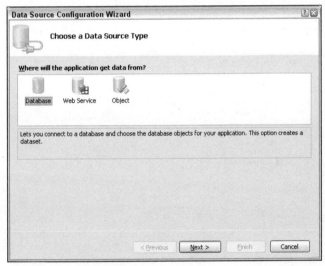

Figure 2-21: Choosing a data source type

9. Select Chapter2Database.mdf (see Figure 2-22) from the drop-down list and click Next.

10. A dialog appears warning you that the database file isn't local to the current project. Click Yes to copy the file to the output directory of the project.

11. Save the connection string using the suggested name, and click Next.

12. The wizard has loaded the database information. Select Tables, as shown in Figure 2-23, and click Finish.

13. Double-click Chapter2DatabaseDataSet.xsd in Solution Explorer to view the generated data set, as shown in Figure 2-24.

14. Open the default form for the project, Form1, by double-clicking Form1.cs in the Solution Explorer window. Add a ListBox control to the form, and name it personBox.

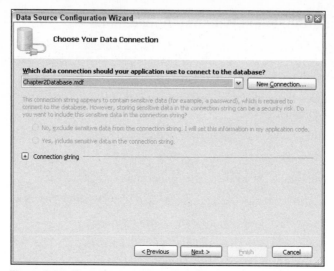

Figure 2-22: Choosing a data connection

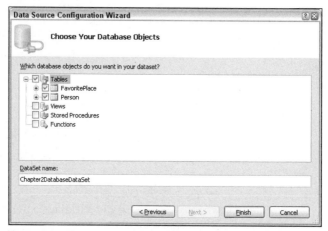

Figure 2-23: Selecting database objects

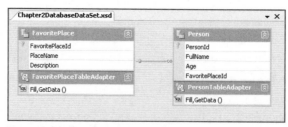

Figure 2-24: Chapter2DatabaseDataSet.xsd

15. Select the `personBox` control on the form and click the small black arrow in the top-right corner to open the ListBox Tasks window.

16. In the ListBox Tasks window, select Use Data Bound Items, and then select the `Person` table as the data source (see Figure 2-25).

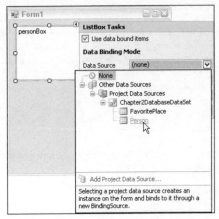

Figure 2-25: Data binding to the ListBox control

17. Next select `FullName` for the Display Member and `PersonId` for the Value Member.

18. Run the application (press F5) and verify that — with hardly any work — you have created a list box containing the list of names from the database.

19. Quit the application.

20. Add three label controls to the right of the `ListBox`:

❑ Have the first label display the words **Favorite Place:** in bold text.

❑ Name the second label `placeNameLabel`, and set its `Text` property to `placeNameLabel` so you can identify it easily.

❑ Set the `Text` and `Name` properties of the third label to `descriptionLabel`. Set its `AutoSize` property to `false` and resize it to make room for description information.

Resize the form, which should now look similar to the one shown in Figure 2-26.

Figure 2-26: Form layout

21. Double-click the form to view its code and add a new member as follows:

```
public partial class Form1 : Form
{
```

```
Chapter2DatabaseDataSetTableAdapters.FavoritePlaceTableAdapter
    favoritePlaceTableAdapter =
    new Chapter2DatabaseDataSetTableAdapters.FavoritePlaceTableAdapter();
```

22. Modify the `Form1_Load()` event handler as follows:

```
private void Form1_Load(object sender, EventArgs e)
{
    // TODO: This line of code loads data into the 'chapter2DatabaseDataSet.Person'
    // table. You can move, or remove it, as needed.
    this.personTableAdapter.Fill(this.chapter2DatabaseDataSet.Person);
    this.favoritePlaceTableAdapter.Fill(
        this.chapter2DatabaseDataSet.FavoritePlace);
    placeNameLabel.Text = "No person selected.";
    descriptionLabel.Text = "";
}
```

23. Return to the Form Designer, and double-click the `ListBox` control to add an event handler for the `SelectedIndexChanged` event.

24. Add code for the event handler as follows:

```
private void personBox_SelectedIndexChanged(object sender, EventArgs e)
{
    if (personBox.SelectedItem != null)
    {
        DataRowView SelectedRowView =
            (personBox.SelectedItem as DataRowView);
        Chapter2DatabaseDataSet.PersonRow selectedPerson =
            SelectedRowView.Row as Chapter2DatabaseDataSet.PersonRow;
        placeNameLabel.Text = selectedPerson.FavoritePlaceRow.PlaceName;
        descriptionLabel.Text = selectedPerson.FavoritePlaceRow.Description;
    }
    else
    {
        placeNameLabel.Text = "No person selected.";
        descriptionLabel.Text = "";
    }
}
```

25. Run the application. This time, selecting a person's name populates the data for the favorite place, as shown in Figure 2-27.

Figure 2-27: Form execution

26. Close the project.

How It Works

In this example you bound controls in a Windows application to the database you created earlier. You did that in two ways:

❑   Declaratively, using visual tools to create a typed data set and bind a table to a list box control

❑   Programmatically, accessing data within the typed data set using event handler code, and using that data to populate two label controls

Binding to a database file required you to navigate to the database file you created in the previous example and copy it to the current project. Then you generated a data source from that database, which produced a typed data set for the database behind the scenes. (You inspected this typed data set before proceeding.)

One of the tables in the database was bound to a `ListBox` control via the typed data set you'd generated. In doing this, VC# created code behind the scenes to populate the `People` table of the data set when the application was executed. You tested that code and saw the data bound to the control.

The next step was to fetch related data for the selected item in the list box and display it in two `Label` controls. You did this programmatically, which first required you to populate the `FavoritePlace` table in the data set. It wasn't populated automatically, because you hadn't specified that you wanted to use this data. However, the data adapter class required to populate this table was generated for you at the same time as the typed data set, so all you had to do was to use the `Fill()` method provided to fill the `FavoritePlace` table, and then it was available for you to use:

```
this.favoritePlaceTableAdapter.Fill(
    this.chapter2DatabaseDataSet.FavoritePlace);
```

With a fully populated typed data set, accessing the linked data was simple. First, you added code to retrieve the selected row of the `Person` table from the `ListBox.SelectedItem` property, by casting the property to a `DataRowView` object.

```
DataRowView SelectedRowView =
    (personBox.SelectedItem as DataRowView);
```

Similar techniques are required for all data-bound controls. The `DataRowView` class is one that you see a lot later in this book.

Next, you extracted the row from the `Person` table, using another class generated at the same time as the typed data set: `Chapter2DatabaseDataSet.PersonRow`. An instance of this class is found in the `DataRowView.Row` property and simply needs to be cast to the correct type:

```
Chapter2DatabaseDataSet.PersonRow selectedPerson =
    SelectedRowView.Row as Chapter2DatabaseDataSet.PersonRow;
```

The auto-generated `PersonRow` class contains several methods and properties to help you navigate through the typed data set data, including simple access to the related `FavoritePlace` row via the `FavoritePlaceRow` property. Using this property, extracting the data you require is simple indeed:

```
placeNameLabel.Text = selectedPerson.FavoritePlaceRow.PlaceName;
descriptionLabel.Text = selectedPerson.FavoritePlaceRow.Description;
```

Using a combination of declarative and programmatic techniques you have created a fully functioning data-reading application in double-quick time. However, there are things missing from this application. Because the data is loaded only once — when the application first executes — any changes to the database while the application is running are not reflected in the display. Also, there is no way to edit the data, although that could be added relatively easily. Both of these issues are addressed in later chapters.

In the next Try It Out, you see how to bind to database data from a web application.

Try It Out   Data Binding in Web Applications

1. Open Visual Web Developer 2005 Express Edition.

2. Click File ⇨ New Web Site. Select the ASP.NET Web Site template, the File System location, and the Visual C# language. Set the web site location to `C:\BegVC#Databases\Chapter02\Ex0203 - Web Data Binding` and click OK.

3. In Solution Explorer, right-click the `App_Data` folder and select Add Existing Item.

4. Navigate to the `Chapter2Database.mdf` file from either of the last two projects, and click Add.

5. Switch to design view for `Default.aspx`.

6. Add a `SqlDataSource` control to the form, and click Configure Data Source from the SqlDataSource Tasks window (accessible by clicking the black arrow in the top-right corner of the `SqlDataSource` control when it is selected).

7. Select the `Chapter2Datasource.mdf` connection and click Next.

8. Save the connection string using the suggested name, and click Next.

9. Select Specify a Custom SQL Statement or Stored Procedure and click Next.

10. Click Query Builder.

11. In the Add Table dialog box, select both tables, as shown in Figure 2-28, click Add, and then click Close.

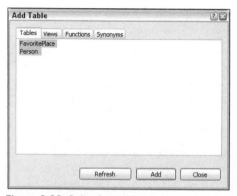

Figure 2-28: Selecting tables

12. In the Query Builder window, select all the columns in `FavoritePlace` and all the columns in `Person` except `FavoritePlaceId`.

13. Click Execute Query to test the generated query, which should result in a display similar to Figure 2-29. The query result is shown in the bottom pane.

Figure 2-29: Query Builder

14. Click OK, Next, and Finish.

15. Add a `GridView` control to the form.

16. In the GridView Tasks window, select `SqlDataSource1` as the data source.

17. Click Auto Format, select the Professional scheme, as shown in Figure 2-30, and click OK.

18. In the GridView Tasks window, enable paging and sorting.

19. In the properties list for the `GridView` control, change the `PageSize` property to `3`.

20. Execute the application in debug mode. When prompted to modify `web.config` to enable debugging, click OK.

21. When the web page you have created is displayed, experiment with pagination by clicking the page numbers at the bottom of the form, and with row ordering by clicking the column headers. The output is shown in Figure 2-31.

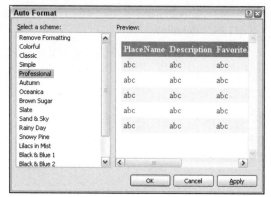

Figure 2-30: Auto-formatting

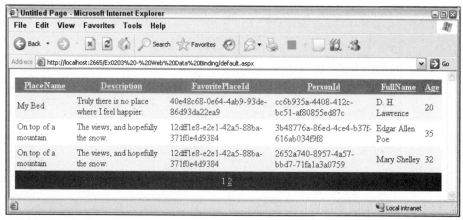

Figure 2-31: Application execution

How It Works

If anything, the web data binding shown here is even more impressive than the windows data-binding example shown earlier. The techniques are more or less the same, but the result is more aesthetically pleasing, thanks to the automatically generated code and automatic formatting. You've also added some additional functionality — pagination and sorting — without having to resort to any code behind modifications.

You started in much the same way as you did in the windows binding example — by adding a data source. This time, however, you edited the data source select query to obtain a single table of data containing information from both the `Person` and `FavoritePlace` tables:

```
SELECT FavoritePlace.PlaceName, FavoritePlace.Description,
       FavoritePlace.FavoritePlaceId, Person.PersonId, Person.FullName,
       Person.Age
   FROM FavoritePlace
   INNER JOIN Person
   ON FavoritePlace.FavoritePlaceId = Person.FavoritePlaceId
```

This query is a join between the two tables based on the `FavoritePlaceId` field, and enables you to see the person data in combination with the related favorite place data in one go.

In configuring the data source, you also configured a connection, which resulted in a `web.config` file being automatically added to the project, with a connection string stored inside:

```
<configuration>
  <appSettings/>
  <connectionStrings>
    <add name="ConnectionString" connectionString="Data Source=
.\SQLEXPRESS;AttachDbFilename=|DataDirectory|\Chapter2Database.mdf;Integrated
Security=True;User Instance=True" providerName="System.Data.SqlClient"/>
  </connectionStrings>
  <system.web>
    ...
  </system.web>
</configuration>
```

In case you haven't come across them before, `web.config` files are where you configure your web sites, and configuration settings such as connection strings are easy to access from your code. Look at the source view for `default.aspx` and you'll see the data source control defined as follows (the `SelectCommand` attribute has been removed here for clarity):

```
<asp:SqlDataSource ID="SqlDataSource1" runat="server"
  ConnectionString="<%$ ConnectionStrings:ConnectionString %>"
  SelectCommand="...">
</asp:SqlDataSource>
```

The `<%$ ConnectionStrings:ConnectionString %>` code uses the connection string stored in `web.config` to define the connection for the data provider. Similar code is available to access other configuration properties stored in `web.config`.

Once the data source was configured, you used it to bind data to a `GridView` control. The `GridView` control, as you'll see later in this book, is extremely powerful; you can use it to view, select, and even edit data. You also have a great deal of control over such things as columns, pagination, and styling. Occasionally, the automatic code generation can cause problems — particularly if there is something specific that you want to do that the wizards can't quite achieve for you, but in general the code generated for you will solve most of your problems and save you a lot of time. Remember that everything here is customizable, and everything can be done manually, should you want to. You can even create your own custom controls and tie them into the data-binding framework, making things flexible indeed.

The code generated for the `GridView` control starts with the opening tag for `<asp:GridView>`:

```
<asp:GridView ID="GridView1" runat="server" AllowPaging="True" AllowSorting="True"
  AutoGenerateColumns="False" CellPadding="4"
  DataKeyNames="FavoritePlaceId,PersonId" DataSourceID="SqlDataSource1"
  ForeColor="#333333" GridLines="None" PageSize="3">
```

This tag defines all the properties for the `GridView` control, including many that were customized by auto formatting the control. The important properties for data binding are the ID of the data source control (in `DataSourceId`) and the names of the key fields in the data (in `DataKeyNames`).

The `<asp:GridView>` element contains child elements that further configure the control. Many of them define the styling of the control:

```
<FooterStyle BackColor="#5D7B9D" Font-Bold="True" ForeColor="White" />
<RowStyle BackColor="#F7F6F3" ForeColor="#333333" />
<EditRowStyle BackColor="#999999" />
<SelectedRowStyle BackColor="#E2DED6" Font-Bold="True" ForeColor="#333333" />
<PagerStyle BackColor="#284775" ForeColor="White" HorizontalAlign="Center" />
<HeaderStyle BackColor="#5D7B9D" Font-Bold="True" ForeColor="White" />
<AlternatingRowStyle BackColor="White" ForeColor="#284775" />
```

These are mostly self-explanatory. Several styles are defined to format the look of the control.

More important, you also have the column specification for the control:

```
<Columns>
  <asp:BoundField DataField="PlaceName" HeaderText="PlaceName"
    SortExpression="PlaceName" />
  <asp:BoundField DataField="Description" HeaderText="Description"
    SortExpression="Description" />
  <asp:BoundField DataField="FavoritePlaceId" HeaderText="FavoritePlaceId"
    ReadOnly="True" SortExpression="FavoritePlaceId" />
  <asp:BoundField DataField="PersonId" HeaderText="PersonId" ReadOnly="True"
    SortExpression="PersonId" />
  <asp:BoundField DataField="FullName" HeaderText="FullName"
    SortExpression="FullName" />
  <asp:BoundField DataField="Age" HeaderText="Age" SortExpression="Age" />
</Columns>
</asp:GridView>
```

This code defines each of the columns in the control, and binds data to these columns. Each of the `<asp:BoundField>` controls shown here defines a single column (there are other column specification controls available, but only these are used in this example). Each has a `DataField` attribute saying what data field to bind to, a `HeaderText` attribute to name the column with a text header, and a `SortExpression` attribute defining how sorting works when the data is sorted by the column. The key fields also have `ReadOnly="True"` because these cannot be changed manually.

There are a lot of things that you could do to improve this application. Some of them are purely aesthetic — for instance, you might want to add more human-readable names to columns (which you can do simply by editing the `HeaderText` attributes for the columns). You might also want to reorder the columns in a more sensible way, and perhaps remove the key columns from view because they don't really give much information to the user.

You could also make data editable. That might be appropriate for the person data, but perhaps you'd restrict editing for favorite places because editing this information would edit it for all users. You might allow users to edit rows by selecting a favorite place for a person using a drop-down selector, and perhaps have a separate page for editing the list of favorite places and their descriptions.

All of this is possible with the techniques you learn later in this book.

Case Study Introduction

As mentioned earlier, this book uses an example database. Instructions for downloading and installing the database can be found in Appendix B. You might be wondering why a database is included rather than you building one as you go along. There are two main reasons:

❑ You can immediately see the sort of structure and detail that databases typically contain.

❑ You don't have to type in lots of data. (That isn't just to save you time and effort; it's also not helpful to have to type in lots of data blind without knowing what it's for or how it will turn out. If you were developing a database in the real world, that wouldn't happen.)

The database is called FolktaleDB and, as the name suggests, contains a collection of folktales. These tales are organized into the following tables:

❑ Story: The pivotal table, it contains the full list of stories that are in the database. Most of the other tables hold details about these stories. The Summary column in the Story table consists of condensed versions of the myths, legends, and fairy tales used so you can familiarize yourself with these tales.

❑ Classification: Each story in the Story table must have a classification, such as Greek mythology or traditional. The types of classification available are listed here.

❑ Ending: Each story in the Story table must be assigned a type of ending, for example, happy or sad. This table has a short selection of possible ending types.

❑ Source: Each story in the Story table must have a source. There are three possible kinds of sources available: unknown author and unknown region, unknown author and known region, known author and known region.

❑ Character: Characters mentioned in the Story table are listed in the Character table. Occupations and e-mail addresses are listed where known ("known" here meaning "made up for the purposes of this book"). Additionally, information about a character's parents is included where available, because some characters are related to each other. There is also a Notes column, which is a useful place to store miscellaneous information.

❑ Species: The species of each character must be specified in the Character table. The Species table contains the names of and information about the most common creatures found in folktales.

❑ CharacterStory: Links characters from the Character table to the relevant stories in the Story table in which they participate.

❑ Address: Some characters have addresses; a few characters have more than one. The addresses are listed in this table.

❑ CharacterAddress: Connects characters from the Character table with their address in the Address table. Because characters can have multiple addresses, it is possible to specify here whether an address is a primary residence for that character.

❑ Location: Contains a list of the locations where stories from the Story table take place. The locations might relate to the addresses in the Address table, but are generalized. For example, if a story takes place in a cottage whose address is listed in the Address table, the location would simply be "cottage."

❑ StoryLocation: Associates stories from the Story table with locations from the Location table. A story can have more than one location.

❏   `Enchantment`: Lists some common folktale spells.

❏   `CharacterEnchantment`: When an enchantment is mentioned in a tale in the `Story` table, the details are recorded here. The information includes the identity of the caster (the one who casts the enchantment), the identity of the subject, the duration of the enchantment in years, and the cure.

❏   `Wish`: Lists some common wishes. (I'm not sure if you can call them folktale wishes, because they aren't really confined to folktales!)

❏   `CharacterWish`: When a character makes a wish in a tale in the `Story` table, the details are documented in this table. It lists the character making the wish, the type of wish, and the outcome of the wish.

The complete database structure and relationships are shown in Figure 2-32. All tables use a GUID column as a primary key.

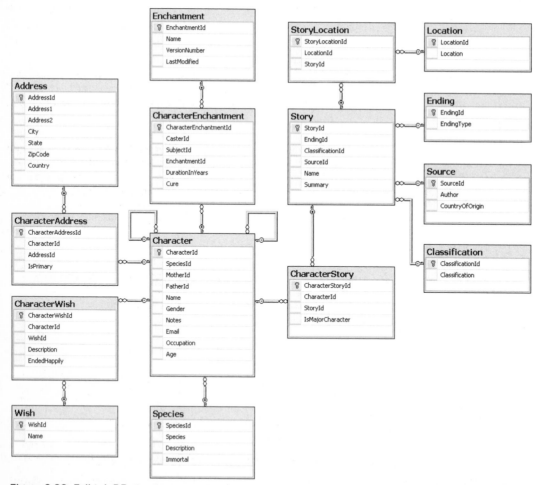

Figure 2-32: FolktaleDB structure

The database is structured so that you can make simple joins between some tables and more complex joins between others. For example, you could retrieve the names of all the stories in the database as follows:

```
SELECT Name FROM Story
```

Or you could get a list of the characters and their species in the database as follows:

```
SELECT Name, Species FROM Character
INNER JOIN Species ON Character.SpeciesId = Species.SpeciesId
ORDER BY Species, Name
```

A more complicated query would be to obtain the number of characters in stories by a particular source, which you could do as follows:

```
SELECT Author, CountryOfOrigin, COUNT(Character.CharacterId) AS CharacterCount
FROM Source
LEFT OUTER JOIN Story ON Story.SourceId = Source.SourceId
LEFT OUTER JOIN CharacterStory ON Story.StoryId = CharacterStory.StoryId
LEFT OUTER JOIN Character ON Character.CharacterId = CharacterStory.CharacterId
GROUP BY Author, CountryOfOrigin
```

The material in the database might not be what you were expecting from a book like this, but I hope it provides some light relief and you enjoy working through the examples. Only the stories in FolktaleDB are frivolous; the design principles you learn are as applicable to customer databases or product catalogs as they are to fairy tale creatures.

There are two final points to note about the database. First, not all of the data it contains is used in the examples in this book. Some extra information is included so you can experiment with it. Second, some of the extra information was added after the examples for the book were written, so don't panic if you see a story, character, or wish in your copy of the database that you can't find in the book!

Summary

In this chapter you covered the rest of the basics that you need to progress on to more advanced techniques.

Specifically, you learned the following:

- ❏   ADO.NET is the tool of choice for accessing databases from code using the .NET Framework.
- ❏   Classes derived from ADO.NET's base data access classes — DbConnection, DbCommand, DbDataReader, and DbDataAdapter — are used to access data in databases and to manipulate databases.
- ❏   ADO.NET's data representation classes — DataTable, DataRelation, DataSet, and some others such as DataRow — are used to contain database data.
- ❏   DBMS-specific classes are derived from ADO.NET's base classes, for example, SqlConnection.
- ❏   The DataSet class is probably the most important ADO.NET class. Its objects are significant and contain a great deal of functionality; their true power is in being used in conjunction with

other objects — including controls for use in web and Windows applications, web services, and XML documents.

❑ Data sets are heavyweight objects, creating an overhead that can be significant in high-performance applications. In addition, transferring data over the Web in the form of a data set can mean transferring large amounts of XML data. However, data sets — and typed data sets in particular — provide a vast array of features that are easy for you to tap into with little code, and the code you do write to manipulate them is often remarkably simple. Without data sets, the capability to have a representation of database data where all edits are recorded in the class, and where those edits can be transmitted back into the database with ease, might require quite a large amount of code and be rather difficult to implement.

❑ Data binding is a technique where data from a database is used to populate controls on a Windows or web form with little effort on your part.

❑ SQL Server Management Studio Express (SSMSE) has a little more functionality than the Database Explorer window in the Express products, but it provides access to the same data. One difference is that there is no need to connect to specific databases in SSMSE. You connect to a DBMS, instead, and automatically have access to all the databases contained therein.

You put theory into practice by working through examples in which you created a database and consumed its data in both Windows and web applications. You also were introduced to the case study database that you will be using in subsequent chapters. The database has been designed to contain everything you need to help investigate all aspects of database design in C# for all kinds of applications.

In the next chapter, you take a step back to cover one aspect of data access in much more detail — viewing data in Windows applications.

Exercises

1. Which ADO.NET class is responsible for connecting to a database, and which class is the SQL-specific version of this class?

2. When accessing databases using ADO.NET you will always use a `DataSet` object. True or false? Why?

3. Which of the following are types of objects in ADO.NET?

    a. Data joiners

    b. Connection objects

    c. Data row objects

    d. Data deleting objects

    e. Primary key objects

    f. Data adapters

4. When using Visual C# Express, why would you not spend a lot of time using SSMSE?

5. Data binding is possible only with a few web and Windows controls, but those controls will do everything that you require, so it doesn't matter. Do you agree with this statement? Why?

6. When data binding in a web site, where are connection strings stored? Why?

Viewing Data

In Chapter 2 you learned a lot about what is possible when consuming data from databases in C# applications. In this chapter you take a far more focused approach and look specifically at viewing data in C# Windows Forms applications using data binding (although a lot of the techniques covered also apply to web applications, which is noted in the text where appropriate). Because you're concentrating on data binding, there won't be a lot of C# code in this chapter — only what is necessary to customize and control data binding. For the most part you'll be using visual tools to achieve your goals.

A lot of the functionality of data binding comes from data sources. You saw these briefly in the last chapter, but now you learn how to add a lot more customization to data sources, including how to automatically generate powerful detail displays to view (and, in the next chapter, edit) record data.

You'll also learn more about the DataGridView control; how to navigate, sort, and filter data; and just generally how to make aesthetically pleasing and powerful data access Windows Forms applications in C#.

In this chapter you learn:

❑   How to configure data sources using wizard tools

❑   How to configure data sources by using the DataSet Designer

❑   How to bind to controls using data sources

❑   How to view data in DataGridView controls

❑   How to view data in detailed forms

❑   How to navigate through data using the BindingNavigator control

❑   How to filter data using parameterized queries and the BindingNavigator control

Creating Data Sources

The first step in binding to data in a database is to create and configure one or more data sources. You were introduced to configuring data sources by using a wizard, and to binding to data by populating a `ListBox` control in the last chapter. Now you examine those techniques in more detail, and thenextend them.

In the sections that follow, you see:

❑ How to configure data sources automatically using wizards

❑ How to perform more customized data source configuration manually, using the DataSet Designer

❑ How to add more advanced features to data sources

Automatic Data Source Configuration

The Data Source Configuration Wizard enables you to perform relatively complicated data source configuration without getting bogged down in the technical details. The wizard starts automatically when you add a database or database connection to your project. Alternatively, if you choose to leave data source configuration until later, you can add a data source based on an existing database connection by selecting Data ➪ Add New Data Source, or by clicking the link or icon in the Data Sources window, as shown in Figure 3-1.

Figure 3-1: Adding a data source using the Data Sources window

Note that Figure 3-1 shows the Data Sources window docked in the same location as the Toolbox and Database Explorer windows. This might not be the case in your installation of Visual C#, so things might look slightly different. At any rate, the key functionality, including the Add New Data Source link, will be the same.

As you know, there is a series of wizard pages — you saw screenshots of them in Chapter 2. You may choose to refer to those figures as you tackle the following sections.

Wizard Page 1: Choose a Data Source Type

On the Data Source Configuration Wizard's first page, you select the type of data source connection you want to make. There are three options:

❑ **Database:** Connect to a local database using either a new or existing connection string.

❑ **Web Service:** Connect to remote data on the Internet using a web service. In Chapter 10, you see how to expose database data using web services, but for now you can ignore this option.

❑   **Object:** Connect to data stored in an object. This is an advanced technique that you can use to bind controls to custom objects; it involves the way you design your classes and reduces the amount of time you spend writing code behind to achieve it. However, as with web services, this isn't an option you need to worry about for now; you'll examine it in more depth in Chapter 8.

To connect to a database, which is after all what you're supposed to be doing in this book, use the first option.

Wizard Page 2: Choose Your Data Connection

On the second page of the wizard, you choose a data connection to connect to the database in which you want to access data. You can either select an existing connection or create a new connection. If you have already added a local database file to your project, you have a connection defined, so go ahead and use that. Alternatively, you can click New Connection and connect to a different database file.

Once you have chosen a connection, you can view it by expanding Connection String at the bottom of the page (click the + sign). This is useful because you can see exactly what string is used. Later, when you are a more advanced database user, you may see something here that you want to change — perhaps one of the more advanced properties of connections. For now, know that the connection string is a set of name/value properties separated by semicolons. Its basic structure is as follows:

```
<Property1>=<Value1>;<Property2>=<Value2>;...;<PropertyN>=<ValueN>
```

Typical properties include those described in the following table. There are many more properties that you can use and properties that may be used interchangeably with other properties for compatibility. The table shows only the ones you are most likely to see and use.

Authentication and Security

When making a new connection, one thing to consider is what authentication method to use. For Windows Forms applications you will typically use Windows authentication, where the account used to access the database is the one used to run the application. This enables you to integrate security in that the application user's credentials are used to access the database. For local databases this isn't a huge issue; the authentication method used to access remote databases is much more important. When the database you are accessing is located elsewhere on your network, Windows authentication must be correctly configured for the application to work. For more remote databases, such as databases accessed over the Internet, you are likely to use SQL Server authentication. This requires you to supply the connection with a username and password. Of course, you must take into account that there's a security risk associated with including a password in a connection string, and you must ensure that the configuration file for the application is secure, write code to request a password before making a connection, or encrypt the sensitive details in the connection string. If you are interested, you can find more information on encrypting connection strings on the MSDN page "Securing Connection Strings," which you can find at `http://msdn2.microsoft.com/en-us/library/89211k9b.aspx` or in your local MSDN installation.

With Visual C# Express, you can connect only to local database files, meaning only database files that are located in your projects or that can be accessed using the file system. Because there's no opportunity to connect to remote databases located on other servers, security isn't so much of an issue in this environment. However, all the techniques you learn here apply to using the more fully featured versions of Visual Studio, and you will likely need to consider security at some point. Also, when using Visual Web Developer Express, you can connect to remote data sources, so you'll have to think about security there.

Property	Description
Data Source	The DBMS instance to use to make the connection. For remote databases, this is the DBMS containing the database. For local databases, it is the DBMS used to manage the connection. This property may be the name of a server, the name of a server and the instance of the DBMS if several DBMSes are installed, or a URI of a remote database — which could be an IP address and port number. For SQL Server Express, the property value is typically `.\SQLEXPRESS`, meaning the local DBMS with the instance name SQLEXPRESS, which is the default value used when SQL Server Express is installed.
AttachDbFilename	The path to the local database file. You may see the string `|DataDirectory|` making up part of the path. That's a dynamically configured string that points to the output directory of a Windows Forms application or the `AppData` directory of a web application.
Initial Catalog	Specifies the name of the database in the DBMS to which a remote database connection can be made.
Integrated Security	If this property is set to `True` or `SSPI` (the values are equivalent), Windows authentication is used, with the running account used to authenticate to the DBMS and database. The default value is `False`.
Connect Timeout	The number of seconds to allow for making a connection. If this time period is exceeded, the attempt to make the connection fails and an exception is thrown.
User Instance	If this property is `True`, a separate instance of the DBMS is run under the user's account. This can be beneficial for process isolation and performance. It is a fairly advanced feature that you may want to research elsewhere. For now, if the automatically generated connection string includes this property and everything works properly, let it be ("if it ain't broke, don't fix it").
User ID	The username used to connect to the database for SQL Server authentication or Windows authentication without integrated security.
Password	The password used to connect to the database for SQL Server authentication or Windows authentication without integrated security.
Persist Security Info	If this property is `True`, the username and password properties are stored in the connection when it is made and can be retrieved from it — even when direct access to the connection string is restricted. This is a potential security risk (although quite a specialized one), so the property's default value is `False`.

This wizard page warns you if you have included sensitive information (username and password) in the connection string. It also gives you the options to remove this information (and set it manually from code) or leave things as they are — which assumes that you will take other measures to protect the information if necessary.

Wizard Page 3: Choose Your Database Objects

At this point in the wizard, the pages become different for web and Windows applications. The pages used in the web application version are covered in Chapter 5.

For Windows applications, the third page is the place where you configure the basic structure of the typed data set that will be generated for use in binding to your controls. This is only a starting point — you can modify the typed data set later. However, it is useful to do all you can now because it will save you work later.

On this page you select the database objects (tables, views, stored procedures, and functions) that you want to be included in the data set. This information is presented in a hierarchical way, and you can select whole categories of objects at once should you want, such as "all the tables." Alternatively, you can expand the selection tree and select individual items. You can even go beyond the table level and select individual columns of tables to include.

As a rule of thumb, include only the data that you want to use. Including additional data only wastes memory and performance, so there is no need to select it. Unless you have a real requirement for them, there's generally no reason to include all database objects.

The dataset will include all relationship and key information for the selected objects, including functionality to navigate to related information from one row to another and so on. Therefore, it's a good idea to simplify application development by including related tables in a single data source rather than creating multiple data sources for them. Having said this, it certainly isn't an error to use multiple data sources for that sort of thing, as long as you are comfortable with the implications. In fact, it may be the preferred way of doing things in some applications. When using data binding, however, having a single data source is generally a good idea because it will enable data-bound controls to communicate with one another without much intervention, and makes much fairly advanced functionality simple to implement.

Each database object is populated from the database using its own data adapter. A single table uses a single data adapter, for example. When data binding to controls, data adapters are instantiated and used as required by data-bound objects, which means that the implications of including additional objects in a typed data set are not as critical as you might have thought. That isn't an excuse to make typed data sets more complicated than they have to be, however.

Completing the Wizard

When you click Finish after selecting objects in page 3, a typed data set is generated in your project. You can view and edit the data set using the techniques given in the "Manual Data Source Configuration" section later in the chapter.

Re-Entering the Wizard

At times the data set you generate with the wizard won't quite be what you want. Perhaps after using the data set for a while you might realize that you should have included an additional table. Conversely, you may recognize that you have included more information than you need and want to "slim down" the data set to improve performance. You can reconfigure the data set manually, but you can also use the wizard to reconfigure the data source.

To do this, select the data source in the Data Sources window and reenter the wizard using the Configure DataSet With Wizard option. The wizard's third page opens, and you can change the objects and details of objects that you have selected.

A word of warning: doing this may overwrite changes that you have made manually to the data set using the DataSet Designer, so be careful!

In the following Try It Out, you create and configure a data source and examine the result. You'll build on the code from it in subsequent Try It Out examples in this chapter.

Try It Out   Using the Automatic Data Source Configuration Wizard

1. Open Visual C# 2005 Express Edition.

2. Create a new Windows application in VC# called Ex0301 - Automatic Configuration.

3. If it isn't currently visible, open the Data Sources window (Data ➪ Show Data Sources).

4. Click Add New Data Source in the Data Sources window.

5. Select Database on the first page of the wizard and click Next.

6. Click New Connection on the second page of the wizard.

7. Browse to the sample database FolktaleDB.mdf in the downloadable code for this book, and then click Open, OK, and Next.

8. Click Yes to copy the database locally, and click Next to save the database connection string in your project with the name FolktaleDBConnectionString and move to the third page of the wizard.

9. Select the Character, CharacterEnchantment, and Enchantment tables, and click Finish.

10. Verify that a typed data set has been added to your project with the name FolktaleDBDataSet .xsd and that it contains the selected tables and relationships between those tables, as shown in Figure 3-2.

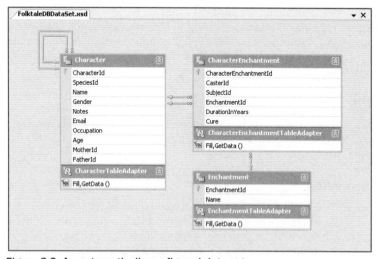

Figure 3-2: An automatically configured data set

11. Save the project in the directory `C:\BegVC#Databases\Chapter03`, with the Create Directory For Solution option unchecked.

12. Close the solution.

13. Close Visual C# 2005 Express Edition.

How It Works

In this example you have used the Data Source Configuration Wizard to automatically configure a data source for three tables contained in this book's sample data source. You will continue to build up this example application throughout the chapter.

Manual Data Source Configuration

Automatic data source configuration takes you only so far. For more involved applications, you have to configure data sources manually. Alternatively, you may feel more comfortable doing things without the aid of a wizard because doing so gives you far greater control over your data and you can be absolutely sure that things are working exactly as you want them to. In addition, sometimes you will want to make minor modifications to a data source, and it can be quicker and easier to do so without using the wizard.

In all these cases, you will use the DataSet Designer.

Adding a Data Source Manually

To add a data source manually, use the `DataSet` project item template, as shown in Figure 3-3, to add a new item to your project.

After you click Add, you are presented with a blank display in the DataSet Designer.

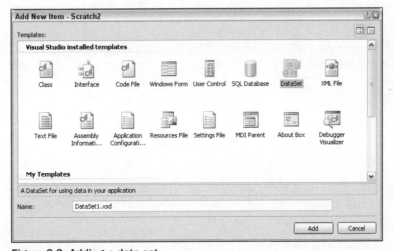

Figure 3-3: Adding a data set

Configuring a Data Set

The next step is to add items to your data set. You can use items from the Toolbox window (shown in Figure 3-4) or you can drag items from the Database Explorer window.

Figure 3-4: Toolbox items for the DataSet Designer

You'll come back to the Database Explorer window shortly. First, take a look at the basic items that make up a data set, as listed in the Toolbox window.

DataTable

A `DataTable` item is a table data structure. Adding it to your data set may sound useful, but it's often not useful at all. Simply adding a data structure doesn't insert any of the other framework that's required to populate that data structure or modify data in a database using that data structure. It doesn't, for example, include a data adapter that can be used to communicate with a database.

However, the other Toolbox items use data tables that work in exactly the same way as the `DataTable` item, so it makes sense to consider it here in isolation from other controls.

Dragging a `DataTable` item to the DataSet Designer results in a new table being added, with no configuration, as shown in Figure 3-5. You can also add a data table by right-clicking in the DataSet Designer main window and selecting Add ➪ DataTable.

Figure 3-5: A freshly
added DataTable item

You can rename the table using the Properties window, by right-clicking on the table and selecting Rename, or by clicking in the title bar of the table when it is selected. You can add columns to the table by right-clicking on the table and selecting Add ➪ Column. Once you have added some columns, you can configure them using the Properties window, which contains a host of properties that are quite self-explanatory or at least look familiar in the context of database tables. You can, for instance, configure the name of the column using the `Name` property, the data type of the column using `DataType`, whether the column can contain null values using `AllowDbNull`, and a default value for the column using `DefaultValue`.

There are also several ways to add primary keys. You can right-click on the table and select Add ➪ Key. That gives you a dialog box in which you can select the column or columns to make up a key, with a checkbox enabling you to select whether the key is the primary key. Alternatively, you can right-click on a column and select either Add ➪ Key in the same way, or you can simply right-click on a column and select Set Primary Key to set it on that column.

That's how you can build up your table, add and edit columns, and configure keys. Figure 3-6 shows a configured data table with two columns, one of which is set as the primary key.

Figure 3-6: A configured
DataTable item

Relation

The `Relation` item is used to add relationships between data tables. You can add a `Relation` item by dragging one from the Toolbox onto the DataSet Designer, by right-clicking the DataSet Designer and selecting Add ➪ Relation, or by right-clicking on a table and selecting Add ➪ Relation.

When you add a `Relation` item, a dialog box appears in which you configure the relationship, as shown in Figure 3-7.

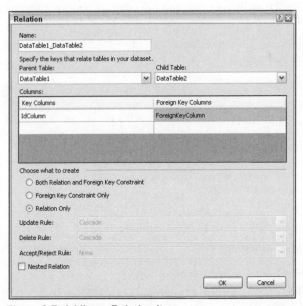

Figure 3-7: Adding a Relation item

The items shown in this dialog box are as follows:

❑ **Name:** Names the relationship.

❑ **Parent Table:** The parent table of the relationship — that is, the table at the "one" end of the one-to-many relationship.

❑ **Child Table:** The child table of the relationship — that is, the table at the "many" end of the one-to-many relationship.

❑ **Columns:** The key columns used to define the relationship. Typically, you have to enter information only in one row here, where the Key Columns entry is the primary key of the parent table, and the Foreign Key Columns entry is the foreign key column in the child table.

❑ **Choose What To Create:** You can choose to create the relationship, place a constraint on the foreign key column (to restrict column values to values that exist in the parent table key column), or both. If a foreign key constraint is added, the next three options become available. If the relationship is added, the Nested Relation option is available. If both are added, all the remaining options are available.

❑ **Update Rule:** Select a rule for what happens to child rows when parent rows are modified. The available options are:

  ❑ **None:** Take no action.

  ❑ **Cascade:** Update values in child rows. This would occur if the value of the primary key in the parent row changed, in which case rows in the child table that referenced that row would have their foreign keys modified to match.

  ❑ **SetNull:** Child rows have their foreign key value set to null if the primary key of the parent row is modified.

  ❑ **SetDefault:** Child rows have their foreign key value set to the default value for the column if the primary key of the parent row is modified.

  Depending on the value chosen for this property, changes to the parent row may result in a situation where the relationship rules are broken and where child rows are left with no parent row (usually referred to as being *orphaned*). This can be a problem, especially when modifying data in a database because it can result in a failure to modify data, depending on the way the relationship is defined in the database. Unless the `DataSet.EnforceConstraints` property is set to `false`, broken relationships result in exceptions being thrown, which of course means that you can write code to catch these exceptions and act on them if desired.

❑ **Delete Rule:** Determines what happens to child rows when a parent row is deleted. The values available for this are the same as for the update rule:

  ❑ **None:** Take no action.

  ❑ **Cascade:** Delete child rows.

  ❑ **SetNull:** Set the foreign key column in child rows to null.

  ❑ **SetDefault:** Set the foreign key column in child rows to the default value.

  As with the update rule, this can result in broken relationships and exceptions.

❑   **Accept/Reject Rule:** Determines what happens to child rows when changes to parent rows are accepted or rejected (canceled). The values available for this are:

  ❑   **None:** Take no action.

  ❑   **Cascade:** Accept or reject changes on child rows.

❑   **Nested Relation:** This setting has no effect on the data table. Instead, it determines what happens when data in the data table is converted to XML. For a nested relationship, child rows are represented as child elements within the element representing the parent row. With this setting set to `false`, child row elements are not contained in parent elements but are located separately. In either case, you can use the foreign key column value to locate parent items, but navigation through data sets in XML form can be simplified with nested elements. The default value is `false`.

When you add a data relation, it's shown in the DataSet Designer using standard database notation (see Figure 3-8).

Figure 3-8: Adding a Relation item

You can modify relationships by right-clicking on them and selecting Edit Relation.

Query

The `Query` item allows you to execute SQL queries against a database. However, these queries are limited in that they can return, at most, a single value. You can't, for example, use a `Query` item to return a set of rows, or even a single row. This is useful because it enables you to group database operations in the data source that would otherwise not have a logical place to exist. Typically, you use a `Query` item to execute scalar-valued or aggregate functions, or to perform operations such as adding, deleting, or modifying rows.

To add a `Query` item, drag it from the Toolbox to the DataSet Designer window, or right-click in the window and select Add ➪ Query. When you do so you are presented with the TableAdapter Query Configuration Wizard. This may seem strange because you are adding a query, not a data adapter. However, the way that queries of this form are implemented is to create a table adapter container for queries (referred to in the wizard as the TableAdapter) and add the queries to it. Once you have added one query, and implicitly created a table adapter, you can add more queries to the same table adapter, thus grouping your queries in one place.

The first page of the TableAdapter Query Configuration Wizard is much the same as the first page of the Data Source Configuration Wizard — you must select a database connection to use. Then you can move on to the second page, shown in Figure 3-9.

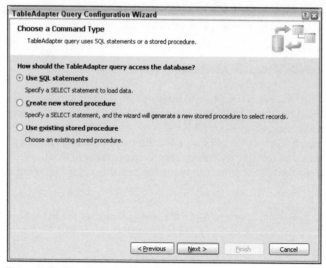

Figure 3-9: Choosing a query command type

On this page you select the type of command that the query should execute. You can choose:

❑ **Use SQL Statements:** Enables you to create any SQL query you might like to as long as it returns either no result or a single result. You can also provide a parameterized query by which you can pass values to be used by the query (such as the ID of a row to delete in a delete query).

❑ **Create New Stored Procedure:** Similar to the preceding option, but the SQL you enter is used to create a stored procedure that is then accessed directly by the Query item. These also can be parameterized.

❑ **Use Existing Stored Procedure:** Creates a command that calls an existing stored procedure in the database, parameterized or not. Care should be taken here to use a stored procedure that returns no results or a single value; otherwise you cannot predict what you'll receive as a return value.

For the first two options, the next stage is to choose the type of SQL statement you are creating, as shown in Figure 3-10.

As you can see, the only option unavailable is Select Which Returns Rows. You can, however, create any other type of SQL statement.

The next step for a SQL command or stored procedure based on a SQL command is to enter the text of the command itself. You can either do that manually or use the SQL command builder, which enables you to design queries graphically. If you want to parameterize your queries, you can supply variable names in the form:

```
@<Variable Name>
```

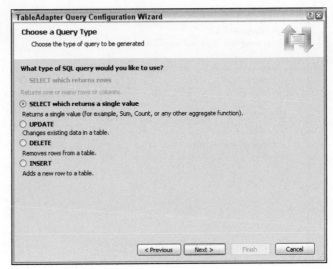

Figure 3-10: Choosing a query type

For example, you could make a query as follows:

```
SELECT StringColumn FROM MyTable WHERE MyTableId = @MyTableId
```

This would return the value for a single column in a single row, where the row is identified by an ID value specified as a parameter called @MyTableId.

If you are using an existing stored procedure, you are presented with a drop-down selector from which to choose a stored procedure to use. Then you will see the parameters that will be generated and the value that will be returned.

Using the commands you generate is something that you will typically do from C# code that you write, although it is equally possible to bind the results of queries to control properties.

TableAdapter

The last object to consider is perhaps the one that you will use most often. Adding a TableAdapter actually results in the addition of several things. First, of course, you add a TableAdapter to which several Query objects will be added. In addition, you are adding a DataTable to contain the results of the select query that is added to the TableAdapter. The DataTable is also used when adding to or modifying database data.

All of this, however, is achieved in a single step.

Adding a TableAdapter can be done using the Toolbox window or by right-clicking in the DataSet Designer and selecting Add ⇨ TableAdapter. In either case, you are presented with the TableAdapter Configuration Wizard. On the first page of this wizard, as with other wizards you have seen, you select or create a data connection to use. The next step is to choose a command type to use, as shown in Figure 3-11.

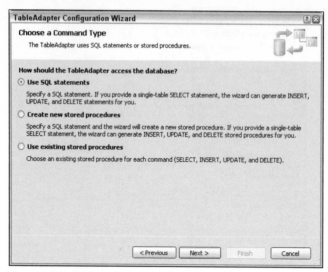

Figure 3-11: Choosing a command type

The options here are as follows:

- **Use SQL Statements:** Enables you to create any SQL query you might like to as long as it returns table data. You can also provide a parameterized query with which you can pass values to be used by the query (such as the value of a column to use to filter the results returned). If you don't use a join to select data from more than one table, the wizard can generate commands to insert, update, and delete data.

- **Create New Stored Procedures:** Similar to the preceding option, but the SQL you enter is used to create a stored procedure that is accessed directly by the `TableAdapter` item. If you don't use a join to select data from more than one table, the wizard can generate stored procedures to insert, update, and delete data.

- **Use Existing Stored Procedures:** Creates a command that uses stored procedures to select, delete, modify, and add data.

Assuming that you take the simplest option, and create a SQL select statement that selects tabular data from a single table, the next step is to create the SQL command. Again, you can use the graphical query builder to help you here, or you can just type the SQL statement in yourself. You can also choose from a selection of advanced options, shown in Figure 3-12.

These options include whether to automatically generate insert, update, and delete statements; whether to generate these statements in such a way as to take concurrency (which is discussed shortly) into account; and whether the select statement is used to refresh data automatically when changes are submitted to the underlying database. The latter options are available only if the first option is selected.

Next, you have a few more options to choose from in the generation of the `TableAdapter`, as shown in Figure 3-13.

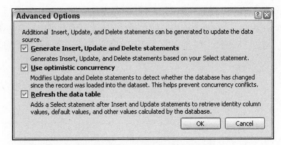

Figure 3-12: Choosing a command type

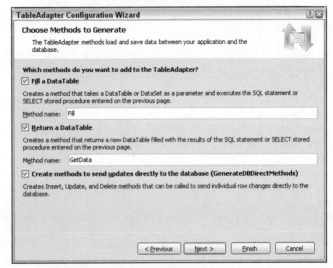

Figure 3-13: Choosing a command type

The options here are as follows:

❑ **Fill A DataTable:** Enables you to generate a method to fill a `DataTable` with results — which you usually want to do. In most circumstances the default name of the method, `Fill()`, is all you need.

❑ **Return A DataTable:** Generates a utility method that you can use to obtain a `DataTable` object from the `TableAdapter` directly, which can be useful in some circumstances as a shortcut. It certainly doesn't hurt to leave this functionality in. You can rename the default value of `GetData()` if you really want to.

❑ **Create Methods To Send Updates Directly To The Database (GenerateDBDirectMethods):** Generates a set of methods that enable you to access the underlying database directly, rather than making changes to a data table and then submitting your changes in one go. This can be useful from your custom C# code. Again, it certainly doesn't hurt to include these methods, unless you have a real reason not to.

The next step generates the `TableAdapter` and related/embedded items. Similarly, if you have chosen to use stored procedures, this completes your configuration. After the wizard has finished its operation, a new object appears in the DataSet Designer window, similar to that shown in Figure 3-14.

Figure 3-14: The TableAdapter Configuration Wizard result

The `DataTable` and `TableAdapter` items (`Story` and `StoryTableAdapter` in Figure 3-14) are linked together.

After you have created a `DataTable` and `TableAdapter` combination this way, there is further configuration that you can perform. For example, you can add additional queries to the `TableAdapter` (including scalar value queries as per the previously mentioned `Query` item). You can also see the queries that have been generated previously by using the Properties window. For example, in the `TableAdapter` shown in Figure 3-14, four queries are generated. In the Properties window, you can see these by looking at the `SelectCommand`, `InsertCommand`, `UpdateCommand`, and `DeleteCommand` properties (expand them and look at the CommandText subproperty). The queries generated here are as follows:

```
SELECT StoryId, EndingId, ClassificationId, SourceId, Name, Summary FROM dbo.Story

INSERT INTO [dbo].[Story] ([StoryId], [EndingId], [ClassificationId], [SourceId],
    [Name], [Summary]) VALUES (@StoryId, @EndingId, @ClassificationId, @SourceId,
    @Name, @Summary);
SELECT StoryId, EndingId, ClassificationId, SourceId, Name, Summary FROM Story
WHERE (StoryId = @StoryId)

UPDATE [Story] SET [StoryId] = @StoryId, [EndingId] = @EndingId,
    [ClassificationId] = @ClassificationId, [SourceId] = @SourceId, [Name] = @Name,
    [Summary] = @Summary
WHERE (([StoryId] = @Original_StoryId) AND ([EndingId] = @Original_EndingId)
    AND ([ClassificationId] = @Original_ClassificationId)
    AND ([SourceId] = @Original_SourceId) AND ([Name] = @Original_Name));
SELECT StoryId, EndingId, ClassificationId, SourceId, Name, Summary FROM Story
WHERE (StoryId = @StoryId)

DELETE FROM [Story] WHERE (([StoryId] = @Original_StoryId)
    AND ([EndingId] = @Original_EndingId)
    AND ([ClassificationId] = @Original_ClassificationId)
    AND ([SourceId] = @Original_SourceId) AND ([Name] = @Original_Name))
```

Some of the automatically generated commands look a little odd. The reasons for this are as follows:

❑ The SELECT command is exactly what you'd expect — the list of columns is selected from the table.

❑ The INSERT statement is also as expected, except that it includes a SELECT statement. This is a result of choosing the Refresh The Data Table option shown earlier; after adding a record, the record is loaded into the data table, using the primary key value StoryId to identify the new row. If you use an identity column for the primary key, the primary key won't be available in this way because it is automatically generated by the database. In this case, the generated SQL code will use SCOPE_IDENTITY(), a SQL Server function that obtains the primary key value for the last row modified. In this example, the select query is used immediately after the insert query, so the function would return the primary key value for the row just added.

❑ The UPDATE statement includes a lot more code than you'd expect, particularly in its WHERE clause (it also has a SELECT statement, but it is just like the one detailed earlier). Because the Use Optimistic Concurrency option was selected, this statement checks the value of every column value against the original row values rather than simply identifying the row to modify by its ID. This means that the row is modified only if all its values are as they were when the row was obtained from the database. If the row has changed, perhaps because of an external modification, the row won't be modified, and an exception will be thrown. This is a simple technique to ensure that concurrency doesn't become a problem. However, it is often overkill, especially in applications where the database data isn't used by multiple users. Unselecting this option results in far simpler SQL code:

```
UPDATE [Story] SET [StoryId] = @StoryId, [EndingId] = @EndingId,
    [ClassificationId] = @ClassificationId, [SourceId] = @SourceId,
    [Name] = @Name, [Summary] = @Summary
WHERE (([StoryId] = @Original_StoryId));
SELECT StoryId, EndingId, ClassificationId, SourceId, Name, Summary FROM Story
WHERE (StoryId = @StoryId)
```

❑ Similarly, the DELETE statement includes concurrency-checking code. Unselecting this option results in the following simple code:

```
DELETE FROM [Story] WHERE ((([StoryId] = @Original_StoryId))
```

Having the extra concurrency-checking code for update and delete commands isn't that serious a problem if you don't need it, although performance may be slightly affected. Perhaps the biggest implication here is that if you include the concurrency check, you have to add additional code to detect concurrency violations and act on them, which can complicate your applications. Of course, you can simply ignore errors, but that may adversely affect the end user experience. You'll learn a lot more about this in Chapter 9.

A final point when adding TableAdapter items this way is that relationships are detected automatically by the wizard. If you add data from one table, and subsequently add data from a second, related table in another TableAdapter, a Relation item is generated for you, matching the relationship defined in the underlying database.

Adding Objects from the Database Explorer Window

You can add data structures to the DataSet Designer directly from the Database Explorer window. You can, for example, drag a table from the Database Explorer to the designer. What happens next is a thing of beauty — everything that you'd otherwise have to do with a wizard happens automatically. The end result is the same as if you'd added a TableAdapter item and configured it using the wizard, but all the options are chosen for you.

If you want to add a subset of the rows in a table, you can — just select the rows you want to add from a table and drag them onto the DataSet Designer as a single unit. You can add stored procedures in the same way.

However, this ease of use comes at a price — flexibility. If you want to perform more advanced operations, you have to use other methods, or customize the resultant objects after you have added them.

In the next Try It Out, you use the DataSet Designer to create a data source manually. Note that some of the instructions in this Try It Out are deliberately kept short — but don't worry if you have to refer to the preceding text and explanations to help you along the way.

Try It Out   Manually Configuring a Data Source

1. In Windows Explorer, copy the contents of the `C:\BegVC#Databases\Chapter03\Ex0301 - Automatic Configuration` directory to a new directory called `C:\BegVC#Databases\Chapter03\Ex0302 - Manual Configuration`.

2. Open the `Ex0301 - Automatic Configuration.sln` solution file from the version of the project stored in the new directory (that is, not the version of the solution file saved in the previous Try It Out, but the new version of the file that you just created by copying the old one). Opening this file opens Visual C# Express 2005.

3. In the Solution Explorer window, rename both the solution and project to `Ex0302 - Manual Configuration`. This also renames the solution and project files.

4. Save all files.

5. Right-click on the project in Solution Explorer and select Add ➪ New Item.

6. Add a new `DataSet` item called `FolkDBDataSet2.xsd`.

7. Right-click in the DataSet Designer for the new data set and select Add ➪ TableAdapter.

8. Use the existing connection, the Use SQL Statements command type, and the following select query:

```
SELECT * FROM Story
```

9. Leave the rest of the options available in the wizard with their default options and click Finish.

10. Drag the `Classification` and `Source` tables from the Database Explorer window onto the DataSet Designer (note that you have to expand the database and database tables to see these tables).

11. Right-click the DataSet Designer and select Add ➪ Query.

12. Use the existing connection and default options, and add the following scalar query with the name `StoryCountQuery`:

```
SELECT COUNT(*) FROM Story
```

13. Right-click `QueriesTableAdapter` (the table adapter you just added) and click Add Query.

14. Add the following query with default options and the name `CharactersByStoryIdCount`:

```
SELECT COUNT(*) FROM CharacterStory WHERE StoryId = @StoryId
```

15. Save all files and close Visual C# 2005.

How It Works

The first thing you did in this Try It Out was to copy the project created in the previous Try It Out to a new project with a different name. The steps required to do this (steps 1–4) are ones that you will carry out several times in this and subsequent chapters (copy the files, open the copied project, rename the solution and project, and save the files). In other Try It Outs, this series of steps will be abbreviated to "Copy project X as project Y." When you see that, you might want to refer back to these steps to make sure you do things correctly.

Once you had a new project to play with, you added a second data source, but this time you did things manually. If all has gone as planned, you should have generated a data set just like the one shown in Figure 3-15.

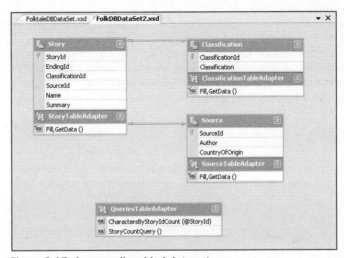

Figure 3-15: A manually added data set

As with the previous Try It Out, you make use of this data set later in the chapter.

Advanced Data Source Configuration

This section introduces you to some of the more advanced techniques you can use to configure data sources, namely:

❑ Filtering data

❑ Modifying data set code

Although these topics aren't covered in depth here, you explore them in more detail later in the book.

Filtering Data

When you bind controls to a data source it is perfectly possible, indeed often desirable, to filter the data in the data set and display a subset of the records contained therein. There is, however, another option for filtering: retrieving only the filtered rows from the database. The advantage is that less data is stored in the data table in the data set; the disadvantage is that the database must be queried every time the filter changes. For rapidly changing data this needn't be a problem because the data is refreshed from the source data when the filter changes, so updates to the database are reflected in the data retrieved.

To do this in practice you must add additional queries to a `TableAdapter` item. This procedure works in much the same way as adding queries to the `TableAdapter` used to group `Query` items, which you saw earlier. The difference, as with the base query for `TableAdapters` linked to `DataTable` items, is that a query used to filter row data returns a set of rows, not a single value (or no value).

To add a query to a `TableAdapter`, right-click it and select Add Query. The query addition works in the same way as adding the base query. You start by selecting the command type (SQL Query, SQL Query To Be Copied To A Stored Procedure, or Existing Stored Procedure). Next, for SQL queries, you choose the type of query, which should be a select query that returns rows for a filter query (you cannot add a query of this type to a stand-alone query object, because you can have only queries that return rows for table adapters with an associated data table). When entering the query, use parameters. For example:

```
SELECT StoryId, EndingId, ClassificationId, SourceId, Name, Summary FROM Story
WHERE EndingId = @EndingId
```

Then name the methods used to execute the query; it is typical to use a name that reflects the filter. For the preceding query you might use `FillByEndingId()` and `GetDataByEndingId()`, as shown in Figure 3-16.

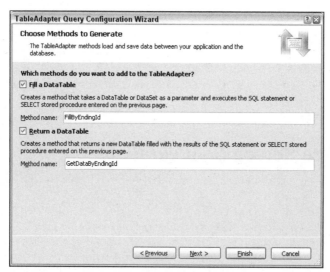

Figure 3-16: Adding a filter query

You can use this query from data-bound controls (or custom code) to retrieve filtered data. There is no limit to the number or complexity of additional queries that you can add to a `TableAdapter` in this way. However, you must make the queries return the same set of columns as the base query; otherwise, the schema of the `DataTable` will fail to load the data successfully and you will receive errors.

It is worth noting that when data-binding controls, you can filter data directly from the wizards used to configure data binding in Windows Forms. Still, there will be times when you want to do this manually, using the DataSet Designer.

Modifying Data Set Code

By now you've probably noticed that generating a typed data set for a data source results in several types of files being added to your project. In particular, a partial class definition is generated for the data set, which defines the typed DataSet class. That class inherits from `System.Data.DataSet` and includes the following:

❑ Nested class definitions for tables, rows, relationships, row-changing events, and row-changing event handlers

❑ Strongly typed methods, properties, and events for accessing rows, columns, and constraints, using the nested type definitions and reacting to data changes

The nested class definitions also contain a variety of methods and properties to ease navigation between rows, retrieving specific rows by their primary key value, and accessing related data. For example, the class definition for a row in a table that is a parent row for child rows in a related table includes a method to retrieve all child rows in one go.

The naming of all these files, classes, and methods uses the database schema information. A data set called `MyDataSet` containing a `TableAdapter` that retrieves data for a table called `MyTable` is defined in a code file called `MyDataSet.Designer.cs`. That file will contain a `DataSet`-derived class called `MyDataSet`, defined in the default project namespace. It will also contain a class derived from `System.ComponentModel.Component` called `MyTableTableAdapter`, defined in the namespace `<default project namespace>.MyDataSetTableAdapters`. This table adapter class contains methods for populating data table classes and making changes to the database, as well as methods corresponding to each query contained in the table adapter.

The exact code generated reflects the structure of the typed data set you define, including many attributes relating to XML serialization and such, as well as the types previously mentioned. The best way to get a feel for this is to play around and see what code is generated. You'll see the ADO.NET classes being used throughout the generated code, and while much of the code won't make a lot of sense at this point, you'll get the idea.

Now, the reason for bringing all this up is that the code generated is only a starting point for typed data set code. Because the code generated is for partial class definitions, you can supply your own code. You shouldn't modify the code in the `<data set>.Designer.cs` file, but you can supply your own code in a file called `<data set>.cs`. That file isn't created by default, but as soon as you want to edit it, it's generated for you. This happens if, for example, you double-click in the DataSet Designer window, or if you right-click on the data set in Solution Explorer and select View Code.

When it is first generated, the code in the file is as follows:

```
namespace <default project namespace>
{
    partial class <data set name>
    {
    }
}
```

In this class definition you can add whatever code you want. For instance, you could add code to manipulate the rows in a data table using more advanced methods. The nested class definitions and table adapter class definitions are also defined as partial class definitions, so you can add code to these classes.

A typical usage of this code is to add methods to row class definitions that set single or multiple column values without accessing the properties directly. For a row in a product table with a Boolean `Discontinued` column, for example, you could add a `MarkAsDiscontinued()` method to set the column value to `false` using a human-friendly named method.

The possibilities are endless. For basic data binding, however, this isn't something you need to do often. The real power comes when you start accessing data programmatically, as you see later in this book.

At this point it's enough to be aware that this functionality exists and that it makes things highly customizable. Now it's time to tackle data binding.

Binding to Data Sources

Once you have created a data source you can start to link form controls to it using data-binding techniques. This can be as simple or a complicated as you want to make it, and may involve a combination of declarative techniques (typically using wizards) and programmatic techniques (customizing behavior using your own code). In this chapter, you examine the simpler end of the scale and use only wizards to bind data to controls. You learn about more advanced customization later in the book.

You can bind data to pretty much any control you like, but using the wizards you will be binding to the following controls:

- ❑ List controls, to display values from a single data column in a list
- ❑ `DataGridView` controls, to display data in a spreadsheet-like format
- ❑ `BindingNavigator` controls, to navigate though multiple records in a table
- ❑ Detail views consisting of primitive controls such as `TextBox` and `Label` controls to display data for single rows

You'll see how to do all of this, but first you need to examine another control that is central to data binding: `BindingSource`.

The BindingSource Control

The BindingSource control is used as an intermediary between data-bound controls and data sources. It provides a common interface containing all the functionality that controls require when binding to data sources. Whenever you bind a control to a data source using wizards, you are actually creating and configuring a BindingSource control instance and binding to that.

This architecture gives you a great deal of flexibility, especially in advanced situations, because you can design data sources in any form you like as long as you provide the capability to communicate with a BindingSource control. That means that you can use non-database data sources, or custom data sources that use whatever esoteric data access mechanism you'd care to think of.

For the most part in this book, however, you'll access typed data set classes using BindingSource controls.

Configuring a BindingSource control is something that, as noted earlier, usually happens automatically. However, to avoid too much stuff happening behind the scenes that you aren't aware of, it's worth delving a little deeper into the workings of this control and seeing how to configure it manually.

You can add an instance of this control to your form manually. It is a nonvisual component, and you won't see it on your form. Instead, you see the instance displayed below the form in the component area, as shown in Figure 3-17.

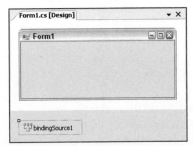

Figure 3-17: A BindingSource component on a form

In Figure 3-17 the BindingSource instance has been added with its default name — bindingSource1. You can change that, of course, but for the purposes of this discussion, it'll be referred to by that name.

> You might like to work through this section with code in front of you, and if you create a new Windows Forms application and add a BindingSource control to the main form, Form1, this is exactly how things will look.

The first step in configuring a BindingSource instance is to set its DataSource property. This can be any of several types of data sources, including ones you create yourself, but most commonly it's a typed data set. Using the Properties window, you can bind to a typed data set in your project, as shown in Figure 3-18. If you are following along in your own application, you'll need to add a data source to your project before this display matches what you see. (After you add a data source, select the bindingSource1 control; then, in the Properties window, select the DataSource property and click the drop-down arrow. From the drop-down list, select the data source to use. For new data sources using a typed data set, you should then expand Other Data Sources and then Project Data Sources to find the data source.)

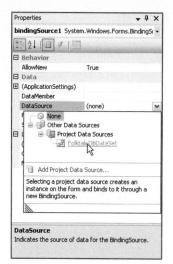

**Figure 3-18: Selecting a data source
for a BindingSource component**

Figure 3-18 demonstrates the selection of a typed data set called `FolktaleDBDataSet` as a data source.
Selecting a typed data set class in this way actually results in an instance of the class being generated.
In this example, selecting a typed dataset with a class `FolktaleDBDataSet` results in a new member
field called `folktaleDBDataSet` being added to your form. It's defined in `Form1.Designer.cs` as
follows:

```
private FolktaleDBDataSet folktaleDBDataSet;
```

It is this member that is used as the data source for the `BindingSource` control.

After you have selected a data source, you set the `DataMember` property of the `BindingSource` control,
which gives more specific information about what data you want to bind to in the data source. When
binding to a typed data set, set this to a data table — which may be populated in any of the ways you
saw earlier in the chapter. In the Properties window you can select from a list of tables in your data set
graphically, as shown in Figure 3-19.

When you add a `DataMember` this way, another new member is added to your code — a data adapter:

```
private <projectNamespace>.FolktaleDBDataSetTableAdapters.StoryTableAdapter
    storyTableAdapter;
```

In addition, code to use this data adapter to populate the relevant table in the data set instance is added
to the `Load` event handler in `Form.cs`:

```
private void Form1_Load(object sender, EventArgs e)
{
    // TODO: This line of code loads data into the 'folktaleDBDataSet.Story' table.
    // You can move, or remove it, as needed.
    this.storyTableAdapter.Fill(this.folktaleDBDataSet.Story);
}
```

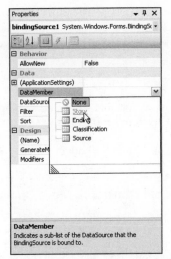

Figure 3-19: Selecting a data member for a BindingSource component

The auto-generated comment tells you that this is added for your convenience and that you can move it to wherever you want it. As things stand, the code means that the data is loaded when the form loads, making it available for use right away — which is often exactly what you want.

Both the data adapter and the typed data set instance are displayed in the components section of the Form Designer, next to the `BindingSource` control. From there you can configure the controls via properties, including modifying whether members are generated in code and so on.

The following table describes a few other `BindingSource` properties that you might want to change, although they are all optional.

Property	Description
AllowNew	Whether the `BindingSource` control allows data-bound controls to add new items.
Filter	A filter expression determining which items will be available to data-bound controls. This doesn't affect the data stored in the underlying data source, unlike adding filter queries, as described earlier in the chapter.
Sort	A comma-separated list of columns to sort by, in SQL format so you can include `ASC` and `DESC` keywords if desired.
Name	The name of the control.
GenerateMember	Whether to generate a field in the form class definition to reference the `BindingSource`.
Modifiers	If adding a field, what access modifier to apply to the field.

You now have a fully configured `BindingSource` control that you can use to bind data to other controls. Alternatively, you can configure a `BindingSource` control as part of your configuration of other controls; as mentioned earlier, the available wizards can do this for you.

Binding to List Controls

There are two Windows Forms list controls that support data binding: `ListBox` and `ComboBox`. In Chapter 2 you used a `ListBox` to perform simple binding. Both of these controls enable you to create a list of items from a data source in two columns, one to display text and the other to display the values of the text items. You can use the same column for both of these purposes.

> ### ListView Control Is More Challenging
>
> You may wonder why the `ListView` control doesn't support data binding. It is, after all, a control that displays lists of items. The `ListView` control is a more complicated way of creating a list of items, and it may have a more complex display than simply a list of strings; it has many options available. For that reason, wizard-based data binding to a `ListView` control isn't available to you. That isn't to say you can't display database data in a control of this type. You can; you just have to take a different approach and write custom code to manage data binding in a `ListView` control. Many people derive a control from this class and add custom data-binding logic to achieve the behavior desired.

With both `ListBox` and `ComboBox` controls, there are three important properties relating to data binding:

❑   `DataSource`: An object reference to a data source

❑   `DisplayMember`: The string name of a column to extract string data to display in the list contained by the control

❑   `ValueMember`: The string name of a column to extract value data for list items

In both controls you can set these properties manually, in the Properties window or in code behind the form, or you can use the Tasks display for the control. You used the latter in Chapter 2, where you bound data to a `ListBox` control. Figure 3-20 shows the ListBox Tasks window when Use Data Bound Items is selected.

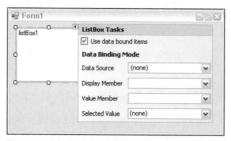

Figure 3-20: Data binding to a ListBox using the Tasks display

Note that a fourth option is available here: Selected Value. It enables you to bind the currently selected value to data. This is typically used when the list needs to be updated according to data displayed elsewhere on a form and is capable of binding to other data set instances that may be in use by other data-bound controls. For now it's best to concentrate on the other three properties.

To bind data to a ListBox or ComboBox, you first select the data source. If you have already created a BindingSource control, you can simply select a table exposed by that control. Alternatively, you can select a table within a typed data set, and all the required plumbing will be installed for you: a data set instance, a BindingSource instance, and a table adapter instance. As with adding a BindingSource control, code also is added to the form Load event handler to populate the typed data set. The ListBox or ComboBox automatically binds to this data after it is loaded, although unless you set the display and value members, you won't actually see anything interesting. Instead, you will see a list of what is obtained when the default ToString() implementation is called for the items bound to the list: When you bind to typed data set data, it will be a list of System.Data.DataRowView objects. This would result in the ListBox containing several entries (one for each row of the bound data), all reading System.Data.DataRowView. Each of these correctly represents a row in the underlying data table, but it's much friendlier to display data from the row so that you can tell which is which.

Binding to DataGridView Controls

When you bind to a DataGridView control you gain a great deal of functionality with little effort. The functionality includes letting users edit and sort data, resize and reorder columns, and so on, simply by applying the relevant properties.

As with the list controls examined in the last section, you can configure data binding to a DataGridView using properties, which you can set using any means you like, including the DataGridView Tasks window, shown in Figure 3-21.

Figure 3-21: The DataGridView Tasks window

Binding to a table data source using the Choose Data Source drop-down again results in the creation of a data set instance, a BindingSource instance, and a table adapter instance. This time, however, more aspects of the data-bound control are configured for you. For instance, you don't have to choose a column to use for item display text or value. Instead, all the columns defined in the table you bind to are displayed. (There might be more than you want, but you can change this later.) Simply selecting a data source is all you need to do to get a functioning interface with which users can interact. With the default options as shown in Figure 3-21, users can even edit the content of the stored data set (although these changes won't be committed to the database without further modification to the application).

One of the most important capabilities of the DataGridView control is modifying the columns that are displayed, including the type of column displayed. The collection of columns in a DataGridView control is accessible by clicking the Edit Columns link in the DataGridView Tasks window to display the Edit Columns window. Figure 3-22 shows an example.

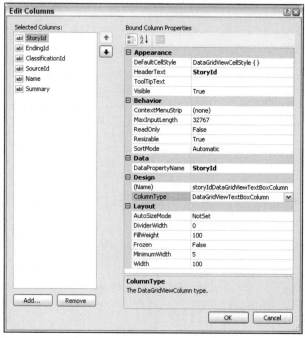

Figure 3-22: The DataGridView column editor

The Edit Columns window is divided into two main areas. On the left is a list of the columns that are currently included in the display, each of which is listed by type and name. In Figure 3-22, six text columns are listed on the left, and the StoryId column is selected (indicated by both the icon in the list on the left and the highlighted property — ColumnType — on the right). On the right is a list of properties associated with the selected column. These properties vary depending on the type of column that is selected, although many of them apply to all types of column. Not every column must bind to a data source column, and similarly not all data source columns must be bound to a DataGridView column.

The available column types are as follows:

❑   DataGridViewTextBoxColumn: A text box used mainly for displaying simple text properties, although also appropriate for other types (especially numeric types).

❑   DataGridViewCheckBoxColumn: A checkbox used mainly for Boolean (bit) column values.

❑   DataGridViewComboBoxColumn: A drop-down list box allowing for selection from a list of items. It is possible to bind the list of available items to another data source, making this a good choice to use at the many end of a one-to-many relationship.

❑ DataGridViewButtonColumn: A button. This isn't used often to bind to data, although it can be used for Boolean data or to call a dialog box containing longer text data. More often it is used to perform an operation on a row, such as confirming changes to the database.

❑ DataGridViewLinkColumn: Similar to DataGridViewButtonColumn but displays as a LinkButton. More commonly used to view the value of long text fields but also to open browser windows for URLs and so on.

❑ DataGridViewImageColumn: An image display for when the database contains image data in binary format.

You'll look at viewing text data and binding additional data to combo boxes in Try It Out sections coming up shortly. But first take a look at the following table, which describes a few of the properties that are available when editing the columns in a DataGridView, in particular those that apply to all column types.

Property	Description
DefaultCellStyle	A collection of style-related properties that you can use to control how the cells in the column look. For example, you can set the foreground and background colors of the cell.
HeaderText	The text displayed in the header for the column. There is no need for this text to match the column name in the underlying database; indeed, it is often more user friendly to use different text here.
ContextMenuStrip	If context menus are in use, this property enables you to associate one with the column.
ReadOnly	Whether the column is editable.
Resizable	Whether users can resize the column.
SortMode	Automatic (sorted by underlying column name and type), Programmatic (write your own code to sort based on this column), or NotSortable (user can't sort based on this column).
AutoSizeMode	How the column automatically sizes itself. There are several options available here, so sizing can depend on the column values, the header text value, the values of only the cells that are visible, and so on.
Frozen	Whether the column moves when the user scrolls the display. By setting this to true you can lock important columns, such as ID values, so that they are always visible, regardless of scrollbar position.

In the following Try It Out, you'll display large text fields.

Try It Out   Displaying Large Text Values

When you have a large amount of text contained in a column (for example, using the `text` data type or `varchar` with a large character limit in SQL Server), displaying it in a single text box in a `DataGridView` is often not the most useful thing that you can do. One popular option is to provide a link that, when clicked, displays text in a pop-up dialog box. Here are the steps to accomplish that:

1.   Copy the project `C:\BegVC#Databases\Chapter03\Ex0302 - Manual Configuration` to a new project, `C:\BegVC#Databases\Chapter03\Ex0303 - Large Text`, using the procedure described in the previous Try It Out.

2.   Open `Form1` in design view.

3.   Add a `DataGridView` control to `Form1`.

4.   In the DataGridView Tasks window, select Dock In Parent Container.

5.   In the DataGridView Tasks window, choose Data Source drop-down, select Other Data Sources ➪ Project Data Sources ➪ FolktaleDBDataSet2, and then click Story.

6.   Resize `Form1` so that all the columns fit in the form without having to scroll horizontally.

7.   In the DataGridView Tasks window, disable adding, editing, and deleting, and then click Edit Columns.

8.   Change the type of the `Summary` column by changing the `ColumnType` property to `DataGridViewLinkColumn`.

9.   Set the `Text` property of the `Summary` column to `Show`, and set `UseColumnTextForLinkValue` to `true`. Click OK to close the Edit Columns dialog box.

10.   Double-click on the `DataGridView` control to add an event handler to the `DataGridView.CellContentClick` event.

11.   Modify the code for the event handler as follows:

```
private void dataGridView1_CellContentClick(object sender,
    DataGridViewCellEventArgs e)
{
    if (dataGridView1.CurrentCell.OwningColumn.DataPropertyName == "Summary")
    {
        string summaryText =
            ((dataGridView1.CurrentRow.DataBoundItem as DataRowView).Row
            as FolkDBDataSet2.StoryRow).Summary;
        MessageBox.Show(summaryText, "Story Summary", MessageBoxButtons.OK);
    }
}
```

12.   Run the application and click Show for a row. The result should look like Figure 3-23.

13.   Close the application and Visual C# Express.

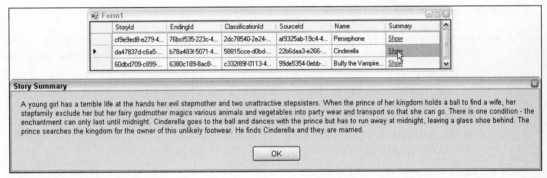

Figure 3-23: Large text view

How It Works

In this example, you did two things. First, you bound a control to a table in one of the data sources you created in a previous Try It Out. Second, you customized the data binding such that the Summary field in the Story table (which is a long text field) can be displayed in a pop-up dialog box.

This customization required a small amount of column manipulation and a small amount of custom code (although not so much as to preclude it from this chapter). It is worth looking at the code in a little more detail because it illustrates some useful properties of DataGridView.

The event hander is executed when the user clicks a cell. The code first checks for the column that the user has clicked:

```
if (dataGridView1.CurrentCell.OwningColumn.DataPropertyName == "Summary")
{
```

The DataGridView.CurrentCell is used to obtain the cell that was clicked. You could use the event arguments object to achieve this, although the DataGridViewCellEventArgs class exposes only indices of the cell. To be sure you are retrieving the column correctly in this case, you should not use indices — in case columns have been deleted, have changed order, and so on.

Once you have the current cell, check that it is referring to the Summary column in the database (and hence is the cell you're after) using the CurrentCell.OwningColumn.DataProperty property. When you are sure that the user has clicked a Show link, you can concentrate on extracting the column value and displaying it:

```
string summaryText =
    ((dataGridView1.CurrentRow.DataBoundItem as DataRowView).Row
    as FolkDBDataSet2.StoryRow).Summary;
MessageBox.Show(summaryText, "Story Summary", MessageBoxButtons.OK);
}
```

That first line of code, which gets `summaryText`, needs more explanation:

1. `dataGridView1.CurrentRow` is a property that exposes the current row in the `DataGridView`, that is, the row containing the cell that was clicked. This property is a `DataGridViewRow` object.

2. The `DataGridViewRow` object obtained this way has a `DataBoundItem` property that exposes the underlying data that was bound to the `DataGridView` and is responsible for the data displayed in the current row. This property is of type `object` because there is no restriction saying that a `DataGridView` must be bound to a database. When binding to a data set, however, the property is actually a `DataRowView` object, so you can cast it to this type.

3. The `DataRowView` class has a `Row` property that provides access to the actual row of data in the data set. This property is of type `DataRow`, and because you know what the actual row type is from the typed data set definition you are using, you can cast this to the appropriate type. Here the type is `FolkDBDataSet2.StoryRow`.

4. From the `FolkDBDataSet2.StoryRow` typed data set row, you can get the value of the `Summary` column by using the `Summary` property.

It is necessary for things to be this way to maintain the flexibility that in possible with the `DataGridView`. If things were made simpler here, you wouldn't be able to bind a `DataGridView` to a different data source, for example. As with all things .NET, if this really becomes a problem you could simply create your own class derived from `DataGridView` and supply it with the necessary plumbing to make this kind of thing easier to achieve — but that may be more trouble than it's worth.

In any case, the result of all this is to obtain the value of the long text value required and to display it to the user.

In the next Try It Out, you look at binding a foreign key column to a table of related data so that a more readable text display is obtained.

Try It Out Binding Combo Boxes to Parent Data

In this exercise, you use a combo box to make it easy to edit a column (although that isn't something explored in this chapter). Here's what to do:

1. Copy the project `C:\BegVC#Databases\Chapter03\Ex0303 - Large Text` to a new project, `C:\BegVC#Databases\Chapter03\Ex0304 - Parent Binding`.

2. Open `Form1` in design view.

3. In the DataGridView Tasks window for the `dataGridView1` control, click Edit Columns.

4. Change the type of the `ClassificationId` column to `DataGridViewComboBoxColumn`.

5. Set the following properties of the `ClassificationId` column:

Property	Value
HeaderText	Classification
DisplayStyle	Nothing
DataSource	Classification table in the FolkDBDataSet2 data set (select Other Data Sources ⇨ Project Data Sources ⇨ FolkDBDataSet2 to get to this item)
DisplayMember	Classification
ValueMember	ClassificationId

6. Click OK to exit the Edit Columns dialog box.

7. Run the application and confirm that human-readable classifications are displayed, as shown in Figure 3-24.

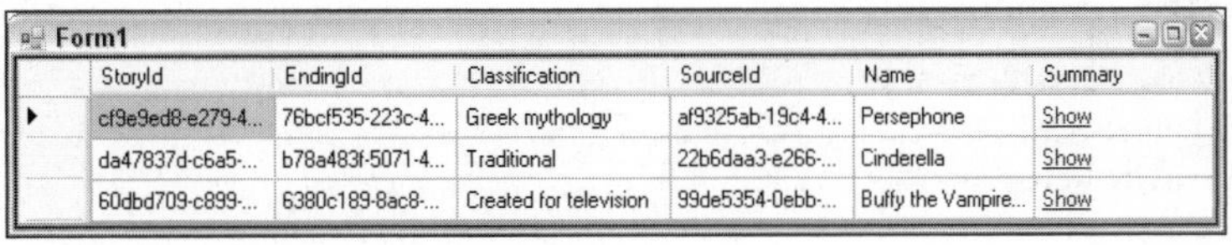

Figure 3-24: Parent binding display

8. Close the application and Visual C# Express.

How It Works

With a simple tweak to the column definition that displays data from the ClassificationId column in the Story table, you are now displaying data from the Classification table. Admittedly, you could do this using a view, or by other means, but the main advantage here is that you get a combo box. In this example, the combo box is disabled, but that doesn't mean that you couldn't enable it for editing data. To do so you would simply have to set the DisplayStyle property for the column to a different value — DropDownButton or ComboBox.

By adding a data source for the list of parent items that was taken from the same typed data set as the data used for the main display, there was no need to create an additional instance of this data set. Instead, Visual C# Express simply added a new binding source and a new table adapter to obtain data from the Classification table and put it into the existing folkDbDataSet2 member variable.

To make this work properly, two more properties were required:

❑ DisplayMember: Determines the column in the parent table to be displayed.

❑ ValueMember: The column in the parent table to link to the foreign key value to determine which row in the parent table to display data from. This is typically the primary key of the parent table, as in this example.

For this exercise, those properties were simple to decide on, particularly because there was only one column other than the ID that was of any interest — the Classification column. There might not be such an obvious choice in other circumstances, such as when you want to display two columns from the Source table. In such situations, you could include additional columns to provide extra information and bind them to the same column in the foreign key table. This would work for editing, too — changing the value of one column would automatically change the value in the other because they are linked by the underlying foreign key value.

Alternatively, you could display related data in a second DataGridView control. You see how to do that later in the book.

The BindingNavigator Control

BindingNavigator is a control that derives from ToolStrip and enables you to navigate through your data using a standardized interface. Essentially, it's a ToolStrip control with a bunch of useful buttons and ready-to-use linking to data sources ready for you to use. Figure 3-25 shows the BindingNavigator control.

Figure 3-25: The BindingNavigator control

The control enables you to move from row to row, one row at a time, jump straight to the first or last row in a data set, and jump to a row by its position by typing in a number. There are also buttons for adding (+) and deleting (x) rows from a data set (you can disable or delete these buttons for read-only data).

All you have to do to get this control to navigate through a data source is set its BindingSource property to an instance of the BindingSource class. That could, for example, be a BindingSource object that you are using to bind to an existing control such as a DataGridView. If this is the case — that the BindingSource is bound to both a data-bound control and the BindingNavigator control — the BindingNavigator control will allow users to navigate through records in the data-bound control.

If this sounds too good to be true, you're probably someone who has spent a great deal of time in the past writing code to achieve just that functionality. Well, now you don't have to.

Try It Out   Using the BindingNavigator Control

The best way to demonstrate the BindingNavigator control is via an example, so follow these steps:

1. Copy the project C:\BegVC#Databases\Chapter03\Ex0304 - Parent Binding to a new project, C:\BegVC#Databases\Chapter03\Ex0305 - BindingNavigator.

2. Open Form1 in design view.

3. Add a BindingNavigator control to the form.

4. In the BindingNavigator Tasks window, select the following:

- ❑ Embed In ToolStripContainer
- ❑ Dock Fill In Form
- ❑ Re-parent Controls
- ❑ Edit Items

5. In the Items Collection Editor dialog box, locate the `BindingSource` property and use the drop-down selector to set it to `storyBindingSource`.

6. Click OK to exit the Items Collection Editor dialog box.

7. Delete the buttons for adding and deleting rows, and also delete the button separator to the left of these rows. To delete a button or separator, click it and press Delete.

8. Run the application and confirm that the navigation control works, and that it updates automatically with the current position as you select rows in the data grid, as shown in Figure 3-26.

Figure 3-26: Using a BindingNavigator control

9. Close the application and Visual C# Express.

How It Works

Most of the work in this example has to do with positioning the `BindingNavigator` control on the form so as not to obscure the data display. Traditionally, this has been quite a fiddly thing to do with Windows Forms, although the automated tasks offered by Visual C# Express make things much easier. By clicking on a few of these tasks in turn, the layout is created for you, and a fine layout it is.

The actual binding of the navigator to data was the work of moments — although this is admittedly in part because a bound `DataGridView` with a `BindingSource` was already in place. By selecting the same `BindingSource` to use with the `BindingNavigator`, all the plumbing was integrated, and everything works as it should.

The only other thing you did in this example was to delete the buttons for adding and deleting rows, and that was purely because you are focusing on data display in this chapter.

Adding a Navigable DataGridView in a Single Step

Okay, it's time to make an admission. After working through the preceding section, it may come as a (slightly annoying) shock that you can skip a lot of what you've seen already. It is possible to add a combination of a `DataGridView` and a `BindingNavigator` control in one step.

To do that you must have already configured a data source, although as you've seen that is something that can easily done with wizards. Once you have a data source you can expand the data source hierarchy in the Data Sources window to the table level, at which point you will find that when you select a table, you get a drop-down list of options. These options are a variety of techniques that you can use to automatically add data to a form, including the three options you've already seen in this chapter and one (Details) that you'll be looking at shortly. Figure 3-27 shows how to select the DataGridView option.

Figure 3-27: Selecting DataGridView

The icon to the left of the table name shows the currently selected option for the table. In Figure 3-27 all the tables have the DataGridView option selected.

After you've selected DataGridView, drag the table to a form and automatically generate both a DataGridView control and a BindingNavigator control, along with the typed data set instance (such as folkDBDataSet2), BindingSource, and table adapter required.

That certainly saves some time, and it probably makes more sense to do things this way around rather than adding a BindingNavigator control later. However, you are still left with responsibility for both laying out and formatting the controls, including the column modifications discussed earlier. That's why you did things this way — it gave you the opportunity to pick up more techniques along the way, without being bogged down by the apparent complexity of function that this technique generates.

Binding to Detail Views

The preceding discussion leads you straight into detail views. A detail view in this context is the display of a single row of data in a more straightforward way, without displaying other data in the table. Rather than this data being displayed in a row of a DataGridView control, a detail view typically consists of a number of component controls, such as text boxes. This gives you much greater control over what is displayed and enables you to make things much more readable. You can, for example, include multiline text boxes for displaying large text data rather than displaying it in a single DataGridView cell, or in a pop-up dialog as you did earlier in this chapter.

You can, if you want to, design a detail view from the bottom up — adding relevant controls to a form, binding their values to data source columns, and adding a BindingNavigator to navigate through row data. However, it is much easier to let Visual C# Express do all this dull work for you. It's much quicker, too. As with the navigable `DataGridView` added in the previous section, you can do all this using the Data Sources window.

There are two things to do before you add a detail view from the Data Sources window. First, select `Details` from the drop-down for the table. Second, make sure that the columns in the table you want to add are associated with the controls you want to add to the form. To do this, expand the table in the Data Sources window and modify each column using the drop-down that appears when you click on it. Figure 3-28 shows an example.

Figure 3-28: Customizing a detail view

The controls that are available for binding to columns vary according to the data type of the column. You can customize the controls, and even supply your own controls, by selecting Customize in the drop-down list (visible in Figure 3-28).

After you've chosen the types of control to bind to, drag the table to your form. An example of the results (using controls as shown in Figure 3-28) is shown in Figure 3-29.

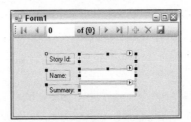

Figure 3-29: Adding a detail view

As with automatically generated `DataGridView` controls, there is more configuration to be done, such as resizing and positioning the controls that are generated for you. Even at this point, however, you have a working application, in which you can navigate through database data and see what's there.

The automatically generated `BindingNavigator` control contains an additional button — Save Data. It enables you to save changes to the data set to the database; you see it in more detail in the next chapter.

Binding to a Detail View

In this exercise, you see for yourself how straightforward it is to bind to a detail view. Just follow these steps:

1. Copy the project `C:\BegVC#Databases\Chapter03\Ex0302 - Manual Binding` to a new project, `C:\BegVC#Databases\Chapter03\Ex0306 - Detail Binding`.

2. Open `Form1` in design view.

3. In the Data Sources window, expand `FolktaleDBDataSet` and `Character`.

4. Set the options for the `Character` table so that it can be added as a detail view.

5. Configure the columns of the `Character` table as follows:

Column	Control to Add
CharacterId	Label
SpeciesId	None
Name	TextBox
Gender	TextBox
Notes	TextBox
Email	TextBox
Occupation	TextBox
Age	TextBox
MotherId	None
FatherId	None

6. Drag the Character table from the Data Sources window onto the form.

7. Position and resize the fields to obtain an aesthetically pleasing layout. The `TextBox` control for the `Notes` column needs to have a `Multiline` property of `True`.

8. Run the application. The result is shown in Figure 3-30.

9. Close the application and Visual C# Express.

Figure 3-30: Parent binding display

How It Works

In this example you created an interface to view and navigate rows in the Character table in the sample database. To do this, you used the automatic creation of a detail view using the Data Sources window (which also gave you a BindingNavigator control for free) and applied some basic formatting to the results.

There are a couple of points to note about the way that you did things in this example. First, the Age column is displayed in a TextBox control, not a NumericUpDown control as you might expect it to be. This is because the Age column is nullable, to cope with immortal beings such as gods. If you use a NumericUpDown control, attempting to set the display to a null value has no effect on the value displayed. That means that you would see the Age column value of the previous row displayed, so that the display would be out-of-date. This could be corrected using custom code, but to keep things simple in this example, that was skipped.

Next, the related data was skipped. This is partly to keep things simple and partly because the current version of Visual C# Express does not deal well with hierarchical data. The Character table contains data of this type because each row has two foreign keys referring to parent records in the same table — linking rows to "mother" and "father" rows where applicable. To bind fields properly to this data, a custom binding scheme must be implemented. Unfortunately, the automatic data binding provided by Visual C# Express is not good enough to implement this hierarchical relationship.

Filtering Data

Filtering the data that's displayed is achieved using additional queries applied to table adapters. Earlier in this chapter you saw how to add such queries. However, using the visual tools means that you can add filter queries automatically, simply by defining the filter you want to apply from your data-bound controls.

Again, this is much simpler than it sounds and best illustrated with an example.

Try It Out   Filtering Data

1. Copy the project C:\BegVC#Databases\Chapter03\Ex0306 - Detail Binding to a new project, C:\BegVC#Databases\Chapter03\Ex0307 - Filtering.

2. Open Form1 in design view.

3. Move the controls that make up the detail view down slightly to make room for an additional tool strip.

4. On the Tasks window for any of the data-bound controls on the form, click Add Query.

5. In the Search Criteria Builder window, add a new query called FillByGender with the following query text (see Figure 3-31), and then click OK:

```
SELECT    CharacterId, SpeciesId, MotherId, FatherId, Name, Gender, Notes,
          Email, Occupation, Age
FROM      Character
WHERE     Gender = @Gender
```

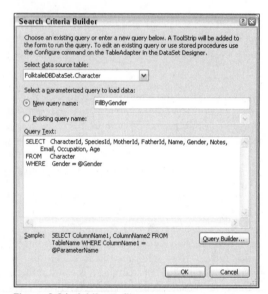

Figure 3-31: Adding a filter query

6. Run the application. Type a gender (Male or Female) into the Gender text box at the top of the form and click FillByGender to filter the results that you can view, as shown in Figure 3-32.

7. Close the application and Visual C# Express.

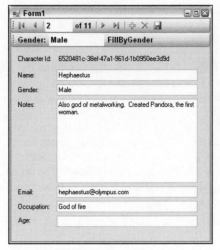

Figure 3-32: Filtered results

How It Works

In this example you filtered the result set that you can browse for through and display details by adding a parameterized query. Including the query automatically generated the following:

❑   A new query in the table adapter for the Characters table in the typed data set

❑   A method to call the parameterized query, defined in the code for the typed data set

❑   A new tool strip

❑   A label/text box/button combination on the new tool strip to configure and run the query

❑   Code that executes when the filter is applied (when the tool strip button is clicked)

This is all great stuff, although there are a couple of issues to be dealt with. First, the text of the button on the tool strip is set to the same name as the new query — in this case, FillByGender. That's not particularly user friendly, and you might want to change it. Also, clicking the button without entering any text still causes the parameterized query to run. Because no entries have an empty string for the value of the Gender column, however, the query returns no results. The code executed for the button-click event handler is responsible for this:

```
private void fillByGenderToolStripButton_Click(object sender, EventArgs e)
{
    try
    {
        this.characterTableAdapter.FillByGender(
            this.folktaleDBDataSet.Character, genderToolStripTextBox.Text);
    }
    catch (System.Exception ex)
    {
        System.Windows.Forms.MessageBox.Show(ex.Message);
    }
}
```

It would be easy to modify this and check for an empty string in the text box. If an empty string were detected, the unfiltered `characterTableAdapter.Fill()` method could be called instead of the `FillByGender()` method, solving the problem.

Ideally, you'd want to put a little more work into this functionality — perhaps supplying the possible values along with the option `All` in a drop-down list. That'd be quite easy to achieve using a mix of automatic and custom data binding and some code behind, and is something else you see a little later in the book.

Note that the queries you add may have more than one parameter (a start date and an end date, for example) or may have none. You could define two queries for gender filtering, for example — one to get the males and one to get the females. These could be applied to buttons on the tool strip in the same way as in this example, although without a text box to enter parameter values. That would simplify the data filtering, streamlining the user experience.

Summary

This chapter has provided you with a crash course in data binding and how you can use visual tools in Visual C# Express to configure data binding. This has been achieved with a minimum of custom code — although at times it has been pointed out where you might add code to add functionality.

Specifically, you have learned:

❑ How to use the Data Source Configuration Wizard to connect to a database data source, including how to select the objects in the database that will make up the data source (the database tables, for example). This led to the creation of a typed data set, which you can examine in the DataSet Designer.

❑ How to use the DataSet Designer to modify typed data sets or create typed data sets manually. You used the graphical interface to configure each of the objects that can be used in data sets (queries, tables, table adapters, and relationships).

❑ How to add additional queries, including parameterized queries, to table adapters, and to simplify the creation of typed data sets by dragging components from the Database Explorer window.

❑ How to bind data to controls using the `BindingSource` control. You saw what this control does, how it fits into the data-binding picture, and what happens when you add one to a form. While this isn't something that you will typically do manually (because the control is added automatically in many circumstances), it was useful to see how the control works and how you can configure it.

❑ How to bind controls — including `ListBox`, `DataGridView`, `BindingNavigator`, and `TextBox` controls — to data in several different ways,

❑ How to perform some simple modifications to enable data to be filtered. You saw how to add a parameterized query to enable filtering functionality and how to use that query to generate a basic user interface to filter data.

In the next chapter you look at how to extend the techniques you've covered in this chapter to edit data and add new rows to tables — again using a minimum of code. You'll also learn a little more about displaying related data, something that was only touched on in this chapter.

Exercises

1. What is a connection string? What sort of information does it contain?

2. What is the limitation placed on SQL queries added to stand-alone Query items in the DataSet Designer?

3. Copy the project `C:\BegVC#Databases\Chapter03\ Ex0304 - Parent Binding` to a new project, `C:\BegVC#Databases\Chapter03\Q0303 - Extended Binding`. Modify the project by replacing the `SourceId` column with two columns bound to the `Author` and `CountryOfOrigin` columns in the `Source` table.

4. The `DataGridView` control is a great way to display any table data and requires practically no configuration. Do you agree with this statement?

Modifying Data

To modify data, you'll use techniques similar to those you learned when data binding to Windows Forms controls in the preceding chapter. Before you do that, however, there is a small amount of theory to get through. Specifically, you need to understand when data modification is possible. The database structure may preclude data modification in many circumstances — by design or otherwise. Should you want to expose your data for editing you must be aware of this and design accordingly. In addition, when using Visual C# Express you must take care to configure the local database correctly to avoid changes being lost when your application is recompiled.

Later in the chapter you see how to modify data using `DataGridView` controls and detail views. You'll find the fundamentals surprisingly simple, but there are some quirks of which you need to be aware. Topics you'll explore include dealing with GUID primary keys, how to cancel data modifications, and how to update multiple related tables in one go. These extra details require some custom code to be written, so this chapter shifts the emphasis slightly from the declarative techniques used in the previous chapter.

You'll also examine a few considerations to take into account when building applications that are capable of modifying data. Some of these are purely cosmetic, and the benefits are simply things that will make the user experience flow better. Some are far more important.

To summarize, in this chapter you look at:

- ❑ Prerequisites for data modification
- ❑ How to modify data using data-bound controls
- ❑ Additional application design considerations

Data Modification Prerequisites

Several factors determine whether it is possible for your applications to modify data. These include, but are not limited to, the structural details of your database. Perhaps more important, however, are the factors that you introduce in the way that your application communicates with the database. This section will help you make sure you provide the appropriate level of access to your data.

Common ways in which database access might be restricted include:

❑ Database security

❑ Database views

❑ Application data sources

Database Security

The first and most fundamental restriction on database access (including modification) is database security. There's no need to worry too much about this yet, because until now you've been using a security configuration that has given you unrestricted access to your databases. Nevertheless, you need to be aware of what is possible because it will affect you later.

No matter how you access a database — using a Windows account or using a built-in DBMS security account — the DBMS assigns you a set of rights. You may have complete control over everything — all objects in all databases as well as adding and removing databases. Alternatively, you may gain access to only a single database or to a single table within a single database. Using SQL Server, you might even have access restricted to individual table columns.

The first thing a DBMS does when you attempt to open a connection is to authenticate you with whatever credentials you have supplied — either a username and password combination or a Windows authentication token. When you do this manually using Windows authentication, you will use the currently logged-in account; in applications there might be a specific account used, or impersonated, according to how the application works.

Only authenticated users can access the DBMS, and authenticated users can perform only the tasks that are authorized by the DBMS. That might be configured by a database administrator, or you might configure it yourself; in either case the account you use determines the level of access permitted. The key point in the context of this section is that access levels may be read-only so that you can read data from database tables but cannot modify data. Alternatively, you may have write-only access to data, where you can add rows to a table but not retrieve the tables — although this situation is less common.

The full list of permissions that a DBMS can apply generally varies according to the specific DBMS used but is likely to include at least the following types:

❑ Read access

❑ Write access

❑ Execute access (for stored procedures and so on)

❑ View definition access

These permissions, or combinations of these permissions, can be applied at the following levels, again depending on the DBMS:

❑ Database

❑ Object inside a database, such as a table, view, or stored procedure

❑ Object contents, such as a column within a table

Some DBMSes, including SQL Server, also enable you to define permissions for roles and then assign users to those roles. There are some built-in roles, such as the system administrator role that gives users complete access to the DBMS and the databases it contains.

The result of all this is that security restrictions placed on the account you use to access a database determine whether you can modify data in the database and, if so, exactly what data can be modified.

Database Views

A *view* is a stored SELECT query that provides an alternative way to access data. Rather than retrieving data from individual tables, or by using complex queries, you can use views that wrap more complicated techniques. A view called ProductView might contain a SQL statement as follows:

```
SELECT Product.ProductId, Product.ProductName, Product.CategoryId,
       Category.CategoryName
FROM Product INNER JOIN Category
ON Product.CategoryId = Category.CategoryId
```

You could then access that information with the following code:

```
SELECT * FROM ProductView
```

Although this is a simple example, it illustrates how views can shorten your code by storing queries in the database. It also means that you have a central location for this storage and that, should the underlying database structure change, you can modify views without having to modify your code.

As their name suggests, views are great for viewing data. They're also good for modifying data, although there are certain restrictions placed on that action. Actually, in many circumstances it is forbidden.

For simple views that show data for a single table, modification by update queries is always possible — with the same rules applied to columns as in the underlying tables (whether null values are allowed, for example). Note, however, that some columns may be hidden when these updates are applied. Deleting rows is also possible, even though this may delete hidden data. Inserting data may or may not be possible, depending on the column specification of the underlying table. If, for instance, one of the columns that is not included in the view does not allow null values and does not have a default value, then inserting a new row will fail.

Where views include joins between two or more tables, additional restrictions apply. Updating rows is possible only if queries are written in such a way as to modify just one of the tables included in a view. This is also something to approach with care because modifying a column value often affects multiple rows in the view — you could be modifying data on the "one" end of a one-to-many relationship. Deleting rows is not possible because that would delete rows from multiple tables. Inserting rows is also not possible.

There are techniques that you can use to get round these limitations, although they are advanced. You can, for example, use INSTEAD OF triggers that effectively intercept operations you perform on a view (such as insert queries) and execute stored procedures that interpret your SQL queries using whatever logic is required. You could use this technique with the ProductView query shown previously to make delete queries delete rows from the Product table but leave the Category table unaffected, for example. (This isn't a technique covered in this book, but if you are interested in it, the MSDN documentation has everything you need to learn more.)

Other factors also can preclude simple data modification through a view, including the following:

❑   Aggregate functions, such as COUNT(*)

❑   Read-only columns in underlying tables

❑   Union queries

❑   Grouping queries

If any of these apply, editing data through the view is not possible unless an advanced technique is used.

Application Data Sources

You've already seen how to create data sources, including how to generate typed data sets from the database schema. As part of that, you know how data adapters used to exchange data between the database and your application are created. They are initialized using either of the following:

❑   **SQL statements:** The Table Adapter Creation Wizard can create update, insert, and delete SQL statements for you, based on what you supply as a select statement.

❑   **Stored procedures:** You must supply your own stored procedures both for retrieving and modifying data.

The first thing to note here is that data modification is possible only if the table adapter includes valid SQL statements or stored procedure commands for its insert, update, or delete commands. These are accessible both in the definition of a typed data set and programmatically, so even a well-designed data source may be broken by client code if these commands are modified in some way, or supplied with incorrect parameters.

Assuming the commands are valid, the restrictions detailed in the preceding sections (security and views) apply.

In addition, data modifications must be made within the constraints applied by the database structure. If foreign key relationships exist and are being enforced, you must not break them. If you attempt to add a new row to a table that has an invalid foreign key, the row insert will fail.

That last point is extremely important when making modifications to multiple tables simultaneously using typed data sets. You've seen how typed data sets can contain data from several tables, including the relationships between those tables. You've also seen how data sets exist in a "disconnected" state, where multiple modifications can be made to the data set without updating the underlying database. Those modifications can then be applied to the database as a bulk operation when you decide to commit them (or they can be discarded should you decide not to). However, table adapters can make changes to only one table in a database at a time. With related data, then, it is essential to update tables in the correct order or the updates will fail.

To illustrate this, consider the Product and Category tables used in several examples so far in this book. If you were to add a new Category row and a new Product row that references the new Category row, then the order in which you make these additions would be important. If you were to attempt to add the Product row first, there would be no Category row to refer to in the database, so the update would fail.

However, if you were to delete a Category row and all its child Product rows, the reverse is true — you must delete rows from the Product table before deleting the row from the Category table.

The correct order in which to modify tables depends on the modifications you make. You'll look at this in more detail later in the chapter.

One final consideration: What happens when identity columns are used for primary keys? In this book, you're using GUID primary keys, but it is also common to use integer values for primary keys, where the values are generated by the database when rows are added. Here, unless you explicitly override certain database functionality, the DBMS will prevent you from adding data to or modifying data in identity columns, which are intended to be maintained purely by the database. This may not seem like a problem, but the following situations can arise:

1. A new row is added to a table at the "one" end of a one-to-many relationship. Internally, the data set assigns a primary key value.

2. A new row is added to a table at the "many" end of a one-to-many relationship that references the row added in step 1 in a foreign key value. The value of the foreign key matches the internally assigned primary key value.

3. The first row is committed to the database, at which point the database assigns it a primary key value using the identity column specification.

4. An attempt is made to commit the second row to the database, at which point a failure occurs because the foreign key column value is invalid.

There are a number of ways to solve the problem:

❑ Override the identity column behavior and insert your own primary key values. This is not recommended, because it can lead to inconsistencies in your database, particularly where multiple users need database access simultaneously.

❑ Before adding the second row, include an additional step to obtain the primary key value that was assigned for the first row by the database and use that value in the second row. The advantage is that the second row will be added successfully; the disadvantage is that the complexity increases.

❑ Never use application-generated primary keys. Instead, you can restrict modifications such that adding a parent row to the database must occur before you can reference that row from a child row. This means that all child rows must contain valid foreign keys by definition.

❑ Add temporary data to the database on-the-fly. This is a powerful but more complicated technique: You add the parent row to the database straightaway, thus obtaining a primary key. If edits are canceled, however, you must delete the row from the database.

As you can see, this is by no means a simple issue, and different techniques apply to different situations. The approach that you take will depend on the specific application you are creating. You'll see some of these techniques implemented in examples in this book.

How to Avoid Data Being Overwritten

You've probably noticed the dialog box shown in Figure 4-1 appearing when you've added an existing database to your example applications.

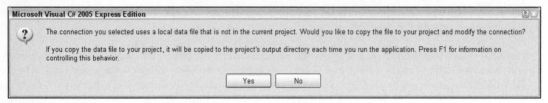

Figure 4-1: Adding a database dialog box

That dialog box appears when you add a connection to a database — when you add a data source and configure a new database connection along the way, for example. It does *not* appear if you insert a database to your project by adding an existing item though the Project ⇨ Add Existing Item menu item or via the Solution Explorer.

The thing to note in this dialog box is the seemingly innocuous text ". . . it will be copied to the project's output directory each time you run the application." In actual fact, this has important implications. The version of the database that you see in the root folder of your application in the Solution Explorer window is not the same version of the database that the application will use. Instead, the database shown in Solution Explorer is copied to the output directory (that is, where your `.exe` file appears, for example, `<project dir>/bin/debug`) every time you run the application. That means that when your application modifies the database, it is actually modifying the temporary version in the output directory, and the next time you run the application, those modifications are lost. This is also the behavior you get when you add a new database to your project.

It's fortunate that the behavior is customizable. If you click on a database in the Solution Explorer window and examine its properties, you'll notice a property called Copy To Output Directory. It can be set to one of the following values:

- ❑ **Do Not Copy:** Never copy the file to the output directory, which means you are responsible for ensuring that the file exists in the output directory if you want the application to work properly.

- ❑ **Copy Always:** The version of the database in the output directory is always overwritten by the "master" version of the database. This is the default setting, and means that changes to the database made by the application will be lost when the application is executed.

- ❑ **Copy If Newer:** Overwrite the database in the output directory only if the "master" version of the database is newer. This means that changes made to the version of the database used by the application will persist and will be visible each time you execute the application. If you replace the version of the database in the Solution Explorer with a new version, any changes made by the application are lost the next time the application is executed because the new version is copied to the output directory and used.

For application development, it can be useful for the database you use to be refreshed each time you run the application so that you can be sure any destructive changes you make to test your application won't break your data. However, to be sure that your application is actually modifying data when you want it to, it's often necessary to change this option to Copy If Newer, which means you can quit and restart your application and verify that changes have been successfully made. Should you want the changes made by the application to be permanent, all you have to do is to copy the version of the database in the `<project dir>/bin/debug` directory and overwrite the version in the root folder of the solution.

Obviously none of this matters in a deployed application, because there will be only one version of the database — the one in the application directory. For deployed applications there is no solution directory, only a single directory that will match the output directory of the application.

Modifying Data from Data-Bound Controls

Many of the examples you've seen have enabled you to edit data by simply using the default settings for controls. At times you've been instructed to remove that functionality, purely because you were concentrating on data display, not modification. However, while data modification was possible in, for instance, `DataGridView` controls in previous examples, if you tried to add a new row, you would most likely have received an exception (error). The main reason is that some fields in the sample database are primary key GUID fields, and they are not assigned default values when you add a new row to a table in a typed data set, and null values aren't permitted for primary keys.

You'll look at this problem and how to deal with it shortly. After that you'll explore a few more subjects related to data modification in a little more detail, specifically using the data-bound controls such as `BindingNavigator` in combination with `DataGridView` and details views.

First, however, work through the following Try It Out.

Try It Out   Simple Data Modification

1. Open Visual C# 2005 Express and create a new Windows application called `Ex0401 - Simple Data Modification`. Save the project in the `C:\BegVC#Databases\Chapter04` directory, with the Create Directory for Solution option unchecked.

2. Add a new SQL Database item to the project, using the default filename `Database1.mdf`. When the Data Source Configuration Wizard appears, click Cancel because there are no objects in the database to build a data source for.

3. Using the Database Explorer window, add a new table to the database with columns as follows:

Column Name	Data Type	Notes
WeatherRecordId	Int	Set as Primary Key, Identity (Identity specification: (`Is Identity = Yes`, `Identity Increment = 1`, `Identity Seed = 1`); no nulls
RecordedDate	Datetime	No nulls
Temperature	decimal(18, 1)	No nulls
Summary	varchar(100)	No nulls
Cloudy	Bit	No nulls
RecorderNo	int	No nulls
Notes	text	Nullable

4. Save the table as `WeatherRecord`.

5. Add a new data source to the project using the new database, with the `WeatherRecord` table included. Use the default filename `Database1DataSet.xsd`.

6. Set the Copy to Output Directory property of the database `Database1.mdf` to Copy If Newer.

7. Open `Form1.cs` in design view, and drag the `WeatherRecord` table onto the form from the Data Sources window (with the `DataGridView` option selected for the table in the drop-down menu for the table in the Data Sources window).

8. Size and position the `DataGridView` control to fill most of the form, and set its `Anchor` property to `Top`, `Bottom`, `Left`, `Right`.

9. Edit the columns of the `DataGridView` control, and remove the `WeatherRecordId` column.

10. Add an event handler to the `RowLeave` event of the `DataGridView` control with code as follows:

```csharp
private void weatherRecordDataGridView_RowLeave(object sender,
    DataGridViewCellEventArgs e)
{
    try
    {
        // Get row
        DataRowView rowView =
            weatherRecordDataGridView[e.ColumnIndex, e.RowIndex]
            .OwningRow.DataBoundItem as DataRowView;
        if (rowView != null)
        {
            Database1DataSet.WeatherRecordRow row =
                rowView.Row as Database1DataSet.WeatherRecordRow;

            // Check values and assign defaults
            if (row.IsNull("RecordedDate"))
            {
                row.RecordedDate = DateTime.Today;
            }
            if (row.IsNull("Temperature"))
            {
                row.Temperature = 32.0M;
            }
            if (row.IsNull("Summary"))
            {
                row.Summary = "Average";
            }
            if (row.IsNull("Cloudy"))
            {
                row.Cloudy = false;
            }
            if (row.IsNull("RecorderNo"))
            {
                row.RecorderNo = -1;
            }

            // Refresh display
```

```
                    weatherRecordDataGridView.Refresh();
                }
            }
        catch (IndexOutOfRangeException)
        {
            // Row was deleted - not a problem, ignore.
        }
    }
```

11. Add an event handler to the `DataError` event of the `DataGridView` control with code as follows:

```
private void weatherRecordDataGridView_DataError(
    object sender, DataGridViewDataErrorEventArgs e)
{
    if (e.Exception is NoNullAllowedException)
    {
        // Can ignore this, as it will just mean the row doesn't get added.
    }
    else
    {
        // Other exceptions you'll want to know about
        e.ThrowException = true;
    }
}
```

12. Run the application and add some data to the rows, as in Figure 4-2.

To add data, simply click in a cell for the row marked with a * and start typing. Use the Tab key to move to the next column in a row, or Shift+Tab to move to the previous column. Changes to rows, including new rows, are saved to the local data when the row loses focus, such as when you select a different row or press Tab when in the last column of the row. If you leave some columns blank, they will be filled in with default values after you select a different row.

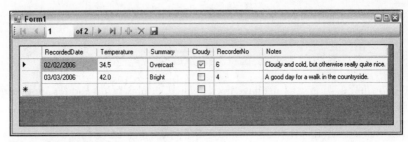

Figure 4-2: Adding data

13. Click the Save Data icon on the tool bar.

14. Quit the application.

15. Run the application again, and confirm that the data is still there.

16. Quit the application and Visual C# Express.

How It Works

In this example application, you've created a data-bound form that is capable of adding and modifying records in a simple one-table database. The columns are designed to use multiple data types.

In fact, the application would work without adding either of the two event handlers (for the RowLeave and DataError events). However, errors would occur when you attempt to add a row without supplying all the required (non-null) data. In particular, to add a false value to the Cloudy column of a new row you'd have to set it to true and then set it back to false. That's because the new row is created with a null value for the column despite the fact that null values aren't allowed. This, unfortunately, is the case even if you set a default value for a column in the database table specification. (Default values in the database are added when you insert a row without specifying a value for a column, rather than when you do specify a value for the column but the value you specify is a null value.)

Open the DataSet Designer for the typed data set in this example (Database1DataSet.xsd) and click on a column (for example Cloudy). Note the DefaultValue property, which has the value <DBNull>. You can change this if you want — which is a good thing to do for columns such as Cloudy that have an obvious choice for a default value (true or false). However, for columns without a well-defined default value (GUIDS and dates, for instance) it's better to set a default dynamically.

That's what is done in the example, in the RowLeave event handler. This event is raised whenever a row (new or existing) loses focus. The event handler starts by obtaining the row as a Database1DataSet.WeatherRecordRow object using code similar to what you've seen before:

```
private void weatherRecordDataGridView_RowLeave(object sender,
    DataGridViewCellEventArgs e)
{
    try
    {
        // Get row
        DataRowView rowView =
            weatherRecordDataGridView[e.ColumnIndex, e.RowIndex]
            .OwningRow.DataBoundItem as DataRowView;
        if (rowView != null)
        {
            Database1DataSet.WeatherRecordRow row =
                rowView.Row as Database1DataSet.WeatherRecordRow;
```

Note that the row in question may just have been deleted, or may be invalid for another reason, so you can avoid errors by adding a little validation and exception handling here.

Next, the code checks each non-nullable column in turn by using the DataRow.IsNull() function. If a null value is found, an appropriate default value is applied:

```
            // Check values and assign defaults
            if (row.IsNull("RecordedDate"))
            {
                row.RecordedDate = DateTime.Today;
            }
            if (row.IsNull("Temperature"))
            {
                row.Temperature = 32.0M;
```

```
        }
        if (row.IsNull("Summary"))
        {
            row.Summary = "Average";
        }
        if (row.IsNull("Cloudy"))
        {
            row.Cloudy = false;
        }
        if (row.IsNull("RecorderNo"))
        {
            row.RecorderNo = -1;
        }
```

In all cases except `RecordedDate`, the default value chosen is a simple constant. These could be entered in the DataSet Designer as described previously if you prefer. To obtain a dynamic date value, however, the `DateTime.Today` property must be evaluated as the row is requested.

After setting values, the `DataGridView` display will be out-of-date, so you refresh it using the `Refresh()` method:

```
            // Refresh display
            weatherRecordDataGridView.Refresh();
        }
    }
```

Finally, you check for an `IndexOutOfRangeException`, which occurs if a row has just been deleted:

```
    catch (IndexOutOfRangeException)
    {
        // Row was deleted - not a problem, ignore.
    }
}
```

You may wonder why the columns aren't checked for null values using code such as the following:

```
if (row.Summary == null)
{
    ...
}
```

The reason is apparent if you look at how the `Summary` property is defined:

```
public string Summary
{
    get
    {
        return ((string)(this[this.tableWeatherRecord.SummaryColumn]));
    }
    set
    {
        this[this.tableWeatherRecord.SummaryColumn] = value;
    }
}
```

In this code, if Summary is null, the expression this[this.tableWeatherRecord.SummaryColumn] evaluates to an instance of the DBNull type. This type cannot be cast to a string value, so an expression is thrown. The same problem applies to columns of other types — including nullable columns.

Of course, you could simply check for an exception and detect null values that way, but since you have an IsNull() method available, why not use it?

The other code you added to the form was an event handler for DataError. That was to deal with the same problem but in different circumstances. This event is called when an error occurs while updating the database or prior to updating the database if validation of the data set fails. It includes errors that might result from setting non-nullable columns to null values, which trigger a NoNullAllowedException exception, so that's what you check for in the code:

```
private void weatherRecordDataGridView_DataError(
    object sender, DataGridViewDataErrorEventArgs e)
{
    if (e.Exception is NoNullAllowedException)
    {
        // Can ignore this, as it will just mean the row doesn't get added.
    }
```

The only time that the NoNullAllowedException will occur in this example is if an attempt is made to save the data to the database while a new row is being edited. That's because if the row loses focus before an attempt to save the data is made, null values will be corrected using the code shown earlier.

In the exception handler code, ignoring the exception prevents an error being raised, but won't mean that the row gets added to the database — so it simply disappears.

When handling a DataError event, set the ThrowException property of the DataGridViewDataErrorEventArgs argument to true if you don't deal with the exception, so that it can be dealt with elsewhere. That's what the remainder of the code does.

```
    else
    {
        // Other exceptions you'll want to know about
        e.ThrowException = true;
    }
}
```

In this example, you didn't have to worry about the primary key at all because it was an integer-valued column with an identity specification. Identity specifications are copied from the database into typed data sets created from database tables. Take a look at the WeatherRecordId column in the DataSet Designer; you'll see three properties — AutoIncrement, AutoIncrementSeed, and AutoIncrementStep — that are used to generate primary key values. That doesn't solve all problems, however, because the values generated here won't necessarily match the ones created by the database, which generates its own values. As discussed earlier, this can be a problem when you add rows to a related table that references a newly generated row by its primary key if that row hasn't yet been added to the database.

Note that the database shown in the Database Explorer window does not display any of the rows you have added using this application, because it is linked to the "master" version of the database. To see the changes you have made, you need to examine the version of the database that has been copied to the output directory. A quick way to do this is to ensure that the Solution Explorer window is showing all files and navigate directly to the copied database file to look at its data.

Adding Rows with GUID Primary Keys

When primary keys have a GUID type, you can't rely on an identity specification to provide you with values. You also can't expect users to type new GUID values themselves unless you are feeling particularly malicious. The solution for `DataGridView` controls is exactly the same as the code you saw in the last example: set the GUID key value in event handlers. That is possible even if the primary key values aren't being displayed in the `DataGridView` control because you are looking at the data that is bound to the row in the control, not what is displayed by the row.

For types of data entry that don't use a `DataGridView`, such as detail views, similar techniques are used, as you'll see shortly.

How BindingNavigator Saves Data

There is nothing magical about the way that the Save Data button in the `BindingNavigator` control saves data to the database. In fact, the code it uses to do so is easily accessible and editable by you.

Take a quick look at the code that is executed when you click the Save Data button in the last example:

```
private void weatherRecordBindingNavigatorSaveItem_Click_1(
    object sender, EventArgs e)
{
    this.Validate();
    this.weatherRecordBindingSource.EndEdit();
    this.weatherRecordTableAdapter.Update(this.database1DataSet.WeatherRecord);
}
```

The code is pretty self-explanatory. First the data is validated, then the current edit operation is committed to the data set by calling `EndEdit()` on the `BindingSource` object that interfaces with the data set, and finally a table adapter is used to update the `WeatherRecord` table in the database using the data in the data set.

The key method here is the table adapter's `Update()`, which you'll use a great deal in this book, particularly when you start moving away from data-bound controls.

Canceling Updates

In the previous example, the save functionality was provided by the `BindingNavigator` control via a Save Data button. However, that control does not supply a button for canceling edits and reverting to the data in the database. Fortunately, that's easy to do.

To cancel edits, you first need to add a new button somewhere, and the `BindingNavigator` control tool bar is as good a place as any. You can supply a bitmap for the button if you want, or you can simply use a text button called something like `CancelButton`, with text reading Cancel Changes or something similar.

Next, you have two things to do in the code for the button event handler:

❑ Commit any changes currently in progress — for example, changes to the record being displayed. This is done in the same way as in the event handler for the Save Data button — by calling the `BindingSource.EndEdit()` method.

❑ Call the `RejectChanges()` method on either the data set as a whole or on an individual table, depending on what data modification you have to cancel.

And that's all there is to it. This will discard any changes you have made to the data set and enable you to start again with the original data.

Updating Data from Detail Views

Updating data from detail views is much like updating data from `DataGridView` controls, except that because you don't have the `DataGridView` events to handle, there are some things you do differently. Rather than responding to `RowLeave` and `DataError` events in the `DataGridView` control, you must hook into events in the `BindingSource` control, instead.

> Using `BindingSource` *events is equally applicable to data-bound* `DataGridView` *controls.*
> *However, responding to* `DataGridView` *events as you did in the last example was a good illustration*
> *of alternative ways of doing things and gave you the chance to learn about some other things, such as*
> *what happens when the* `DataError` *event is raised.*

When a new row is added to a data set by a data-bound control, it is the `BindingSource` control that actually makes the modification to the underlying data. The data-bound control does not communicate with the data source directly. This is great for you in two ways:

❑ There is a central point for you to monitor data changes and respond to modification events.

❑ The framework standardizes the way of doing things, such that the code you must use is both simple and reusable.

New rows are added when, for example, the user begins editing the "new item" row in a `DataGridView` control or clicks the Add New button in a `BindingNavigator` control. At that point, the `AddNew()` method of the `BindingSource` control is called, and the `AddingNew` event fires as part of the method's execution. If you handle this event you can control which object gets added to the data source. Your event handler is passed an object of type `AddingNewEventArgs`, which has an important property: `NewObject`. If you set the property to an object instance, then this object is what gets added to the data source. If you leave this property as null, the default implementation will be executed. So this is the ideal place for dynamically setting default column values, such as GUID primary keys.

With database data sources, you have to be aware of how `BindingSource` controls reference the data they bind to make use of this functionality. The data source of a `BindingSource` control is stored as a `DataView` object in the `BindingSource.List` property. To create a new row, you must use the `DataView.AddRow()`

method, which returns a `DataViewRow` object. You can then set column values through the `DataViewRow` object and then reference it in the `NewObject` property of the event arguments.

The following Try It Out shows that technique in action.

Try It Out   **Detail Modification**

1.   Open Visual C# 2005 Express and create a new Windows application called `Ex0402 - Detail Modification`. Save the project in the `C:\BegVC#Databases\Chapter04` directory, with the Create Directory For Solution option unchecked.

2.   Add a new data source to the project, making a connection to the sample `FolktaleDB.mdf` database file. Copy the file locally to the project and save the connection string with the default name when prompted. When asked to choose database objects, select the `Classification`, `Ending`, `Source`, `CharacterStory`, `StoryLocation`, and `Story` tables. The generated data set is shown in Figure 4-3.

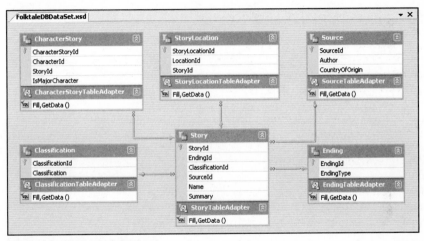

Figure 4-3: Generated data set

You won't be using all of these tables in this example, only `Source`. However, when you expand this example later in the chapter, you'll find it easier to have these data structures in place.

3.   Open `Form1.cs` in design view.

4.   In the Data Sources window, select Details for the drop-down option for the `Source` table. Also, expand the `Source` table and select None for the drop-down option for the `SourceId` field.

5.   Drag the `Source` table from the Data Sources window to the form. Reposition the controls and resize the form to get an aesthetically pleasing display. Make the two text boxes for the column data fill as much of the width of the form as possible, and add `Right` to their `Anchor` property. Change the `Text` property of the form to Story Source Editor.

6.   Add a button to the `BindingNavigator` control called `cancelButton`. (Select the `BindingNavigator` control, and then select `Button` from the Add ToolStripButton drop-down menu using the icon on the right of the `BindingNavigator` control). Set the

`DisplayStyle` property of the new button to `Text`, and its `Text` property to Cancel Changes. (You may need to make the Story Source Editor form wider to see the button.)

7. Double-click the Cancel Changes button to add an event handler, and then add the following code to the event handler method:

```
private void cancelButton_Click(object sender, EventArgs e)
{
    // Reject changes
    sourceBindingSource.EndEdit();
    folktaleDBDataSet.RejectChanges();
}
```

8. In the `Form1` design view window, select the `sourceBindingSource` component, and add an event handler to its `AddingNew` event with code as follows:

```
private void sourceBindingSource_AddingNew(object sender, AddingNewEventArgs e)
{
    // Get data table view
    DataView dataTableView = sourceBindingSource.List as DataView;

    // Create row from view
    DataRowView rowView = dataTableView.AddNew();

    // Configure defaults
    rowView["SourceId"] = Guid.NewGuid();
    rowView["Author"] = "New author";
    rowView["CountryOfOrigin"] = "Unknown";

    // Set new row
    e.NewObject = rowView;

    // Navigate to new row
    sourceBindingSource.MoveLast();
}
```

9. In Solution Explorer, set the Copy to Output Directory property of the database `FolktaleDB.mdf` to Copy If Newer.

10. Run the application. Edit the data for a record or two, and add a new record using the Add New button. You should see a new record generated for you with default data in place, as shown in Figure 4-4.

Figure 4-4: Added record

11. Experiment with saving/canceling changes, and quit and restart the application to check that your changes persist.

12. Try deleting a record for which you know there are existing entries in the Story table (Joss Whedon, for example). If you try to save the data with the Save Data button after deleting the record, an exception will occur, as shown here:

```
The DELETE statement conflicted with the REFERENCE constraint
"FK_Story_Source". The conflict occurred in database
"C:\BEGVC#DATABASES\CHAPTER04\EX0402 - DETAIL
MODIFICATION\BIN\DEBUG\FOLKTALEDB.MDF", table "dbo.Story", column 'SourceId'.
The statement has been terminated.
```

13. Terminate the application and Visual C# Express.

How It Works

In this example you again assembled an application for modifying data in just a few steps, and the application is a useful starting point for the techniques you'll learn in the rest of this chapter. This time, rather than using a DataGridView display, you created a simple detail view display — simple in that only two fields are displayed and they both contain text column data.

The basic procedure is much the same as before — define a data source, add controls using the Data Sources window interface, and customize things to streamline functionality. The customization consists of the following:

❑   Add "cancel changes" functionality.

❑   Add default values for new rows.

❑   Make database changes persistent for testing.

The first change adds the capability to cancel changes. As discussed earlier, this simply requires you to commit in-progress changes to the data source, and then reject all changes made to the data source:

```
private void cancelButton_Click(object sender, EventArgs e)
{
    // Reject changes
    sourceBindingSource.EndEdit();
    folktaleDBDataSet.RejectChanges();
}
```

Next you added code to set the default values for new rows, using the technique described immediately before the example — by handling the BindingSource.AddingNew event. The code for the event handler starts by getting a reference to the data source in the form of a DataView:

```
private void sourceBindingSource_AddingNew(object sender, AddingNewEventArgs e)
{
    // Get data table view
    DataView dataTableView = sourceBindingSource.List as DataView;
```

Using this view, you created a new DataRowView:

```
    // Create row from view
    DataRowView rowView = dataTableView.AddNew();
```

Through the `DataRowView` you set the default row properties, including a dynamically generated GUID to use as the primary key of the new row:

```
// Configure defaults
rowView["SourceId"] = Guid.NewGuid();
rowView["Author"] = "New author";
rowView["CountryOfOrigin"] = "Unknown";
```

Then you set the `AddingNewEventArgs.NewObject` property for the new row, ready for use by the binding source:

```
// Set new row
e.NewObject = rowView;
```

One final step, added purely for usability, instructs the `BindingSource` control to navigate to the last record in its data source — namely, the one just added:

```
// Navigate to new row
sourceBindingSource.MoveLast();
}
```

That makes it easy for users to edit what they have added immediately.

After making the database update only if newer to persist modifications, the next thing you did was test things out by making some changes. All of this worked fine apart from one thing — you were unable to delete rows that have child rows because the database restraint forbids it.

There are several ways to deal with this problem, depending on the behavior you want to achieve. You could modify the constraint to cascade deletions, such that deleting a parent row deletes all child rows. That has the advantage of being easy to implement (it's just a database change) but is a little brutal. Alternatively, you could forbid such a deletion unless no child rows exist. This is also quite easy to implement with some coding but reduces usability if removing parent and child rows together is what the user wants to do.

The best solution, which you will implement shortly, is to give the user the choice. The user should be warned that child rows will be deleted but should have the final say over whether that should happen.

To detect that a row has child rows, however, you need to populate the data set with data from more than one table (or use a view that indicates whether child rows exist, although for now you'll concentrate on the former, simpler option). Because you need to start using multiple tables at once to do this, it's time to look at binding to and modifying such data.

Updating Multiple Tables

Earlier in the chapter you saw that modifying multiple tables in one operation isn't a simple thing to do if the tables are related. With relationships in place, you need to ensure that the updates you make are performed in the right order or errors will occur.

To formalize this, consider a situation in which `TableA` has a one-to-many relationship with `TableB`. That means that `TableB` has a foreign key referencing the primary key of `TableA`. Assuming that the foreign key relationship must be maintained, you can state the following:

❑   If a row is added to `TableB`, then the referenced row in `TableA` must already exist.

❑   If a row is deleted from `TableA`, then any child rows in `TableB` that reference the row must already have been modified (either deleted or updated with a difference foreign key value).

From these statements it is possible to infer the correct order of doing things to cater for both additions and deletions, which is as follows:

1.   Add new rows and update existing rows to the parent table (`TableA`) — but don't delete any rows.

2.   Make changes to the child table (`TableB`) — additions, modifications, and deletions.

3.   Delete rows from the parent table (`TableA`).

If you follow this order, all modifications will be performed successfully.

The preceding works fine with two related tables. In practice you will probably have a more complex arrangement of relationships. However, it is relatively simple to extend this to such arrangements. If `TableB` has a one-to-many relationship with `TableC`, for example, then you simply need to replace step 2 with three steps just like the existing steps 1–3, but replace `TableA` with `TableB` and `TableB` with `TableC`:

1.   Add new rows and update existing rows to the parent table (`TableA`) — but don't delete any rows.

2.   *Extra steps*:

2.1. Add new rows and update existing rows to the parent table (`TableB`) — but don't delete any rows.

2.2. Make changes to the child table (`TableC`) — additions, modifications, and deletions.

2.3. Delete rows from the parent table (`TableB`).

3.   Delete rows from the parent table (`TableA`).

And so on.

This means a slight modification in the way you use table adapters to update a database. Typically, you update a table in the database using code as follows:

```
tableATableAdapter.Update(myDatabaseDataSet.TableA);
```

To update a subset of the changes to a table, you must obtain a new data table containing only the changes you want to commit. You can do this using the `DataTable.GetChanges()` method, passing a `DataRowState` enumeration value (or combination of values) to say what changes you want to obtain. This method returns a new `DataTable` instance, which you can cast to the correct type and then use in the `Update()` method. For example:

```
MyDatabaseDataSet.TableA tableAChanges =
    myDatabaseDataSet.TableA.GetChanges(DataRowState.Added | DataRowState.Modified)
    as MyDatabaseDataSet.TableA;
```

This gets the changes corresponding to added or modified rows in a data table called `tableAChanges`. You can then commit these changes as follows:

```
tableATableAdapter.Update(tableAChanges);
```

Be sure to check data tables generated in this way for null values — which happens if there are no changes of the specified type.

The `DataRowState` enumeration contains the values `Added`, `Deleted`, `Detached`, `Modified`, and `Unchanged`. Here, `Detached` means that the row isn't part of a data table (either it hasn't been added or it has been removed), so it isn't a value you will use in this situation.

In the following Try It Out you modify the earlier example application to permit modification of two related tables: `Source` and `Story`.

Try It Out   Multi-Table Modification

1. Copy the project `C:\BegVC#Databases\Chapter04\Ex0402 - Detail Modification` to a new project, `C:\BegVC#Databases\Chapter04\Ex0403 - Multi-Table Modification`, and then open the new project.

2. Open `Form1` in design mode, and then switch to the Data Sources window and expand the `Source` table. Note that there is a second, nested version of the `Story` table that appears under the `Source` table, as shown in Figure 4-5.

Figure 4-5: The child Story table

3. Ensure that there is enough space on `Form1` to hold a `DataGridView` control, and then drag the nested version of the `Story` table to the form underneath the source detail view controls. Make the `DataGridView` fill the area underneath these controls, and set its `Anchor` property to `Top`, `Bottom`, `Left`, `Right` so that it will resize with the form.

4. Open the Edit Columns dialog box for the `DataGridView` control.

5. Remove the `StoryId` and `SourceId` columns.

6. Move the `Name` column to the top of the column list and change its `AutoSizeMode` property to `AllCells`.

7. For the `EndingId` column:

   a. Change the `HeaderText` property to `Ending`.

   b. Change the `ColumnType` property to `DataGridViewComboBoxColumn`.

   c. Change the `DataSource` property to the `Ending` table, found under Other Data Sources ⇨ Project Data Sources ⇨ FolktaleDBDataSet, as shown in Figure 4-6.

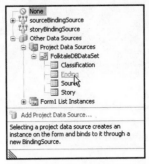

Figure 4-6: The Ending table data source

   d. Change the `DisplayMember` property to `EndingType`.

   e. Change the `ValueMember` property to `EndingId`.

   f. Change the `Width` property to `120`.

8. For the `ClassificationId` column:

   a. Change the `HeaderText` property to `Classification`.

   b. Change the `ColumnType` property to `DataGridViewComboBoxColumn`.

   c. Change the `DataSource` property to the `Classification` table, found under Other Data Sources ⇨ Project Data Sources ⇨ FolktaleDBDataSet.

   d. Change the `DisplayMember` property to `Classification`.

   e. Change the `ValueMember` property to `ClassificationId`.

   f. Change the `Width` property to `120`.

9. Change the `AutoSizeMode` property of the `Summary` column to `Fill`.

10. Add the following event handler for the `storyBindingSource.AddingNew` event:

```
private void storyBindingSource_AddingNew(object sender, AddingNewEventArgs e)
{
    // Get data table view
    DataView dataTableView = storyBindingSource.List as DataView;

    // Create row from view
```

```
DataRowView rowView = dataTableView.AddNew();

// Configure defaults
rowView["StoryId"] = Guid.NewGuid();
rowView["SourceId"] = (sourceBindingSource.Current as DataRowView)["SourceId"];
rowView["EndingId"] = (endingBindingSource[0] as DataRowView)["EndingId"];
rowView["ClassificationId"] =
    (classificationBindingSource[0] as DataRowView)["ClassificationId"];
rowView["Name"] = "New story";
rowView["Summary"] = "Story summary";

// Set new row
e.NewObject = rowView;

// Navigate to new row
storyBindingSource.MoveLast();
}
```

11. In the design view for `Form1`, add a `CharacterStoryTableAdapter` component to the form called `characterStoryTableAdapter`, and a `StoryLocationTableAdapter` component called `storyLocationTableAdapter`. If these components do not appear in the Toolbox, then compile the project first.

12. Modify `Form1_Load()` as follows:

```
private void Form1_Load(object sender, EventArgs e)
{
    this.classificationTableAdapter.Fill(this.folktaleDBDataSet.Classification);
    this.endingTableAdapter.Fill(this.folktaleDBDataSet.Ending);
    this.storyTableAdapter.Fill(this.folktaleDBDataSet.Story);
    this.sourceTableAdapter.Fill(this.folktaleDBDataSet.Source);
    this.characterStoryTableAdapter.Fill(this.folktaleDBDataSet.CharacterStory);
    this.storyLocationTableAdapter.Fill(this.folktaleDBDataSet.StoryLocation);
}
```

13. In the design view for `Form1`, set the `DeleteItem` property of the `sourceBindingNavigator` control to `(none)`.

14. Add a new event handler for the Delete button as follows:

```
private void bindingNavigatorDeleteItem_Click(object sender, EventArgs e)
{
    if (Validate() && (sourceBindingSource != null))
    {
        // Flag
        bool deleteRow = true;

        // Get row to be deleted
        DataRowView rowView = sourceBindingSource.Current as DataRowView;
        if (rowView == null)
        {
            return;
        }
```

```
FolktaleDBDataSet.SourceRow row =
    rowView.Row as FolktaleDBDataSet.SourceRow;

// Check for child rows
FolktaleDBDataSet.StoryRow[] childRows = row.GetStoryRows();
if (childRows.Length > 0)
{
    DialogResult userChoice = MessageBox.Show("If you delete this source "
        + "row you will also delete its child story rows. Continue?",
        "Warning", MessageBoxButtons.YesNo, MessageBoxIcon.Warning);
    if (userChoice == DialogResult.Yes)
    {
        // Delete row and child rows
        foreach (FolktaleDBDataSet.StoryRow childStory in childRows)
        {
            // Delete child CharacterStory rows
            FolktaleDBDataSet.CharacterStoryRow[] characterStoryRows =
                childStory.GetCharacterStoryRows();
            foreach (FolktaleDBDataSet.CharacterStoryRow
                childCharacterStory in characterStoryRows)
            {
                childCharacterStory.Delete();
            }

            // Delete child StoryLocation rows
            FolktaleDBDataSet.StoryLocationRow[] storyLocationRows =
                childStory.GetStoryLocationRows();
            foreach (FolktaleDBDataSet.StoryLocationRow
                childStoryLocation in storyLocationRows)
            {
                childStoryLocation.Delete();
            }

            // Delete Story row
            childStory.Delete();
        }
    }
    else
    {
        deleteRow = false;
    }
}

// Delete row?
if (deleteRow)
{
    sourceBindingSource.RemoveCurrent();
    sourceBindingSource.EndEdit();
}
}
}
```

15. Modify the event handler for the Save Data button as follows:

```
private void sourceBindingNavigatorSaveItem_Click(object sender, EventArgs e)
{
    this.Validate();
    this.sourceBindingSource.EndEdit();
    this.storyBindingSource.EndEdit();

    // Save added / edited parent rows
    FolktaleDBDataSet.SourceDataTable tableChanges =
        folktaleDBDataSet.Source.GetChanges(
        DataRowState.Added | DataRowState.Modified)
        as FolktaleDBDataSet.SourceDataTable;
    if (tableChanges != null)
    {
        sourceTableAdapter.Update(tableChanges);
    }

    // Save child row modifications
    characterStoryTableAdapter.Update(folktaleDBDataSet.CharacterStory);
    storyLocationTableAdapter.Update(folktaleDBDataSet.StoryLocation);
    storyTableAdapter.Update(folktaleDBDataSet.Story);

    // Save deleted parent rows
    FolktaleDBDataSet.SourceDataTable tableDeletes =
        folktaleDBDataSet.Source.GetChanges(DataRowState.Deleted)
        as FolktaleDBDataSet.SourceDataTable;
    if (tableChanges != tableDeletes)
    {
        sourceTableAdapter.Update(tableDeletes);
    }

    // Accept changes
    folktaleDBDataSet.AcceptChanges();
}
```

16. Run the application and modify some data. The interface should look similar to Figure 4-7.

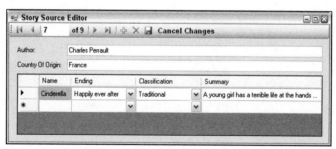

Figure 4-7: The Story editing interface

17. Test the functionality of adding and removing data. Remove a source with story rows (and accepting the confirmation) and then add a new source and add a story to the source before saving all changes. The operation should be successful.

18. Close the application and Visual C# Express.

How It Works

In this example, you first added a related table to the form by using a nested item in the Data Sources window. Doing this means that you automatically bind a filtered view of the data to the control, so with no additional code whatsoever you get a list of child rows in a `DataGridView`, where the `Story` rows displayed are determined by the selected item in the `Source` table. If you use the top-level version of the `Story` table as displayed in the Data Sources window, this filtering is not automatic, and you'd have to write your own code to achieve that functionality.

The Data Sources window is far from perfect in this respect. For more complex relationships, you will have to write your own code. Hierarchical relationships also cause problems — and have even been known to confuse Visual C# Express to the point of crashing. In the FolktaleDB database, the `Character` table is hierarchical — it has `MotherId` and `FatherId` foreign key fields that refer to other rows in the same table. You might like to experiment with data binding to this table in your own applications, but beware the results! For this table you really need to write custom code, which is something you'll see later in the book.

Back to the current example, the next thing you did was format the columns used in the `DataGridView`. You hid the primary key field (there is no real need to display GUID values to users, after all) and replaced two of the three foreign keys with drop-down selectors. The third primary key, `SourceId`, was removed because it was redundant (the parent source row is already displayed on the form). You also formatted the layout of the remaining columns to fill the available area, keeping enough space for each to display all information — with the exception of the `Summary` column, which you deal with properly in the next section.

Then you added the custom functionality required to add new `Story` rows, delete rows from multiple tables, and save data to multiple tables in the right order. Adding rows to the `Story` table uses much the same code as adding rows to the `Source` table. Apart from adding the code as an event handler for the `AddingNew` event of a different `BindingSource` control, the only real change was in the default values used:

```
// Configure defaults
rowView["StoryId"] = Guid.NewGuid();
rowView["SourceId"] = (sourceBindingSource.Current as DataRowView)["SourceId"];
rowView["EndingId"] = (endingBindingSource[0] as DataRowView)["EndingId"];
rowView["ClassificationId"] =
    (classificationBindingSource[0] as DataRowView)["ClassificationId"];
rowView["Name"] = "New story";
rowView["Summary"] = "Story summary";
```

Note that the foreign keys are configured here to give initial values. The `SourceId` field comes from the parent row, and the other two foreign keys (`EndingId` and `ClassificationId`) are set to the first row in the respective parent tables.

Next, you added the additional code required to delete items. The first step here was to include the related information in the `CharacterStory` and `StoryLocation` tables. Because those tables were not bound to anything, you had to add the table adapters manually, and added code in `Form1_Load()` to populate them. With that data in place, it is possible to remove child rows in these tables when `Story` rows are deleted, as you will see shortly.

To implement a custom scheme for deleting `Source` table rows, you first had to replace the existing code for deleting items from the `Source` table. You disabled the existing code by clearing the `sourceBindingNavigator.DeleteItem` property, which was initially set to the `id` of the `Delete` button. This property hooks up the specified button to internal deletion code, which you wanted to replace so that you could add additional validation and functionality. The code you added started with some basic checks to see that deletion was possible, and then obtained the row to be deleted (exiting immediately if no row is found):

```
private void bindingNavigatorDeleteItem_Click(object sender, EventArgs e)
{
    if (Validate() && (sourceBindingSource != null))
    {
        // Flag
        bool deleteRow = true;

        // Get row to be deleted
        DataRowView rowView = sourceBindingSource.Current as DataRowView;
        if (rowView == null)
        {
            return;
        }
```

Next comes the important bit — the code checks to see if the row to be deleted from the `Source` table has child rows in the `Story` table:

```
        FolktaleDBDataSet.SourceRow row =
            rowView.Row as FolktaleDBDataSet.SourceRow;

        // Check for child rows
        FolktaleDBDataSet.StoryRow[] childRows = row.GetStoryRows();
        if (childRows.Length > 0)
        {
```

If rows exist, a dialog box is displayed to confirm the deletion of child rows:

```
            DialogResult userChoice = MessageBox.Show("If you delete this source "
                + "row you will also delete its child story rows. Continue?",
                "Warning", MessageBoxButtons.YesNo, MessageBoxIcon.Warning);
```

If the user clicks Yes, the child rows are deleted (as well as child rows for the `Story` row in the `CharacterStory` and `StoryLocation` tables, if any exist):

```
            if (userChoice == DialogResult.Yes)
            {
                // Delete row and child rows
```

```
        foreach (FolktaleDBDataSet.StoryRow childStory in childRows)
        {
            // Delete child CharacterStory rows
            FolktaleDBDataSet.CharacterStoryRow[] characterStoryRows =
                childStory.GetCharacterStoryRows();
            foreach (FolktaleDBDataSet.CharacterStoryRow
                childCharacterStory in characterStoryRows)
            {
                childCharacterStory.Delete();
            }

            // Delete child StoryLocation rows
            FolktaleDBDataSet.StoryLocationRow[] storyLocationRows =
                childStory.GetStoryLocationRows();
            foreach (FolktaleDBDataSet.StoryLocationRow
                childStoryLocation in storyLocationRows)
            {
                childStoryLocation.Delete();
            }

            // Delete Story row
            childStory.Delete();
        }
    }
```

Alternatively, a flag is set to prevent deletion of the parent row if the user clicks No:

```
        else
        {
            deleteRow = false;
        }
    }
```

Finally, the parent row is deleted if necessary:

```
    // Delete row?
    if (deleteRow)
    {
        sourceBindingSource.RemoveCurrent();
        sourceBindingSource.EndEdit();
    }
    }
}
```

The last code modification was the code for updating the database, which followed the scheme laid out prior to this example. First the form is validated, and pending changes to the underlying data set are committed:

```
private void sourceBindingNavigatorSaveItem_Click(object sender, EventArgs e)
{
    this.Validate();
    this.sourceBindingSource.EndEdit();
    this.storyBindingSource.EndEdit();
```

Next, parent row additions and modifications are committed to the database:

```
// Save added / edited parent rows
FolktaleDBDataSet.SourceDataTable tableChanges =
    folktaleDBDataSet.Source.GetChanges(
    DataRowState.Added | DataRowState.Modified)
    as FolktaleDBDataSet.SourceDataTable;
if (tableChanges != null)
{
    sourceTableAdapter.Update(tableChanges);
}
```

That's followed by all child row modifications:

```
// Save child row modifications
characterStoryTableAdapter.Update(folktaleDBDataSet.CharacterStory);
storyLocationTableAdapter.Update(folktaleDBDataSet.StoryLocation);
storyTableAdapter.Update(folktaleDBDataSet.Story);
```

There's no need here to worry about rows being added to the `CharacterStory` or `StoryLocation` tables, because that functionality does not exist in the application. Instead, you only have to worry about deleting a `Story` row with child rows in these tables, so performing updates in this order is enough to avoid errors.

Finally, you make the parent row deletions:

```
// Save deleted parent rows
FolktaleDBDataSet.SourceDataTable tableDeletes =
    folktaleDBDataSet.Source.GetChanges(DataRowState.Deleted)
    as FolktaleDBDataSet.SourceDataTable;
if (tableChanges != tableDeletes)
{
    sourceTableAdapter.Update(tableDeletes);
}
```

Then it's necessary to clear all the changes in the data set so that no attempt is made to commit them a second time:

```
// Accept changes
folktaleDBDataSet.AcceptChanges();
}
```

And that completes the code for this example. Now you can modify data in a far more user-friendly way and have the capability to automatically delete child rows if required.

Updating Long Text Data for DataGridView Displays

In Chapter 3 you saw how to view long text data in a DataGridView control by using a pop-up dialog. It is possible to write similar code to ease the editing of long text data in a pop-up window. There isn't a lot to say about this because the code should mostly be familiar to you, so the best way to see what to do is through another Try It Out.

Try It Out   Text Modification

1. Copy the project C:\BegVC#Databases\Chapter04\Ex0403 - Multi-Table Modification to a new project, C:\BegVC#Databases\Chapter04\Ex0404 - Text Modification, and then open the new project.

2. Open Form1 in design mode, and then open the Edit Columns dialog box for the storyDataGridView control.

3. Add a new unbound column called EditSummaryButton of type DataGridViewButtonColumn, with the header text Edit Summary, as shown in Figure 4-8.

Figure 4-8: The EditSummaryButton column

4. Move the new column to a position just before the Summary column, change its Text property to Edit Summary, and change its UseColumnTextForButtonValue property to True.

5. Set the ReadOnly property of the Summary column to True.

6. Accept the column changes, and add a new form to the project called SummaryEditor.

7. Change the Text property of the new form to Edit Summary.

8. Add a multiline TextBox and two Button controls to the form called summaryBox, okButton, and cancelButton. Set the Text property for okButton and cancelButton to OK and Cancel, respectively. Set the Anchor properties of the controls to Top, Bottom, Left, Right for the text box and Bottom, Left for the buttons. Finally, set the ScrollBars property of the text box to Vertical. The layout of the controls appears in Figure 4-9.

9. Set the AcceptButton property of the SummaryEditor form to okButton and the CancelButton property to cancelButton.

Figure 4-9: The SummaryEditor form

10. Add event handlers for the two buttons as follows:

```
private void okButton_Click(object sender, EventArgs e)
{
    this.DialogResult = DialogResult.OK;
}

private void cancelButton_Click(object sender, EventArgs e)
{
    this.DialogResult = DialogResult.Cancel;
}
```

11. Add the following public property to the SummaryEditor form by editing the code for the form directly:

```
public string SummaryText
{
    get
    {
        return summaryBox.Text;
    }
    set
    {
        summaryBox.Text = value;
    }
}
```

12. Switch back to Form1, and add an event handler for the CellContentClick event by double-clicking the storyDataGridView control. Add code as follows:

```
private void storyDataGridView_CellContentClick(
    object sender, DataGridViewCellEventArgs e)
{
    // Check for summary column
    if (storyDataGridView.CurrentCell.OwningColumn.HeaderText == "Edit Summary")
    {
        // Check for nulls
        if (storyDataGridView.CurrentRow.DataBoundItem == null)
```

```
        {
            return;
        }

        // Get row
        FolktaleDBDataSet.StoryRow dataRow =
            (storyDataGridView.CurrentRow.DataBoundItem as DataRowView).Row
            as FolktaleDBDataSet.StoryRow;

        // Get summary text
        string summaryText = "";
        if (!dataRow.IsNull("Summary"))
        {
            summaryText = dataRow.Summary;
        }

        // Use dialog to display / edit text
        SummaryEditor editor = new SummaryEditor();
        editor.SummaryText = summaryText;
        DialogResult result = editor.ShowDialog();
        if (result == DialogResult.OK)
        {
            // Update data
            dataRow.Summary = editor.SummaryText;
        }
    }
}
```

13. Run the application and edit the content of a `Summary` column for a `Story` using the new editor button. Figure 4-10 shows a typically convoluted tale from Greek mythology.

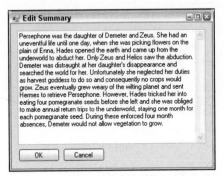

Figure 4-10: The SummaryEditor form

14. Close the application and Visual C# Express.

How It Works

As noted earlier, none of the code here is particularly complicated. The form you added to edit data from the `Summary` column is simply a standard text editing form that you've probably used many times in applications. The only thing to remark on it is how the text displayed is exposed as a public property.

The text property is accessed in the event handler that is called when a cell of the DataGridView is clicked. The event handler starts by checking the column that was clicked:

```
private void storyDataGridView_CellContentClick(
    object sender, DataGridViewCellEventArgs e)
{
    // Check for summary column
    if (storyDataGridView.CurrentCell.OwningColumn.HeaderText == "Edit Summary")
    {
```

A check is made for null data (for example, if the cell that was clicked is the cell for a nonexistent row, such as the one that appears at the bottom of the DataGridView row before a new row is added).

```
        // Check for nulls
        if (storyDataGridView.CurrentRow.DataBoundItem == null)
        {
            return;
        }
```

If a row is available, it's obtained and its Summary column data is extracted:

```
        // Get row
        FolktaleDBDataSet.StoryRow dataRow =
            (storyDataGridView.CurrentRow.DataBoundItem as DataRowView).Row
            as FolktaleDBDataSet.StoryRow;

        // Get summary text
        string summaryText = "";
        if (!dataRow.IsNull("Summary"))
        {
            summaryText = dataRow.Summary;
        }
```

That's then displayed in the SummaryEditor form:

```
        // Use dialog to display / edit text
        SummaryEditor editor = new SummaryEditor();
        editor.SummaryText = summaryText;
        DialogResult result = editor.ShowDialog();
```

And, if the user clicks OK, the text is used to update the column:

```
        if (result == DialogResult.OK)
        {
            // Update data
            dataRow.Summary = editor.SummaryText;
        }
    }
}
```

All in all, there's nothing that complicated about this example. However, it provides a user-friendly way for users to edit long text information, and it is well worth building in this sort of functionality should you need it in your applications. Your users will thank you.

Saving Data When the Application Closes

One more thing that data modification applications should do — purely from a usability point of view — is warn users if they attempt to quit the application without saving data. That simply means handling the FormClosing event, as demonstrated in the following Try It Out.

Try It Out   Saving Data on Application Termination

1.   Copy the project C:\BegVC#Databases\Chapter04\Ex0404 - Text Modification to a new project, C:\BegVC#Databases\Chapter04\Ex0405 - Handling FormClosing.

2.   Open the code for the Form1 form and copy the code from the sourceBindingNavigatorSaveItem_Click() event hander into a new private void method called SaveData(). Replace the code in the event handler as follows:

```
private void sourceBindingNavigatorSaveItem_Click(object sender, EventArgs e)
{
    SaveData();
}
```

3.   Open Form1 in design mode, and add an event handler to the form for the FormClosing event as follows:

```
private void Form1_FormClosing(object sender, FormClosingEventArgs e)
{
    // Check for changes
    if (folktaleDBDataSet.HasChanges())
    {
        DialogResult result = MessageBox.Show("Do you want to save the changes "
            + "you have made to the database before closing?", "Save changes?",
            MessageBoxButtons.YesNoCancel, MessageBoxIcon.Warning);
        if (result == DialogResult.Cancel)
        {
            // Return to application
            e.Cancel = true;
        }
        else if (result == DialogResult.Yes)
        {
            // Save data before quitting
            SaveData();
        }
    }
}
```

4. Run the application, make some changes, and then close the application. The dialog box shown in Figure 4-11 should appear.

Figure 4-11: The SummaryEditor form in action

5. Select No to abort changes, and then close Visual C# Express.

How It Works

The two things you did in this example were to encapsulate the code for saving data to the database in a method of its own, and to add a new event handler to monitor attempts to close the application. If the application is closed and changes have been made (as detected by the `folktaleDBDataSet.HasChanges()` method), the user is prompted to take action. If the user clicks Yes, data is saved and the application terminated. If the user clicks No, the application terminates without saving changes. Cancel aborts the close operation and returns to the data editing form.

This simple code should really be included in all your data modification applications — just in case!

Summary

In this chapter you have seen how to make data-bound controls in Windows applications capable of saving data. This involved mostly declarative techniques, although some code customization was necessary to deal with a few quirks that exist in database editing. You also saw how to perform some more complicated tasks, such as what to do in the situation when related rows are deleted. Finally, you looked at ways to improve the usability of data access applications.

Specifically, you have learned:

❑ That databases are not always updatable. Database security may prevent you from accessing a database, or may limit you to accessing certain tables, or even certain columns in certain tables, depending on the security configuration. You also saw how views can restrict data modification and how data sources may need additional configuration to enable you to modify data through them.

❑ How Visual C# Express deals with "master" copies of local database files. Depending on the value of the Copy to Output Directory property of the local database file, Visual C# Express may copy a fresh version of the database to the output directory of your project each time the project is executed. You learned how this can be advantageous in testing, but how it can be useful to disable that functionality to persist changes.

❑ How to modify simple database data in `DataGridView` controls. You used data-bound `DataGridView` controls to modify data using the data structures created for data binding and saw how to use the control to modify data.

❑ How to set column default values for adding new data using various techniques — including dynamically setting column data values programmatically. This technique is often required, such as when generating GUID primary key values, as you saw in the example.

❑ How to cancel data modifications.

❑ How to update data from detail views.

❑ Techniques for dealing with multiple related tables, including the order of execution required to update the database when using related data. You saw how it is often necessary to apply subsets of changes to individual tables in a specific order to avoid foreign key reference problems in your databases. Specifically, it is necessary to add and update rows in a parent table before applying changes to child tables, before finally deleting rows from a parent table.

❑ How to create a more user-friendly interface, including dialog boxes for the modification of long text data and prompts to ensure that changes are not lost when applications are closed down.

The next chapter covers a lot of the same ground as in this and the previous chapter but in the context of web applications. Web applications can do the same things as Windows applications but in a slightly differently way, as you will see.

Exercises

1. What are the two ways in which you can initialize data adapters?

2. During development, which Copy to Output Directory property value should you use if you want to be sure that your application is modifying data when you want it to?

3. You have four tables:

❑ `TableA`, which has a one-to-many relationship with `TableB`.

❑ `TableB`, which has a one-to-many relationship with `TableC`.

❑ `TableC`, which has a one-to-many relationship with `TableD`.

❑ `TableD`.

If you want to make changes to all of these tables at the same time, in what order would you apply the changes?

4. Copy the project `C:\BegVC#Databases\Chapter04\Ex0401 - Simple Data Modification` to a new project, `C:\BegVC#Databases\Chapter04\Q0404 - Canceling Edits`. Modify the project by adding a button to the `BindingNavigator` control to cancel edits.

5. What event would you handle in a Windows application if you want to prevent data from being lost when the application is terminated?

Databases and the Internet

Data binding in web applications is a little different than the data binding in Windows applications that you've looked at in previous chapters. Because the underlying technology you use for database access — ADO.NET — is the same for both web and Windows applications, much of what you do in this chapter will seem familiar. However, web applications do work in a slightly different way, so there are other techniques to learn. In addition, you'll use Visual Web Developer Express rather than Visual C# 2005 Express.

In the first part of this chapter you explore the differences between web and Windows applications and the implications of their differences when databases enter the picture. The rest of the chapter tackles database access in ASP.NET, the environment for writing web applications in the .NET Framework. You'll learn how to connect to databases in ASP.NET, which is one area where you have more flexibility than in Windows applications — at least those created in Visual C# 2005 Express. You'll also examine data sources, which are used to access data through connections in the same way that data sources are used in Windows applications, and the ASP.NET controls that you can use to bind data to. Additionally, you'll learn the differences between the controls, how templates are used to format data as HTML, and how to view and edit data in both list and detail views.

Specifically, in this chapter you learn:

- ❑ How web and Windows applications differ, and what this means when dealing with databases
- ❑ How to connect to data from ASP.NET web applications
- ❑ How to configure ASP.NET data sources
- ❑ What controls are available for data binding in ASP.NET
- ❑ How to format data as HTML
- ❑ How to view and edit data in list and detail views

Web versus Windows Applications

There are many differences between web and Windows applications, some obvious and some not so obvious. Before .NET you could think of these applications as two different creatures. Now, however, with the .NET Framework used for all types of applications, that isn't the case. The presentation layer may be as different as ever, but business and data layer code may well be identical, and even shared, when considering these types of applications. Most important in the context of this book, ADO.NET is used for data access in both cases.

It is possible that Windows applications will at some point cease to exist in the form that you know them today. The current direction of development suggests that a common language will be used to design both web and Windows applications, with extensive use of remote web services to provide functionality in both cases. For now, however, you still have to approach them differently, and in this section you consider the key differences.

Perhaps the most obvious disparity is the manner in which you use the application types. Windows applications are executed as applications in their own right. Web applications are accessed via a browser application. There are many of these browsers available (Internet Explorer, Firefox, Netscape, and others) and multiple platforms to consider (Windows, Macintosh, Linux, portable devices, and so on). This immediately introduces additional complexity because you will probably want to cater to as many browsers and platforms as possible.

You can design your Windows applications with a user interface over which you have complete control. That's not the case for web applications. While the user interface ends up as "platform-neutral" HTML and script code, various browsers are notoriously bad at rendering that information in the same way. Proprietary implementations abound, and what works great in one browser may not work at all — or generate errors — in others.

Rendering web applications on portable devices requires yet another approach to cope with small screens, limited display capabilities, and so on. Many web applications are simply not suitable for display on such devices, and in many cases you may need to supply alternative gateways to your information.

The upshot is that if you want your web applications to work on as many browsers as possible, you will need to test, test, and test again. You may also have to think carefully about what functionality to include — especially if such functionality is critical to your applications. To maximize compatibility, you may need to make do with applications that aren't as fully featured as you'd like. Of course, that's only the case if you need this interoperability. For a corporate, nonpublic web site, you can limit the browser used to view the site to, say, Internet Explorer, and make use of the available features freely.

To some extent, this difference between web and Windows applications isn't important from the point of view of this book, although you certainly shouldn't disregard it completely if web applications are your main area of interest.

Far more significant is the essentially disconnected nature of web applications. From the point of view of the server on which the web application runs, users exist only when an exchange of information takes place between the browser (client) and the application (server). Because of some clever tricks that go on behind the scenes, this is often completely transparent to users. In ASP.NET, view state and session state are used to provide a fluid environment for web applications to run in so that the server can keep track of application state between requests for information. This enables users to interact with the server as if permanently connected to it, even if that is not the case. In many cases you, the developer, can also forget about this because ASP.NET is designed to make this as easy as possible. Still, there are times when you will need to have a greater degree of control over such things, which is something you never have to worry about in Windows applications.

The other main difference between web and Windows applications is that you will, more than likely, have to cater to more than one user accessing your data at the same time. For popular web sites you may have to deal with many users — thousands or even hundreds of thousands. For editable data, then, concurrency is much more of an issue and, of course, security becomes more important. Performance is also something to take into account in such circumstances, and there are a number of ways to improve that. You can, for example, cache requests for data such that information is exchanged with the database much less frequently than it is exchanged with users.

It is worth reiterating here that SQL Server Express is not suitable for large-scale applications. Instead, you're much better off using something akin to the full version of SQL Server. That doesn't mean that you can't use SQL Server Express for development. As has already been noted in this book, Microsoft has made it relatively easy to transfer databases between these DBMSes.

Depending on your application requirements and projected usage, there are a number of architectural solutions in web application design. You may, for example, choose to host the database remote from the web application, on a different server located elsewhere on the same LAN as the web application or at a more remote location using web services to exchange data between the web server and a remote database server. In most cases, you do not want to use a local database file as you've seen being used for Windows applications in previous chapters. There are many reasons for this, but perhaps the most compelling is that hosting your database on a web server will affect the performance of web applications, whereas using a remote database enables you to streamline things by having a specialized database server. For this reason, in this chapter you will use a database hosted by SQL Server Express and access it remotely from your web application. This architecture is more likely to mirror the real-world situations you will encounter, although here the "remote" database will exist on the same machine as the web application.

To summarize, writing web applications that include database access code is in some ways exactly the same as writing Windows applications that do the same thing (by virtue of a common underlying technology), and in some ways different (because of the architecture and cross-platform interoperability requirements). The remainder of this chapter takes these similarities and differences into account, and highlights key points as and when they come up.

Data Binding in ASP.NET

As with Windows applications, data binding in ASP.NET relies on the combination of a connection, a data source, and a data-bound control. Unlike Windows applications, there is no `BindingNavigator` control mediating between data sources and data-bound controls, and data binding typically does not use typed data sets. You can use typed data sets if you want, although that requires programmatic data access rather than declarative data binding.

In previous chapters you saw how controls could be made to communicate with each other by, for example, using the selection in one control to filter the results of another. This is also possible in ASP.NET, but the mechanism is different and involves configuring multiple, filtered data sources. You'll see how this is achievable later in this chapter.

In the following sections you'll work through ASP.NET data binding from the bottom up. You'll start by looking at data connections, and then move on to data sources before being introduced to the data-bound controls that are available for you. After that, you learn about templates, which control the HTML output for data-bound controls in various modes (display, item selection, and editing items). Finally, you round things off with some more extensive examples demonstrating how to view and edit data in list and detail views using the data-bound controls.

ASP.NET Data Connections

When data binding in ASP.NET, data connections are defined with connection strings in the application configuration file `web.config`. Behind the scenes, as you might expect, ADO.NET connection objects are used, but that implementation is shielded from you.

Most of the time you configure data connections as part of the configuration of data sources. However, it's possible to configure connections independently, using the Database Explorer window (as you did in the example in Chapter 2). Whichever way you do it, the interface for creating a new connection is the same. The main difference is that when you add a connection as part of data source configuration you have the option of storing the connection string in `web.config`. Connection strings aren't stored in a shared location until you do this; instead, they are hard-coded into the data source, as you will see a later in this chapter.

When you add a connection, you choose the data source and provider, as shown in Figure 5-1. The Change Data Source dialog box displays when you click the Change button in the Add Connection window that appears when you add a new connection.

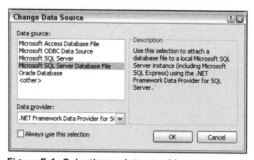

Figure 5-1: Selecting a data provider

Be careful not to confuse "data source" as it appears in Figure 5-1 with the notion of a "data source control" in ASP.NET. In Figure 5-1, the term "data source" is used in its literal sense — the source from which to obtain data. Data source controls, on the other hand, are used to bind data to controls on an ASP.NET page — and you'll learn a lot more about this subject shortly.

The two types of data sources you are looking at in this section are Microsoft SQL Server (for databases hosted in an instance of Microsoft SQL Server or SQL Server Express) and Microsoft SQL Server Database File (for local database files). For Microsoft SQL Server data sources, you have the option of choosing either the .NET Framework Data Provider for SQL Server data provider or .NET Framework Data Provider for OLE DB. The latter offers an alternative, less specialized access mode for databases, and should be used only in circumstances where you are having trouble with the default provider or where you are accessing a non-SQL Server database that supports this type of access. In practice, when using SQL Server or SQL Server Express, there should never be a reason to use this provider type. No alternative provider is available for local database files.

Local Database File Connections

Local database file connections in ASP.NET work the same way as in Windows applications, although things are simplified because Visual Web Developer Express doesn't prompt you to copy database files locally when you add a connection to them. Instead, it simply opens a connection to the database file in the location that you specify. Be careful when you do this because you may want to provide a unique instance of the database to your application, which is really the main reason why you'd want to use a local database file rather than having a remote connection.

In addition, there are authorization issues associated with using a local database file that isn't part of the web application directory structure. By default, web servers typically aren't configured to allow web applications to access locations such as these. This may not be a problem — for example, if you are able to perform additional configuration of your web server to allow such access, or if you are using Windows authentication where user accounts have the privileges required to access the database file in the location where it resides. However, you should certainly think carefully about implementing such schemes because changes to security can result in problems down the line. Those problems might include the introduction of potential security vulnerabilities and the additional configuration requirement that may have to be duplicated later, such as if you move your web site to an alternative web server.

Generally, a better option is to include the local database files in the directory structure of your project — specifically, putting the database files in the App_Data folder of your web application. You aren't forced to use this folder, but it's a good idea to do so because content in that folder is not served in response to web requests (from browsers, for example). This basic security feature is a good one and means that you can be more certain that no unauthorized access to your database is permitted. Instead, only code in your web application can directly access the database, so users get indirect access only through the application.

You can add an existing database to a web application project either by dragging it to the App_Data folder from Windows Explorer or by right-clicking the folder, selecting Add Existing Item, and navigating to the current location of the database .mdf file. You can add a new database file in a similar way. In both cases, a connection to the database file is automatically created, and you can view the database contents using the Database Explorer window.

Remote Connections

More often than not, web applications access databases remotely, either using a local SQL Server instance or (more likely in a production environment) a remote SQL Server instance. By default, SQL Server 2005 Express does not allow remote connections. However, you can enable that functionality using the SQL Server Configuration Manager configuration application that is installed with SQL Server 2005 Express. You can find this through the Start menu via All Programs ➪ Microsoft SQL Server 2005 ➪ Configuration Tools ➪ SQL Server Configuration Manager. Open it, expand SQL Server 2005 Network Configuration, select Protocols for SQLEXPRESS, right-click Named Pipes, and click Enable — as shown in Figure 5-2.

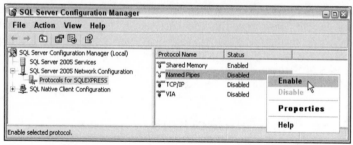

Figure 5-2: Enabling remote access for SQL Server 2005 Express

You can also use the TCP/IP protocol for remote connections, and depending on the architecture of your system, that may be preferable. For remote connections as discussed in this chapter, where the database server still resides on the same computer as the web application, named pipes is fine.

You will receive a warning that the change won't take effect until the service is stopped and restarted. The quickest way to do that is to open a command prompt window and type the following commands:

```
net stop "SQL Server (SQLEXPRESS)"
net start "SQL Server (SQLEXPRESS)"
```

Alternatively you can use the Computer Management tool and restart the service using the Services page, as shown in Figure 5-3.

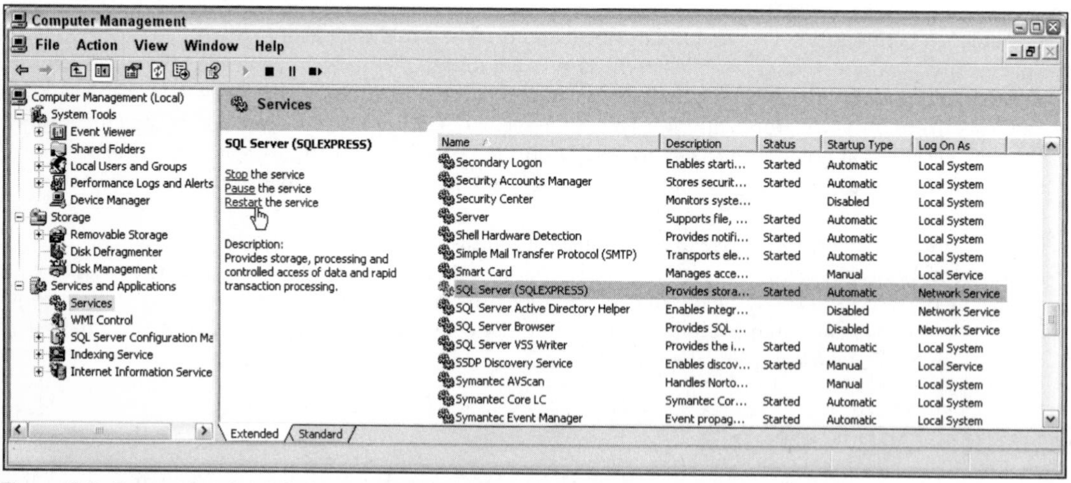

Figure 5-3: Restarting the SQL Server 2005 Express service

With this functionality enabled, you can connect to any database hosted in SQL Server Express. To see these databases, you can use Microsoft's SQL Server Management Studio Express (SSMSE), which you were introduced to in Chapter 2. Among other things, SSMSE (see Figure 5-4) enables you to create and edit databases, as well as connect to existing database files.

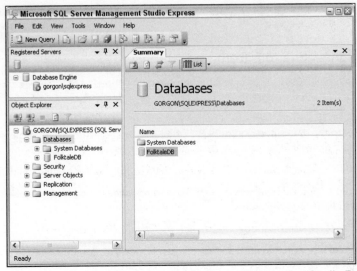

Figure 5-4: Databases in Microsoft SQL Server Management Studio Express

The Databases folder in your version of SSMSE may be empty. In the Try It Out section coming up shortly you'll add the FolktaleDB database you see in Figure 5-4 to SQL Server Express for use in later examples.

To connect to a remote database in Visual Web Developer Express, you must first select the Microsoft SQL Server data source, as discussed in the introduction to this section. Then you can select a database to connect to using the dialog box shown in Figure 5-5.

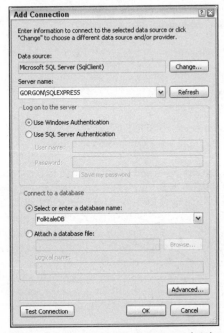

Figure 5-5: Connecting to a remote database

In the following Try It Out, you add the FolktaleDB database to Microsoft SQL Server and connect to it from a web application.

Try It Out   Connecting to a Remote Database

1. If you haven't already done so, enable remote connections in SQL Server 2005 Express, as discussed in the previous section.

2. Copy the `FolktaleDB.mdf` and `FolktaleDB_log.ldf` files in the downloadable code for this book to the data directory for SQL Server Express — which by default is `C:\Program Files\Microsoft SQL Server\MSSQL.1\MSSQL\Data`.

3. Open All Programs ➪ Microsoft SQL Server 2005 ➪ SQL Server Management Studio Express CTP.

4. Connect to your local SQL Server 2005 Express instance (`<computer name>\SQLEXPRESS`) using Windows authentication.

5. In the Object Explorer window, right-click the Databases folder and then click Attach.

6. Click the Add button, navigate to the location where you copied `FolktaleDB.mdf`, select `FolktaleDB.mdf`, and click OK; then click OK again.

7. Close SQL Server Management Studio Express.

8. Open Visual Web Developer Express.

9. If the Database Explorer window is not visible, display it by selecting the View ➪ Database Explorer menu option.

10. In the Database Explorer window, click the Connect To Database icon.

11. Change the data source for the connection to Microsoft SQL Server, and connect to the FolktaleDB database, as discussed earlier (and shown in Figure 5-5).

Your SQL Server Instance may not appear in the Server name drop-down list. If that's the case, you can type it in manually (`<computer name>\SQLEXPRESS`).

12. Click OK to add the connection.

13. Close Visual Web Developer Express.

How It Works

In this example, you added a database to SQL Server 2005 Express and created a connection to it in Visual Web Developer Express. There are a few points to note.

First, this process of attaching a database is an excellent way to copy databases from one location to another. As well as attaching databases through SQL Server Management Studio Express, you can also detach them, then copy the files to a new location and reattach them. This procedure does mean that there will be some "downtime" when the database is unavailable, but that can be kept to a minimum if you work fast. Never copy database files to another location and attach them if they haven't already been detached from their original location, because that may cause errors.

Second, note that the name of the database wasn't preserved — to simplify access to the database the name was manually added. This isn't essential, but it does make sense to avoid excessively long database names. After all, once the database is hosted in this way, the file location is to a large extent irrelevant.

Third, and possibly most important, never attempt to host a database file that is also accessed as a local database file, either by a Windows application, as in previous chapters, or by web applications. Owing to the way things work with SQL Server 2005 Express, this leads to all sorts of trouble and may result in the database file becoming unusable.

Finally, in this example you didn't actually add a connection to a web application. Instead, you added it to the collection of connections stored in the Visual Web Developer Express environment. Connections added this way are available for use in any applications you develop, as you see in the Try It Out in the next section.

ASP.NET Data Source Controls

Several data source controls are available to you in ASP.NET, all of which expose data that can be bound to other controls. In this chapter you use `SqlDataSource`, which, as its name suggests, exchanges data with a SQL Server database. It is worth being aware of the other data source controls, however, because ASP.NET data-binding techniques can also be applied to them. In other words, you can apply the techniques you learn in this chapter to those controls as and when you need to. They are:

❑   `AccessDataSource`: Connects to data stored in Microsoft Access databases.

❑   `ObjectDataSource`: Exposes data stored in objects for data binding. This can be used to great effect to bind your own objects to display controls, and in fact has its place in the context of databases. Later in the book you see how to populate objects with data and manipulate this data using advanced techniques. This data source type can be used in combination with those techniques to display such data.

❑   `XmlDataSource`: Enables you to bind to data stored in XML files. It also allows you to transform the XML using XSLT to customize the data that other controls bind to.

❑   `SiteMapDataSource`: Exposes data from the site map for your web application so that you can display dynamically generated navigation controls, bread-crumb trails, and so on.

When you add a `SqlDataSource` control to an ASP.NET page from the Visual Web Developer Toolbox, the following code is added:

```
<asp:SqlDataSource ID="SqlDataSource1" runat="server"></asp:SqlDataSource>
```

Further configuration can be applied to the control either by manually adding attributes to it or by using the Configure Data Source Wizard. The wizard is available in the SqlDataSource Tasks window when in Design view, as shown in Figure 5-6.

In this section you concentrate on using the wizard but also look at the effects in the code for the data source control, should you want to do things manually in the future.

Figure 5-6: Accessing the Configure Data Source Wizard

Data Source Configuration

The first page of the Configure Data Source Wizard — titled Choose Your Data Connection — is where you choose a data connection to use for the data source. It can be a connection stored in the Visual Web Developer environment, such as the one you added earlier in this chapter, a local database connection to a file in the `App_Data` directory for your application, or any other sort of connection that you have added. You can also add a new connection at this point. After selecting a connection you can see the connection string that will be used.

On the next page of the wizard, you are given the option to save the connection string to the configuration file if it doesn't already exist there. In most circumstances you want to do this, and typically you want to use the default name for the connection string that is suggested for you. This is especially useful if your application contains multiple `SqlDataSource` controls because changing the connection string for all of them can be achieved simply by changing the connection string in the configuration file (`web.config`).

The next page of the wizard is where you configure the data accessed by the data source. One way to do that is by using a custom SQL select statement or stored procedure, in much the same way as you did in Windows applications in the previous chapters. However, you can also use the wizard to generate the code for you, and it can add filtering, ordering, and other customizations for you.

To do this, select the Specify Columns From A Table Or View option in the wizard, as shown in Figure 5-7.

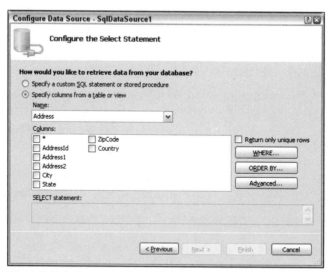

Figure 5-7: Data source data configuration

Then select a table or view in the Name drop-down, and select the columns to display (or * for all columns) in the Columns pane. As you do so, the SELECT statement that will be used is displayed in the SELECT Statement pane. On the right side of this wizard page are additional options. You can, if you want, choose to return only unique rows by selecting the Return Only Unique Rows option. For example, in Figure 5-7 you can see the columns in the `Address` table of the FolktaleDB database. You could select just the `Country` column from the table and choose to return only unique countries, so you get a list of the countries used in the addresses stored with no duplicates. Doing so adds a DISTINCT option to the SQL statement used to obtain data. Here's the generated SQL:

```
SELECT DISTINCT [Country] FROM [Address]
```

You'll look at the other options available on this page of the wizard shortly.

On the next page of the wizard, test the query that you have generated and see the results that are returned. Once you are satisfied that things are working as they should, finish the wizard.

Once the wizard completes, you will notice that attributes corresponding to your choices have been added the markup for the control in Source view. For example:

```
<asp:SqlDataSource ID="SqlDataSource1" runat="server"
    ConnectionString="<%$ ConnectionStrings:FolktaleDBConnectionString %>"
    SelectCommand="SELECT DISTINCT [Country] FROM [Address]"></asp:SqlDataSource>
```

If you elected to save the connection string in the application configuration file, the ConnectionString attribute will look similar to this one. The `<%$ ConnectionStrings:XXX %>` placeholder instructs ASP.NET to use the named connection string stored in the web.config file.

If one doesn't already exist for the application, the web.config file is automatically added by the wizard. It contains a `<connectionStrings>` section similar to the following:

```
<configuration>
  <appSettings/>
  <connectionStrings>
    <add name="FolktaleDBConnectionString"
      connectionString="Data Source=GORGON\SQLEXPRESS;Initial
        Catalog=FolktaleDB;Integrated Security=True"
      providerName="System.Data.SqlClient" />
  </connectionStrings>
  <system.web>
    ...
  </system.web>
</configuration>
```

Here you can see both the connection string and the provider required to make a connection to the database.

Filtering Options

Clicking the WHERE button (on the right in Figure 5-7) on the Configure The Select Statement page of the wizard gives you access to a wealth of filtering options for your data. The filtering can also take a number of forms — it doesn't just have to be a hard-coded filter value. Figure 5-8 shows the filtering dialog box with one filter added and another one in progress.

The Column drop-down is a list of the columns in the table or view you have selected. From there you select a column to filter by — which needn't be one that is included in the results returned by your SQL query. Next, select a comparison operator in the Operator drop-down; = is the most common, but you can use any logical operator as well as LIKE and NOT LIKE for text comparisons.

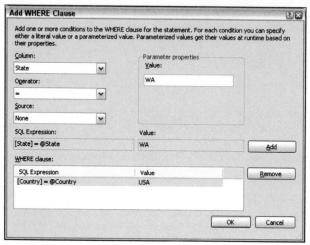

Figure 5-8: Data source filter configuration

In the Source drop-down, select how to obtain the value for comparison — which is where the real power of data source filtering comes in. In Figure 5-8, the selected value is None, which simply means you have to provide a hard-coded value to filter by — in the Value text box on the right. The other options, shown in the table that follows, provide alternative text boxes to configure them.

Source	Usage
None	Set a single, hard-coded value to compare to in the Value text box.
Control	Obtain a value from a control elsewhere on the page. Specify the control using the Control ID drop-down list.
Cookie	Extract a value from a cookie stored on the client. Use Cookie Name to specify the name of the cookie.
Form	Use a value from an HTML form field, identified using the Form Field text box.
Profile	Obtain a value from the ASP.NET user profile for the current user, where the profile property to use is specified by Property Name.
QueryString	Extract a value from a named querystring parameter, specified by the QueryString field.
Session	Extract a value from session state, using the identifier specified by the Session field.

In addition, all the options other than Value allow you to specify a default value for comparison with the Default Value text box, in case the value is unobtainable for whatever reason.

These options enable you to dynamically filter data sources in response to a variety of circumstances. Using the QueryString type, for example, you can provide URLs for filtered views of data with no additional coding, which can be extremely useful. Another practical parameter source type is `Control`, which as you will see a little later in this chapter, enables you to filter one data-bound control from the selection in another data-bound control.

As you add filters (you can provide as many as you like), they appear in the WHERE clause pane at the bottom of the dialog box, as shown in Figure 5-8.

Ordering Options

Click the Order By button on the Configure The Select Statement page of the wizard to add an `ORDER BY` clause to the SQL statement used to obtain data. Again, you do this in a user-friendly way with a dialog box, as shown in Figure 5-9.

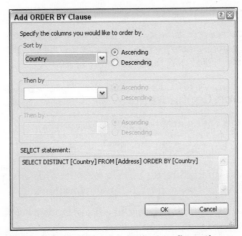

Figure 5-9: Data source order configuration

You can select up to three columns to order data by, and each can be ordered in ascending or descending fashion.

In practice this isn't the primary way in which you order data, because data-bound controls can sort rows themselves — that's why the options here aren't as full as those for filtering data. However, it is useful to be able to set the default ordering in this way.

Additional Options

Finally, the wizard has two options filed under the Advanced button, as shown in Figure 5-10.

As with Windows application data sources, you can automatically generate `INSERT`, `UPDATE`, and `DELETE` statements according to the `SELECT` statement you have provided. This is necessary if you want to modify data through your data source (and, to be honest, it's a little strange that this is classified as "advanced" because it is fairly fundamental functionality).

Select the first option and the second option becomes available. It formats the `UPDATE` and `DELETE` statements using optimistic concurrency — which works in exactly the same way as for Windows applications.

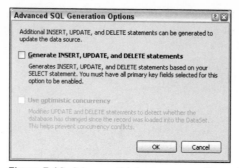

Figure 5-10: Advanced data source configuration

In certain circumstances, these options may not be available, perhaps because of the specific query you are using as a SELECT statement or because of the tables or views you are using. Sometimes these options are not available until you save the wizard changes and then reopen the wizard, so if you expect them to be available and they aren't, this is the first thing to try.

Try It Out   Data Source Configuration

In this Try It Out, you create a data source for use in later exercises.

1. Open Visual Web Developer Express.

2. Create a new web site in the directory `C:\BegVC#Databases\Chapter05\Ex0501 - Data Source Configuration`, using the File System location and Visual C# language.

3. The `Default.aspx` page should appear in editing mode by default, in Source view — change the view of this page to Design view.

4. Add a `SqlDataSource` control to the form using the Toolbox window.

5. In the SqlDataSource Tasks window, click Configure Data Source.

6. Select the remote connection to the FolktaleDB database (added in the previous Try It Out) from the drop-down and click Next.

7. Save the connection string using the default name and click Next.

8. Select all columns from the `Species` table.

9. Click WHERE. Configure a QueryString filter as follows:

Column	Immortal
Operator	=
Source	QueryString
QueryString field	Immortal
Default value	false

10. Click Add to add the filter. Click OK to return to the Configure Data Source dialog box.

11. Click ORDER BY. Order the data by the Species field, ascending. Click OK.

12. Finish the wizard.

13. Save the project and exit Visual Web Developer.

How It Works

In this example you've added a data source that you will use in subsequent Try It Outs. As such, there isn't much to comment on here, although it is worth looking at the code that has been generated:

```
<asp:SqlDataSource ID="SqlDataSource1" runat="server"
  ConnectionString="<%$ ConnectionStrings:FolktaleDBConnectionString %>"
  SelectCommand=
    "SELECT * FROM [Species] WHERE (([Immortal] = @Immortal) ORDER BY [Species]">
  <SelectParameters>
    <asp:QueryStringParameter DefaultValue="false" Name="Immortal"
      QueryStringField="Immortal" Type="Boolean" />
  </SelectParameters>
</asp:SqlDataSource>
```

Note the @Immortal parameter. Its value is specified using the <asp:QueryStringParameter> element in the <SelectParameters> child element of the control. That element includes all of the configuration you selected in the form of attributes.

Additional Data Source Control Functionality

There are a couple of additional techniques that you can use with SqlDataSource objects that are worth being aware of but which won't be covered in depth here. First, a SqlDataSource object is capable of retrieving data in two ways: It can either use a DataSet object as internal storage or obtain results on-the-fly using a DataReader. To choose which method to use, you set the DataSourceMode property, which takes a value from the SqlDataSourceMode enumeration. This enumeration has two members, SqlDataSourceMode.DataReader and SqlDataSourceMode.DataSet. Using a DataSet has a slightly higher overhead but does enable additional functionality, such as paging when binding data to a GridView control (which you learn about shortly) and caching (which you learn about in Chapter 10).

Second, you can use the Select() method to obtain the data from a SqlDataSource object. This can be useful in code-behind situations where you want to manipulate data obtained using a SqlDataSource control — and it saves you from having to write code behind to obtain data in the first place. The result of this method depends on the DataSourceMode property. If that property is set to SqlDataSourceMode .DataSet, the method returns a DataView; otherwise, it returns an IDataReader interface. To use the result, cast it to the appropriate type.

ASP.NET Data Display Control Summary

So far in this chapter you've seen how to connect up plumbing that enables you to access data using declarative data-binding techniques. The next step is to provide a means to display and edit that data, and ASP.NET provides a variety of controls to which you can bind data for that purpose: `GridView`, `DataList`, `Repeater`, `FormView`, and `DetailsView`. This section introduces you to these controls.

GridView

The `GridView` control enables you to display multiple rows of data in tabular form. Its display consists of a table showing the data from rows and columns of the underlying data table.

This control contains rich functionality including pagination, sorting, and even editing, and also gives you a great deal of flexibility in styling. In Chapter 2 you saw how to connect a `GridView` control to a database and style it to look good in surprisingly few steps. In many ways, this control is analogous to the `DataGridView` control you used in Windows applications in previous chapters. As with `DataGridView`, you can use `GridView` to choose from an assortment of column types to display data in various ways, such a text fields, checkboxes, and so on.

The main difference between `GridView` and `DataGridView` is that `GridView` renders its data using HTML, to make it available to web browsers. To achieve this, you supply the control with a selection of templates to render data in different ways according to the situation. You look at templates in more detail a little later in the chapter.

Figure 5-11 shows a `GridView` control in action, with sorting, pagination, and row selection functionality included.

	Name	Occupation	Age	Gender	Email	Notes
Select	Aphrodite	Goddess of love		Female	aphrodite@olympus.com	Also goddess of beauty and protecter of sailors
Select	Apollo	God of prophecy		Male	apollo@olympus.com	
Select	Ares	God of war		Male	ares@olympus.com	Handsome but cruel
Select	Artemis	Goddess of the hunt		Female	artemis@olympus.com	Goddess of the moon
Select	Athena	Goddess of wisdom		Female	athena@olympus.com	Goddess of practical crafts and warfare; also patron goddess
Select	Buffy	Vampire slayer	21	Female	buffy@slayer.com	Californian superhero
Select	Cinderella	Household drudge	18	Female	cinderella@scullery.com	Despised stepdaughter
Select	Cronus	Former supreme god	2600	Male	cronus@titan.org	Dethroned
Select	Demeter	Goddess of the harvest		Female	demeter@olympus.com	
Select	Dione	Uncertain - may have been a Titaness		Female		Became one of Saturn's moons in 1684

Figure 5-11: GridView control in action

DataList

The `DataList` control also displays multiple records, but the formatting of items is different from that of `GridView`. Instead of restricting you to a tabular layout with each row corresponding to a data table row, the `DataList` control displays all the information from each row sequentially, and you define exactly how the columns in each row are formatted.

You can display items in a table or flow layout. With a table layout, each table cell contains the information from a single data row, formatted according to the templates you supply. In this mode, you can choose how many columns the table should display simply by setting the RepeatColumns property, meaning that you can alter the layout with ease.

No tabular formatting is supplied in flow layout; instead, you control the layout of items using whatever HTML code you choose. In this layout, each item is wrapped in a <span> element.

In today's web world, attention is moving away from using <table> controls to control web page layout as they are increasingly seen as cumbersome. If you are the sort of person that keeps up with such things you will probably prefer to use the flow layout wherever possible.

As with GridView, this control enables you to provide selecting and editing functionality, although in this case you have to code the functionality manually — the wizards won't help you out. However, this isn't such a difficult thing to achieve and can be a powerful technique.

Figure 5-12 shows a formatted DataList view.

Name: Cronus Gender: Male Notes: Dethroned Email: cronus@titan.org Occupation: Former supreme god Age: 2600	Name: Demeter Gender: Female Notes: Email: demeter@olympus.com Occupation: Goddess of the harvest Age:
Name: Metis Gender: Female Notes: First wive of Zeus Email: metis@firstwives.org Occupation: Titaness Age:	Name: Athena Gender: Female Notes: Goddess of practical crafts and warfare; also patron goddess of Athens Email: athena@olympus.com Occupation: Goddess of wisdom Age:
Name: Aphrodite Gender: Female Notes: Also goddess of beauty and protecter of sailors Email: aphrodite@olympus.com Occupation: Goddess of love Age:	Name: Hephaestus Gender: Male Notes: Also god of metalworking. Created Pandora, the first woman. Email: hephaestus@olympus.com Occupation: God of fire Age:

Figure 5-12: DataList control in action

Repeater

The Repeater control is essentially a stripped-down version of the DataList control. Repeater provides a read-only view of data where you have complete control over the HTML that is output for each item. Rather than giving you a host of options for layout types, Repeater gives you access to its display using a basic set of templates and outputs only the HTML that you supply.

This control is most useful for outputting data when you need the HTML to exactly match your specification. If you use it, however, you may have to provide your own code for any more advanced functionality, such as pagination or item editing.

FormView

The `FormView` control provides a view of a single row in a data table. The data to display is often decided by an item selection in a list control such as a `GridView` control elsewhere on the page. Alternatively, you can allow paging in `FormView`, enabling you to navigate through multiple data rows.

This control supports a variety of templates so you can control how it is rendered in various modes. You can provide templates to edit data as well as to just view it. The `FormView` display generated in all circumstances is much like that of the `DataList` control, where you have a high degree of control over the layout of each column of data in a row and you can arrange them however you want.

Figure 5-13 shows a formatted `FormView` control including pagination.

Figure 5-13: FormView control in action

DetailsView

The `DetailsView` control, like the `FormView` control, displays a single record, can provide automatic pagination, and allows the editing of data as well as its display. The main difference between these controls is that `DetailsView` displays each column of data as a row with two columns. The left column gives the name of the field, and the right column its value.

Another important aspect of `DetailsView` is that it can generate controls for editing, deleting, and adding new records without your having to perform any additional configuration. This is possible because the tabular layout makes the positioning of controls to change between modes a simple matter. (In `FormView`, the greater flexibility in display makes it impossible for that functionality to be added automatically.)

Figure 5-14 shows a formatted instance of this control.

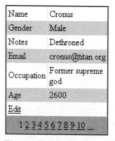

Figure 5-14: DetailsView control in action

Figure 5-15 shows the same control in edit mode using automatically generated templates.

Figure 5-15: DetailsView control in edit mode

An Introduction to Templates

Templates are the way in which bound data is rendered as HTML. There are several templates available, and each of the data-bound controls discussed in the previous section uses a different selection of them.

A template is a chunk of HTML and ASP.NET code that forms a distinct, reusable unit. For data binding, the most important things that a template can contain are data-binding expressions. A data-binding expression is a placeholder that can be used dynamically to insert bound data at a specific point in a template, and can also provide a two-way link between properties of ASP.NET controls and data columns. For example, the `Text` property of a `TextBox` control can be bound to a data column, and modifications to that property are reflected as modifications to the underlying data (should changes be committed, that is).

One of the most commonly used templates is `ItemTemplate`. Used in `DataList`, `Repeater`, and `FormView` controls, this template renders a row of a data table as HTML. Depending on whether the control it is used in displays lists of rows or just a single row, the template may be used one or more times on a page. In the ASP.NET code for the page, an item template is created by enclosing HTML code, ASP.NET controls, and data-binding expressions in an `<ItemTemplate>` element, which in turn is a child element of the element representing the data-bound control — `<asp:DataList>` in the following example:

```
<asp:DataList id="MyDataList" runat="server" DataSourceID="SqlDataSource1" ... >
   ...
   <ItemTemplate>
      <!--Template specification-->
   </ItemTemplate>
   ...
</asp:DataList>
```

Data-binding expressions in the template specification have the following syntax:

```
<%# data binding expression %>
```

There are two key methods that you can use in data-binding expressions: `Eval()` and `Bind()`. `Eval()` returns the value of a data column as a text string but does so in a read-only way. This method is useful for writing out literal values for data columns, or binding text values to, for example, `Label` controls. It takes a single string parameter that is the name of the column to be bound. For example:

```
<ItemTemplate>
  The value of the Occupation column for this row is: <%# Eval("Occupation") %>
</ItemTemplate>
```

Using this `ItemTemplate` specification, every row rendered in a data-bound control will output a single line of text that includes the value of a single data column.

For nullable columns, the text is still output for null values, with the data-binding expression replaced with an empty string.

It is possible, by clever use of placeholders with bound properties, to output text conditionally:

```
<ItemTemplate>
  <asp:PlaceHolder ID="nonNullOccupationBox" runat="server"
    Visible='<%# Eval("Occupation") != DBNull.Value %>'>
    The value of the Occupation column for this row is: <%# Eval("Occupation") %>
  </asp:PlaceHolder>
  <asp:PlaceHolder ID="nullOccupationBox" runat="server"
    Visible='<%# Eval("Occupation") == DBNull.Value %>'>
    This row has a null value for its Occupation column.
  </asp:PlaceHolder>
</ItemTemplate>
```

The `Bind()` method works in a similar way to `Eval()` but provides two-way binding, which is useful, for example, in providing users with a way to edit data. Editing data is usually achieved in a different template, `EditItemTemplate`:

```
<EditItemTemplate>
  Occupation:
  <asp:TextBox ID="occupationBox" runat="server"
    Text='<%# Bind("Occupation") %>' />
</EditItemTemplate>
```

Templates can contain as many data-binding expressions for data columns as you want. You can even repeat column data if required.

When you add data-bound controls to a page and supply them with a data source, ASP.NET automatically generates a selection of templates for you depending on the control type. Typically these templates simply output each column in a row in the order in which the columns are obtained from the data source. While these automatically generated templates may not be exactly what you want, they do provide a useful starting point from which you can evolve your own code.

The full set of templates available to you is as follows:

❑   `ItemTemplate`: Controls the output of individual items in a list control or the main item display area for a single-item display control.

❑ `AlternatingItemTemplate`: For list controls, this (optional) template can be used to provide different formatting for alternate items, which can aid users in reading the data in the way that alternating background colors are often used in tables.

❑ `SelectedItemTemplate`: Replaces the `ItemTemplate` template for an item that is selected.

❑ `EditItemTemplate`: Replaces the `ItemTemplate` template for an item that is in edit mode.

❑ `InsertItemTemplate`: Used when new items are being added.

❑ `HeaderTemplate`: Contains code to be rendered prior to items in a list or above the main item content in single item display controls. Data-binding expressions will not bind to an item in this template.

❑ `FooterTemplate`: Contains code to be rendered after items in a list or below the main item content in single item display controls. Data-binding expressions will not bind to an item in this template.

❑ `SeparatorTemplate`: Contains HTML code that renders between each item in a list control. Data-binding expressions will not bind to an item in this template.

❑ `EmptyDataTemplate`: If an item contains no data, the contents of this template are rendered instead of the contents of `ItemTemplate`. Data-binding expressions will not bind to an item in this template, because the item in question is null.

❑ `PagerTemplate`: The HTML to display for the pagination control for a data-bound control. Controlling the pagination control with this template can be fairly involved and can require code behind, and as such it is not covered in this book.

The templates available to each of the data-bound controls are shown in the table that follows.

Template	GridView	DataList	Repeater	FormView	DetailsView
`ItemTemplate`		X	X	X	
`AlternatingItemTemplate`		X	X		
`SelectedItemTemplate`		X			
`EditItemTemplate`		X		X	
`InsertItemTemplate`				X	
`HeaderTemplate`		X	X	X	X
`FooterTemplate`		X	X	X	X
`SeparatorTemplate`		X	X		
`EmptyDataTemplate`	X			X	X
`PagerTemplate`	X			X	X

Many of the data-bound controls also make use of style properties to control the display of items and rows. For example, the `GridView` control includes `RowStyle` and `AlternatingRowStyle` properties, and `DataList` has (among others) an `ItemStyle` property. These can be useful for applying styling to items without having to tinker with templates. To some extent, however, these properties are superseded in modern web pages, where CSS styling is fast becoming the normal way to do things.

That being said, styling with properties can be a nice way to get things looking good quickly, especially in a prototyping situation. In addition, Visual Web Developer Express provides a number of auto-format style templates that you can apply to any of the data-bound controls. You used one of these in the example in Chapter 2. The auto-format templates are also a good way to get a starting point from which you can develop your own look and feel.

Viewing and Editing Data in List Views

Now it's time to start using the data-bound controls you've been learning about in this chapter.

Viewing Data

When you add a data-bound control to a page, the Tasks window for the control appears automatically. If you already have a `SqlDataSource` control in place, you can select it from the Choose Data Source drop-down in the Tasks window. Once you do so, the schema for the data is obtained, and the data-bound controls automatically generate default templates to display data from the data source.

At this point, everything is in place to view data, and you can run the web application and see your results. However, you are likely to want to change things a little and add additional functionality.

The following Try It Out illustrates how the default display looks for `GridView` and `DataList`, and then you edit things to change the layout.

Try It Out   List Data

1. Copy the `C:\BegVC#Databases\Chapter05\Ex0501 - Data Source Configuration` example directory from the previous Try It Out to a new directory, `C:\BegVC#Databases\Chapter05\Ex0502 - List Data`.

2. Open Visual Web Developer Express.

3. Select the File ⇨ Open Web Site menu item and open the web site `C:\BegVC#Databases\Chapter05\Ex0502 - List Data`.

4. In Design view for the `Default.aspx` page, select the `SqlDataSource` control and, in the SqlDataSource Tasks window, click Refresh Schema. Click OK in the dialog box that appears.

5. Add a `GridView` control, and select the `SqlDataSource1` data source for the data source of the `GridView` control.

6. Add a `DataList` below the `GridView` control, and select the same data source.

7. In Source view, add the following code near the top of the file:

```
<form id="form1" runat="server">
  <div>
    <a href="Default.aspx?Immortal=true">Show Immortals</a><br />
    <a href="Default.aspx">Show Non-Immortals</a><br />
    ...
```

8. Run the application in debug mode. If prompted by the Debugging Not Enabled dialog box, select the Modify the `web.config` file to enable debugging option and click OK. Figure 5-16 shows what the output should look like.

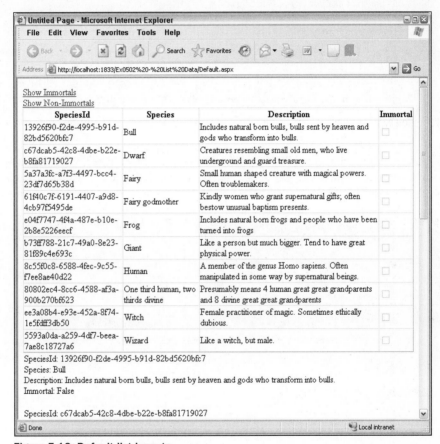

Figure 5-16: Default list layouts

9. Test the links at the top of the page to change the display filter.

10. Close the web page.

11. In Design view, click the `SpeciesId` column in the `GridView` control, and in the GridView Tasks window select Remove Column.

12. In the GridView Tasks window, click Auto Format and choose the Classic scheme.

13. In Source view, modify the `ItemTemplate` for the `DataList` control as follows:

```
<ItemTemplate>
  <strong>Species:</strong>
  <asp:Label ID="SpeciesLabel" runat="server" Text='<%# Eval("Species") %>' />
  <asp:PlaceHolder ID="immortalBox" runat="server"
    Visible='<%# Bind("Immortal") %>'>
    <small>(Immortal)</small>
  </asp:PlaceHolder>
  <br />
  <strong>Description:</strong>
  <asp:Label ID="DescriptionLabel" runat="server"
    Text='<%# Eval("Description") %>' />
  <br />
  <br />
</ItemTemplate>
```

14. In Design view, in the DataList Tasks window, click Property Builder.

15. On the General page of the DataList1 Properties dialog box, set Columns to 3 and Direction to Horizontal, and then click OK.

16. In the DataList Tasks window, click Auto Format and choose the Slate scheme.

17. Run the application again, and verify changes as shown in Figure 5-17, which shows the view for Immortal Species.

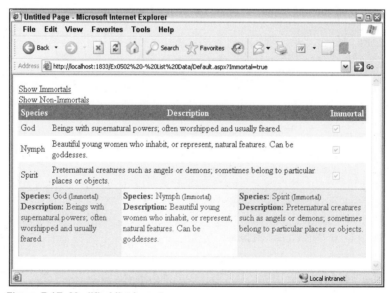

Figure 5-17: Modified list layout

18. Close the application, saving changes if prompted. Close Visual Web Developer Express.

How It Works

In this example, you use the data source configured earlier in the chapter to display data in two different types of data-bound lists. You also reformat the lists using a combination of automatic formatting and ASP.NET code modification, and use the QueryString filter for the data source to filter the data using URLs.

Starting from the top, the first thing you did was to refresh the schema for the data source. This is sometimes necessary, such as when you copy a web application from one place to another, and ensures that the data-bound controls can generate default templates correctly. After adding the display controls, you added two simple hyperlinks, one of which included the QueryString Immortal=true. That QueryString parameter is used by the data source control to set a SQL query parameter, as discussed earlier in the book, and filters the data. The filtered data is immediately available to the data-bound controls, and the display changes accordingly.

Next, you formatted the GridView control by removing a column and applying auto-formatting. This changed the ASP.NET code for the control as follows:

```
<asp:GridView ID="GridView1" runat="server" AutoGenerateColumns="False"
  DataKeyNames="SpeciesId" DataSourceID="SqlDataSource1" CellPadding="4"
  ForeColor="#333333" GridLines="None">
  <Columns>
    <asp:BoundField DataField="Species" HeaderText="Species"
      SortExpression="Species" />
    <asp:BoundField DataField="Description" HeaderText="Description"
      SortExpression="Description" />
    <asp:CheckBoxField DataField="Immortal" HeaderText="Immortal"
      SortExpression="Immortal" />
  </Columns>
  <FooterStyle BackColor="#507CD1" Font-Bold="True" ForeColor="White" />
  <RowStyle BackColor="#EFF3FB" />
  <EditRowStyle BackColor="#2461BF" />
  <SelectedRowStyle BackColor="#D1DDF1" Font-Bold="True" ForeColor="#333333" />
  <PagerStyle BackColor="#2461BF" ForeColor="White" HorizontalAlign="Center" />
  <HeaderStyle BackColor="#507CD1" Font-Bold="True" ForeColor="White" />
  <AlternatingRowStyle BackColor="White" />
</asp:GridView>
```

You can see that a number of properties have been set on the GridView control, and a number of style elements have been added. The code for this is readable, and you can see at a glance how the properties of the style elements map to the display you see. Note that several styles are defined that aren't currently being used — for selected and edit-mode rows, for example. These are associated with the auto-format style chosen, and will be usable a little later.

You also can see how the columns for the control are defined, by using controls nested in a <Columns> element. The GridView control doesn't use templates in the same way as other controls do; instead, it binds its columns to data columns. There are a number of column types that you can see here, such as columns for including edit controls, which you will see in the next section. In this example, BoundField columns are used for simple text data display and a CheckBoxField column displays Boolean data from the Immortal column.

Moving on, wizards were used to auto-format the DataList control and change the basic layout (to a three-column view). More important, you edited the ItemTemplate for the control, enabling you to completely overhaul the display. You did this by adding HTML code and adding a `PlaceHolder` control to output the text "(Immortal)" if the value of the `Immortal` data column is `true`. Here's the code:

```
<asp:PlaceHolder ID="immortalBox" runat="server"
  Visible='<%# Bind("Immortal") %>'>
  <small>(Immortal)</small>
</asp:PlaceHolder>
```

Because the `Immortal` column is a Boolean value, it was possible to simply bind the column data to the `Visible` property of the `PlaceHolder` control, which is also Boolean. By switching the display filter using the hyperlinks added earlier, you can see this conditional display in action.

Additional Configuration

As discussed earlier in this chapter, the `GridView` control is capable of additional functionality, such as selecting, paging, and sorting data. You can configure this simply by checking the appropriate boxes in the GridView Tasks window, shown in Figure 5-18.

Figure 5-18: GridView Tasks window

In addition, you can set a number of other properties for pagination, such as `PageSize` to set the number of items to display on a page. These properties are shown in Figure 5-19.

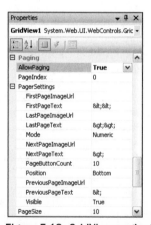

Figure 5-19: GridView pagination properties

Most of these properties are to control the display of the pager control, which appears at the bottom of the GridView control. You can replace the default text for the various controls (first page, previous page, next page, and last page), replace the text for these controls with images, set the position of the pager control (Top, Bottom, or TopAndBottom), choose the number of page numbers that are displayed, and change the mode of the pager. The pager mode can be any of the following:

- ❏   Numeric: Shows only page numbers
- ❏   NextPrevious: Shows only next and previous page controls.
- ❏   NextPreviousFirstLast: Shows next, previous, first, and last page controls.
- ❏   NumericFirstLast: Shows page numbers and first and last page controls.

These properties provide you with a fair amount of flexibility in the pagination of the control. To have more control, you can set the Visible property of the pagination control to false and write your own code.

When column selection is enabled, an additional column is added to the control. By default it has the text "Select" and enables users to select rows by clicking on it. The code added for this column, which you can see in Source view in the <Columns> section, is as follows:

```
<asp:CommandField ShowSelectButton="True" />
```

You can change the text displayed by setting the SelectText property for this column specification.

The CommandField *column specification is used for a number of things, including adding edit commands, as you will see in the next section.*

With selection enabled, the SelectedIndex property of the control changes according to the selected row. You can use this in code behind to access the selected data row, and it also provides the basis for master/detail views, which you'll look at later in the chapter.

When sorting is enabled, each column heading is rendered as a link; and clicking a link causes the control to sort data by that column. This is controlled by the column specifications for each column. You can modify the behavior using the Edit Columns option in the GridView Tasks window, shown in Figure 5-20.

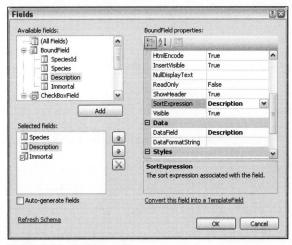

Figure 5-20: Column editor

In this dialog box, you can control all aspects of columns, including adding and removing columns, reordering columns, changing the types of columns, and changing sort behavior. By changing the SortExpression property for a column, you can change which field is sorted by when the column header is clicked. If you clear this property, you can prevent sorting by the selected column.

As with Windows applications, you can also add additional types of columns here, such as the command columns used to edit data.

All of this functionality — pagination, sorting, and selecting — is also available in DataList controls. However, you have to do a lot of the work by hand for that control. For pagination and sorting, you need to modify the data returned by the data source. For selection (and editing), you have to add button type controls (Button, LinkButton, or ImageButton) to the ItemTemplate of the DataList, and set the CommandName property of the button to the appropriate value (select for item selection). You also have to handle the SelectedIndexChanged event for the DataList control in code behind and re-bind data when an item is selected by calling the DataList.DataBind() method.

The following modification adds a select button to the previous example:

```
<asp:DataList ... OnSelectedIndexChanged="DataList1_SelectedIndexChanged">
    <ItemTemplate>
        ...
        <br />
        <asp:LinkButton runat="server" ID="selectButton" CommandName="select"
          Text="Select" />
        <br />
        <br />
    </ItemTemplate>
    ...
</asp:DataList>
```

The code for the SelectedIndexChanged event is added to the code behind the form as follows:

```
protected void DataList1_SelectedIndexChanged(object sender, EventArgs e)
{
    DataList1.DataBind();
}
```

Editing Data

To enable item editing in a GridView, simply add the required column for control editing. The column will display an Edit link for items that aren't in edit mode, and Update and Cancel links for items that are in edit mode. Because of the nature of the GridView control, where each data field is clearly defined in a grid cell, the control can add the required edit controls (such as TextBox controls) for you.

To facilitate this, the Column Editor dialog box that was introduced in the last section enables you to add just such a column, as shown in Figure 5-21.

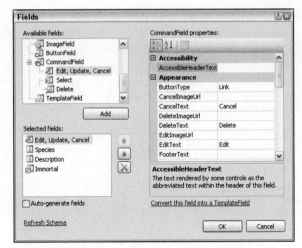

Figure 5-21: Column editor showing edit buttons

When you have added this column, shown as Edit, Update, Cancel in the Available Fields pane, the functionality is in place. You can modify the added controls using the `ButtonType` property for the column, and employ links or buttons with customizable text or images by using other properties of the column. You can also add a column containing a delete command in the same way. The one thing you can't do here is provide functionality to add a new column — to do that you must use some code behind. You'll see all of this in action in an example shortly.

For the `DataList` control you must do a little more work. As well as adding a button, as you saw in the last section for selecting items, you must also provide a template containing bound controls such as text boxes. There are also more event handlers to deal with. Again, you'll see this in the following Try It Out.

One more thing to be aware of — it is only possible to update data through a data source if that data source is configured with the commands required to update data. In the Try It Out that follows, you modify the existing data source accordingly.

Try It Out   Editing List Data

1. Copy the `C:\BegVC#Databases\Chapter05\Ex0502 - List Data` example directory from the previous Try It Out to a new directory, `C:\BegVC#Databases\Chapter05\Ex0503 - Modifying List Data`.

2. Open Visual Web Developer Express.

3. Select File ➪ Open Web Site and open the web site `C:\BegVC#Databases\Chapter05\Ex0503 - Modifying List Data`.

4. In Design view for the `Default.aspx` page, select the `SqlDataSource` control and, in the SqlDataSource Tasks window, click Refresh Schema. Click OK in the first dialog box that appears, and then No in the next two dialog boxes to avoid regenerating the fields and keys for `GridView1` and `DataList1`.

5. In Design view for `Default.aspx`, in the SqlDataSource Tasks window for the `SqlDataSource1` data source, click Configure Data Source and then click Next to open the Configure The Select Statement page of the wizard.

Copying a web site from one location to another can result in the loss of some "hidden" information for the project. The information, which is stored in the solution file used for the project, cannot be copied when a web application is copied. Part of that information is the extended configuration of database queries, and the Configure The Select Statement page of the wizard may have the Specify A Custom SQL Statement Or Stored Procedure option selected and the query may not be visible on the page. If that's the case, you will have to select the Specify Columns From A Table Or View option and then configure the query again. To do so, follow steps 8–12 of the earlier Try it Out, "Data Source Configuration," before continuing with this example.

6. Click Advanced. (You must ensure that Specify Columns From A Table Or View is selected, otherwise the Advanced option will not be available.) Select Generate INSERT, UPDATE, and DELETE statements. Click OK, Next, and Finish to complete the wizard.

7. In the GridView Tasks window for `GridView1`, click Edit Columns.

8. Add Edit, Update, Cancel, and Delete columns to the `GridView` control.

9. In Source view, edit `ItemTemplate` and add an `EditItemTemplate` template to the `DataList` control as follows:

```
<asp:DataList ...>
  <ItemTemplate>
    ...
    <br />
    <asp:LinkButton ID="editButton" runat="server" CommandName="edit"
      Text="Edit" />
    <br />
    <br />
  </ItemTemplate>
  <EditItemTemplate>
    <strong>Species:</strong>
    <asp:TextBox ID="SpeciesBox" runat="server" Text='<%# Bind("Species") %>' />
    <br />
    <strong>Immortal:</strong>
    <asp:CheckBox ID="ImmortalBox" runat="server"
      Checked='<%# Bind("Immortal") %>' />
    <br />
    <strong>Description:</strong>
    <asp:TextBox ID="DescriptionBox" runat="server"
      Text='<%# Bind("Description") %>'
     TextMode="MultiLine" Height="100px" />
    <br />
    <asp:LinkButton ID="updateButton" runat="server" CommandName="update"
      Text="Update" />
    <br />
    <asp:LinkButton ID="cancelButton1" runat="server" CommandName="cancel"
      Text="Cancel" />
    <br />
    <br />
  </EditItemTemplate>
  ...
</asp:DataList>
```

10. Add event handlers for the `EditCommand`, `CancelCommand`, and `UpdateCommand` events of the `DataList` control as follows:

```csharp
protected void DataList1_EditCommand(object source, DataListCommandEventArgs e)
{
    DataList1.EditItemIndex = e.Item.ItemIndex;
    DataList1.DataBind();
}
protected void DataList1_CancelCommand(object source, DataListCommandEventArgs e)
{
    DataList1.EditItemIndex = -1;
    DataList1.DataBind();
}
protected void DataList1_UpdateCommand(object source, DataListCommandEventArgs e)
{
    string speciesId =
     DataList1.DataKeys[e.Item.ItemIndex].ToString();
    string species =
        ((TextBox)e.Item.FindControl("SpeciesBox")).Text;
    string immortal =
        ((CheckBox)e.Item.FindControl("ImmortalBox")).Checked.ToString();
    string description =
        ((TextBox)e.Item.FindControl("DescriptionBox")).Text;

    SqlDataSource1.UpdateParameters["SpeciesId"].DefaultValue
        = speciesId;
    SqlDataSource1.UpdateParameters["Species"].DefaultValue
        = species;
    SqlDataSource1.UpdateParameters["Immortal"].DefaultValue
        = immortal;
    SqlDataSource1.UpdateParameters["Description"].DefaultValue
        = description;

    SqlDataSource1.Update();

    DataList1.EditItemIndex = -1;
    DataList1.DataBind();
}
```

11. Modify the `SpeciesId` update parameter for `SqlDataSource1` in the Source view for `Default.aspx` as follows (remove the `Type` parameter):

```xml
<UpdateParameters>
  <asp:Parameter Name="Species" Type="String" />
  <asp:Parameter Name="Description" Type="String" />
  <asp:Parameter Name="Immortal" Type="Boolean" />
  <asp:Parameter Name="SpeciesId" />
</UpdateParameters>
```

12. Add the following code to the bottom of the page in Source view:

```xml
    </asp:DataList>
    <br />
    <asp:LinkButton ID="addButton" runat="server">Add Species</asp:LinkButton>
  </form>
</body>
</html>
```

13. Add the following event handler for this `LinkButton` by double-clicking the control in Design view:

```
protected void addButton_Click(object sender, EventArgs e)
{
    SqlDataSource1.InsertParameters["SpeciesId"].DefaultValue
        = Guid.NewGuid().ToString();
    SqlDataSource1.InsertParameters["Species"].DefaultValue
        = "New Species";
    SqlDataSource1.InsertParameters["Immortal"].DefaultValue
        = "False";
    SqlDataSource1.InsertParameters["Description"].DefaultValue
        = "";

    SqlDataSource1.Insert();
    DataList1.DataBind();
    GridView1.DataBind();
}
```

14. Modify the `SpeciesId` insert parameter for `SqlDataSource1` in the Source view for `Default.aspx` as follows (remove the `Type` parameter):

```
<InsertParameters>
    <asp:Parameter Name="SpeciesId" />
    <asp:Parameter Name="Species" Type="String" />
    <asp:Parameter Name="Description" Type="String" />
    <asp:Parameter Name="Immortal" Type="Boolean" />
</InsertParameters>
```

15. Run the application and experiment with editing data. The changes you make will be permanent, so be careful; use the Add Species link to add some dummy records to play with if necessary. Figure 5-22 shows edit views for the two list view controls.

16. Quit the application and Visual Web Developer Express.

How It Works

In this example you made four modifications:

- ❑ Configured the data source to allow data modification
- ❑ Made the `GridView` control capable of editing and deleting rows
- ❑ Made the `DataList` control capable of editing items
- ❑ Provided a means to add new items

Let's examine each of these in turn.

First, you modified `SqlDataSource1` using the wizard, and created UPDATE, INSERT, and DELETE statements based on the SELECT statement. In the code behind, this added code for the SQL statements and a whole bunch of parameters to use when modifying data using this control.

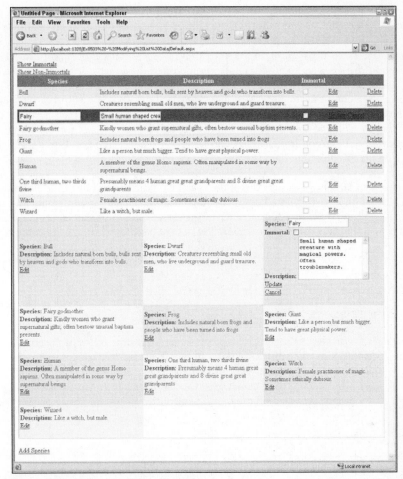

Figure 5-22: List controls in edit mode

It is extremely important to note that at the time of this writing there is a slight problem when using GUID values for column data in combination with SqlDataSource controls. The control incorrectly identifies the column type as object, and in fact doesn't let you specify that the column is a GUID value. You can work around this simply by not specifying a type for the parameter corresponding to the GUID column. That's why, at two points in the example, you removed the Type parameters for the SpeciesId column. This applies only when you have to write update code yourself. The GridView control apparently takes this into account — in any case, it doesn't generate errors and successfully updates data without complaining. Until a fix appears, you must make this change if you want to update data through a SqlDataSource control using custom code, such as that used for the DataList or LinkButton controls in the example.

After you made this change you made the `GridView` control capable of editing and deleting items. That was the work of moments — simply adding the required columns was enough to add the functionality.

Sadly, making the `DataList` control do the same thing was a slightly more complicated affair, and a number of modifications were required. First, you modified the `ItemTemplate` to add a button to enter edit mode, and added an `EditItemTemplate`, which had data-bound controls and two buttons for confirming/discarding changes. The three buttons have specific `CommandName` properties that are required to give rise to the functionality desired. The `DataList` control recognizes the `CommandName` property of any button clicked. Still, the command names are easy to remember: `edit` for a button to put an item into edit mode, `update` to confirm changes, and `cancel` to cancel changes. While it isn't used here, you can also use `delete` to delete an item, and, as you saw earlier in the chapter, `select` to select an item.

Because the `DataList` control is unaware of the specific bindings you have used in your templates and the way in which you have formatted data, you must also write code to implement any such commands. In this case, you wrote code to respond to each of the three commands that can occur. First, the code for the Edit button, in the `DataList1_EditCommand()` event handler method, is as follows:

```
protected void DataList1_EditCommand(object source, DataListCommandEventArgs e)
{
    DataList1.EditItemIndex = e.Item.ItemIndex;
    DataList1.DataBind();
}
```

This sets the `DataList.EditItemIndex` property, which stores the index of the currently edited item. The code uses a value extracted from the event arguments passed to it to find the index of the item in which the user has clicked the Edit button. This value is stored in the `DataListCommandEventArgs.Item.ItemIndex` property. Once this value has been set, the `DataBind()` method must be called on the `DataList` control to update the display in response to this change.

The code for the Cancel button, in `DataList1_CancelCommand()`, reverses the change:

```
protected void DataList1_CancelCommand(object source, DataListCommandEventArgs e)
{
    DataList1.EditItemIndex = -1;
    DataList1.DataBind();
}
```

By setting the `DataList.EditItemIndex` property to –1 you effectively say "no item being edited," so the code clears the edit mode. `DataBind()` is called for the same reason as before.

Finally, you wrote code for updating data in `DataList1_UpdateCommand()`. The code for this event handler starts by obtaining the ID of the current item from the `DataList.DataKeys` collection, using the item index obtained from the `DataListCommandEventArgs.Item.ItemIndex` property:

```
protected void DataList1_UpdateCommand(object source, DataListCommandEventArgs e)
{
    string speciesId =
     DataList1.DataKeys[e.Item.ItemIndex].ToString();
```

Next, new values for the updated column values were obtained from the controls in the `EditItemTemplate`. To do this, individual controls are acquired by calling the `FindControl()` method in the `Item` property of the event arguments. By passing the `ID` value of a control, this method gets it for you, and once you have cast it to the correct type you can access its properties:

```
string species =
    ((TextBox)e.Item.FindControl("SpeciesBox")).Text;
string immortal =
    ((CheckBox)e.Item.FindControl("ImmortalBox")).Checked.ToString();
string description =
    ((TextBox)e.Item.FindControl("DescriptionBox")).Text;
```

To use the `SqlDataSource` control to update a database you must use the `UpdateParameters` collection of the control, which is found in the definition of the control in the ASP.NET code. Once these parameters have values set (which, somewhat strangely, is achieved by setting the `string` value `DefaultValue` for the parameter) you can call the `Update()` method of the control and commit changes:

```
SqlDataSource1.UpdateParameters["SpeciesId"].DefaultValue
    = speciesId;
SqlDataSource1.UpdateParameters["Species"].DefaultValue
    = species;
SqlDataSource1.UpdateParameters["Immortal"].DefaultValue
    = immortal;
SqlDataSource1.UpdateParameters["Description"].DefaultValue
    = description;

SqlDataSource1.Update();
```

Finally, you should clear the edit mode after making changes, which happens in the same way as for the Cancel button:

```
DataList1.EditItemIndex = -1;
DataList1.DataBind();
}
```

With these changes, and the modification to the update parameter type as discussed earlier, the `DataList` control is capable of editing data.

The other change, adding an Add button to add new rows to the `Species` table, used code similar to that used in the Update button event handler. The difference is that hard-coded default values are used rather than bound values (you could, of course, provide a simple form for user-defined values, should you want). Also, the `InsertParameters` parameter collection is used to parameterize the SQL statement used to add the data, and the `Insert()` method is called to make the change.

There are, as you might expect, a lot more things you can achieve with data-bound list controls. However, it's about time you looked at the other type of data-bound controls, those that deal with individual table rows. You'll be seeing data-bound lists again a little later in this chapter when you look at how to construct master/detail views.

Viewing and Editing Data in Detail Views

Many of the techniques used for detail views are similar to those used for list views. Data binding, the use of templates, and styling are achieved in much the same way. In this section, you look at the `FormView` and `DetailsView` controls for viewing, editing, and creating single data table rows.

Configuring a `FormView` or `DetailsView` control is something that, as with list view controls, you can achieve with a mix of automatic configuration from a data source and modifications to the ASP.NET code. When you have added either of these controls to a page, you can configure the control from the data source by selecting the data source from the control's Tasks window. You can then format the display of the controls using the same sort of auto-formatting you saw for list views.

With the `DetailsView` control, rows are added for each data column, and appropriate controls are added for data visualization. As with the `GridView` control, you can modify the types of fields that are added. The `DetailsView` control includes a Field Editor dialog box (similar to the Column Editor dialog box) that you can use to configure columns in a `GridView`. Here you can change field types such as text fields and checkbox fields, and also add command fields for data modification and pagination.

The `FormView` control generates an `ItemTemplate` for you when you bind it to a data source. Unlike the `DataList` control, however, `FormView` (if the data source is configured for data modification) also generates `EditItemTemplate` and `InsertItemTemplate` templates for you. And it adds the commands necessary to use these templates, such that there is little that you need to do to edit data through this control.

In the following Try It Out, you use the same data source as in previous examples to view data in `FormView` and `DetailsView` controls.

Try It Out   **Row Data**

1. Copy the `C:\BegVC#Databases\Chapter05\Ex0503 - Modifying List Data` example directory from the previous Try It Out to a new directory, `C:\BegVC#Databases\Chapter05\Ex0504 - Row Data`.

2. Open Visual Web Developer Express.

3. Select the File ⇨ Open Web Site menu item and open the web site `C:\BegVC#Databases\Chapter05\Ex0504 - Row Data`.

4. Delete the `GridView`, `DataList`, and Add Species button controls from the `Default.aspx` page.

5. Remove all the code behind from `Default.aspx.cs` that you added in the previous Try It Out example.

6. Refresh the schema for the `SqlDataSource` control as in previous examples, and then add a `DetailsView` control to the page.

7. From the DetailsView Tasks window, select the `SqlDataSource1` data source.

8. Click the `SpeciesId` row of the control, and in the DetailsView Tasks window, click Remove Field.

9. In the DetailsView Tasks window, enable Paging, Inserting, Editing, and Deleting.

10. Auto-format the control with the Classic scheme.

11. Add a `FormView` control to the page.

12. From the FormView Tasks window, select the `SqlDataSource1` data source.

13. From the FormView Tasks window, enable Paging.

14. In Source view, in the code for the `FormView` control, remove the label and display for the `SpeciesId` field from each of the three templates.

15. Auto-format the control with the Classic scheme.

16. Add event handlers for the `ItemInserting` event for both the `FormView` and `DetailsView` controls, with code as follows:

```
protected void DetailsView1_ItemInserting(object sender,
    DetailsViewInsertEventArgs e)
{
    e.Values.Add("SpeciesId", Guid.NewGuid());
}
protected void FormView1_ItemInserting(object sender, FormViewInsertEventArgs e)
{
    e.Values.Add("SpeciesId", Guid.NewGuid());
}
```

17. Run the application and experiment with browsing, editing, inserting, and deleting data using both the detail view controls. The display should like similar to Figure 5-23.

18. Quit the application and Visual Web Developer Express.

Figure 5-23: Detail view controls

How It Works

The configuration and formatting of the controls in this example hardly needs much comment — the procedure was nearly identical to that used in list views in the preceding section. It is, however, worth scrutinizing the result in a little more detail.

First, note the field specification for the DetailsView control:

```
<asp:DetailsView ...>
  ...
  <Fields>
    <asp:BoundField DataField="Species" HeaderText="Species"
      SortExpression="Species" />
    <asp:BoundField DataField="Description" HeaderText="Description"
      SortExpression="Description" />
    <asp:CheckBoxField DataField="Immortal" HeaderText="Immortal"
      SortExpression="Immortal" />
    <asp:CommandField ShowDeleteButton="True" ShowEditButton="True"
      ShowInsertButton="True" />
  </Fields>
  ...
</asp:DetailsView>
```

The code used here is similar indeed to the column specification for the GridView control. As with that control, it isn't necessary to specify template details for editing items — the controls required are instead inferred from the controls used in the field specification section. In addition, you can see where the command buttons are specified, in the CommandField control. You can change the text displayed for these commands (or use images instead) by modifying this specification.

Also, examine the code in the templates specified for the FormView control — for example, EditItemTemplate:

```
<EditItemTemplate>
  Species:
  <asp:TextBox ID="SpeciesTextBox" runat="server" Text='<%# Bind("Species") %>'>
  </asp:TextBox><br />
  Description:
  <asp:TextBox ID="DescriptionTextBox" runat="server"
    Text='<%# Bind("Description") %>'>
  </asp:TextBox><br />
  Immortal:
  <asp:CheckBox ID="ImmortalCheckBox" runat="server"
    Checked='<%# Bind("Immortal") %>' /><br />
  <asp:LinkButton ID="UpdateButton" runat="server" CausesValidation="True"
    CommandName="Update" Text="Update">
  </asp:LinkButton>
  <asp:LinkButton ID="UpdateCancelButton" runat="server" CausesValidation="False"
    CommandName="Cancel" Text="Cancel">
  </asp:LinkButton>
</EditItemTemplate>
```

This also looks familiar — the code is almost identical to that used in the analogous DataList control template used in the previous Try It Out — apart from a few minor cosmetic differences.

The other thing you did in this example was handle the `ItemInserting` event for both detail view controls. This provides for the GUID primary key field in the `Species` table, which must be generated from code — as you saw in the chapters on Windows data binding. The `ItemInserting` event fires when the user clicks the Update button but before data is added to the database. In both cases, simple code was used to generate a primary key GUID value:

```
e.Values.Add("SpeciesId", Guid.NewGuid());
```

Both the `DetailsViewInsertEventArgs` and `FormViewInsertEventArgs` argument types allow you to do this by exposing the about-to-be-added item though a `Values` property that is a dictionary collection of name/value pairs.

Master/Detail Views

The last topic to cover in this chapter is how to deal with master/detail views — an extremely common scenario that uses a list view and a detail view in combination. Selecting an item in the list view causes it to be displayed in the detail view, where it can be edited. In this situation, you don't need pagination functionality in the detail view because the list view fulfils that purpose.

The data-binding framework in ASP.NET has been designed with this situation in mind and makes it surprisingly easy to implement. In fact, you've seen pretty much everything that you need to do to implement this. However, in the Try It Out that follows, a few tips and tricks are introduced to streamline matters.

Try It Out   Master/Detail Views

1. Copy the `C:\BegVC#Databases\Chapter05\Ex0503 - Modifying List Data` example directory from the earlier Try It Out to a new directory, `C:\BegVC#Databases\Chapter05\Ex0505 - Master-Detail View`.

2. Open Visual Web Developer Express.

3. Select the File ⇨ Open Web Site menu item and open the web site `C:\BegVC#Databases\Chapter05\Ex0505 - Master-Detail View`.

4. Remove the `DataList` control from `Default.aspx`.

5. Remove all the code behind from `Default.aspx.cs` that you added in the earlier Try It Out example except the code for `addButton_Click`. In this event handler, remove the following line of code:

   ```
   DataList1.DataBind();
   ```

6. In the Source view for `Default.aspx`, modify the column specification for the `GridView` control as follows:

   ```
   <Columns>
       <asp:TemplateField HeaderText="Species" SortExpression="Species">
       <ItemTemplate>
   ```

```
        <asp:LinkButton ID="speciesLabel" runat="server"
          Text='<%# Bind("Species") %>' CommandName="Select" />
      </ItemTemplate>
    </asp:TemplateField>
  </Columns>
```

7. Refresh the schema for `SqlDataSource1` as in earlier examples, and then add a new `SqlDataSource` control to the page after the existing `SqlDataSource1` control.

8. For the new data source, use the existing `FolktaleDBConnectionString`, and configure the select command to obtain all columns from the `Species` table.

9. Add the following `where` clause specification:

Column	SpeciesId
Operator	=
Source	Control
Control ID	GridView1

10. Choose to generate data modification SQL statements for the data source.

11. Complete the Data Source Configuration Wizard.

12. Add a `DetailsView` control to the page and select the `SqlDataSource2` data source.

13. Remove the `SpeciesId` field from the `DetailsView` control.

14. Auto-format the control using Classic scheme, and enable editing and deleting.

15. Add event handlers for the `ItemDeleted` and `ItemUpdated` events for the `DetailsView` control with code as follows:

```
protected void DetailsView1_ItemDeleted(object sender,
    DetailsViewDeletedEventArgs e)
{
    GridView1.DataBind();
}
protected void DetailsView1_ItemUpdated(object sender,
    DetailsViewUpdatedEventArgs e)
{
    GridView1.DataBind();
}
```

16. In the Source view for `Default.aspx`, wrap the controls in the following HTML:

```
    ...
    </asp:SqlDataSource>
    <hr />
    <div style="float: left;">
      <asp:GridView ...>
        ...
      </asp:GridView>
    </div>
    <div>
```

```
      <asp:DetailsView ...>
         ...
      </asp:DetailsView>
   </div>
   <br style="clear: left;"/>
   <hr />
   <asp:LinkButton ID="addButton" runat="server"
     OnClick="addButton_Click">Add Species</asp:LinkButton>
   <br />
   </div>
 </form>
</body>
</html>
```

17. Execute the application, and note that items selected in the master control are displayed in the detail view and can be modified there. Figure 5-24 shows the application in action.

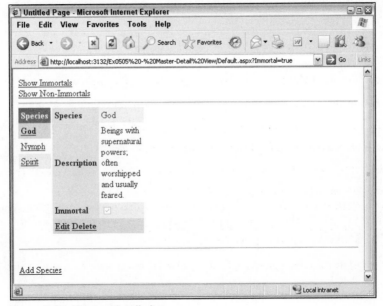

Figure 5-24: Master/detail view

How It Works

In this example you have used the data source from earlier in the chapter along with a second, filtered data source to create a master/detail view. You started by clearing out an old control and its associated code behind, including a reference to the control in the code for the Add Species button. Next you reformatted the `GridView` control to show a single row from the `Species` table — the title field also called `Species`. In doing so you used a new type of bound column specification: `TemplateField`.

The `TemplateField` column specification allows you to override the default layout of columns in a `GridView` control and provide the HTML to use for a column using familiar templates. You can use `ItemTemplate`, `EditItemTemplate`, and `InsertItemTemplate` templates in this control, as well as

HeaderTemplate and FooterTemplate, if desired. You use this control in this example to remove the necessity of having a second column whose only function is to supply a link button to select items. Instead, the Species field is rendered as the text of a link button and allows the user to select items by clicking their title:

```
<asp:TemplateField HeaderText="Species" SortExpression="Species">
  <ItemTemplate>
    <asp:LinkButton ID="speciesLabel" runat="server"
      Text='<%# Bind("Species") %>' CommandName="Select" />
  </ItemTemplate>
</asp:TemplateField>
```

Next, you added a second SqlDataSource control. It uses an advanced filter mechanism, as described earlier in the chapter, to choose items according to the selected item in another control — namely, the ListView control. ASP.NET makes this easy — you simply specify the ID of the control to use for filtering and the field to filter by, and it connects everything up without your having to worry about it any further. The new data source control returns only a single result, filtered according to the SpeciesId field.

> This could be extended to filter-related data. A table using SpeciesId as a foreign key, such as Character, could be filtered using the same master selection control. This would result in a filtered set of results, which might number more that one, which you could then page through and navigate using techniques already encountered in this chapter.

One further modification was necessary (apart from the cosmetic changes) — the ItemDeleted and ItemUpdated events for the DetailsView control were handled. That's necessary because changing the underlying data will cause the master list view to go out of date unless you manually refresh it by calling its DataBind() method:

```
GridView1.DataBind();
```

With this in place, the master/detail view is complete — with a minimum of effort, and just a few tweaks required to get everything working properly. In general, remember the following when creating master/detail views:

❑ Use two data sources, where one is filtered by the master view.

❑ The detail view may not appear if no data is available after filtering, so controls making up this control may not always be visible, which can affect layout and functionality.

❑ When data changes are made, both data sources need refreshing.

Summary

In this chapter, you extended your knowledge of data-binding techniques to cover web applications. You saw how things differ from Windows applications, but also how many of the techniques used are similar or analogous to those required to implement data binding in Windows applications.

You were introduced to all of the controls in ASP.NET that are responsible for data binding — both those that work as data sources and those that display data — and saw how they interrelate. You also put theory into practice and saw these controls in action, and you learned a few helpful tips and tricks along the way.

Specifically, you learned:

❑ How web and Windows applications differ. You saw that there are many similarities, especially when dealing with data access, but also some major differences. For example, Windows applications are typically used by only one person at a time, while web applications may have to deal with thousands of simultaneous users.

❑ How to configure SQL Server 2005 Express for remote connections by enabling the named pipes protocol (and/or the TCP/IP protocol).

❑ How to configure connections in web applications — including remote connections.

❑ How the `SqlDataSource` control is used for data access, and how to configure it to connect to your data.

❑ How to sort, filter, and update data using a `SqlDataSource`. You saw how parameters can be used by `SqlDataSource` controls and how these parameters can be obtained from a number of sources. You can, for example, use `querystring` parameters from URLs, values stored in session state, and so on.

❑ What the data-bound controls in ASP.NET are and key features about them.

❑ How to use the data-bound controls to display list and detail data. You saw how the `GridView` and `DataList` controls can be configured to display data exposed by a `SqlDataSource` control, and you customized the display by changing the columns shown and the schemes used for HTML rendering.

❑ How to get around an ASP.NET problem that makes dealing with GUID data more difficult than it need be, noting how the parameters used by data source controls fail to recognize the GUID data type, and instead use `object`. By removing this type specification, you avoid data update errors.

❑ How to edit data in list and detail views by using the other templates that are included in the data-bound controls.

❑ How to visualize and edit data in master/detail relationships. You used a combination of a `GridView` and a `DetailsView` control to implement this scheme, and saw why it is necessary to use a second, filtered data source for the detail view.

The next chapter delves deeper into the realm of ADO.NET and you learn to perform data access programmatically.

Exercises

1. Which of the following are valid reasons to use remote database connections in ASP.NET rather than local database files?

    a. Security

    b. Convenience

    c. Performance

  d. Data caching

  e. Flexibility

  f. Functionality

2. How would you configure a data source filter to remember filter settings for a user between sessions?

3. Which of the following data-bound controls are available in ASP.NET?

  a. Repeater

  b. DataGrid

  c. DataView

  d. DataList

  e. ItemView

  f. FormView

  g. DetailsForm

4. Copy the project `C:\BegVC#Databases\Chapter05\Ex0505 - Master-Detail View` to a new project, `C:\BegVC#Databases\Chapter05\Q0504 - List Filtering`. Modify this project by replacing the `DetailsView` control with a `DataList` control that displays entries from the `Character` table filtered by the existing `GridView` control. Display data in a three-column horizontal table layout and use the Classic auto-format scheme. None of the GUID data in the `Character` table should be displayed. The width of each item should be 200 pixels. Figure 5-25 shows the expected result.

Figure 5-25: Exercise 4 goal

Accessing Databases Programmatically

As you have seen throughout this book, ADO.NET is the technology used to access databases. Until now, however, you've almost exclusively used declarative data-binding techniques to access data — using controls and wizards to do a lot of the hard work for you rather than coding database access by hand.

However, data binding often doesn't give you quite the degree of control that you need in your applications, or might not do things as efficiently as you like. Also, data binding is geared toward applications with a visual interface, which doesn't include many application types, such as Windows services. Or you might want to provide a completely custom-built user interface that doesn't use the data-bound controls you've encountered in this book.

In any of these circumstances you can use the ADO.NET classes independently of other database access techniques. From your code you can make connections, execute SQL statements, manage database objects, and manipulate data — all without any data binding whatsoever. The downside is that you have to remember to do everything properly, without missing important steps, and often without the help of wizards. The upside is that you obtain an almost limitless flexibility to make your applications work exactly the way you want them to, without having to deal with some of the quirks of data-bound controls.

In this chapter you look at how you can achieve this flexibility. You learn to:

❑ Configure and use ADO.NET database connections

❑ Execute commands through a database connection

❑ Read data with data readers

❑ Use data adapters to exchange data with a database

❑ Use `DataSet` and `DataTable` objects

For the most part, in this chapter you experiment with code in console applications. The techniques you learn will apply equally to web and Windows applications, but by using console applications there's less extraneous code, so the database access code is clearer. The ADO.NET classes that enable you to access databases, as well as the relationships between these classes, were introduced in Chapter 2. In this chapter, you formalize that information and learn to manipulate these classes in your C# code.

Database Connections

The first step in accessing databases programmatically is to configure a connection object. Then you can execute commands against it, obtain data readers, exchange data with a data set using data adapters, and otherwise manipulate database data.

As you have seen in previous chapters, the ADO.NET class used to connect to databases is SqlConnection. In this section you learn to create, configure, and use instances of this class, and explore connection pooling in the .NET Framework.

Creating Connections

SqlConnection objects are simple to use, and can be instantiated in the usual way:

```
SqlConnection conn = new SqlConnection();
```

Once instantiated, you can configure the connection with a connection string using the SqlConnection.ConnectionString property:

```
conn.ConnectionString = "<connection string>";
```

Alternatively, you can combine these steps into one by using a constructor:

```
SqlConnection conn = new SqlConnection("<connection string>");
```

In both these code fragments, "<connection string>" is the connection string used to connect to the database. As you saw in Chapter 3, connection strings consist of properties in the form of name/value combinations that define the connection. Those properties include the DBMS to connect to, the name of the database (or database file location), and security information.

Rather than writing connection strings manually, you can use the Database Connection window that you've seen in previous chapters, which means that you can use the connection configuration wizard. Once you have done so, you can see the connection string in the properties for the connection, as shown in Figure 6-1.

Figure 6-1: Obtaining connection strings from database connections

You cannot edit the connection string via the Properties window, but you can select the text displayed and copy it to your application. You can modify the connection string manually or by using the Modify Connection command to reconfigure the connection using the standard wizard. You can access this command by right-clicking on the connection in the Database Explorer.

This technique has another advantage — it means that you can edit the database through the Database Explorer window, making use of standard visual techniques to do so, without having to rely on code.

Once you have a connection string, either created by hand or using the Database Connection window, you have to decide where to store it. There is nothing to stop you from hard-coding the string in your application wherever it is required by your code, but that isn't an ideal solution — the string may be used multiple times, so changing it would mean changing it wherever it appears. Alternatively, you can use a variable or constant to define the connection string, centralizing it. That's an improvement, but still requires a recompile to change the connection string if it needs changing. You can also use external storage, such as registry settings or a data file. One frequently used way, which you examine in more detail in a moment, is to use an application configuration file (`app.config` in Windows/console applications or `web.config` for web applications).

Using a configuration file means that no recompiling is necessary to change the string, and you can change it either in a text editor or programmatically without much effort. However, it does mean that you are exposing the connection string in plain text format, which may be an issue in some security-critical uses (especially if username and password information is stored in the connection string). Typically, configuration files are the best option. The final choice of which method to use, however, is up to you.

In a configuration file, connection strings can be stored wherever you like, but there is a location that's already configured for this purpose — the `<connectionStrings>` element. It is a child element of the root `<configuration>` element, and contains a number of `<add>` elements defining connection strings. The following code is an example of a configuration file for a Windows or console application with a connection string in place:

```xml
<?xml version="1.0" encoding="utf-8" ?>
<configuration>
  <connectionStrings>
    <add name="MyConnectionString" connectionString="
      Data Source=.\SQLEXPRESS;
      AttachDbFilename=C:\BegVC#Databases\FolktaleDB.mdf;
      Integrated Security=True;
      Connect Timeout=30;
      User Instance=True"/>
  </connectionStrings>
</configuration>
```

To access this information from your code, use the `System.Configuration.ConfigurationManager` class, which is included in the `System.Configuration.dll` library (not included by default to console applications). The preceding connection string could be accessed as follows:

```csharp
SqlConnection conn = new SqlConnection(
    ConfigurationManager.ConnectionStrings["MyConnectionString"].ConnectionString);
```

With this code in place, changes to connection strings stored in the application configuration file will automatically be utilized in your code.

Once a connection is configured with a connection string, some connection string properties become accessible through properties on the `SqlConnection` object. For example, you can obtain the name of the database through the `SqlConnection.Database` property, or the name of the SQL Server instance in use through the `SqlConnection.DataSource` property. Properties such as these aren't used frequently, but can be used for example to display connection information in a Windows application.

Connection State

At any one time, a connection can be said to be open or closed. Databases are only accessible through connections when they are open. However, database connections consume resources, and so they should be open for only as long as the database is being used by your code. They should be closed the rest of the time, or you may introduce a memory leak in your application as well as potentially blocking other applications from accessing the database. The state of a connection can be determined by using the `SqlConnection.State` property, which contains a value from the `ConnectionState` enumeration. The enumeration includes the values `ConnectionState.Open` and `ConnectionState.Closed`, as well as some other values that are not currently used in the SQL Server provider implementation.

You open a connection with the `SqlConnection.Open()` method. When you are finished with it, you can close it using the `SqlConnection.Close()` method. It is extremely important to remember that connections are *not* closed automatically when they go out of scope — you must perform this operation manually.

It's also possible to close connections through data reader objects, as you will see shortly, or to use a `using` block to close the connection automatically:

```
using (SqlConnection conn = new SqlConnection(
    ConfigurationManager.ConnectionStrings["MyConnectionString"].ConnectionString))
{
    conn.Open();
    ...
}
```

Once the last line of code in the `using` block completes, the connection closes. That's because the `using` block causes the `Dispose()` method of the `SqlConnection` object to be called, which closes the connection.

Another common way to close connections is to use a `try...catch...finally` structure:

```
SqlConnection conn = new SqlConnection(
    ConfigurationManager.ConnectionStrings["MyConnectionString"].ConnectionString);
try
{
    conn.Open();
    ...
}
catch (Exception ex)
{
    // Handle exception.
}
finally
{
    conn.Close();
}
```

There is no need to test the `SqlConnection.State` property in the `finally` block because attempting to close a connection that is already closed does not generate an exception (although there may be a tiny processing overhead in closing a connection more than once).

Connection Pooling

Making a connection to a database takes time and processor cycles. Under the hood, the provider must open channels, allocate resources, and authenticate to the database. If the process is repeated each and every time you want to manipulate a database, noticeable delays can occur in your applications. For that reason, the .NET Framework uses *connection pooling* to make things work more efficiently. That means the provider maintains a number of connections to your database, which are available to your code when requested. When you close a connection in your code, the underlying connection in the connection pool does not close — instead, it is released and remains open and ready for subsequent code to use. When you open a new connection, the framework first looks in the pool to see if there are any open connections that aren't currently in use. If there is one, you are passed a reference to the pooled connection, and the process of physically opening a new connection is not necessary. If no pooled connection is available, a new connection is created and opened, and added to the pool for future recycling. Pools have a maximum number of connections, and if that number is exceeded, either a new pool is created, or application execution pauses until a connection becomes available.

Connection pooling makes for a highly optimized, extremely scalable system. The exact mechanism differs according to the provider in use, and often you don't have to do anything to enable it. For the SQL Server provider, connection pooling is enabled by default, with a maximum of 100 concurrent connections supported in the pool.

Connection pooling can be controlled by modifying the connection string or programmatically manipulating the provider. Both of these are advanced topics and won't be covered in this book. However, it is well worth knowing what connection pooling is, and how it optimizes your applications, which is why it's mentioned here. It also explains why, when you first run an application, there is a slight delay before a connection is opened, while subsequent data access is much faster — because the connection used to access the database is created and opened on first use, and then recycled for later use.

Database Commands

`SqlCommand` objects are used to execute commands against a database through `SqlConnection` objects. There are a number of ways that the `SqlCommand` class can be used, and a number of different possible return values. In this section you examine the various usages of this class, as well as how to use parameters and what SQL injection attacks are and how to protect against them.

Creating Commands

The `SqlCommand` object has four constructors that allow varying degrees of control over the properties of the instantiated command object. The simplest of these is the default constructor:

```
SqlCommand cmd = new SqlCommand();
```

The most complicated constructor takes three parameters as follows:

```
SqlCommand cmd = new SqlCommand("<command string>", <connection>, <transaction>);
```

Here `<command string>` is a string that defines the command, such as a SQL statement. The form of the string depends on the command type, as detailed in the next section. If this is not set in the constructor, you can set it later using the `SqlCommand.CommandText` property. `<connection>` is a reference to the `SqlConnection` object that will be used to transmit the command to the database. You have to supply one of these or you can't execute the command (and, of course, the connection must be open before the command can execute). Again, you can either set this in the constructor, or you can set it later using the `SqlCommand.Connection` property. Finally, `<transaction>` is used to enlist the command in a transaction, a subject that is covered in Chapter 9.

The other two constructors for `SqlCommand` take as their parameters either a single string for the command text, or the command text string and a connection object respectively:

```
SqlCommand cmd = new SqlCommand("<command string>");
SqlCommand cmd = new SqlCommand("<command string>", <connection>);
```

Command Types

Three types of commands are supported by the SQL Server client, and the type of command represented by a `SqlCommand` instance is determined by its `SqlCommand.CommandType` property. The type of the command influences how the test in the `CommandText` property is interpreted. The `CommandType` property takes a value from the `CommandType` enumeration, which has three values as follows:

❑ `CommandType.Text`: The default value for the `CommandType` property, specifying that the `CommandText` property is a SQL command. This command may be parameterized, as discussed later in this section.

❑ `CommandType.TableDirect`: With this value, `CommandText` should be the name of a table or view. When the command is executed, all rows and all columns are returned from the specified table.

❑ `CommandType.StoredProcedure`: This value means that `CommandText` contains the name of a stored procedure. If the specified stored procedure requires parameters, they must be specified in the manner described later in this section.

For example, you might create a table direct command as follows:

```
SqlCommand cmd = new SqlCommand("MyTable", conn);
cmd.CommandType = CommandType.TableDirect;
```

Command Execution Methods

Depending on the type and text of the command, different results are to be expected. Many commands will return rows from a table, but there are also commands that don't return any result, or a different type of result. Rather than having a single `Execute()` method, `SqlCommand` objects have several methods for executing a command, and you must choose the one that will provide the result you want.

The available methods for executing commands are as follows:

❏ ExecuteNonQuery(): Use this when no result is expected from the command. This applies to insert, update, and delete commands. In actual fact, this method does have a return value, of type int, which informs you of the number of rows that have been affected by the command. You don't have to use this return value, but it can be helpful — after a delete command to verify that a row was actually been deleted, for example. The name of this method is a little misleading because all types of SQL commands can be termed queries; it stems from the fact that an alternative use of the word "query" refers only to SQL commands that return data.

❏ ExecuteReader(): Use this when the command is expected to return row data. This includes most select commands as well as table direct commands and many stored procedures, and is probably the most frequently used command execution method. It is overloaded, and includes an optional parameter that you can use to set the command behavior. (Command behavior is discussed in a moment.) The return value of this method is a SqlDataReader object.

❏ ExecuteScalar(): Use when you are expecting a single result of whatever type. This applies when, for example, you are obtaining an aggregate function result such as the sum of values in a single column, or a count of rows matching certain criteria. It isn't appropriate for select commands that return single rows of data — in such circumstances you should use ExecuteReader(). If the query in fact returns row data, the first column of the first row obtained will be returned by this method. The return value of this method is of type object.

❏ ExecuteXmlReader(): If the command you are executing returns XML data (for example, a SQL query using the FOR XML clause), you can use this method to obtain an XmlReader object that you can use to access the data. It works only for single rows of data — if the command returns more than one row, any rows after the first are not accessible though the XmlReader.

There are also asynchronous versions of ExecuteNonQuery(), ExecuteReader(), and ExecuteXmlReader() that you can use where appropriate. For example, to obtain a data reader object using asynchronous methods, you would call BeginExecuteReader() and then either poll the IAsynchResult interface returned for the result or wait for a callback function to be called and obtain the result using EndExecuteReader(). This model follows the standard pattern for calling methods asynchronously in the .NET Framework — a subject that is beyond the scope of this book. There are, however, plenty of good references around, both in books and on the Internet, should you require this behavior.

As noted, for ExecuteReader() you can specify a command behavior to be used by the command object. To do this, specify one or more values from the CommandBehavior enumeration (you can combine values using bitwise logic — that is, by using the | operator). The enumeration has the following values:

❏ CommandBehavior.Default: No affect; this results in the default behavior.

❏ CommandBehavior.CloseConnection: When you use this behavior the connection will be closed when you close the data reader. This can be a useful way to ensure that connections are closed when, for example, you call a method that performs data access and returns a data reader object. In this situation you might not have access to the underlying connection, which may have gone out of scope. However, you can rest assured that the connection will be closed when you close the data reader that you have obtained.

❑ CommandBehavior.KeyInfo: This option means that additional information, including information regarding the primary key of the table, is obtained as part of the query. If you intend to use the result of the command to examine the schema of the table, use this option. There are some (advanced) considerations to take into account when using it because of the SQL statement that is generated (see MSDN documentation for details), although they won't affect you in most situations.

❑ CommandBehavior.SchemaOnly: With this option only schema information is returned, not actual data. This option is often used in combination with CommandBehavior.KeyInfo to obtain full schema information.

❑ CommandBehavior.SequentialAccess: Ensures that data is only readable in a sequential fashion, meaning that you must read column data in the order in which it is returned. Once a column is read through a SqlDataReader that uses this option, you cannot read it again, nor can you read columns that precede it in result order. With this option enabled, it is possible to read large binary data fields using GetChars() and GetBytes() methods.

❑ CommandBehavior.SingleResult: Notifies the SQL provider that only a single result should be returned by the command, enabling optimization to take place. When a single result is to be returned, however, it makes more sense to use the ExecuteScalar() method, making this option somewhat redundant in most situations.

❑ CommandBehavior.SingleRow: Notifies the SQL provider that only a single row will be returned by the command. Again, this enables additional optimization to take place. Having said that, the implementation of this option is optional by providers, and it is unclear whether the SQL Server provider performs any such optimization.

Parameterized Commands

When you execute SQL statements, there is nothing to stop you from including all of the information in the statement in the CommandText property of the command. However, it can often be useful to parameterize some parts of the SQL statement. That both aids in protecting against SQL injection attacks (see the next section for details), and enables you to reuse commands. In addition, this technique is necessary for stored procedures that use parameters because these parameters cannot be included in the command text if you use the CommandType.StoredProcedure command type.

To use parameters in SQL statements, you provide placeholders (variable names) in the command text. The placeholders take the form of a variable name preceded by an @ character. For example:

```
SELECT * FROM MyTable WHERE MyId = @MyId
```

Here, @MyId represents a parameter.

Similarly, the definition of a stored procedure that uses parameters includes one or more parameters using the same syntax. The main difference with stored procedures is that parameters may be in or out parameters, in much the same way that you can exchange data with methods by passing parameters using the ref or out keywords.

To use parameterized commands, either queries or stored procedures, you must add corresponding parameters to the SqlCommand.Parameters collection, which is an instance of the SqlParametersCollection class and contains SqlParameter objects. Add parameters by using the `SqlParametersCollection.Add()` method, either by passing a pre-configured parameter or (more normally) by specifying the properties of the parameter to add. You can either specify simply the name of the parameter to add; the name and data type of the parameter; the name, data type, and column length of the parameter; or the name, data type, column length, and source column of the parameter. The last of these, which includes a source column name, enables the value of the parameter to be obtained from existing data, and is not commonly used. In all cases where a data type is specified, a value from the `SqlDbType` enumeration is used. It generally isn't necessary to specify the column length for a parameter.

Once a parameter is configured, you can set its value using the `SqlParameter.Value` property. Because the `SqlParametersCollection.Add()` method returns a reference to the added parameter, it is common practice to set the value of a parameter in the same line of code — despite the fact that this leads to slightly odd-looking syntax, as this example shows:

```
SqlCommand cmd = new SqlCommand("SELECT * FROM MyTable WHERE MyId = @MyId", conn);
cmd.Parameters.Add("@MyId", SqlDbType.UniqueIdentifier).Value = MyGuidVar;
...
```

When you use this technique, parameters are added as an input parameter. Should you want to use an output (or bidirectional) parameter, you can instantiate the parameter independently, like this:

```
SqlParameter myParam = new SqlParameter("@MyOutputParam", SqlDbType.Int);
myParam.Direction = ParameterDirection.Output;
...
```

The default direction is `ParameterDirection.Input`, and you can also use `ParameterDirection` `.InputOutput` for bidirectional values and `ParameterDirection.ReturnValue` if the parameter is the return value of, for example, a stored procedure.

Protecting Against SQL Injection

When executing SQL statements that are in part configured by users, you have to beware of SQL injection attacks (sometimes referred to as SQL insertion attacks). For example, let's say that you assemble a SQL statement using user input where the user enters a value for a string valued `ItemName` field of a record, that is:

```
SELECT * FROM MyTable WHERE ItemName = '<user input>'
```

In code this might be assembled using the following:

```
Console.WriteLine("Enter Id:");
string userInput = Console.ReadLine();
string query = "SELECT * FROM MyTable WHERE MyTableId = '" + userInput + "'";
...
```

At first glance there doesn't seem to be anything wrong with this. However, malicious users might enter something like this:

```
Take this!';DELETE FROM MyTable;--
```

making the combined SQL statement(s):

```
SELECT * FROM MyTable WHERE ItemName = 'Take this!';DELETE FROM MyTable;--'
```

This is actually three SQL commands. The first is a select statement, the second is a dangerous delete statement, and the third is a comment. If you were to execute this command you'd be in for a nasty surprise — the data in `MyTable` would be deleted.

Obviously that isn't a good thing, and you should take steps to prevent it. You can validate user input, perhaps replacing `'` characters with `''` as follows:

```
userInput = userInput.Replace("'", "''");
```

This is a useful first line of defense, and also prevents more minor problems, say, when the string in the parameter includes an apostrophe. You can also ensure that the account used to access your database doesn't have permission to perform such a destructive SQL query by configuring your database accordingly.

A better way to deal with this, however, is to use parameterized queries to assemble SQL statements. Parameters are automatically escaped in that way, and are also validated in other ways to ensure that this type of attack is impossible.

While this protection is extremely easy to implement, it's surprising how many people forget to do it — and risk losing an awful lot of data to this sort of attack. Some people have estimated that up to 50 percent of large-scale e-commerce web sites — and up to 75 percent of smaller sites — may be vulnerable to SQL injection attacks.

In the following Try It Out, you configure a connection and execute a command through it.

Try It Out   Executing Commands

1. Open Visual C# Express and create a new Console application called `Ex0601 - Executing Commands`. Save the project in the `C:\BegVC#Databases\Chapter06` directory, with the Create Directory For Solution option unchecked.

2. Add the `FolktaleDB.mdf` database file to the project by selecting Project ➪ Add Existing Item. If the Datasource Configuration Wizard appears, click Cancel.

3. Add an application configuration file to the project selecting Project ➪ Add New Item. Use the default filename `App.config`.

4. Obtain the connection string to the database using the Database Explorer window (which should automatically have added a connection to the database you added), and use it to add a connection string to the `App.config` file called `FolktaleDBConnectionString`, as follows:

```xml
<?xml version="1.0" encoding="utf-8" ?>
<configuration>
  <connectionStrings>
    <add name="FolktaleDBConnectionString"
      connectionString="Data Source=.\SQLEXPRESS;
      AttachDbFilename=
        C:\BegVC#Databases\Chapter06\Ex0601 - Executing Commands\FolktaleDB.mdf;
      Integrated Security=True;
```

```
                User Instance=True"/>
        </connectionStrings>
    </configuration>
```

5. Add a project reference to `System.Configuration` by selecting Project ⇨ Add Reference.

6. In `Program.cs`, add using statements at the top of the file as follows:

```
using System.Data;
using System.Data.SqlClient;
using System.Configuration;
```

7. Add the following code in `Program.cs`:

```
static void Main(string[] args)
{
    // Configure connection.
    SqlConnection conn = new SqlConnection(ConfigurationManager
        .ConnectionStrings["FolktaleDBConnectionString"].ConnectionString);

    // Get user input table name.
    Console.WriteLine("Enter table to count records for:");
    string tableName = Console.ReadLine();
    if (tableName.IndexOf(';') != -1)
    {
        Console.WriteLine("SQL injection attack detected. Press ENTER to close.");
        Console.ReadLine();
        return;
    }
    tableName = tableName.Replace("'", "''");

    // Create command.
    string query = "SELECT COUNT(*) FROM " + tableName;
    SqlCommand cmd = new SqlCommand(query, conn);
    int rowCount = -1;

    // try...catch...finally for command execution.
    try
    {
        // Open connection.
        conn.Open();

        // Execute command.
        rowCount = (int)cmd.ExecuteScalar();
    }
    catch (Exception ex)
    {
        // Process exception.
        Console.WriteLine(ex.Message);
    }
    finally
    {
        // Close connection.
        conn.Close();
    }
```

```
                    // Output result.
                    Console.WriteLine("There are {0} rows in table [{1}].", rowCount, tableName);

                    // Close application.
                    Console.WriteLine("Press ENTER to close.");
                    Console.ReadLine();
              }
```

8. Execute the application and type the name of a table in the FolktaleDB database (for example `Character`). The result is shown in Figure 6-2.

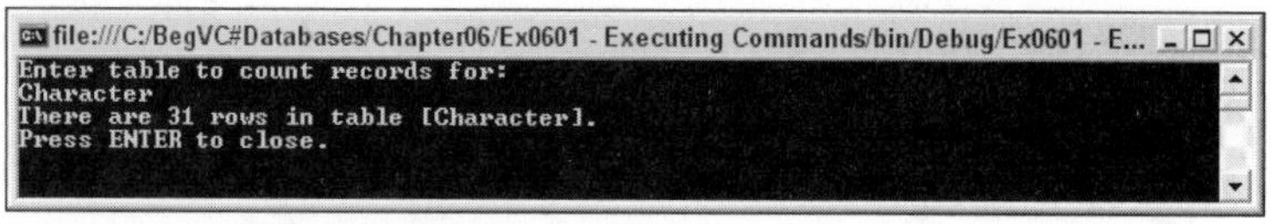

Figure 6-2: Obtaining a table row count

9. Execute the application again and try a SQL injection attack with the string `Character;` `DELETE FROM Story;`. The result is shown in Figure 6-3.

Figure 6-3: Stopping a SQL injection attack

10. Close the application and Visual C# Express.

How It Works

In this example you made a connection to the `FolktaleDB` database (with a connection string stored in an application configuration file) and executed a command against it. The command is a simple one that uses the aggregate `COUNT()` function to count the rows in a database table, where that table is specified by the user. For example:

```
SELECT COUNT(*) FROM Character
```

The table name entered by the user first passes through a basic SQL injection attack protection routine — the code searches for the semicolon character used to separate commands. You could be a lot more advanced here, perhaps checking the entries against a list of table names, or even (and this is the preferable way of doing things) making the user choose from a list of tables rather than using free text entry. This way there is no possibility of SQL injection because none of the SQL statements used come directly from user input.

Once a valid table name is entered (or at least one that doesn't appear to be a SQL injection attack), the application assembles a SQL statement, executes it, and displays the result. Because the result is a single value, the `SqlCommand.ExecuteScalar()` method is used, and the result is cast to an `int` value.

The database access code uses exception handling as discussed earlier in the chapter. If something goes wrong, the exception message is simply output to the user, although you could easily replace that code with something more advanced.

Data Reader Objects

The `SqlDataReader` class is used to read data obtained by executing a command. As you saw in Chapter 2, it provides a forward-only cursor on data, where after reading data from a row, you can move on to the next row, but not back to rows that have already been read. In most cases, however, you can read columns in any order — unless the command used to generate the reader specifies sequential access as described in the previous section.

The `SqlDataReader` class provides an extremely fast, optimized way to read data from a database. In this section you learn how to use it and what it is capable of.

Creating Data Reader Objects

`SqlDataReader` objects can be obtained only by executing commands using the `SqlCommand.ExecuteReader()` method. There is, therefore, no public constructor for creating instances of the `SqlDataReader` class.

Creating a data reader consists of the following tasks:

1. Configure a connection.
2. Configure a command that obtains row data.
3. Execute the command using the `ExecuteReader()` method.

Typically, you keep the connection open for the minimum amount of time, which means opening the connection just before Step 3, and closing it once you have finished using the data reader. If the command uses `CommandBehavior.CloseConnection`, you can close the connection at the same time you close the data reader.

You can see this in action with an extension of the earlier code for opening a connection:

```
SqlConnection conn = new SqlConnection(
    ConfigurationManager.ConnectionStrings["MyConnectionString"].ConnectionString);
try
{
    SqlCommand cmd = new SqlCommand("SELECT * FROM MyTable", conn);
    conn.Open();
    SqlDataReader reader = cmd.ExecuteReader();
    ...
}
catch (Exception ex)
{
```

```
        // Handle exception.
    }
    finally
    {
        conn.Close();
    }
```

Reading Data

Once you've got a `SqlDataReader` instance, the next thing to do is to read data with it. You will want to do one or more of the following:

❑ Read schema data.

❑ Read row data.

❑ Read other properties of the data reader, such as whether any rows are contained in it, and if so how many.

When you have finished reading data through a data reader, close it using the `SqlDataReader.Close()` method to avoid memory leaks.

Schema Data

You can obtain schema information for the data contained in a `SqlDataReader` object in two ways: one column at a time (ignoring any columns that you don't require), or in a single step, populating a `DataTable` with schema information. The latter technique uses the `SqlDataReader.GetSchemaTable()` method, which takes no parameters and returns a `DataTable` instance.

When using `GetSchemaTable()`, the `DataTable` object returned will contain a row for each column in the data in the data reader. Each row contains 30 columns with information about a column in the data reader, including column indexes, names, types, sizes, key information, and so on, as well as the name of the SQL Server instance used to obtain the data, and names of base database columns used to obtain the data.

Using this method enables you to perform advanced tasks, such as dynamically transforming the data in the data reader, because you have access to all the information about the data that you could possibly want. Although it provides you with all the basic information about columns, and as such serves a number of uses, in most cases it's much more information than you need. The fact that it is likely to get more information than you want, however, means that you usually want to get information for individual columns as and when you need to.

The other way to obtain schema information, column by column, is often more suitable (and can be much faster). It involves using the following property and methods:

❑ `SqlDataReader.FieldCount`: Obtains the number of columns in the rows in the data reader as an `int` value.

❑ `SqlDataReader.GetName()`: Obtains the name of a specified row (where the row is specified using its `int` index).

❑ `SqlDataReader.GetDataTypeName()`: Obtains the name of the data type of a specified row (where the row is specified using its `int` index) in the form of a `string`.

If you know the name of a column and want to find out what index to use to access values from it, you can use `SqlDataReader.GetOrdinal()`, passing the string name of the column, and get the index of the column in the form of an `int` value.

You can also get column type information from the values returned when you read data from a data reader.

All of the information detailed here is available as soon as you obtain a `SqlDataReader` instance. There's no need to load a row into the reader as described in the next section. However, the underlying connection must be open to use the schema properties and methods.

Row Data

When you first obtain a `SqlDataReader` object, it does not allow data access to any row in the result set. Think of a data reader as needing to have a row "loaded" for you to access it, and until you tell it to load a row, there won't be any data for you to look at. In fact, if you try to read data before you load a row, you get an `InvalidOperationException` with the message "Invalid attempt to read when no data is present."

Use the `Read()` method to load a row. It attempts to load the next row in the result set (the first row if this is the first time the method is called) and returns a Boolean value to let you know whether it has been successful. If there are no rows in the result set, or if all the rows have already been read, you receive a value of `false`. It is usual to call this method as part of a `while` loop as follows:

```
// Obtain data reader.
while (reader.Read)
{
    // Process row.
}
// No more rows to process.
```

With this code structure, you process every row in the result set in turn. You can use `SqlDataReader.HasRows`, a Boolean property, to find out if there are any rows before you use the loop. You cannot, however, use the data reader to find out how many rows are accessible. If you wanted to do this you'd have to use the `COUNT(*)` aggregate function in a separate query, or keep a running count as you process rows, and then find out how many there were after you've finished with them.

One common mistake people make when first using the `SqlDataReader` class is to confuse the `Read()` method with the `NextResult()` method. After all, `NextResult()` does sound as if it would do exactly what has been described here. But that is not the case. The `NextResult()` method actually moves to the next set of results, which can occur if the SQL query or stored procedure used in the command returns multiple result sets. The following code sample illustrates this:

```
SqlConnection conn = new SqlConnection(
    ConfigurationManager.ConnectionStrings["MyConnectionString"].ConnectionString);
try
{
    SqlCommand cmd =
        new SqlCommand("SELECT * FROM MyTable1; SELECT * FROM MyTable2;", conn);
    conn.Open();
    SqlDataReader reader = cmd.ExecuteReader();
```

```
        do
        {
            while (reader.Read())
            {
                // Process row.
            }
        } while (reader.NextResult());
        reader.Close();
    }
    catch (Exception ex)
    {
        // Handle exception.
    }
    finally
    {
        conn.Close();
    }
```

Unlike with `Read()`, there is no need to call `NextResult()` to load the first result set, hence the use of a `do...while` loop. Of course, because the code you use to process rows from each result set may be different, you may not use this kind of structure at all, and simply process each result set in turn using different code.

Typically, however, it is much less of a headache to use separate commands and readers to process individual result sets, and will make things a lot easier if you have to return to your code at a later date. The key thing to take away from this discussion is not to call `NextResult()` when you actually mean to call `Read()`.

Once a row is loaded, you want to process it by extracting column information. As you know, there are a large number of methods you can use to extract column data as specific data types, each of which takes an integer column index value and returns a result of the specified type. For integer data you could use `SqlDataReader.GetInt32()`, for example. There are also methods that use native SQL Server types as well, such as `SqlDataReader.GetSqlInt32()`. And you can obtain values in the form of `object` references using `SqlDataReader.GetValue()`, or simply by using the indexer for the data reader. The following lines of code are equivalent:

```
object columnVal1 = reader.GetValue(0);
object columnVal2 = reader[0];
```

In most cases, you will use the indexer because it involves less code, although it requires you to cast values to their proper types. Note that the SQL types, from the `System.Data.SqlTypes` namespace, can only be obtained using the `GetSqlXXX()` methods.

Besides involving less typing, the indexer of `SqlDataReader` has another advantage — it is overloaded to enable you to access columns by name. For example:

```
object columnVal = reader["MyColumn"];
```

Admittedly, this has the disadvantage of being slower because the index of the specified column must be obtained by the data reader before it can return a value, but that's relatively minor, and it certainly makes your code look readable.

When using the typed methods to obtain column values, you should be aware of what happens in the case of null values. When dealing with value types, null values are not permitted. Calling `GetGuid()` when there is a null result in the data row, for example, causes an exception to be raised. You can handle the exception and act accordingly, or use the `SqlDataReader.IsDBNull()` method, which tells you if the column at the specified index contains a null value. If you detect a null value, you can avoid calling a typed method to obtain the value, knowing that doing so would result in an exception. However, using `GetSqlGuid()` in the same situation does not raise an exception. Instead, the value returned is an instance of the correct SQL data type (in this case `SqlGuid`). Attempting to access the value of this object using its `Value` property (for example `SqlGuid.Value`) raises an exception. Instead, check the Boolean `IsNull` property of the object (`SqlGuid.IsNull` in this case) before using the `Value` property. Finally, when using `GetValue()` or an indexer to access data, null values result in a return value of type `System.DBNull`, and no exception.

Another way of getting at row data is to use the `SqlDataReader.GetValues()` or `SqlDataReader.GetSqlValues()` methods. Both have a single parameter, a reference to an array of `object` type objects. The result is that the array is filled with values from the row, one for each column, in column order. It doesn't matter if the size of the array you pass doesn't match the number of columns — if the array is too small, only the first columns are filled; if it is too big, then some members of the array aren't affected by the method call.

These methods don't raise exceptions for null values but, as discussed earlier, using the SQL type version of the method (`GetSqlValues()`) may obtain items that generate exceptions if you access their `Value` property and they contain null values.

To optimize performance, only a single object reference is generated by the data reader when you obtain object references to column values. Obtaining two objects by calling the same method of the reader actually means that you have two references to the same object. This is worth being aware of if you change column values for any reason.

Finally, you can also use `SqlDataReader` objects to obtain the values of large amounts of binary or text data using the `GetBytes()`, `GetSqlBytes()`, `GetChars()`, and `GetSqlChars()` methods. This is possible only if the `CommandBehavior.Sequential` access behavior is specified for the command that generates the data reader.

Other Properties

There are a few other properties that you might want to access for `SqlDataReader` objects. Two of these, `FieldCount` and `HasRows`, you've already looked at — they're used to obtain the number of columns in a row and whether the reader contains any rows respectively. There is also `IsClosed`, a Boolean property telling you if the reader is closed, and `RecordsAffected`, which tells you how many rows have been affected (if any) by the command that generated the data reader, or the value –1 if it is not applicable to the current command. These two properties are the only ones that are available for a closed data reader, and you should close the reader before using `RecordsAffected` to ensure a correct value for it.

In more advanced situations, you can use the `VisibleFieldCount` property to obtain the amount of non-hidden columns. For example, if a table uses a primary key consisting of a combination of more than one column, but only some of these columns are returned by a query, the data reader must obtain additional columns to have a valid primary key reference, despite not being asked for them, and those columns will be hidden.

Finally, there is a `Depth` property, intended to give you a "nesting level" for the currently loaded row. However, this property is meaningless when using the SQL Server data provider, and as such is not implemented by the `SqlDataReader` class.

Connections for Data Reader Objects

While a data reader is in use, its underlying `SqlConnection` object is unavailable for any other use. You can access the underlying connection through the `SqlDataReader.Connection` property should you need to, but all you'll be able to do is close the connection by calling its `Close()` method. You can't, for example, execute another command through the connection.

In the following Try It Out, you use a data reader to obtain table data.

Try It Out   Data Readers

1. Copy the project `C:\BegVC#Databases\Chapter06\Ex0601 - Executing Commands` to a new project, `C:\BegVC#Databases\Chapter06\Ex0602 - Data Readers`. (Copy and rename the directory, open it in Visual C# Express, and rename the solution and project.)

2. Open `app.config` and change the path to the local database file to include the new project directory rather than `Ex0601 - Executing Commands`.

3. Modify the code in `Program.cs` as follows:

```
static void Main(string[] args)
{
    // Configure connection.
    SqlConnection conn = new SqlConnection(ConfigurationManager
        .ConnectionStrings["FolktaleDBConnectionString"].ConnectionString);

    // Get user input table name.
    Console.WriteLine("Enter table from which to output data:");
    string tableName = Console.ReadLine();
    if (tableName.IndexOf(';') != -1)
    {
        Console.WriteLine("SQL injection attack detected. Press ENTER to
close.");
        Console.ReadLine();
        return;
    }
    tableName = tableName.Replace("'", "''");

    // Create command.
    string query = "SELECT * FROM " + tableName;
    SqlCommand cmd = new SqlCommand(query, conn);
    // Line removed.

    // try...catch...finally for command execution.
    try
    {
        // Open connection.
        conn.Open();
```

```
            // Execute command.
            SqlDataReader reader = cmd.ExecuteReader();

            // Output data.
            while (reader.Read())
            {
                for (int index = 0; index < reader.FieldCount; index++)
                {
                    Console.Write(reader.GetName(index) + ": "
                        + reader[index].ToString() + "; ");
                }
                Console.WriteLine();
            }

            // Close reader.
            reader.Close();
        }
        catch (Exception ex)
        {
            // Process exception.
            Console.WriteLine(ex.Message);
        }
        finally
        {
            // Close connection.
            conn.Close();
        }

        // Close application.
        Console.WriteLine("Press ENTER to close.");
        Console.ReadLine();
    }
```

4. Execute the application and enter a table name — `Character`, for example. Figure 6-4 shows the result.

5. Close the application and Visual C# Express.

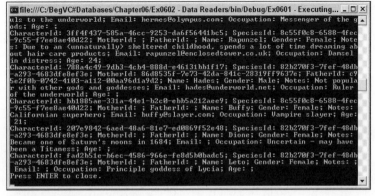

Figure 6-4: Table data output

How It Works

In this example, some modifications are made to the code from the previous example to use a data reader to read output from a user-specified table. This time the query used is a simple select everything statement:

```
string query = "SELECT * FROM " + tableName;
```

Using this SQL query in your command, you can obtain a data reader using the `ExecuteReader()` method:

```
SqlDataReader reader = cmd.ExecuteReader();
```

Next you have a `while` loop of the type discussed earlier in this chapter to output data from each row of the result. When the results have been exhausted, `reader.Read()` returns `false` and the loop terminates:

```
while (reader.Read())
{
```

In the `while` loop, the number of columns to output is accessed with the data reader's `FieldCount` property and used to initialize a `for` loop. In the `for` loop, the name and value of each column is output in turn:

```
for (int index = 0; index < reader.FieldCount; index++)
{
    Console.Write(reader.GetName(index) + ": "
        + reader[index].ToString() + "; ");
}
```

To space out results a little, an extra line of whitespace is added between each row:

```
Console.WriteLine();
}
```

Finally, the reader is closed because it is no longer required:

```
reader.Close();
```

The output of this example is a little garbled, and displays perhaps more data than strictly necessary. Formatting this data wouldn't require anything complicated, however.

Data Adapter Objects

The techniques laid out in the first part of this chapter are essentially all you need to access data. By using command and data reader objects through configured connections, you can interact with data in databases in any way you want. In fact, many developers look no further than this.

However, there are additional classes in the .NET Framework to make things easier for you. Using commands and data readers is a powerful approach, but can be time-consuming and involve a lot of code. Reading data into your own data-aware classes (something that you'll look at later in the book) means coding those classes, usually from the ground up.

Alternatively, you can make use of classes such as DataTable, DataSet, and so on. These can be populated using SqlDataAdapter and, optionally with the help of a SqlCommandBuilder object, changes to data can be made to the database with a minimum of effort.

There's one point of view that says using these classes is unnecessary and adversely affects performance — mostly stemming from the fact that classes such as DataSet are "heavyweight." That means the functionality offered by DataSet objects is designed to be as flexible as possible, and therefore includes an overhead related to additional code that you might never need. This is a perfectly valid stance, and if you are writing an application that must be as fast and sleek as possible, then these classes probably aren't the best choice for you. For most circumstances, however, they will serve your needs admirably.

In this section you will look at four things:

❑ Configuring data adapters

❑ Extracting data from a database using the Fill() and FillSchema() methods

❑ Modifying database data using the Update() method

❑ Customizing behavior using SqlDataAdapter properties

You'll concentrate here on exchanging data with DataTable objects. You'll explore the functionality of DataTable and DataSet objects in more detail later in this chapter; for now it is enough to know that these objects store database data and communicate with the database using data adapters.

Configuring Data Adapters

The first step in using a data adapter is to configure a SqlDataAdapter object to access your data. The SqlDataAdapter class has a number of constructors that you can use in addition to the default constructor, allowing you to quickly configure an instance of the class. Initial configuration requires two things:

❑ A select statement or SqlCommand object that can fetch data (if a select statement is used then it is used to generate a SqlCommand internally).

❑ A connection string or SqlConnection object (if a connection string is used, it's to generate a SqlConnection internally, and if a SqlCommand object with a connection is used, then that connection is used).

If you use the default constructor, you can configure both of these by supplying a SqlCommand instance to the SqlDataAdapter.SelectCommand property. Alternatively you can use a constructor where you pass a SQL select statement and a connection string, a SQL select statement and a SqlConnection object, or just a SqlCommand object. For example, you could do the following:

```
SqlConnection conn = new SqlConnection(
    ConfigurationManager.ConnectionStrings["MyConnectionString"].ConnectionString);
SqlCommand cmd = new SqlCommand("SELECT * FROM MyTable", conn);
SqlDataAdapter adapter = new SqlDataAdapter(cmd);
```

Alternatively, you could use:

```
SqlDataAdapter adapter = new SqlDataAdapter("SELECT * FROM MyTable",
    ConfigurationManager.ConnectionStrings["MyConnectionString"].ConnectionString);
```

The end result is the same, but the advantage of the first technique is that you have direct references to the `SqlCommand` and `SqlConnection` objects used by the data adapter.

Once you have configured a data adapter this way, you can use the `Fill()` and `FillSchema()` methods to populate data and schema information in a `DataTable` — either one that is a standalone instance or one in a `DataSet`. You'll do this in the next section.

To allow data to be modified through a `SqlDataAdapter`, there are three more properties that you need to set: `DeleteCommand`, `InsertCommand`, and `UpdateCommand`. Each of these is a parameterized `SqlCommand` object and is used to delete, insert, and update rows respectively. You can make these by hand if you want, or, alternatively you can use a `SqlCommandBuilder` to make the commands for you.

The `SqlCommandBuilder` is a simple one to use. All you have to do is instantiate it with a reference to the adapter with which it should be associated — that's it. For example:

```
SqlCommandBuilder builder = new SqlCommandBuilder(adapter);
```

Then, when the data adapter needs to obtain a delete, insert, or update command, it asks the command builder to generate one. It achieves this by looking at the select command that the data adapter has already configured, communicating with the database to obtain any additional information it needs (such as primary key column names), and creating SQL commands accordingly. This class is how the data-binding controls you've seen in earlier chapters generate commands for you. There are options to choose from when generating commands, accessible through the `SqlCommandBuilder.ConflictOption` property. This property uses the `ConflictOption` enumeration, which has the following members:

❑   `ConflictOption.CompareAllSearchableValues`: The default option, it results in the longest SQL commands. Records are identified by all their column values, so if any of the data in a row has changed since it was obtained, it won't be modified by this command.

❑   `ConflictOption.CompareRowVersion`: Any columns that use the `Timestamp` data type are used to check the version of a row. If the row data has changed since it was obtained, data won't be overwritten.

❑   `ConflictOption.OverwriteChanges`: Only the primary key is used to identify rows, so data changes since last access are overwritten. This gives you the shortest SQL statements, but in multi-user situations, it may cause you problems.

The fact that the `SqlCommandBuilder` object requires a connection to the database to generate commands is one reason why some people object to using it. In reality, however, it makes use of schema information that must be obtained to fill a `DataTable` anyway, so the overhead is small, and it is a convenient way of doing things.

The data returned by the select command in the data adapter must return at least one primary key or unique column or `SqlCommandBuilder` won't be able to identify the rows to be modified in the generated commands.

In the following Try It Out, you use the `SqlCommandBuilder` class to generate commands.

Try It Out   Generating Commands

1. Copy the project `C:\BegVC#Databases\Chapter06\Ex0602 - Data Readers` to a new project, `C:\BegVC#Databases\Chapter06\Ex0603 - Generating Commands`. (Copy and rename the directory, open it in Visual C# Express, and rename the solution and project.)

2. Open `app.config` and change the path to the local database file to include the new project directory rather than `Ex0602 - Data Readers`.

3. Modify the code in `Program.cs` as follows:

```
static void Main(string[] args)
{
    // Initialize.
    Console.WriteLine("Initializing.");
    SqlConnection conn = new SqlConnection(ConfigurationManager
        .ConnectionStrings["FolktaleDBConnectionString"].ConnectionString);
    conn.StateChange += new StateChangeEventHandler(conn_StateChange);
    SqlCommand cmd = new SqlCommand("SELECT * FROM Classification", conn);
    SqlDataAdapter adapter = new SqlDataAdapter(cmd);
    SqlCommandBuilder cmdBuilder = new SqlCommandBuilder(adapter);

    Console.WriteLine(
        "Getting commands with ConflictOption.OverwriteChanges.");
    cmdBuilder.ConflictOption = ConflictOption.OverwriteChanges;
    SqlCommand deleteCmd = cmdBuilder.GetDeleteCommand();
    Console.WriteLine("Delete command: {0}", deleteCmd.CommandText);
    SqlCommand insertCmd = cmdBuilder.GetInsertCommand();
    Console.WriteLine("Insert command: {0}", insertCmd.CommandText);
    SqlCommand updateCmd = cmdBuilder.GetUpdateCommand();
    Console.WriteLine("Update command: {0}", updateCmd.CommandText);

    Console.WriteLine();
    Console.WriteLine(
        "Getting commands with ConflictOption.CompareAllSearchableValues.");
    cmdBuilder.ConflictOption = ConflictOption.CompareAllSearchableValues;
    deleteCmd = cmdBuilder.GetDeleteCommand();
    Console.WriteLine("Delete command: {0}", deleteCmd.CommandText);
    insertCmd = cmdBuilder.GetInsertCommand();
    Console.WriteLine("Insert command: {0}", insertCmd.CommandText);
    updateCmd = cmdBuilder.GetUpdateCommand();
    Console.WriteLine("Update command: {0}", updateCmd.CommandText);

    // Close application.
    Console.WriteLine("Press ENTER to close.");
    Console.ReadLine();
}

static void conn_StateChange(object sender, StateChangeEventArgs e)
{
    Console.WriteLine("Connection state changed from {0} to {1}.",
        e.OriginalState, e.CurrentState);
}
```

4. Execute the application. The result is shown in Figure 6-5.

5. Close the application and Visual C# Express.

```
file:///C:/BegVC#Databases/ConsoleScratch/bin/Debug/ConsoleScratch.EXE
Initializing.
Getting commands with ConflictOption.OverwriteChanges.
Connection state changed from Closed to Open.
Connection state changed from Open to Closed.
Delete command: DELETE FROM [Classification] WHERE (([ClassificationId] = @p1))
Insert command: INSERT INTO [Classification] ([ClassificationId], [Classificatio
n]) VALUES (@p1, @p2)
Update command: UPDATE [Classification] SET [ClassificationId] = @p1, [Classific
ation] = @p2 WHERE (([ClassificationId] = @p3))

Getting commands with ConflictOption.CompareAllSearchableValues.
Delete command: DELETE FROM [Classification] WHERE (([ClassificationId] = @p1) A
ND ([Classification] = @p2))
Insert command: INSERT INTO [Classification] ([ClassificationId], [Classificatio
n]) VALUES (@p1, @p2)
Update command: UPDATE [Classification] SET [ClassificationId] = @p1, [Classific
ation] = @p2 WHERE (([ClassificationId] = @p3) AND ([Classification] = @p4))
Done, press ENTER to exit.
```

Figure 6-5: Generated command output

How It Works

In this example, a `SqlCommandBuilder` object generates delete, insert, and update commands for a data adapter that uses the select command:

```
SELECT * FROM Classification
```

To track database connections, once the connection is configured, an event handler is attached to its `StateChange` event, which is called when the state of the connection changes (from open to closed, for example):

```
SqlConnection conn = new SqlConnection(ConfigurationManager
    .ConnectionStrings["FolktaleDBConnectionString"].ConnectionString);
conn.StateChange += new StateChangeEventHandler(conn_StateChange);
```

The event handler simply outputs the original and new states of the connection:

```
static void conn_StateChange(object sender, StateChangeEventArgs e)
{
    Console.WriteLine("Connection state changed from {0} to {1}.",
        e.OriginalState, e.CurrentState);
}
```

Next, the code configures a data adapter, and attaches a `SqlCommandBuilder` to it:

```
SqlCommand cmd = new SqlCommand("SELECT * FROM Classification", conn);
SqlDataAdapter adapter = new SqlDataAdapter(cmd);
SqlCommandBuilder cmdBuilder = new SqlCommandBuilder(adapter);
```

The generated commands are retrieved using some of the methods of `SqlCommandBuilder`: `GetDeleteCommand()`, `GetInsertCommand()`, and `GetUpdateCommand()`. Each of these methods retrieves a `SqlCommand` instance for the associated command. The commands are used to output the SQL statements they contain to the console.

The first time this happens in the code, the `ConflictOption` of the `SqlCommandBuilder` is set to `ConflictOption.OverwriteChanges`:

```
Console.WriteLine(
    "Getting commands with ConflictOption.OverwriteChanges.");
cmdBuilder.ConflictOption = ConflictOption.OverwriteChanges;
SqlCommand deleteCmd = cmdBuilder.GetDeleteCommand();
Console.WriteLine("Delete command: {0}", deleteCmd.CommandText);
SqlCommand insertCmd = cmdBuilder.GetInsertCommand();
Console.WriteLine("Insert command: {0}", insertCmd.CommandText);
SqlCommand updateCmd = cmdBuilder.GetUpdateCommand();
Console.WriteLine("Update command: {0}", updateCmd.CommandText);
```

The process is repeated using `ConflictOption.CompareAllSearchableValues`.

The result of the code tells you several things. First, because of the output triggered when the connection state changes, you can see that the connection is opened and closed automatically when the `SqlCommandBuilder` generates commands. This happens at the time the first generated command is requested, that is, when `GetDeleteCommand()` is called for the same time (you can see this where the text is output just before this method is executed). You also can see that the connection is opened only once, and from that point on, the `SqlCommandBuilder` has all the information it needs to generate commands — event commands using different `ConflictOption` property values.

Additionally, you can see the SQL statements generated for the various commands. For the delete command, the SQL differs in the WHERE clause — when all values are being checked, the WHERE clause looks at the values of two columns:

```
DELETE FROM [Classification] WHERE (([ClassificationId] = @p1))

DELETE FROM [Classification] WHERE (([ClassificationId] = @p1) AND
([Classification] = @p2))
```

The insert commands are identical because no WHERE clause is required to identify an existing row:

```
INSERT INTO [Classification] ([ClassificationId], [Classification]) VALUES (@p1,
@p2)
```

The update commands differ in the same way as the delete commands — in their WHERE clause:

```
UPDATE [Classification] SET [ClassificationId] = @p1, [Classification] = @p2 WHERE
(([ClassificationId] = @p3))

UPDATE [Classification] SET [ClassificationId] = @p1, [Classification] = @p2 WHERE
(([ClassificationId] = @p3) AND ([Classification] = @p4))
```

In all cases the statements are parameterized using simple parameter names: @p1, @p2, and so on. The naming of the parameters isn't important — the data adapter is capable of working out which parameter is for which column. If you supply your own commands for the data adapter, you can, if you want, use friendly names such as @ClassificationId.

Extracting Database Data

Now that you can create and configure data adapters, it's time to use them to work with data in `DataTable` and `DataSet` objects. In this section, you learn to get data from your database into a `DataTable`.

In actual fact, this is an easy thing to do. Once you have a configured data adapter, you simply have to call its `Fill()` method, passing a reference to the `DataTable` that you want to fill with data:

```
DataTable dataTable = new DataTable();
adapter.Fill(dataTable);
```

The result of this code (which assumes that `adapter` is a configured data adapter) is that the `DataTable` object `dataTable` is filled with the data obtained using the data adapter's `SelectCommand` command. You can also use the `Fill()` method to populate a table in a `DataSet`, something that you look at later in the chapter.

There is, however, a slight problem with the code. While the `Fill()` method transfers data, it does not transfer schema information, which includes such things as primary key information, relationships with other tables, and so on.

There are two ways to deal with that problem. The first is to use the data adapter to infer schema information from the database. If you are using a `SqlCommandBuilder` to generate commands, the data adapter already gets this information for you, so it is a logical step to use the schema obtained for this purpose to configure a `DataTable`. To do so, you use the `FillSchema()` method. This method requires additional information regarding how to configure the schema in the `DataTable`, using a value from the `SchemaType` enumeration. For now, use the `SchemaType.Mapped` option — for reasons that will become clear in the section on customizing the behavior of data adapters a little later in the chapter. The code to populate the schema of a `DataTable` and then fill it with data is as follows:

```
DataTable dataTable = new DataTable();
adapter.FillSchema(dataTable, SchemaType.Mapped);
adapter.Fill(dataTable);
```

As with obtaining commands using `SqlCommandBuilder`, *these methods automatically open and close connections that aren't already open. If the connection used by the data adapter in the preceding code is not open, this code means that the connection will be opened and closed twice, once for the* `FillSchema()` *method and once for* `Fill()` *— an unnecessary overhead. To avoid that happening, always open and close connections manually when using this technique to populate a* `DataTable`.

Alternatively, you can use the `Fill()` method with a `DataTable` object that already has a schema matching the schema for the data retrieved by the data adapter. And you don't have to create a schema yourself (although you can if you really want to). In previous chapters you saw how typed data sets can be configured from data sources. Part of this configuration, which you can do using wizards or bit by bit, is the creation of classes derived from `DataTable` that include schema information ready for you to use (as well as handy properties and methods for accessing the data they contain). Again, you look at this a little later in the chapter, when you see how `DataSet` and typed data set objects fit into the picture.

Modifying Database Data

Once you have data loaded into a `DataTable` object you can read and manipulate it to your heart's content. However, any changes you make won't be applied to the data stored in the database until you use the data adapter to transfer them to the database.

> *A key factor here is that you are working with disconnected data — something that is discussed in much greater detail in Chapter 9.*

Applying changes through a data adapter is just as easy as getting the data into a `DataTable` as previously described. In fact, it is even easier because you don't have to worry about schema information when making changes — it's already configured.

All you have to do, then, is call the `Update()` method of the data adapter and pass the `DataTable` object containing the changes that you want to make:

```
adapter.Update(dataTable);
```

This does two things. First, all changes in the `DataTable` are applied to the database using the commands stored in the data adapter. Second, all changes in the `DataTable` are accepted, such that no attempt is made to apply them to the database again if the `Update()` method is called again in the same way. This is important because you want the `DataTable` to reflect the current state of the database. In fact, in a multi-user situation you may want to refresh the content of the `DataTable` each time you update the database in case extra rows have been added or existing rows modified.

As you know from previous chapters, the order in which updates are made to a database is important — especially when dealing with multiple, related tables. To recap, if you have two tables in a one-to-many relationship — parent table `TableA` and child table `TableB`, for example — changes must be applied in the following order:

1. Add new rows and update existing rows to the parent table (`TableA`) — but don't delete any rows.

2. Make changes to the child table (`TableB`) — additions, modifications, and deletions.

3. Delete rows from the parent table (`TableA`).

You also saw that you can achieve this by using the `GetChanges()` method of a data adapter to obtain just the changes of the type you want to apply — in order. For example:

```
// Parent table additions and modifications.
DataTable dataTableAChanges1 = dataTableA.GetChanges(
    DataRowState.Added | DataRowState.Modified)
if (dataTableAChanges1 != null)
{
    adapterA.Update(dataTableAChanges1);
}
```

```
// Child table changes.
adapterB.Update(dataTableB);

// Parent table deletions.
DataTable dataTableAChanges2 = dataTableA.GetChanges(DataRowState.Deleted)
if (dataTableAChanges2 != null)
{
    adapterA.Update(dataTableAChanges2);
}

// Accept changes in parent table.
dataTableA.AcceptChanges();
```

As the `GetChanges()` method creates a new `DataTable`, calling `Update()` does not accept changes to the original `DataTable`. That's why the `AcceptChanges()` method is called on `dataTableA` in this code sample.

You can expect update errors to occur when databases are used by multiple users simultaneously. This can happen because another user has modified data since you accessed it, in such a way as to cause concurrency problems. Attempting to update a row already deleted is an example. The simplest — and most brutal — ways of dealing with this are either to overwrite changes made by previous database accesses (although this won't work in all cases, such as the "update deleted row" situation) or to abort all changes when a problem arises. Either of these approaches, however, is likely to cause problems and angry e-mails from users. In Chapter 10 one of the more advanced topics you examine is how to deal with individual errors as they occur, on a row-by-row basis. You'll also see how to make update operations transactional so that an irreconcilable error in one database update can cause other updates to be rolled back — an essential part of database interaction.

Customizing Data Adapter Behavior

As with all things .NET, you have lots of control over the way the `SqlDataAdapter` class works. Much of the customization you can perform is done using various properties, which the first part of this section examines. A more advanced technique, which is touched on here, is table mappings: by configuring them, you can control exactly how data is transferred between databases and `DataTable` objects.

SqlDataAdapter Properties

In addition to those you've already seen, the `SqlDataAdapter` class has several properties that you can use to control its behavior. The following table details the ones that aren't related to table mappings.

Table Mappings

Table mappings determine how data columns in the database map to data columns in a `DataTable`. This isn't something that you need to worry about often — most of the time you want a column called `MyColumn` in a table called `MyTable` in the database to be placed in a column of the same name in a table of the same name in your `DataTable` object. Sometimes, for whatever reason, you may want to change that behavior. Perhaps the column name in the database is too verbose for you, or perhaps you have a table with the same name in a different database and want to distinguish between the two.

Property	Description
AcceptChangesDuringFill	Determines whether rows added to a DataTable have their AcceptChanges() method called. If it's set to false, each row added by calling Fill() is marked as having been inserted. The default is true.
AcceptChangesDuringUpdate	This property's default value is true, which means that the default behavior of SqlDataAdapter is to call AcceptChanges() on each row after its changes have been committed to the database. If this isn't the behavior you want, set this property to false.
ContinueUpdateOnError	With this property set to true (the default), any row update errors result in an exception being thrown. When it's set to false, no exception is thrown, and the update continues with the next modified row. (This is important when dealing with concurrency errors, as you'll see in Chapter 10.)
FillLoadOption	Determines how data is written to the DataTable if existing data exists in the table. It has three possible values: LoadOption.OverwriteChanges: The default option; row data is written to both the original and current values for rows in the table. LoadOption.PreserveChanges: Only the original values of rows are affected, so any changes already made to data in the DataTable are preserved. LoadOption.Upsert: Overwrites the current version of the rows, but not the original version, so that changes can be undone to a point prior to calling Fill() if desired.
ReturnProviderSpecificTypes	Whether to return provider-specific types or CLS-compliant types. The default is false, although as you've seen you can get data in the form of types from the System.Data.SqlTypes namespace to handle data in a form that closely matches SQL database types — without changing this property.
UpdateBatchSize	This int property specifies how many rows are processed for each round trip to the DBMS. The default value, 1, is fine for most applications, but you can set this to a larger number or 0 to use the maximum amount of rows that the DBMS can handle. This can improve performance, but can also lead to problems when update errors occur (see the MSDN documentation for details).

To control table mapping you use the `SqlDataAdapter.TableMappings` property, which is a collection of `DataTableMapping` objects. Typically, a single data adapter has a single `DataTableMapping` object because it is likely to be associated with a single table. It is possible, however, that a stored procedure or SQL command might return multiple result sets for multiple tables, and if that happens, you can use more than one `DataTableMapping` object. Each `DataTableMapping` object has three properties that you need to configure:

- ❑ `SourceTable`: Name of the table in the database.
- ❑ `DataSetTable`: Name of the table that identifies it in a collection of `DataTable` objects in a `DataSet`.
- ❑ `ColumnMappings`: A collection of `ColumnMapping` objects, each of which maps a column in the database to a column in the `DataTable`.

Each `ColumnMapping` object has two properties to configure:

- ❑ `SourceColumn`: Name of the column in the database.
- ❑ `DataSetColumn`: Name of the column in the `DataTable`.

To set up a table mapping, you add a new item to the `SqlDataAdapter.TableMappings` property of type `DataTableMapping`, which you can do easily using a constructor of this type:

```
adapter.TableMappings.Add("SourceTableName", "DataSetTableName");
```

Then you can add column mappings in the same way:

```
adapter.TableMappings["SourceTableName"].Add(
    "SourceColumn1Name", "DataSetColumn1Name");
adapter.TableMappings["SourceTableName"].Add(
    "SourceColumn2Name", "DataSetColumn2Name");
...
```

Initially, there are no table mappings for a data adapter, and even when you add them you might add them only for some columns. When the data adapter is filling a data set and it encounters a column with no mapping, what happens next depends on the `SqlDataAdapter.MissingMappingAction` property, which has three possible values:

- ❑ `MissingMappingAction.Passthrough`: The default value; the same column name is used in the `DataTable` as in the database.
- ❑ `MissingMappingAction.Ignore`: Unmapped columns are not added to the `DataTable`.
- ❑ `MissingMappingAction.Error`: An exception of type `InvalidOperationException` is raised for unmapped columns.

When columns get added to a `DataTable`, either mapped or because of the `MissingMappingAction.Passthrough` option, they must fit into the schema for the table. Earlier you saw how primary key information is not added to databases by default — by configuring the schema of the table prior to adding data you cause this information to be retained. In actual fact, what happens when a column value is added to a `DataTable` is a little more complicated, and again you have some control over what happens.

What happens is this: when an attempt is made to write a column value to a `DataTable`, the schema of the `DataTable` is first checked to see if a data column with the same name as the column (or the mapped name of the column if there is a column mapping) exists. If it does, the data is added. If it doesn't, the value of the `SqlDataAdapter.MissingSchemaAction` property comes into play. This property can take one of four values:

- ❑ `MissingSchemaAction.Add`: A column is added to the schema using the (mapped or unmapped) name of the column. However, information such as whether the column is a primary key is omitted. This is the default value.

- ❑ `MissingSchemaAction.AddWithKey`: A column is added to the table schema, and if the column is part of a primary key, that is recognized, and the `DataTable` column is configured accordingly. You can use this option rather than populating the schema of a `DataTable` before filling the `DataTable` with table data.

- ❑ `MissingSchemaAction.Ignore`: If the column doesn't exist in the schema, its values are not added to the `DataTable`.

- ❑ `MissingSchemaAction.Error`: If the column doesn't exist in the schema, an exception of type `InvalidOperationException` is thrown.

By using table and column mappings and the `MissingMappingAction` and `MissingSchemaAction` properties, you have complete control over the way data maps between the database and a `DataTable`.

Earlier in the chapter you saw that the `SqlDataAdapter.FillSchema()` method takes a parameter of type `SchemaType` and you used the value `SchemaType.Mapped` for that parameter. Now you can see what this means — schema information is added to the `DataTable` using any table mappings defined for the data adapter. The alternative option, `SchemaType.Source`, ignores any table mappings that you might have defined.

In the following Try It Out, you use a data adapter with table mappings to obtain table data.

Try It Out   **Using Data Adapters**

1. Copy the project `C:\BegVC#Databases\Chapter06\Ex0603 - Generating Commands` to a new project, `C:\BegVC#Databases\Chapter06\Ex0604 - Data Adapters`. (Copy and rename the directory, open it in Visual C# Express, and rename the solution and project.)

2. Open `app.config` and change the path to the local database file to include the new project directory rather than `Ex0603 - Generating Commands`.

3. Modify `Program.cs` as follows:

```
static void Main(string[] args)
{
    // Initialize.
    Console.WriteLine("Initializing.");
    SqlConnection conn = new SqlConnection(ConfigurationManager
        .ConnectionStrings["FolktaleDBConnectionString"].ConnectionString);
    conn.StateChange += new StateChangeEventHandler(conn_StateChange);
    SqlCommand cmd = new SqlCommand("SELECT * FROM Classification", conn);
    SqlDataAdapter adapter = new SqlDataAdapter(cmd);
    SqlCommandBuilder cmdBuilder = new SqlCommandBuilder(adapter);
```

```csharp
        // Prepare table
        DataTable classTable = new DataTable("Classes");

        // Configure mappings
        adapter.TableMappings.Add("Classification", "Classes");
        adapter.TableMappings["Classification"].ColumnMappings.Add(
            "Classification", "Class");
        adapter.TableMappings["Classification"].ColumnMappings.Add(
            "ClassificationId", "Id");

        // try...catch...finally for adapter execution.
        try
        {
            // Open connection.
            conn.Open();

            // Get data.
            adapter.Fill(classTable);
        }
        catch (Exception ex)
        {
            // Process exception.
            Console.WriteLine(ex.Message);
        }
        finally
        {
            // Close connection.
            conn.Close();
        }

        // Output data.
        foreach (DataRow row in classTable.Rows)
        {
            Console.WriteLine("{0}: {1}", row["Id"], row["Class"]);
        }
```

```csharp
        // Close application.
        Console.WriteLine("Press ENTER to close.");
        Console.ReadLine();
    }

    static void conn_StateChange(object sender, StateChangeEventArgs e)
    {
        Console.WriteLine("Connection state changed from {0} to {1}.",
            e.OriginalState, e.CurrentState);
    }
```

4. Execute the application. The result is shown in Figure 6-6.

5. Close the application and Visual C# Express.

Figure 6-6: Application output

How It Works

In this example you use the data adapter configured in the previous example to obtain data from the Classification table in the database. However, to make things a little more interesting, you change the mappings for the table, such that the Classification table is loaded into a table called Classes, with its columns renamed as well.

After the initialization code, a DataTable is prepared to hold the data:

```
DataTable classTable = new DataTable("Classes");
```

The naming of the table here is important — it is the same as the name used in the mapping. If you like, change the name here, or omit it entirely — you will get errors when data is output. Because a schema isn't being loaded into the table in this example, the mappings only result in a table called Classes being filled with data. A table called anything else isn't configured, and no data is added to it, hence the error.

Next, table and column mappings are added in the way specified earlier:

```
adapter.TableMappings.Add("Classification", "Classes");
adapter.TableMappings["Classification"].ColumnMappings.Add(
    "Classification", "Class");
adapter.TableMappings["Classification"].ColumnMappings.Add(
    "ClassificationId", "Id");
```

Then data is obtained in the standard way:

```
try
{
    conn.Open();
    adapter.Fill(classTable);
}
catch (Exception ex)
{
    Console.WriteLine(ex.Message);
}
finally
{
    conn.Close();
}
```

225

Finally, the data is output using the `DataTable.Rows` collection of `DataRow` objects. This code also verifies that the mappings have been correctly applied, because the column names used here are the mapped column names:

```
foreach (DataRow row in classTable.Rows)
{
    Console.WriteLine("{0}: {1}", row["Id"], row["Class"]);
}
```

It is worth noting that the database connection is only opened and closed once. All of the round trips to the server — getting schema information, generating commands, and obtaining data — are executed in one go, with one open connection. That is the optimal way of doing things.

DataSet Objects

In Chapter 2 you learned that `DataSet` objects are capable of representing a "chunk" of a database in memory, including tables, relationships, and key information. You also saw that the `DataSet` class is capable of transforming data to and from XML data, and that typed data sets can be used to simplify the code syntax required to use `DataSet` objects.

Since then, you have used typed `DataSet` objects extensively in data binding, but as yet you haven't had much cause to interact with them directly, short of some simple code in applications that use data binding.

In this section you learn more about `DataSet` and typed dataset objects and see how they can be useful even without data binding.

Populating DataSet objects

`DataSet` objects can be filled with data by using a data adapter such as `SqlDataAdapter`, which you've been learning about in this chapter. You can simply pass a `DataSet` instance to the `SqlDataAdapter.Fill()` method as follows:

```
DataSet ds = new DataSet();
adapter.Fill(ds);
```

This results in a table (a `DataTable` object) being added to the `DataSet` with the name `Table`. There is nothing wrong with this, although typically you want to use a more sensible table name, which you can do with a `string` parameter as follows:

```
DataSet ds = new DataSet();
adapter.Fill(ds, "MyTable");
```

If a table called `MyTable` already exists in the `DataSet`, it's filled with the data from the data adapter; otherwise, it's added. `DataSet` table names are case sensitive; if in the preceding example a table called `myTable` exists in the `DataSet` then a new table called `MyTable` is added and the `myTable` table is ignored.

When using this syntax, the table name that you pass is actually the source table name, so the actual table name as used in the DataSet may be different if table mapping is in use. Consider the code in the previous Try It Out that had a table mapping from the Classification table in the database to a DataTable called Classes. In that situation you'd have to add data to the DataSet as follows:

```
DataSet ds = new DataSet();
adapter.Fill(ds, "Classification");
```

However, when accessing the data you'd have to use the following:

```
foreach (DataRow row in ds.Tables["Classes"].Rows)
{
    Console.WriteLine("{0}: {1}", row["Id"], row["Class"]);
}
```

This code accesses the DataTable called Classes in the DataSet, using an indexer that takes a table name to access the table.

*As an exercise, you might make the modifications suggested to the code for the previous Try It Out —
you'll find that little modification is necessary to achieve the same result.*

The beauty of the DataSet class is that you can fill it with multiple tables. All you have to do to achieve this in your code is to use different names when you call Fill():

```
DataSet ds = new DataSet();
adapter1.Fill(ds, "MyTable1");
adapter2.Fill(ds, "MyTable2");
```

Here two different data adapters are used — adapter1 and adapter2 — which presumably are configured to fetch data from tables names MyTable1 and MyTable2 respectively.

As with individual DataTable objects, it is often desirable to fill table schema information before filling table data. Again, you can use the FillSchema() method to do this:

```
DataSet ds = new DataSet();
adapter.FillSchema(ds, SchemaType.Mapped, "MyTable");
adapter.Fill(ds, "MyTable");
```

This code fetches primary key and extended column information, which you can then access through the DataTable stored in the DataSet if you want.

Unfortunately, relationships between tables (such as the one-to-many relationship between the parent table Classification and the child table Story) are not obtained when you call these methods. That's a shame because DataSet objects enable you to navigate through data using such relationships — functionality that is essential in many applications, particularly those with master/detail views. You could, if you wanted to, code this functionality manually. You could find the primary key value of a row in the parent table and then search through child rows to find those that reference the key using a foreign key. However, that's a long-winded approach, and you really are a lot better off defining the relationships so that you can use more optimized code, as described in the following section.

Defining and Using Table Relationships

Many times in this book already you've made use of the fact that tables can be related to each other — for example, in a one-to-many relationship. You have seen how data-bound controls can display information from two or more tables in a master/detail view. To achieve that using DataSet objects populated from a database, you must add relationships manually.

A DataSet object's Relations property contains a list of relationships between tables. This property is of type DataRelationCollection, which holds a collection of DataRelation objects. To add a relationship between two tables, you must add a DataRelation object that defines the relationship. The easiest way to do that is to use the following code:

```
// DataSet ds created and populated with schema and data from two tables.
ds.Relations.Add(
    "ParentTable_ChildTable",
    ds.Tables["ParentTable"].Columns["ParentTableId"],
    ds.Tables["ChildTable"].Columns["ParentTableId"]
);
```

Here, a relationship called ParentTable_ChildTable is created between two tables called ParentTable and ChildTable. Both of these tables have a column called ParentTableId (it is the primary key of ParentTable and a foreign key in ChildTable). These columns are accessed in the form of DataColumn objects via the Columns property of the DataTable class, and used in this method call to DataRelationCollection.Add to define the relationship.

You don't have to name relationships in this manner, although it does help to identify them, particularly when using them to navigate between rows as you'll see shortly. And you can substitute arrays of Data-Column objects for the individual DataColumn objects in the preceding example, should one or both tables have compound primary keys. Note that if one of the parameters is of type DataColumn[], they must both be of this type. Also, you can optionally specify an additional Boolean parameter that determines whether constraints are added to the tables in the relationship (the default is true). If a constraint is added, the DataSet ensures that all foreign key values in the child table match a primary key value in the parent table.

Once a relationship is defined this way, you can use it in your code. To do so, use the DataRow.GetChildRows() method. This method gets child rows according to a DataRelation, which you can specify either by passing a DataRelation object or by name. Child rows are then returned as a DataRow[] array. For example:

```
DataRow parentRow = ds.Tables["ParentTable"].Rows[0];
DataRow[] childRows = parentRow.GetChildRows("ParentTable_ChildTable");
```

This way you have all child rows in the form of an array, which you can then process however you like.

In the following Try It Out, you fill two tables in a DataSet, configure a relationship between those tables, and then use that relationship to navigate through related data.

Try It Out   Using DataSets

1. Copy the project C:\BegVC#Databases\Chapter06\Ex0604 - Data Adapters to a new project, C:\BegVC#Databases\Chapter06\Ex0605 - DataSets. (Copy and rename the directory, open it in Visual C# Express, and rename the solution and project.)

2. Open `app.config` and change the path to the local database file to include the new project directory rather than `Ex0604 - Data Adapters`.

3. Modify `Program.cs` as follows:

```
static void Main(string[] args)
{
    // Initialize.
    Console.WriteLine("Initializing.");
    SqlConnection conn = new SqlConnection(ConfigurationManager
        .ConnectionStrings["FolktaleDBConnectionString"].ConnectionString);
    conn.StateChange += new StateChangeEventHandler(conn_StateChange);
    SqlCommand cmd1 = new SqlCommand("SELECT * FROM Classification", conn);
    SqlCommand cmd2 = new SqlCommand("SELECT * FROM Story", conn);
    SqlDataAdapter adapter1 = new SqlDataAdapter(cmd1);
    SqlDataAdapter adapter2 = new SqlDataAdapter(cmd2);
    SqlCommandBuilder cmdBuilder1 = new SqlCommandBuilder(adapter1);
    SqlCommandBuilder cmdBuilder2 = new SqlCommandBuilder(adapter2);

    // Prepare DataSet
    DataSet ds = new DataSet();

    // try...catch...finally for adapter execution.
    try
    {
        // Open connection.
        conn.Open();

        // Get schemas and data.
        adapter1.FillSchema(ds, SchemaType.Mapped, "Classification");
        adapter2.FillSchema(ds, SchemaType.Mapped, "Story");
        adapter1.Fill(ds, "Classification");
        adapter2.Fill(ds, "Story");
    }
    catch (Exception ex)
    {
        // Process exception.
        Console.WriteLine(ex.Message);
    }
    finally
    {
        // Close connection.
        conn.Close();
    }

    // Add relation
    ds.Relations.Add(
        "Classification_Story",
        ds.Tables["Classification"].Columns["ClassificationId"],
        ds.Tables["Story"].Columns["ClassificationId"],
        true);

    // Navigate relation
    foreach (DataRow classificationRow in ds.Tables["Classification"].Rows)
    {
```

```
            Console.WriteLine("Classification: {0}",
                classificationRow["Classification"]);
            DataRow[] childRows = classificationRow.GetChildRows(
                "Classification_Story");
            if (childRows.Length > 0)
            {
                foreach (DataRow storyRow in childRows)
                {
                    Console.WriteLine("Story: {0}", storyRow["Name"]);
                }
            }
            else
            {
                Console.WriteLine("No stories.");
            }
            Console.WriteLine();
        }

        // Close application.
        Console.WriteLine("Press ENTER to close.");
        Console.ReadLine();
    }

    static void conn_StateChange(object sender, StateChangeEventArgs e)
    {
        Console.WriteLine("Connection state changed from {0} to {1}.",
            e.OriginalState, e.CurrentState);
    }
```

4. Execute the application. The result is shown in Figure 6-7.

5. Close the application and Visual C# Express.

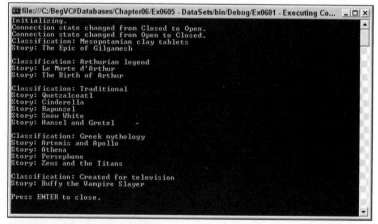

Figure 6-7: Application output

How It Works

After the now-familiar initialization, you created not one, but two select commands for two tables, `Classification` and `Story`, which have a one-to-many relationship. You also created two adapters and, for completeness, used command builders for these adapters:

```
SqlCommand cmd1 = new SqlCommand("SELECT * FROM Classification", conn);
SqlCommand cmd2 = new SqlCommand("SELECT * FROM Story", conn);
SqlDataAdapter adapter1 = new SqlDataAdapter(cmd1);
SqlDataAdapter adapter2 = new SqlDataAdapter(cmd2);
SqlCommandBuilder cmdBuilder1 = new SqlCommandBuilder(adapter1);
SqlCommandBuilder cmdBuilder2 = new SqlCommandBuilder(adapter2);
```

Next you created a `DataSet` to hold the data and relationships:

```
DataSet ds = new DataSet();
```

After opening the connection in the usual `try...catch...finally` structure, you filled two tables in the `DataSet` with schema information and data:

```
adapter1.FillSchema(ds, SchemaType.Mapped, "Classification");
adapter2.FillSchema(ds, SchemaType.Mapped, "Story");
adapter1.Fill(ds, "Classification");
adapter2.Fill(ds, "Story");
```

When the connection was closed again, you added the relationship between the tables to the `DataSet.Relations` collection, naming the relationship `Classification_Story`. You used the `ClassificationId` column from both table to define the relationship:

```
ds.Relations.Add(
    "Classification_Story",
    ds.Tables["Classification"].Columns["ClassificationId"],
    ds.Tables["Story"].Columns["ClassificationId"],
    true);
```

Next you proceeded to navigate the relationship, starting with a loop over each row in the `Classification` table:

```
foreach (DataRow classificationRow in ds.Tables["Classification"].Rows)
{
    Console.WriteLine("Classification: {0}",
        classificationRow["Classification"]);
```

You used the `DataRow.GetChildRows()` method to obtain child rows, passing the name of the relationship defined earlier, which results in an array of rows from the `Story` table:

```
DataRow[] childRows = classificationRow.GetChildRows(
    "Classification_Story");
```

You then proceeded to output information based on the rows returned, using a similar `foreach` loop:

```
if (childRows.Length > 0)
{
    foreach (DataRow storyRow in childRows)
    {
        Console.WriteLine("Story: {0}", storyRow["Name"]);
    }
}
```

or reported no rows if no child rows were found:

```
else
{
    Console.WriteLine("No stories.");
}
Console.WriteLine();
```

All in all, simple. However, defining relationships like this can be a bit of a drag, and as you've seen in previous chapters, typed `DataSet` classes make things a lot clearer.

Typed DataSet Classes

In Chapter 3 you spent a great deal of time looking at adding typed `DataSet` classes, which you achieved by adding data sources. By adding a data source that uses data from a database, either using wizards or by designing them using the DataSet Designer, you saw how to create and customize typed `DataSet` classes. You used those classes by binding them to controls via the `BindingSource` control. The `BindingSource` control was responsible for instantiating the typed `DataSet` class, filling it with data, and so on.

Outside the data-binding environment, things are much the same, although you won't use `BindingSource` and instead will fill instances of typed `DataSet` classes yourself. The important thing is that by adding a data source to your project, you generate all the classes you need to exchange data with your database in a type-safe way. That means you no longer have to worry about configuring commands for accessing data, using default data adapters, adding relationships manually, or taking convoluted routes to manipulate data in `DataSet` objects.

The first thing to look at when considering typed `DataSet` classes is what code and classes are created for you, starting with classes. For the purposes of this discussion, you'll consider a typed `DataSet` class called `MyDataSet` that accesses two tables, `TableA` and `TableB`, where `TableA` has a one-to-many relationship with `TableB` via a column called `TableAId` (primary key in `TableA`, foreign key in `TableB`). `TableA` has an additional string column called `StringColumn`, and `TableB` has an integer column called `IntColumn`.

The most obvious class generated is `MyDataSet`. This is the typed data set class itself, and derives from `DataSet`. As such, it offers all the functionality that `DataSet` does — and more. The two tables, `TableA` and `TableB`, are already initialized, complete with schema information as specified in the DataSet

Designer. Both of these tables are stored as classes derived from `DataTable`, and are accessible in the normal way through the `MyDataSet.Tables` property. However, they are also made available through named properties: `MyDataSet.TableA` and `MyDataSet.TableB`, respectively. Using this mode of access gives you access to the tables in the form of their derived classes, `TableADataTable` and `TableBDataTable`, which you'll look at in a moment.

If you look at the code for the `MyDataSet` class, you can see much of the initialization that it performs in a method called `InitClass()`. The method starts by setting a few basic properties of the class, such as its name, namespace, and serialization mode (which affects how it gets serialized to XML):

```
private void InitClass()
{
    this.DataSetName = "MyDataSet";
    this.Prefix = "";
    this.Namespace = "http://tempuri.org/MyDataSet.xsd";
    this.EnforceConstraints = true;
    this.SchemaSerializationMode =
        System.Data.SchemaSerializationMode.IncludeSchema;
```

Next, the two table members are initialized. These are available in the class as private members, and are also part of the `Tables` collection inherited from `DataSet`:

```
    this.tableTableA = new TableADataTable();
    base.Tables.Add(this.tableTableA);
    this.tableTableB = new TableBDataTable();
    base.Tables.Add(this.tableTableB);
```

Finally, a relationship between these tables is added using a `DataRelation` object as described earlier in this chapter. It's also stored as a private member as well as being in the base `Relations` collection:

```
    this.relationFK_TableB_TableA = new System.Data.DataRelation(
        "FK_TableB_TableA",
        new System.Data.DataColumn[] {this.tableTableA.TableAIdColumn},
        new System.Data.DataColumn[] {this.tableTableB.TableAIdColumn},
        false);
    this.Relations.Add(this.relationFK_TableB_TableA);
}
```

You can already see that things will be easier for you, with properties more suited to readable code, and relationships defined ready for you to use. But there's more, which you can see in the table classes — `TableADataTable`, for example. This class is defined as part of the `MyDataSet` definition, and so is actually referred to as `MyDataSet.TableADataTable`; inside the `MyDataSet` namespace. Again, type-specific code is added, such as rows being exposed through the following indexer:

```
public TableARow this[int index]
{
    get
    {
        return ((TableARow)(this.Rows[index]));
    }
}
```

Another class, `MyDataSet.TableARow`, is used to provide easy access to row data (you'll look at this in a moment). `TableADataTable` also includes a revealing initialization method, `InitClass()`. The method, shown in the following code, configures the data columns used by the class (which again are stored as private members and exposed through properties — `TableAIdColumn` and `TableAStringColumn`), serialization settings for table data serialization to XML, and primary key information (using the `Constraints` collection). Some of the code to achieve this hasn't been discussed yet, but it's all fairly readable.

```
private void InitClass()
{
    this.columnTableAId = new System.Data.DataColumn(
        "TableAId", typeof(int), null, System.Data.MappingType.Element);
    base.Columns.Add(this.columnTableAId);
    this.columnStringColumn = new System.Data.DataColumn(
        "StringColumn", typeof(string), null, System.Data.MappingType.Element);
    base.Columns.Add(this.columnStringColumn);
    this.Constraints.Add(new System.Data.UniqueConstraint(
        "Constraint1", new System.Data.DataColumn[] {this.columnTableAId}, true));
    this.columnTableAId.AutoIncrement = true;
    this.columnTableAId.AllowDBNull = false;
    this.columnTableAId.ReadOnly = true;
    this.columnTableAId.Unique = true;
    this.columnStringColumn.MaxLength = 50;
}
```

In case you're wondering, the table name (`TableA` in this case) is set in the constructor for this class, rather than in the initialization method.

Moving on, you have the classes representing table rows, `TableARow` and `TableBRow`, both of which are derived from `DataRow`. Again, these are defined local to the `MyDataSet` class, and have additional members defined for your convenience. `TableARow` includes properties for easy access to the columns in the table, which it obtains using the inherited indexer and casts to the right types for you. The indexer is accessed by passing the column type defined in `TableADataTable`. For example, `TableAId`:

```
public int TableAId
{
    get
    {
        return ((int)(this[this.tableTableA.TableAIdColumn]));
    }
    set
    {
        this[this.tableTableA.TableAIdColumn] = value;
    }
}
```

If columns are nullable, which `StringColumn` is, additional code is produced to generate exceptions when null values are accessed. For example:

```
public string StringColumn
{
    get
    {
```

```
        try
        {
            return ((string)(this[this.tableTableA.StringColumnColumn]));
        }
        catch (System.InvalidCastException e)
        {
            throw new System.Data.StrongTypingException(
        "The value for column \'StringColumn\' in table \'TableA\' is DBNull.", e);
        }
    }
    set
    {
        this[this.tableTableA.StringColumnColumn] = value;
    }
}
```

In columns, additional methods are required to test for a null value and to set a null value:

```
public bool IsStringColumnNull()
{
    return this.IsNull(this.tableTableA.StringColumnColumn);
}

public void SetStringColumnNull()
{
    this[this.tableTableA.StringColumnColumn] = System.Convert.DBNull;
}
```

In addition, the relationships between tables are used to generate typed versions of the `GetChildRows()` method you used earlier to navigate relationships. For `TableARow`, the following method is generated to access child rows in `TableB`:

```
public TableBRow[] GetTableBRows()
{
    return ((TableBRow[])(base.GetChildRows(
        this.Table.ChildRelations["FK_TableB_TableA"])));
}
```

This method simply uses the base `GetChildRows()` method with the relationship defined for the table and casts the result to an array of type `TableBRow[]`.

The classes generated also include event-raising code enabling you to deal with row changing, row changed, row deleting, and row deleted events. Again, these are named according to the data. For `TableA`, they're defined in the `TableADataTable` class with the names `TableARowChanging`, `TableARowChanged`, `TableARowDeleting`, and `TableARowDeleted`. A typed delegate called `MyDataSet.TableARowChangeEventHandler` is used for these events, with event arguments defined as `MyDataSet.TableARowChangeEvent` objects. This event argument class includes a typed `Row` property to access, say, the `TableARow` object raising the event directly.

Finally, typed data adapter classes are generated in a namespace called `MyDataSetTableAdapters` (the name varies according to the name of the data set class). In this case, `TableATableAdapter` and `TableBTableAdapter` classes are generated. These classes don't derive from `SqlDataAdapter` because it is a sealed class and can't be inherited from. However, they use a private member of type `SqlDataAdapter` to achieve data adapter functionality. The member is configured in a method called `InitAdapter()`. This method is defined in the `TableATableAdapter` class in a typical way. It starts by configuring table mappings:

```
private void InitAdapter()
{
    this._adapter = new System.Data.SqlClient.SqlDataAdapter();
    System.Data.Common.DataTableMapping tableMapping =
        new System.Data.Common.DataTableMapping();
    tableMapping.SourceTable = "Table";
    tableMapping.DataSetTable = "TableA";
    tableMapping.ColumnMappings.Add("TableAId", "TableAId");
    tableMapping.ColumnMappings.Add("StringColumn", "StringColumn");
    this._adapter.TableMappings.Add(tableMapping);
```

This uses code you've already seen in this chapter, and caters to any name changes you may apply to the DataSet Designer.

The rest of the code in this method configures the select, delete, insert, and update commands used by the data adapter. These are not assembled using a command builder but in a more long-winded fashion, which leads to more optimized operation because the commands don't need to be inferred when required. That code isn't reproduced here because it's quite long and doesn't show you much that you haven't already seen — commands are created, SQL statements or stored procedures used according to the settings in the DataSet Designer, and parameters added.

The data adapter includes a single `Fill()` method with a slightly different signature than the one used by `SqlDataAdapter`:

```
public virtual int Fill(MyDataSet.TableADataTable dataTable)
{
    this.Adapter.SelectCommand = this.CommandCollection[0];
    if ((this.ClearBeforeFill == true))
    {
        dataTable.Clear();
    }
    int returnValue = this.Adapter.Fill(dataTable);
    return returnValue;
}
```

To use this method, you pass an instance of the correctly typed table. That's simple enough to do from your code because if you instantiate the typed `DataSet` class, you have access to a table of the correct type through, for example, the `MyDataSet.TableA` property.

`Fill()` also optionally clears data in the table being filled, according to the value of the `TableATableAdapter.ClearBeforeFill` property.

Similarly, several versions of the `Update()` method are provided, one of which takes a parameter of type `MyDataSet.TableADataTable`.

As noted in Chapter 3, all of these types are defined as partial class definitions, meaning that you can extend the code used here in any way you like. In the following Try It Out, you modify the previous example to use a typed `DataSet` class called `FolktaleDBDataSet`, employing the default classes generated.

Using Typed Data Sets

1. Copy the project `C:\BegVC#Databases\Chapter06\Ex0605 - DataSets` to a new project, `C:\BegVC#Databases\Chapter06\Ex0606 - Typed DataSets`. (Copy and rename the directory, open it in Visual C# Express, and rename the solution and project.)

2. Open `app.config` and change the path to the local database file to include the new project directory rather than `Ex0605 - DataSets`.

3. If the Data Sources window is not visible, display it by selecting Data ➪ Show Data Sources.

4. From the Data Sources window, add a new data source connecting to the existing local database file `Folktale.mdf`. In the data source configuration wizard, select the tables `Classification` and `Story` and leave the data set name with its default value.

5. Modify `Program.cs` as follows:

```
static void Main(string[] args)
{
    // Initialize.
    Console.WriteLine("Initializing.");
    FolktaleDBDataSetTableAdapters.ClassificationTableAdapter classificationAdapter
        = new FolktaleDBDataSetTableAdapters.ClassificationTableAdapter();
    FolktaleDBDataSetTableAdapters.StoryTableAdapter atoryAdapter
        = new FolktaleDBDataSetTableAdapters.StoryTableAdapter();

    // Prepare DataSet
    FolktaleDBDataSet ds = new FolktaleDBDataSet();

    // try...catch for adapter execution.
    try
    {
        // Get schemas and data.
        classificationAdapter.Fill(ds.Classification);
        atoryAdapter.Fill(ds.Story);
    }
    catch (Exception ex)
    {
        // Process exception.
        Console.WriteLine(ex.Message);
    }

    // Navigate relation
    foreach (FolktaleDBDataSet.ClassificationRow classificationRow
        in ds.Classification)
    {
        Console.WriteLine("Classification: {0}", classificationRow.Classification);
        FolktaleDBDataSet.StoryRow[] childRows = classificationRow.GetStoryRows();
        if (childRows.Length > 0)
        {
            foreach (FolktaleDBDataSet.StoryRow storyRow in childRows)
```

```
            {
                    Console.WriteLine("Story: {0}", storyRow.Name);
            }
        }
        else
        {
            Console.WriteLine("No stories.");
        }
        Console.WriteLine();
    }

    // Close application.
    Console.WriteLine("Press ENTER to close.");
    Console.ReadLine();
}

static void conn_StateChange(object sender, StateChangeEventArgs e)
{
    Console.WriteLine("Connection state changed from {0} to {1}.",
        e.OriginalState, e.CurrentState);
}
```

6. Execute the application. The result should be exactly the same as in the previous Try It Out.

7. Close the application and Visual C# Express.

How It Works

Apart from the initial configuration of this class, modifications to the code were more about removing existing code than about adding new code. There was no longer a need to configure connections, commands, or command builders; obtain schema information for tables; or configure a relationship between tables. As you saw in the previous section, all of this information is already in place when you use a typed `DataSet`.

The first code modification obtains two typed data adapters:

```
FolktaleDBDataSetTableAdapters.ClassificationTableAdapter classificationAdapter
    = new FolktaleDBDataSetTableAdapters.ClassificationTableAdapter();
FolktaleDBDataSetTableAdapters.StoryTableAdapter atoryAdapter
    = new FolktaleDBDataSetTableAdapters.StoryTableAdapter();
```

Next, the new typed `DataSet` class is initialized:

```
FolktaleDBDataSet ds = new FolktaleDBDataSet();
```

This typed `DataSet` is then filled with data in a simplified exception-handling block with the new `Fill()` methods:

```
try
{
    // Get schemas and data.
    classificationAdapter.Fill(ds.Classification);
    atoryAdapter.Fill(ds.Story);
```

```
    }
    catch (Exception ex)
    {
        // Process exception.
        Console.WriteLine(ex.Message);
    }
```

Finally, the code used to navigate the relationship is re-written using the new, strongly typed methods and properties in the classes generated by the data source:

```
foreach (FolktaleDBDataSet.ClassificationRow classificationRow
    in ds.Classification)
{
    Console.WriteLine("Classification: {0}", classificationRow.Classification);
    FolktaleDBDataSet.StoryRow[] childRows = classificationRow.GetStoryRows();
    if (childRows.Length > 0)
    {
        foreach (FolktaleDBDataSet.StoryRow storyRow in childRows)
        {
            Console.WriteLine("Story: {0}", storyRow.Name);
        }
    }
    else
    {
        Console.WriteLine("No stories.");
    }
    Console.WriteLine();
}
```

As you can see, using code in this way is much easier. Perhaps the only disadvantage is that each data adapter opens and closes a connection independently. However, that's something that you can customize if you want — the data adapters have a `Connection` property that you can use to set your own connection to use, which you could open and close manually to prevent the extra processing. To be honest, however, unless you are using a lot of data adapters, this overhead will be minimal because connection pooling will be used, and the improved code simplicity is more than worth the cost in most applications.

Summary

In this chapter you have extended your knowledge of ADO.NET to the point where you can use it in your applications without data binding to controls. You have learned to perform basic operations such as making connections and executing commands as well as using data readers to read data, and data adapters and `DataSet` objects to obtain disconnected data for reading and modification. You've also seen how to use powerful typed `DataSet` classes to make your code simpler and save you a lot of work.

Specifically, you have looked at:

❑   How to make database connections using the `SqlConnection` class, and how to store connection strings in `web.config` and `app.config` configuration files. You learned why the state of the connection (open or closed) is important, and how connection pooling can improve application performance.

❑ How to create execute commands of various types using the `SqlCommand` class, how to execute SQL queries and stored procedures, and how to use parameters to pass values to commands.

❑ How to defend against SQL injection attacks, which required you to think more about exactly what SQL command you send to a database and how that command will be interpreted. You saw how parameters set by users should be checked before you use them, especially if you use user input to generate SQL queries manually.

❑ How to read schema, row, and other data using data readers. You used the `SqlDataReader` class to read data sequentially, and learned that this quick, efficient access is often all you need to use in your applications.

❑ How to configure data adapters. You saw how `SqlDataAdapter` objects require commands to interact with a database, although it is possible to generate those commands automatically using `SqlCommandBuilder`. You also saw how you can use data adapters to read schema data, and how to customize data adapter behavior by using table mappings.

❑ How to use `DataSet` objects to store and manipulate `DataTable` objects. You used data adapters to exchange data between a `DataSet` instance and a database, and you defined relationships between tables in a `DataSet`.

❑ How to create, use, and customize typed `DataSet` classes.

In the next chapter you learn to use additional database features such as views and procedures to streamline your database applications, and how to use custom code in place of `DataSet` objects to facilitate database access.

Exercises

1. When you dispose of a connection it is discarded and cannot be used again. True or false? Why?

2. In what ways could you obtain schema information from a database table?

3. Which of the following ADO.NET classes would you use to read and display data in the most efficient way possible?

    a. SqlCommand

    b. DataSet

    c. SqlDataReader

    d. SqlConnection

    e. SqlDataAdapter

    f. DataTable

4. If you had a table with a column called `ThisIsAnExtremelyLongAndSillyColumnName`, how would you put data from this column into a `DataTable` with a column name of `SensibleName` when using a data adapter?

Views and Stored Procedures

Now that you've covered the basics of database access, using both data binding and programmatic techniques, it's time to delve deeper into getting the best out of databases. So far all of the access you've performed has been using simple select statements taking data from single database tables. In many circumstances that's all you need, and you can do a lot with the data you obtain by manipulating it in your code. However, by changing the way you obtain data from a database, you can go a lot further and reduce the amount of work that you have to do in your applications to use the data you want.

Views and stored procedures help you do this. You can use views to work with data combined from multiple tables, instead of using data from those tables individually and then having to navigate relationships yourself. Of course you can use select statements with joins to combine data when you fetch it, but by defining views you can improve performance since the DBMS is capable of optimizing their behavior. There can also be security bonuses because you can restrict data access to views rather than underlying table data.

Stored procedures are another way in which you can improve the functionality of your applications. Like views, stored procedures can provide you with alternative ways of accessing data, but they also enable you to do a lot more and they assemble result sets in complex ways to suit your needs. Again, this is something that you could do using C# code in your application — but stored procedures can encapsulate algorithms and generally make your life easier. They can perform multiple tasks in one go, make use of conditional and looping logic, and, like views, their behavior is optimized by the DBMS.

To summarize, in this chapter you learn:

❑ How to create and use database views
❑ How to create and use stored procedures

Database Views

A view, as you learned in Chapter 1, is a stored SQL query that you can access as if it were a table. This means that you can use simpler syntax to access your data, as you will see in this section.

You were introduced to the subject of performing joins between tables when executing select statements in Chapter 1. For example, you can obtain data from `ProductCategory` and `Product` tables with a one-to-many relationship defined by a `ProductCategoryId` column as follows:

```
SELECT * FROM Product INNER JOIN ProductCategory
    ON Product.ProductCategoryId = ProductCategory.ProductCategoryId
```

This acquires column data from both tables, with a result set consisting of one row for each row in the `Product` table, with additional data from the `ProductCategory` table being included in each row. That means data may well be duplicated in the result set because data from rows in the `ProductCategory` table may be reproduced once or many times (or not at all). However, while the result includes this redundancy, it does mean that you have easy access to data from the parent table `ProductCategory` without having to navigate through relationships between these tables in your code.

Queries such as this would be an ideal use for a view, called something like `Product_with_Category`. You could read data from that view as if it were a table containing all the linked data, and that can simplify code in your application that displays this information.

Alternatively, you could use a view to list rows in the `ProductCategory` table along with the number of rows in the `Product` table that are child rows, like this:

```
SELECT COUNT(ProductId) AS ProductCount, ProductCategory.ProductCategoryId,
    ProductCategory.CategoryName
FROM ProductCategory INNER JOIN Product
ON ProductCategory.ProductCategoryId = Product.ProductCategoryId
GROUP BY ProductCategory.ProductCategoryId, ProductCategory.CategoryName
```

This uses the `COUNT()` aggregate function to count rows according to the grouping specification in the `GROUP BY` clause of the statement. A view containing this query might be called something like `Category_ProductCount`.

These queries can be executed directly from your code, but once a view has been defined, you can use simpler syntax. For example:

```
SELECT * FROM Category_ProductCount
```

You can also reference views from other views, making even more complicated result sets that are still just as easy to access from your code.

Another situation in which views can be useful is where you want to protect data in underlying tables. Because you can apply different access rules to tables and views, you could, for instance, allow users to access views but prevent them from directly accessing data in the tables that store the data used in the view.

In the following sections, you look at creating and using views, and examine considerations for updating data through views.

Creating Views

You can create views in two ways:

- ❏ Graphically, using Visual C# Express, SQL Server Management Studio Express, or another visual tool
- ❏ Using SQL script

You can even create views on-the-fly from applications if you need to. Many advanced users prefer to create views from script because it offers more flexibility. It also enables you to copy views from one location to another with ease — you can generate the script required to create a table at its source location, and then execute the script against a remote server. Assuming all the other database objects required by the view exist (tables, functions, stored procedures, and so on), the view will be recreated exactly as it was in its original location.

Let's first look at graphically creating views, and then move on to the script required to achieve the same ends.

Graphical View Creation

The graphical tool used to create views in Visual C# Express is the same as the one used in SQL Server Management Express, so in this section most techniques apply to both. About the only real difference is how you open the tool in the first place. In Visual C# Express you have two options, both of which become available when you are looking at a database connection in the Database Explorer window. With a project open, select an open database connection and you can add a view using the Data ➪ Add New ➪ View menu option. Alternatively, if you haven't got a project open or if you just prefer, you can expand the database, right-click the Views folder, and choose Add New View as shown in Figure 7-1.

Figure 7-1: Creating a view

In SQL Server Management Studio Express, you can create a view in an existing database by right-clicking the Views folder in a database and selecting New View, or though the Summary window that you can see when the Views folder is selected. (To add a new view in the Summary window, right-click in the Summary window and select New View.)

Whichever method you choose to add a view, the main display changes to the view creation tool. In actual fact, in Visual C# Express this tool is the general tool used to design queries, and as such is referred to as the Query Designer tool. Because views consist primarily of a query, however, the usage is the same. When the tool opens, you are immediately prompted with the Add Table dialog box, as shown in Figure 7-2.

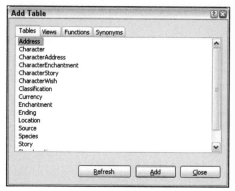

Figure 7-2: Add Tables dialog box

From this tool you can add references to tables, views, functions, and synonyms (synonyms are alternative names for other database objects), so the name of the dialog box is slightly misleading. Any database objects you select here are added to the FROM clause of the query that defines your new view. You don't have to configure your query this way, as you will see shortly, but it is a helpful starting point.

As you add objects from the Add Table dialog box, relationships between them are automatically detected from foreign key relationships and used to define the nature of the table joins to add to your query. For example, adding the Story, CharacterStory, and Character tables from the FolktaleDB database adds the following FROM clause:

```
FROM dbo.Story INNER JOIN
    dbo.CharacterStory ON dbo.Story.StoryId = dbo.CharacterStory.StoryId INNER JOIN
    dbo.Character ON dbo.CharacterStory.CharacterId = dbo.Character.CharacterId
```

That may not be the exact relationship you want to add, but it is easy enough to change, as you will see.

Once you have added database objects using this query (or not added them, as the case may be), they and any relationships between them are visible at the top of the View Editor display. The query generated for the view can be seen below it. Figure 7-3 shows a full display.

The View Editor is divided into the following four sections (from top to bottom):

❑ **Diagram pane:** Shows the tables, views, and other objects that return tabular data in your query. It also shows the relationships between those objects and the fields output by the query, as well as additional information such as fields used for grouping, and primary key fields in bold.

❑ **Criteria pane:** Shows the specification of your query in tabular form when you modify the query with output columns, grouping columns, filtering information, sorting information, and so on.

❑ **SQL pane:** Displays the text of the SQL query you have created.

❑ **Results pane:** Displays the results of your testing your query.

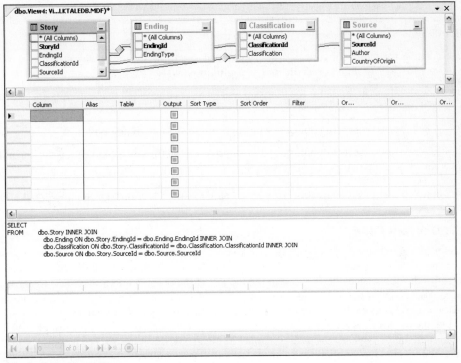

Figure 7-3: View Editor

The top three panes all enable you to edit the query. You can do so graphically in the diagram pane, schematically in the criteria pane, or using SQL in the SQL pane. Any modifications you make in any of these panes are automatically applied to all three panes — so, for example, if you add a table in the SQL pane, it appears in the diagram pane. There are some circumstances when the diagram pane does not display information from your query, such as when you use the UNION keyword to join two result sets together. In that case the diagram pane is unavailable.

In both Visual C# Express and SQL Server Management Studio Express an additional toolbar — the View Builder toolbar (see Figure 7-4) — appears when you are building a view. In a slightly modified form, that toolbar is also used when you add other types of SQL objects such as queries.

Figure 7-4: View Builder toolbar

Here's a brief description of the View Builder toolbar buttons' functions:

❑   Toggles diagram pane open/closed

❑   Toggles criteria pane open/closed

❑   Toggles SQL pane open/closed

❑   Toggles results pane open/closed

These first four buttons are shown active in Figure 7-4, as reflected in the display shown in Figure 7-3.

❑   Executes your query and shows you the results

❑   Verifies the syntax of your SQL query without executing it (useful when the query modifies data or takes a long time to execute; not as useful in views)

❑   Toggles the edit mode for the diagram and criteria panes such that columns are added as GROUP BY columns (more on this shortly)

❑   Click to add objects to your query through the Add Table dialog box

❑   Click to add objects to your query via a derived table for you to edit (more details on this shortly)

In the following sections, you explore each of the panes in the View Builder in more detail.

Using the Diagram Pane

The diagram pane displays the objects that make up your query. Each table is displayed as a window, which you can move around or resize as you see fit without affecting the query. This can help you to understand the query visually. The icon in the top left of the object's window reflects the type of object it is. (All of the objects in Figure 7-3 are tables, and they all have the same icon.) Hover the mouse pointer over any of the objects in the diagram pane and a ToolTip displays additional information — the name of a table, the name and data type of a column, or the specification of a join, for example. When you select an item in this pane, its properties display in the Properties window. For instance, you can see additional data type information for columns, although you can't edit that information through the display.

The most basic use of the diagram pane is to select which columns from the available objects will be included in your view. Each column has a checkbox to its left; select the checkbox for each column you want to include in the query, or check the box for * (all columns) to select all the columns in the object.

You can also add columns to the GROUP BY clause of your query in the diagram pane. To do so, click the Add Group By button in the View Builder toolbar, and then select columns the same way as before. To go back to adding columns in the normal way, click the Add Group By button again to unselect it. If you add a column as a GROUP BY column, an icon appears to the right of the column name; the icon looks the same as the Add Group By button in the toolbar.

Add an ORDER BY clause to a query by right-clicking a column and selecting either Sort Ascending or Sort Descending. You can clear sort specifications for columns by right-clicking and selecting the appropriate option. You can also clear filter expressions for columns through the right-click menu, although you cannot add filter expressions using the diagram pane. If a sort or filter specification is used for a column, an icon is displayed to the right of the column name. It is possible, depending on your query, for a single column to have icons for sort, filter, and group-by specifications.

You can also modify the joins between objects in the diagram pane, although again you cannot add new joins through this pane. Right-click a relationship to delete it; change it to a right, left, or full outer join by selecting combinations of the Select All Rows From options; and view and edit the join using the Join Condition And Type property. This property also has an editor associated with it, which you can open via the Properties window. The Join dialog box is shown in Figure 7-5.

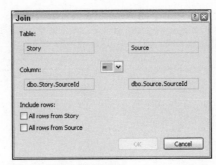

Figure 7-5: Join dialog

The Join dialog box also enables you to select the type of join by including all rows from one or both objects in the join, and you can change the operator used in the join if you want.

Additionally, you can use the diagram pane to add a *derived table*. A derived table is an intermediate, dynamic table that you can use in your query. In effect, using a derived table is like having a view that references another view, but with the referenced view being defined as part of the referencing view. This additional step enables more complex result processing, although it can make things more confusing. To add a derived table, use the toolbar icon or right-click in the design pane and select Add New Derived Table. Either way, once you have added a derived table you cannot edit it further using the design pane, although you can see and select its columns once they are defined. You can define derived tables only in the SQL pane.

In some circumstances you may be able to design queries completely using the diagram pane. More often than not, however, you need to use one of the other panes to complete your query.

Using the Criteria Pane

Columns and other items that you add to your query appear in the criteria pane. You can configure your query by entering information in this pane. Specifically, the rows in the criteria pane display the following information:

❑ Columns selected as output columns from the tables and other objects in the query

❑ Calculated column specifications, including function calls and aggregate functions

❑ Aliases for selected columns, including names for calculated columns

❑ Query sorting specifications

❑ Query filter specifications

❑ Columns used to group data

When designing other types of queries in the criteria pane, you can also set other information here, such as new values used in insert and update queries.

The layout of the criteria pane consists of a number of rows with columns as follows:

❑ **Column:** Enter the name of a column from a table or other object in the query, or enter a column specification. If you are entering the name of an existing column, you can use a drop-down selector in this column, as shown in Figure 7-6. You can choose all the columns in a table by selecting * for that table, for example dbo.Story.*. (The dbo part of this name refers to the schema for the table as defined in the database.)

Column	Alias	Table	Output	Sort Type	Sort Order	Filter	Or...
			▣				
dbo.Story.*			▣				
dbo.Story.StoryId			▣				
dbo.Story.EndingId			▣				
dbo.Story.ClassificationId			▣				
dbo.Story.SourceId			▣				
dbo.Story.Name			▣				
dbo.Story.Summary			▣				
dbo.Classification.*			▣				

Figure 7-6: Column selection

❑ **Alias:** Type the alias to be used for a column, or the name to use for a calculated column. If multiple columns are specified (if * is used, for example), this column is unavailable.

❑ **Table:** Specifies the table from which the column is to be taken, if appropriate. For some columns, such as where columns in two or more tables in the query have the same name, you can use a drop-down to change the table that the column is taken from. This setting is unavailable for calculated columns.

❑ **Output:** Use the checkbox to specify whether the column will be output as part of the query result. It is possible to sort or filter by a column without having it output.

❑ **Sort Type:** If the column is part of the sorting specification for your query, specify whether it is sorted in Ascending or Descending order. You can select the type by using a drop-down, which also includes the entry Unsorted to clear the column value.

❑ **Sort Order:** Where multiple columns in the query are used to sort the results, set the order in which sorting is applied by entering numbers in this column. The lower the number, the greater the priority given to sorting by the specified column. For example, you might order people's names by last name, then first names, so you would have a lower number for the priority of sorting for the last name column.

❑ **Filter** and **Or**: If the data column is used to filter data (that is, used in a WHERE or HAVING clause), you can set the criteria here. Where multiple filter expressions exist for a single column, you can use multiple rows in the criteria pane to combine them using the AND operator, or use the Or columns to include multiple criteria combined using OR. You can add additional Or columns by pressing the Tab key in the rightmost one.

The order in which data columns and other output data appears in the criteria pane will match the order that columns are returned in the query result, which in the case of views means the order of columns in the view. You can reorder columns in the criteria view by dragging the row for the data column to the position you require using the selection column to the left of the Column column. Of course, you can reorder columns in the SQL pane if you prefer — the reordering is automatically reflected in the criteria pane if you do so.

If the query you are designing includes a grouping specification, the behavior of the criteria pane alters slightly. First, the drop-down in the Column column enables you to select COUNT(*) and COUNT_BIG(*) aggregate functions directly — COUNT_BIG(*) works the same way as COUNT(*) but returns a different data type (a bigint instead of an int). An additional column called Group By appears in the criteria pane. You use it to specify how the column is handled in the query — either it is part of the grouping specification or part of an aggregate function. You can select values for this column from a drop-down, which includes entries for grouping, various aggregate functions, user-defined aggregate functions, and WHERE clause filtering. To include a HAVING clause, for example, you would set this column to Group By and enter the filter expression in the Filter column.

At times, particularly where column grouping is specified, the same column in the query may be displayed in multiple rows of the criteria pane. This happens when, for instance, a column is used both to group the query and also in the WHERE clause of a query. Although that may appear a little confusing at first, it makes perfect sense.

Using the SQL Pane

The final way to edit a SQL query is to type it directly into the SQL pane. In some circumstances, such as when UNION is used to merge the results of multiple queries, or where derived tables are used, this is your only option — although once you have created your query, you may be able to tweak it using the diagram and criteria panes. Using the SQL pane is a more advanced practice, but you may well find that, once you are more accustomed to SQL syntax, you use it as much as or more than the other panes.

In particular, the SQL pane is a great place for cutting and pasting queries from other sources. Perhaps you have experimented with a query using alternative tools, or someone has e-mailed you a SQL query. Rather than having to recreate that query using the graphical tools, you can simply paste it into this pane.

The View Builder tool often modifies any queries you enter here, including adding full column specifications with schema and table names where appropriate, or reformatting your SQL code in other ways. In most cases, the result makes your SQL code more readable and removes any possible ambiguity, although it is always worth checking the results to ensure that the rewriting results in the query you were after and has not changed its meaning. In those rare circumstances where the View Builder changes your query beyond what was expected, you still have the option to add views using script, so you won't ever be completely defeated by this behavior.

When using the SQL pane (or the criteria pane), the Properties window displays general properties for your query. Use the properties to add a description to your query, specify that the DISTINCT keyword should be used, add OLAP-specific extensions to grouping queries, bind the view to your schema (essential for indexing), and add TOP clause information. You can do all of this manually, of course, but it's nice to have this additional functionality at your disposal when you require it. For other types of queries, you can use these properties to provide an update specification.

Using the Results Pane

The last part of the View Builder tool is the results pane. To test the query used in your view, click the Execute Query button in the toolbar, choose the Query Designer ➪ Execute SQL menu item, or press Ctrl+R. The query result is shown in this pane, in tabular form. If you execute a query and then edit the query, an icon appears in the top left of the results pane to indicate that the query results are out of date and that you have to execute the query again to update them.

Some queries (although not those used for views) may return multiple result sets. In those cases, the controls at the bottom of the results pane enable you to navigate between result sets.

There isn't really much more to say about this pane. As with other data displays, you can resize columns to see data and scroll through them if they don't fit in the pane.

Saving Your View

Once you have used the View Builder tool to create a query that you want to use in a view, the final step is to save it to the database, where it is stored and available for you to use from your applications. Simply click the Save icon in the toolbar, use the File menu, or press Ctrl+S. When you first save the view, you are prompted for a name for the view and it is saved to the database under that name.

Modifying Views

You can also use the View Builder tool to edit existing views. To do so, navigate to the view in the Database Explorer window, and double-click it, or right-click and select Open View Definition. The View Builder displays exactly as before, but with the panes already full with the information specifying the view. You can then proceed to modify the view as appropriate.

Script View Creation

Before moving on to using a view in an application, it is worth looking at what happens under the hood. When you use the View Builder in Visual C# Express or in SQL Server Management Studio Express, what actually happens is the execution of a SQL statement that creates the view — or that modifies an existing view.

You can, if you prefer, skip the design step and simply do this yourself — create and execute a SQL script that creates or modifies a view. It's actually a surprisingly simple thing to do because most of the SQL required consists of the SQL query that defines the view. All that remains is to wrap the view in the SQL necessary to say that you are creating or modifying a view. To create a view, that means using the CREATE VIEW keywords as follows:

```
CREATE VIEW <view name>
AS
<view specification>
```

And to modify a view:

```
ALTER VIEW <view name>
AS
<view specification>
```

For completeness, you can also delete a view using the DROP keyword:

```
DROP VIEW <view name>
```

For example, you could define a view that includes data from the Story table in FolktaleDB combined with parent data from the Classification, Ending, and Source tables as follows:

```
CREATE VIEW [dbo].[StoryInfo]
AS
SELECT     dbo.Story.StoryId, dbo.Story.Name, dbo.Story.Summary,
           dbo.Classification.Classification, dbo.Ending.EndingType,
```

```
             dbo.Source.CountryOfOrigin
FROM         dbo.Story
INNER JOIN dbo.Classification
    ON dbo.Story.ClassificationId = dbo.Classification.ClassificationId
INNER JOIN dbo.Ending
    ON dbo.Story.EndingId = dbo.Ending.EndingId
INNER JOIN dbo.Source
    ON dbo.Story.SourceId = dbo.Source.SourceId
```

You can execute this script through any method that you can use to execute queries — including the Query Designer in Visual C# Express and SQL Server Management Studio Express, and through code by using a SqlCommand object.

Attempting to create a view using a name that already exists in the database creates an error, as does attempting to alter or delete a view that doesn't exist. You can test whether a view exists in the database already — either visually by examining the database yourself, or programmatically by searching for information about the view in the sys.views table. This table, which is a system view that is included in all databases maintained by SQL Server and SQL Server Express, includes information about each view you define. Each view is assigned an ID value that is stored in a column in the sys.views table called object_id. You can get the ID of a view from its name using the OBJECT_ID() function: for example, OBJECT_ID('[dbo].[StoryInfo]').

Knowing this, it is common to use the EXISTS() function to look for a row in the sys.views table to test for the existence of a view. This function returns a Boolean value, and might be used as follows:

```
IF EXISTS(SELECT * FROM sys.views WHERE object_id = OBJECT_ID('[dbo].[StoryInfo]'))
DROP VIEW [dbo].[StoryInfo]
```

Here, Boolean logic is used in a SQL statement to test for the existence of the [dbo].[StoryInfo] view. If EXISTS() returns true, the view exists, and the DROP VIEW statement is executed to delete the view, avoiding errors caused by nonexistent views.

As you no doubt suspect, there are more techniques that you can use when creating and editing views, many of which are only possible when creating views directly from SQL code as described here. There are more keywords and there is additional syntax, both of which you can add to introduce additional functionality. These are advanced techniques, however, and won't be covered in this book.

Now it's time for an example in which you create and use a view in a Windows application.

Try It Out   Using Views

1. Open Visual C# Express and create a new Windows application called Ex0701 - Using Views. Save the project in the C:\BegVC#Databases\Chapter07 directory, with the Create Directory For Solution option unchecked.

2. Add the FolktaleDB.mdf database to your project as a local database file. If prompted by the Data Source Configuration Wizard, click Cancel.

3. In the Database Explorer window, expand the database and right-click on Views. Click Add New View.

4. Add the `Story`, `Classification`, `Ending`, and `Source` tables to the view (in that order) using the Add Table dialog box, and then click Close.

5. In the diagram pane of the View Builder, select the following columns for the view in order:

    a. `StoryId`, `Name`, and `Summary` from the `Story` table

    b. `EndingType` from the `Ending` table

    c. `Classification` from the `Classification` table

    d. `Author` and `CountryOfOrigin` from the `Source` table

6. Sort the view by the value of the `Name` column, in ascending order. (Use the drop-down in the `Sort Type` column.)

7. Verify that the SQL query contains the following query (edit it if necessary):

```
SELECT TOP (100) PERCENT dbo.Story.StoryId, dbo.Story.Name,
dbo.Story.Summary,
            dbo.Ending.EndingType, dbo.Classification.Classification,
            dbo.Source.Author, dbo.Source.CountryOfOrigin
FROM        dbo.Story
INNER JOIN dbo.Classification
    ON dbo.Story.ClassificationId = dbo.Classification.ClassificationId
INNER JOIN dbo.Ending
    ON dbo.Story.EndingId = dbo.Ending.EndingId
INNER JOIN dbo.Source
    ON dbo.Story.SourceId = dbo.Source.SourceId
ORDER BY dbo.Story.Name
```

8. Execute the query and check that there are no syntax errors and that results are returned.

9. Save the view with the name `StoryInfo`.

10. Close the View Designer window.

11. Set the `Text` property of `Form1` to `Story Info`.

12. Add a new data source to the project called `FolktaleDBDataSet`, retrieving all columns from the `StoryInfo` view.

13. Using the Data Sources window, add a details view of the `FolktaleDBDataSet` data source, including all columns except `StoryId`. Make the `TextBox` for `Summary` a multi-line `TextBox` with a vertical scrollbar, and arrange the controls as shown in Figure 7-7.

To recap, to add a details view, use the drop-down for the `StoryInfo` view in the Data Sources window to set the type of control to add for the view to Details, and then expand the view and use the drop-down for `StoryId` to set the control to add for `StoryId` to None. Finally, drag the StoryInfo view to the form.

14. Set the `Anchor` property for all the `TextBox` controls except the one for `Summary` to Top, Left, Right. Set the `Anchor` property for the `Summary` `TextBox` to Top, Left, Right, Bottom.

15. Run the applications and verify that you can view rows from the `Story` table with data included from the `Classification`, `Ending`, and `Source` tables.

16. Close the application and Visual C# Express.

Figure 7-7: Form layout

How It Works

In this example you created a simple viewing application for data in the `FolktaleDB` database. However, rather than including several tables and having to configure data binding using assorted master/detail views, you created a single view that gets exactly the data you need in the form that you need it.

The view uses simple `INNER JOIN` table joins of the form you were introduced to in Chapter 2 and have seen throughout this chapter.

> For obscure reasons known only to the designers of SQL Server, views can sort data only if the view query includes a `TOP` clause. You can, however, simply include the (seemingly redundant) `TOP` clause `TOP (100) PERCENT`, which is exactly what the View Builder adds for you when you include a sorting specification as you did in this example.

Once the data source is created from the view, the data-binding behavior is exactly the same as it is for binding to simple table data. Because the view includes all the information you need, it isn't necessary to select data from multiple tables or perform any complicated tricks when designing the form.

Notice that the Save Data icon is unavailable while the application is running. You can edit data in the application, but there's no way to save your changes. In fact, saving data from modifications to this view would be tricky, for reasons such as the following:

❑　You would need to generate your own primary keys (something you've seen how to do, but still not something that's trivial).

❑　If modifications are made to the linked columns (`EndingType`, `Classification`, `Author`, and `CountryOfOrigin`) changing them to other linked values, you need to look up the IDs for those columns and change them in the underlying `Story` table.

❑　If a similar modification is made but the changed value doesn't exist in a parent table, you have to decide whether to change the value of the parent table (which affects all child records) or add a new, alternative row in the parent table.

❑　If you want to add new rows to parent tables, you need to generate ID values, etc. — and you must be careful of the order in which you update the database.

All in all, it is not an easy thing to do — and can lead to more difficulty than you'd expect. It may even be more work than if you simply use the tables without resorting to views.

Using a view this way is great for viewing data, but when it comes to updating data, views are seldom ideal. The same applies to views that summarize data using grouping and aggregate functions — these are great for obtaining data in novel ways and saving you work in your application code, but not for updating data.

This isn't to say that it is impossible to update data through a view, however, as you see in the next section.

Updating Data Through Views

To modify data in a view, the view must meet certain requirements. If those conditions are satisfied, modifications to the data in the view result in modifications to the underlying data tables. These rules are:

❑ The view cannot contain a row grouping specification or aggregate functions.

❑ The view cannot include the DISTINCT keyword.

❑ The view cannot be a union of multiple result sets.

❑ If the view contains multiple tables, only data from one table at a time can be updated in a single operation.

❑ Restrictions on modifications to underlying data tables apply — a read-only column in a base table cannot be modified through a view, for example.

There are ways round some of these, although they involve advanced techniques such as using triggers to update data in multiple tables simultaneously, and so won't be covered here.

Another concern is where views provide a filtered view of data in an underlying table (or tables). Here, modifying or adding rows could result in the new or modified row not being visible in the view. It is possible to prevent this by setting a WITH CHECK OPTION clause when creating a view manually in View Builder. With that option, updates that would result in a new or modified row being hidden from the view are forbidden, and result in errors.

When you use data-binding techniques in Visual C# Express and use a view, as you did in the previous example, it is unfortunately impossible to get modification commands to be generated for you automatically. However, it is a relatively simple process to create your own commands, as you will see in the following Try It Out.

Try It Out   Updating Data Using Views

1. Copy the solution directory for the previous Try It Out, C:\BegVC#Databases\Chapter07\ Ex0701 - Using Views, to a new directory, C:\BegVC#Databases\Chapter07\Ex0702 - Updating Views. Open the copied solution file and rename the solution and project.

2. Open the DataSet Designer for the `FolktaleDBDataSet` typed `DataSet` class.

3. Examine the properties of the `StoryInfoTableAdapter` data adapter, and verify that no commands exist to insert, delete, or update rows.

4. In the Properties window, select `(New)` for the `UpdateCommand` property, expand this property and click . . . in the `CommandText` sub-property.

5. Cancel the Add Table dialog box in the Query Builder window, and add the following SQL command text:

```
UPDATE StoryInfo
SET    Name = @Name, Summary = @Summary
WHERE  StoryId = @StoryId
```

6. Add a SQL command to the `DeleteCommand` property in the same way, with the following SQL text:

```
DELETE FROM Story
WHERE  StoryId = @StoryId
```

7. In `Form1`, right-click the Save Data button in the binding navigator and change its status to Enabled. Double-click the Save Data button to add an event handler, and add the following code:

```
private void storyInfoBindingNavigatorSaveItem_Click(object sender, EventArgs e)
{
    this.storyInfoTableAdapter.Update(this.folktaleDBDataSet.StoryInfo);
}
```

8. In the Solution Explorer window, change the Copy to Output Directory property for `FolktaleDB.mdf` to Copy If Newer.

9. Run the application, and modify a record, change the view to a different record, and then click the Save Data button.

10. Close the application, and then run it again to verify that changes made to the `Name` and `Summary` fields have been applied but that other changes have been discarded.

11. Delete a record, and then save the data. Either the record will be deleted or, more likely, the following error should occur:

```
The DELETE statement conflicted with the REFERENCE constraint
"FK_CharacterStory_Story". The conflict occurred in database
"C:\BEGVC#DATABASES\CHAPTER07\EX0702 - UPDATING VIEWS\BIN\DEBUG\FOLKTALEDB.MDF",
table "dbo.CharacterStory", column 'StoryId'.
The statement has been terminated.
```

This error occurs because the records in the Story *table have a one-to-many relationship with records in the* CharacterStory *table. As you have seen earlier in the book, the database enforces these relationships so that it is impossible to delete a row from the* Story *table if it is referenced by rows in the* CharacterStory *table. To delete the* Story *row, it's necessary to identify the rows in the* CharacterStory *table that reference the* Story *row and delete those first. Alternatively, you could alter the database such that the child rows are deleted when the parent row is deleted. However, that's not done in this example.*

12. Close the application and Visual C# Express.

How It Works

This exercise modifies the earlier example application to allow data to be modified and updated through the view you created for that application. You modified the data adapter in the typed `DataSet` class defined by the data source, adding queries to update and delete data.

The update query includes three parameters, `@Name` and `@Summary`, which update data, and `@StoryId`, which identifies the row to update. The `StoryInfo` view can be updated directly using this query because only one of the tables in the view is updated. Unfortunately, as evidenced by the running application, only the `Name` and `Summary` fields are updateable — the fields in the joined tables that are included in the view are, for the purposes of this example, read-only. You could easily reflect this in the presentation of the application by disabling the relevant `TextBox` fields on the form.

For the delete query, you delete rows directly in the `Story` table, using the `StoryId` value taken from the view (because it is one of the fields included in the view). You cannot delete rows in the `StoryInfo` table because it would be unclear exactly what data you want to delete. It's unlikely that you would want to delete parent table rows through this application, so the command works well.

In both cases, it is interesting to note that adding parameters to the queries results in the automatic creation of parameters for the queries, and the automatic binding of them to the appropriate fields. So, while there is a small amount of work involved when updating through views this way, Visual C# Express still helps you out.

In addition to making the query changes, you also enabled data updating though the application and added an event handler to perform updates. However, that's a consequence of the controls already having been created from the data source, rather than something that is necessary every time you make a view updateable this way. If you were to start from scratch and add these extra queries before designing the form and binding data to controls, you would find that this step is unnecessary. That's because the additional queries would be detected and used at the time the controls are created and bound.

You have probably noted the absence of an insert command for adding rows to this view. While such an operation is possible, it involves more coding than the other modifications — such as a dialog box appearing to prompt for foreign keys, or a method to choose from parent rows in drop-down controls on the form rather than using text boxes. It also involves additional coding to obtain existing values in the parent tables, and to add the required foreign key references in a new row in the `Story` table. You might want to take on this challenge yourself as an exercise; there's certainly nothing in it that you shouldn't be able to do using the techniques you've already learned in this book. Because you wouldn't learn anything new, however, that project isn't covered in any detail here.

Stored Procedures

Stored procedures, as you learned in Chapter 1, are blocks of SQL code that can be executed in one go, much like methods are executed in C# objects. Stored procedures are a lot like views in many ways. You can use then to wrap a portion of SQL script in the same way, and the return value of a stored procedure can be a tabular result set just like a view. However, additional functionality is available in stored procedures above and beyond what is to be had in views.

Perhaps the most important difference between views and stored procedures is that stored procedures can use parameters. You can pass parameters to stored procedures to customize the results. For instance, you can create a stored procedure that returns a filtered result set, with a parameter defining the filter. In practice, this involves using the parameter value in the WHERE clause of a SQL query; here's an example:

```
SELECT * FROM Story WHERE ClassificationId = @ClassificationId
```

Here, the parameter @ClassificationId is used to filter results from the Story table. Alternatively, you could use a more complicated query with joins, and filter by a value in the Classification table rather than a GUID-valued ID for a more human-readable mode of operation:

```
SELECT Story.* FROM Story INNER JOIN Classification
ON Story.ClassificationId = Classification.ClassificationId
WHERE Classification = @Classification
```

You could, of course, create these queries yourself, replacing the parameter value with the value you want programmatically. The advantage of using a stored procedure here is threefold:

❑   The syntax required to use the stored procedure is simpler than using the query directly.

❑   The DBMS optimizes the behavior of stored procedures, and the speed of operation is likely to be faster (although this difference may be practically insignificant).

❑   By using a stored procedure, the actual processing is encapsulated in the database, meaning that if you were to change the database structure, you could change the stored procedure at the same time and not have to recompile your code to account for those changes — assuming the changes weren't that major.

This is only the beginning, however. Stored procedures can use more than one parameter, and parameters can be input or output parameters — so the return value of a stored procedure may not be all the data that is returned by the stored procedure. It might in fact return additional information at the same time. For example, in the preceding filtered query example you could include an additional output parameter that returns the percentage of the total rows in the Story table that the returned rowset represents. Now, doing this isn't something that you can do in a single operation. You'd have to first get the total count of rows in the Classification table, then count the rows in the filtered rowset, then use these values to calculate a percentage, and finally return this result as an output parameter. To perform such operations, the syntax that you can use inside a stored procedure is far more flexible than that for views. You can use variables, branching, Boolean logic, cursors to read results of inner query operations and process them sequentially, and more. In fact, in many respects programming a stored procedure is more akin to programming in a language such as C# than typical database querying. Also, with the latest version of SQL Server (and SQL Server Express) it is even possible to write stored procedures in C# — a subject you look at in the last chapter of this book.

Stored procedures can do more than simply return data, tabular or otherwise. You can use them to modify database data — if you want, you can even completely replace update, insert, and delete operations in your application code with stored procedure calls (and there is a school of thought that says this is a good idea). Recall from earlier chapters how, when data binding to controls, you can select stored procedures for data retrieval and modification. Again, this is a technique that you can use to encapsulate database modification. The result set you work on through the stored procedures you have created might not even refer to a single table. It might involve joined data much like the views you've seen earlier in this chapter. However, because the operation of data modification operations is completely controlled by you, many of the limitations of data modification through views are instantly resolved — although you may still face awkward decisions when coding the stored procedures, such as which tables to update in what circumstances, and whether to allow rows to be added to multiple tables simultaneously.

In this section, you look at creating and using stored procedures, and then explore additional programming structures (such as looping and branching) that you can use in them.

Creating Stored Procedures

One consequence of the additional flexibility of stored procedures is that there is no graphical designer associated with creating them in Visual C# Express or SQL Server Management Studio Express. You must use script to create them. Doing so is akin to creating views by script, although instead of using CREATE VIEW, you use CREATE PROCEDURE. Similarly you can use ALTER PROCEDURE to modify an existing stored procedure and DROP PROCEDURE to delete a stored procedure.

When you create stored procedures using Visual C# Express or SQL Server Management Studio Express, some template code is created for you. Let's examine those templates, and then look at the structure of stored procedure creation scripts in more detail.

Stored Procedure Creation Templates

As with views, you can create stored procedures through the user interface of Visual C# Express by right-clicking the Stored Procedures folder inside a database and selecting Add New Stored Procedure. You can do the same in SQL Server Management Studio Express, although you will find the Stored Procedures folder nested inside a folder called Programmability inside the database, as shown in Figure 7-8.

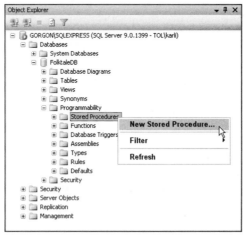

Figure 7-8: Adding a stored procedure in SQL Server Management Studio Express

In both cases, you are provided with a template script to use as a starting point from which to design your stored procedure. Here's the template in Visual C# Express:

```
CREATE PROCEDURE dbo.StoredProcedure1
    /*
    (
    @parameter1 int = 5,
    @parameter2 datatype OUTPUT
    )
    */
AS
    /* SET NOCOUNT ON */
    RETURN
```

The first line defines the name of the stored procedure, dbo.StoredProcedure1. Your first step in creating a stored procedure is likely to be changing this name to one that suits you. Then, there are four distinct regions:

❑   The parameter specification for the stored procedure (commented out in this case)

❑   The AS keyword signifying the end of the parameter specification — SQL code after it determines the operation of the stored procedure

❑   The body of the stored procedure, which in this template consists of a single, commented out, command

❑   The RETURN keyword, which terminates the stored procedure (and, as you will see shortly, can be used to provide simple return values)

You'll see what the code in these sections means shortly.

The template in SQL Server Management Studio Express is different, and at first glance seems far more daunting:

```
-- ==================================================
-- Template generated from Template Explorer using:
-- Create Procedure (New Menu).SQL
--
-- Use the Specify Values for Template Parameters
-- command (Ctrl-Shift-M) to fill in the parameter
-- values below.
--
-- This block of comments will not be included in
-- the definition of the procedure.
-- ==================================================
SET ANSI_NULLS ON
GO
SET QUOTED_IDENTIFIER ON
GO
-- ==================================================
-- Author:      <Author,,Name>
-- Create date: <Create Date,,>
-- Description: <Description,,>
-- ==================================================
```

```
CREATE PROCEDURE <Procedure_Name, sysname, ProcedureName>
    -- Add the parameters for the stored procedure here
    <@Param1, sysname, @p1> <Datatype_For_Param1, , int> =
        <Default_Value_For_Param1, , 0>,
    <@Param2, sysname, @p2> <Datatype_For_Param2, , int> =
        <Default_Value_For_Param2, , 0>
AS
BEGIN
    -- SET NOCOUNT ON added to prevent extra result sets from
    -- interfering with SELECT statements.
    SET NOCOUNT ON;

    -- Insert statements for procedure here
    SELECT <@Param1, sysname, @p1>, <@Param2, sysname, @p2>
END
GO
```

In fact, much of it is placeholder code for template parameters, as described in the comment at the beginning of the code. Follow the instruction there and press Ctrl+Shift+M to see the dialog box shown in Figure 7-9.

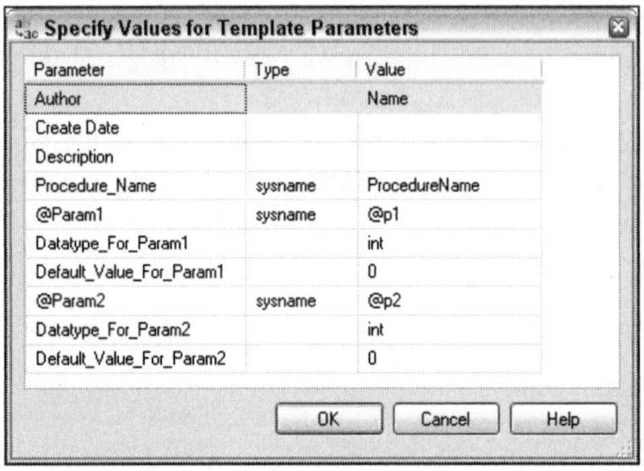

Figure 7-9: Specifying template parameters for a stored procedure

Each row in the dialog box specifies values to use in one of the placeholders in the stored procedure template, each of which consists of three comma-separated values enclosed in angle brackets. The first three parameters, Author, Create Date, and Description, are used to fill in the comments in the stored procedure. These are optional by definition, although it is good practice to add comments to your stored procedures, especially if you are part of a large development team.

The next parameter, ProcedureName, is the name of the stored procedure. The type, sysname, is simply the internal data type that SQL Server uses to store names of stored procedures, tables, variables, and so on, and isn't something that you should worry about or change.

The remaining template parameters enable you to stipulate two parameters for your stored procedure, by specifying the name, data type, and default value for each one. Although two parameters may be enough, it's likely you will be editing the script manually to add more.

Click OK with the default values shown in Figure 7-9, and the script changes as follows:

```
-- =============================================
-- Author:        Name
-- Create date:
-- Description:
-- =============================================
CREATE PROCEDURE ProcedureName
    -- Add the parameters for the stored procedure here
    @p1 int = 0,
    @p2 int = 0
AS
BEGIN
    -- SET NOCOUNT ON added to prevent extra result sets from
    -- interfering with SELECT statements.
    SET NOCOUNT ON;

    -- Insert statements for procedure here
    SELECT @p1, @p2
END
GO
```

And from this point you can continue to modify the script and create your stored procedure. The code is similar to that used in the template supplied by Visual C# Express, although less is commented out. One interesting note is the use of BEGIN and END keywords surrounding the body of the stored procedure. These keywords are used frequently in stored procedure design. They are analogous to the curly braces used in C# code to denote blocks of code, and are used in the same way as you will see later in this chapter. You can, for example, use them to mark out sections of code to be executed conditionally in IF code blocks.

One statement supplied by both the templates is SET NOCOUNT ON. This option is commonly used in stored procedures because most SQL statements that you execute return a count of the rows that have been affected. Stored procedures might execute a number of SQL statements, so returning this data can interfere with the data that the procedure is intended to return. Unless you actually want that information, it is good practice to include the command in your stored procedures, which is why both templates include it.

The following sections explore each of the sections of code in a stored procedure definition.

Stored Procedure Name

The first part of the stored procedure definition is the name of the stored procedure. You may notice a difference in the two templates shown in the previous section — the one used in Visual C# Express includes the owning schema of the stored procedure: dbo. (For small applications, or applications that aren't used by many users, you may well have only one owner for all database objects, typically dbo, which is shorthand SQL Server parlance for "database owner.") In general, this is something that you should include; having specific owners for SQL Server objects enables you to apply security settings via each owner.

You can, if you want, include a semicolon and a number for your stored procedure after the name. For example:

```
CREATE PROCEDURE dbo.ProcedureName;1
```

You can create multiple stored procedures with the same name but using different numbers. Those procedures are then considered to be grouped together, and can be deleted in one go with a single command:

```
DROP PROCEDURE dbo.ProcedureName
```

Additionally, the PROCEDURE keyword can be shortened to PROC if you want — the two words are interchangeable in SQL syntax. However, for clarity I use the full version, PROCEDURE, in this book.

Parameter Specification

The first part of a stored procedure definition is the parameter specification. It's an optional section because you can have stored procedures that don't include parameters. If you include parameters you can, again optionally, enclose them in parentheses. The Visual C# Express template includes the parentheses, but the SQL Management Studio Express template doesn't. Using parentheses is a matter of preference — personally, I tend to include them because they look more like C# methods that way, but it's entirely up to you whether you use them.

Each parameter of a stored procedure is specified in the following way:

```
<Parameter Name> <Parameter Data Type>
```

Parameter names must start with the @ symbol. The parameter data type is a SQL Server data type, and may optionally include additional specification. For example, for string parameters you should specify the maximum length of the string, such as varchar(200), but you wouldn't need anything else for an int. You can specify multiple parameters for a stored procedure in a comma-separated list.

You can also specify the following extra information:

❑ For cursor return types (see later in the chapter), you must use the VARYING keyword. It signifies that the return type is a non-scalar value, and can therefore return multiple values. This means that you can return result sets via a parameter.

Stored procedures that return cursors can't be used via ADO.NET, only from other SQL script.

❑ You can make parameters optional by specifying a default value — which works even if the default value is NULL. Just use the = operator followed by the value you want to specify.

❑ To denote an output parameter, use the OUTPUT keyword.

Each of the options you use must be included in the order in which it appears in this list. You cannot, for instance, use OUTPUT before VARYING.

For example, the following parameter specification is for three parameters: an integer value called @MyIdentifier that has a default value of −1; a string search pattern called @MySearch (presumably used in a LIKE filter) with a default value of '%'; and an output parameter called @ExtendedInfo that returns a result set via a cursor.

```
(
    @MyIdentifier int = -1,
    @MySearch varchar(50) = '%',
    @ExtendedInfo CURSOR VARYING OUTPUT
)
```

You can also apply a few advanced options at the end of the parameter specification for a stored procedure. They determine how the stored procedure is executed. Although they aren't covered here, you can check the MSDN documentation for further details.

> *You can specify up to 2,100 parameters for a stored procedure. However, I've yet to hear of a stored procedure that requires anything close to that number. If you ever find this limit too low, you ought to reconsider the design of your stored procedure.*

Indicate the end of the completed parameter specification with the AS keyword.

Stored Procedure Body

Following the AS keyword, you define the body of the stored procedure. This region of the stored procedure definition is where you really have to put the work in; it is the SQL code here that provides the implementation of the stored procedure. Later sections of this chapter explain how to add more complicated operations such as looping and branching. Here you will explore the basics.

The first thing to note is the use of parameters in the stored procedure body. You can insert these as you please throughout the SQL statements you use. For example, suppose you pass a string variable to a stored procedure called @MySearch (as in the example in the previous section), used to filter results:

```
SELECT * FROM MyTable WHERE MySearchableField LIKE @MySearch
```

This uses the value of @MySearch in a text search comparison, including wildcard values and so on.

Output parameter values must be set before terminating the stored procedure, or they will have a NULL value. To do so, use the SET keyword as follows:

```
SET <parameter name> = <value>
```

For example:

```
SET @MyReturnedString = 'Everything is hunky-dory.'
```

You can also use this technique to set the values of local variables, which you might use for intermediate storage as part of the execution of your stored procedure. To use a local variable you must first declare it using the DECLARE keyword and specifying its name and data type; for example:

```
DECLARE @MyTempInt int
```

Declaring and setting cursor type variables requires different code, as you will see later in this chapter.

How do you return results from stored procedures? Note the use of the RETURN keyword in the stored procedure template generated by Visual C# Express. It terminates execution of the stored procedure, ignoring any subsequent statements and exiting all structures such as conditional blocks of code. But it isn't the means by which you return result sets for stored procedures that require that functionality. You can return a result using the RETURN keyword, but it can only be an integer value; for example:

```
RETURN 1
```

This return value is optional, as is the RETURN keyword itself — there is no need to finish your stored procedure with it.

Instead, results are returned from a stored procedure as they are encountered. Every time you execute a SELECT statement, for example, the result is returned (unless you store the result in a variable), so a stored procedure may return multiple result sets. In the previous chapter you saw how to prepare for this eventuality when you read query results using a SqlDataReader object, using the SqlDataReader.NextResult() method to move from one returned result to the next.

This means that in many cases, a stored procedure consists solely of a single SELECT statement. There is no need to use any additional code to return that result, so a simple stored procedure body may be a simple as the SELECT statement shown at the beginning of this section. The complete script for that stored procedure would be:

```
CREATE PROCEDURE dbo.MySearch
    (
    @MySearch varchar(50) = '%'
    )
AS
    SET NOCOUNT ON
    SELECT * FROM MyTable WHERE MySearchableField LIKE @MySearch
```

Note that you don't have to return tabular data using SELECT. If you wanted to return a result that was a single, scalar value you could simply use SELECT to do that. For example:

```
SELECT 'See other result set for results.' AS NoteText
```

You can also return variable values (and parameters) in the same way.

Another often-used technique is to use the RETURN keyword even when returning result sets in this way so that the value returned by RETURN can be used as a status code. It won't interfere with the results of the stored procedure as returned by SELECT statements, and can be interpreted independently. Similarly, if your stored procedure doesn't return any results, but results in a database modification of some kind, you might also want to use the RETURN keyword to return a result status code.

Using Stored Procedures

You can use a stored procedure in two ways — either from your C# applications using ADO.NET or through script execution. The latter is important because it enables you to execute stored procedures from other SQL code, including the SQL code in other stored procedures. So stored procedures can call other stored procedures, which means that there is even more that you can achieve with them.

Using Stored Procedures from C# Code

You have already seen all the objects and techniques that you need to call stored procedures from C# code. In outline, you make a connection, configure a command object to call the stored procedure, set any parameters to use (input or output) through the command object, and then execute the command. Depending on the stored procedure, you might proceed to inspect scalar or tabular results, or simply continue without requiring any kind of result returned to you. You can also use values returned by any output parameters, and data readers to parse multiple tabular result sets.

In the following example, you create and use a stored procedure in a Windows application.

Try It Out   Stored Procedure Execution

1. Open Visual C# Express and create a new Windows application called Ex0703 - Using Sprocs. Save the project in the C:\BegVC#Databases\Chapter07 directory, with the Create Directory For Solution option unchecked.

2. Add the FolktaleDB.mdf database to your project as a local database file. If prompted by the Data Source Configuration Wizard, click Cancel.

3. In the Database Explorer window, expand the database and right-click Stored Procedures. Select Add New Stored Procedure.

4. Add a new stored procedure as follows:

```
CREATE PROCEDURE dbo.GetStoriesByEnding
(
    @EndingType varchar(100)
)
AS
    SELECT dbo.Story.StoryId, dbo.Story.EndingId, dbo.Story.Name,
            dbo.Story.Summary, dbo.Ending.EndingType
    FROM dbo.Story INNER JOIN dbo.Ending
        ON dbo.Story.EndingId = dbo.Ending.EndingId
    WHERE dbo.Ending.EndingType = @EndingType
```

5. Add a new data source to the project called FolktaleDBDataSet using the Data Source Configuration Wizard. Select the Ending table and the GetStoriesByEnding stored procedure to add to the data source.

6. Verify that the data set is correctly configured by opening it in the DataSet Designer and comparing it to Figure 7-10.

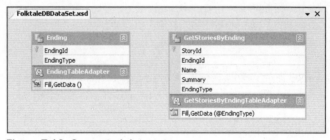

Figure 7-10: Generated data set

7. Open Form1 in design view, and set its Text property to Stories by Ending.

8. From the Data Sources window, drag the GetStoriesByEnding item onto Form1 to create a DataGridView and associated controls.

9. Remove the StoryId and EndingId columns from the DataGridView control, and position the control as shown in Figure 7-11 with its anchor property set to Top, Bottom, Left, or Right.

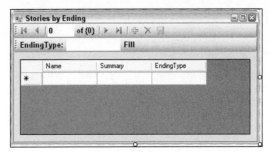

Figure 7-11: Control positioning

10. Execute the application. When it's running, type the text **Sad** in the EndingType text box and click Fill to obtain the stories with sad endings.

11. Close the application.

12. Right-click on the EndingType text box, and select Convert To ⇨ ComboBox from the context menu.

13. Change the width of the combo box to 200, its DropDownStyle property to DropDownList, and its name to endingTypeToolStripComboBox.

14. Add an event handler for the SelectedIndexChanged event of the combo box, and move the existing code from the Click event of the Fill button into the event handler — changing the control name reference as follows:

```
private void endingTypeToolStripComboBox_SelectedIndexChanged(object sender,
    EventArgs e)
{
    try
    {
        this.getStoriesByEndingTableAdapter.Fill(
            this.folktaleDBDataSet.GetStoriesByEnding,
            endingTypeToolStripComboBox.Text);
    }
    catch (System.Exception ex)
    {
        System.Windows.Forms.MessageBox.Show(ex.Message);
    }
}
```

15. Remove the old event handler for the Fill button Click event, and remove the Fill button from the form.

16. Add a form load event handler and the following code:

```
private void Form1_Load(object sender, EventArgs e)
{
    try
    {
        // Get endings and fill dropdrown.
        FolktaleDBDataSetTableAdapters.EndingTableAdapter endingTableAdapter =
            new FolktaleDBDataSetTableAdapters.EndingTableAdapter();
```

```
            endingTableAdapter.Fill(folktaleDBDataSet.Ending);
            foreach (FolktaleDBDataSet.EndingRow endingRow in folktaleDBDataSet.Ending)
            {
                endingTypeToolStripComboBox.Items.Add(endingRow.EndingType);
            }

            // Select first item
            endingTypeToolStripComboBox.SelectedIndex = 0;
            getStoriesByEndingTableAdapter.Fill(
                this.folktaleDBDataSet.GetStoriesByEnding,
                endingTypeToolStripComboBox.Text);
        }
        catch (System.Exception ex)
        {
            System.Windows.Forms.MessageBox.Show(ex.Message);
        }
    }
```

17. Run the application and select an ending from the drop-down to filter the stories, as shown in Figure 7-12.

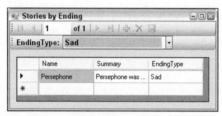

Figure 7-12: Application result

18. Close the application and Visual C# Express.

How It Works

This example creates a stored procedure that obtains a filtered list of results from the Story table using a stored procedure. The stored procedure uses a familiar select statement with a single text parameter to filter its result. You created an application using data binding to use the stored procedure, and modified the application to improve its usability.

It is good to see that the wizard for adding a data source is just as happy to use stored procedures as it is tables and other objects. It even uses the parameter to create a custom Fill() method for ease of use, and binds the method to controls on the form. Look at the generated code to see how the parameter is used, and how the custom Fill() method is designed to accept a value to use for the parameter, which is why you can use code as follows:

```
getStoriesByEndingTableAdapter.Fill(
    this.folktaleDBDataSet.GetStoriesByEnding,
    endingTypeToolStripComboBox.Text);
```

Of course, the automatically generated code is not the only way to access the stored procedure. You can use a `SqlCommand` object as follows:

```
public SqlDataReader GetSprocResult(SqlConnection conn, string paramValue)
{
    // Use command object and param valueto access stored procedure and return
    // data reader with CommandBehavior.CloseConnection behavior.
    SqlCommand cmd = new SqlCommand("GetStoriesByEnding", conn);
    cmd.CommandType = CommandType.StoredProcedure;
    cmd.Parameters.Add("@EndingType", SqlDbType.VarChar, 100).Value = paramValue;
    conn.Open();
    return cmd.ExecuteReader(CommandBehavior.CloseConnection);
}
```

This example, however, takes the data-binding route. Another reason to do it is that adding the data source to your form results in controls being created to set the parameter through the user interface. As you saw when you tried the application for the first time, however, the generated controls aren't ideal in this situation. That's because there are a limited number of options available for the parameter, so it makes more sense to use a drop-down list to select from them.

That isn't something that you can use wizards and automatic formatting to achieve. However, you can make the modification without too much effort, as the second part of the example shows — the control used to select the ending is converted to a combo box and then a small amount of custom code is added to achieve the desired result. Part of this simply removes the existing Fill button and changes the event handler code to automatically fetch new results when desired. The rest of the code adds a form load handler to populate the drop-down list using the Ending table — which you had already added to the data source. You started by fetching rows from this table as follows:

```
FolktaleDBDataSetTableAdapters.EndingTableAdapter endingTableAdapter =
    new FolktaleDBDataSetTableAdapters.EndingTableAdapter();
endingTableAdapter.Fill(folktaleDBDataSet.Ending);
```

You used those results to populate the drop-down:

```
foreach (FolktaleDBDataSet.EndingRow endingRow in folktaleDBDataSet.Ending)
{
    endingTypeToolStripComboBox.Items.Add(endingRow.EndingType);
}
```

Finally, you selected the first item in the list, triggering the event handler for the combo box, and also providing some initial results to work with:

```
endingTypeToolStripComboBox.SelectedIndex = 0;
getStoriesByEndingTableAdapter.Fill(
    this.folktaleDBDataSet.GetStoriesByEnding,
    endingTypeToolStripComboBox.Text);
```

All in all, nothing complicated, although it is something that you might think would be possible to achieve automatically.

Using Stored Procedures from SQL Script

At times you will want to access stored procedures, either system-stored procedures or those you've created, from SQL script. For example, one system-stored procedure that you might want to use occasionally is called `sp_changedbowner`. It enables you to change the SQL Server account that owns a database.

You can do this through applications, of course, but you can also execute stand-alone queries. In Visual C# Express you can create and execute a query through the New Query option, available through the Database Explorer window or the Data menu. In SQL Server Management Studio Express you can open a new query window to add and execute queries. In either case, the SQL keyword you use to execute queries is, unsurprisingly, `EXECUTE`. You can also use an alternative, short form of this keyword: `EXEC`. You use both forms of the keyword by including the name of the stored procedure to execute and the parameters you want to use.

SQL Server Management Studio Express includes a useful tool to generate a code template for executing a stored procedure. To use it, you simply have to right-click on a stored procedure and select Script Stored Procedure as ⇨ EXECUTE To ⇨ New Query Editor Window. For the `GetStoriesByEnding` stored procedure added in the previous example, this results in the following SQL script being generated:

```
DECLARE @RC int
DECLARE @EndingType varchar(100)

-- TODO: Set parameter values here.

EXECUTE @RC = [FolktaleDB].[dbo].[GetStoriesByEnding]
    @EndingType
```

All you need to do to complete the execution is set the `@EndingType` parameter using the `SET` keyword and run the script to obtain the result. The script assumes that you are using an integer result code (as described earlier in the chapter), which is stored in the variable `@RC` should you want to use it. If you are not interested in the result, or in setting parameters manually, you can simply use the following code:

```
EXECUTE [FolktaleDB].[dbo].[GetStoriesByEnding] 'Sad'
```

You can specify the parameters for stored procedures with or without parentheses — it makes no difference to the execution behavior. You can also use the `NULL` or `DEFAULT` keyword to pass null values or use default values specified by the stored procedure definition. If you want to use an output parameter's result, you must use a variable for the parameter and include the keyword `OUTPUT`, like this:

```
DECLARE @OutputParam int
EXECUTE [FolktaleDB].[dbo].[SprocWithOutput] 5, @OutputParam OUTPUT
```

Here, the stored procedure called `SprocWithOutput` has two parameters, the first an `int` and the second an `int` output parameter. If the `OUTPUT` keyword is omitted, no value is assigned to `@OutputParam` after executing the script.

You can also specify parameters by name instead of by position. To do so, you use the syntax `@Parameter = value`; for example:

```
EXECUTE [FolktaleDB].[dbo].[GetStoriesByEnding] @EndingType = 'Sad'
```

You can specify any number of parameters for stored procedures this way, and even omit those that have default values defined.

Finally, in Visual C# Express you can also execute queries by right-clicking them in the Database Explorer window and selecting Execute. If the stored procedure requires parameters, you have to enter them, as shown in Figure 7-13.

Similarly, in SQL Server Management Express you can execute stored procedures using a dialog box, as shown in Figure 7-14.

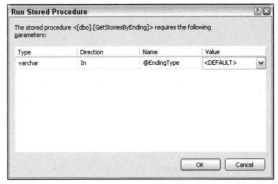

Figure 7-13: Executing a stored procedure through Visual C# Express

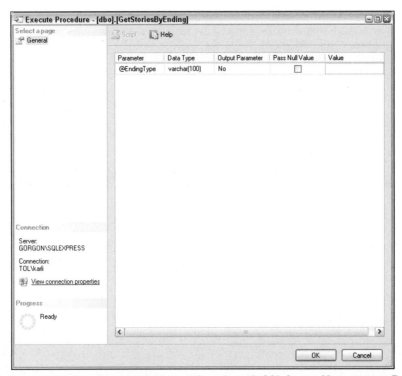

Figure 7-14: Executing a stored procedure through SQL Server Management Express

Updating Data Through Stored Procedures

One thing missing from the example in the previous section was the capability to modify data. When you use stored procedures to obtain results, you typically use additional stored procedures to modify those results — creating one to edit, one to insert, and one to delete rows in the database. You then use those stored procedures in the definition of the data source. You can do this through the DataSet Designer by right-clicking the table created for the stored procedure and selecting Configure. The dialog box shown in Figure 7-15 appears, which you can use to add additional stored procedures.

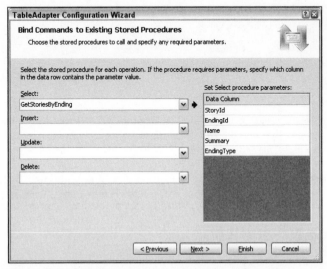

Figure 7-15: Data source stored procedure configuration

To modify results in the example, you would need to make a few choices about what happens when, such as when ending type names are added or modified, and design stored procedures accordingly. This is not a simple thing to do, and involves additional logic either in the application or by using some of the more advanced stored procedure structures that you'll be looking at in the next section.

In many cases, such as when only a single table is accessed through a stored procedure, it's quite easy to add the stored procedures required to edit data. For example, the following four stored procedures allow complete access to and modification of the Ending table:

```
CREATE PROCEDURE [dbo].[EndingSelect]
AS
    SELECT EndingId, EndingType FROM Ending
GO


CREATE PROCEDURE [dbo].[EndingInsert]
(
    @EndingType varchar(100)
)
AS
    INSERT INTO Ending (EndingType) VALUES (@EndingType)
GO
```

```
CREATE PROCEDURE [dbo].[EndingUpdate]
(
    @EndingId uniqueidentifier,
    @EndingType varchar(100)
)
AS
    UPDATE Ending SET EndingType = @EndingType WHERE EndingId = @EndingId
GO

CREATE PROCEDURE [dbo].[EndingDelete]
(
    @EndingId uniqueidentifier
)
AS
    DELETE FROM Ending WHERE EndingId = @EndingId
GO
```

Note the use of the GO keyword to separate stored procedure definitions. In longer pieces of SQL script you often need to include this keyword, which means "execute all SQL statements up to this point." In this code extract, it separates the stored procedure definitions and avoids errors that would otherwise occur if the SQL interpreter understood all of the SQL code to be part of a single definition for EndingSelect.

Admittedly, this isn't the most interesting use of stored procedures, although as has already been pointed out, it can be argued that all database access should take place through stored procedures.

Conditional Logic and Looping

When you write C# applications, you use conditional logic and looping structures a great deal, and you'll do the same when you begin writing and using more advanced stored procedures.

The following is a list of the logic and branching structures that you can use in SQL:

❑ **Simple branching using** GOTO: This suffers from all the problems associated with using similar structures in programming languages of the past. It can be useful to jump quickly from one place to another in script code, but can rapidly result in your code becoming confusing, and make debugging practically impossible. Briefly: Avoid unless you really have to.

❑ **Looping using** WHILE: This is the only loop type available in SQL. It repeats a statement (or block of statements delimited with BEGIN and END) until a condition returns true. By using counters, it's easy to use this structure as a C#-style for...next type loop.

❑ **Branching using** IF **and** ELSE: Conditional execution of a statement (or block of statements delimited with BEGIN and END) based on a Boolean evaluation. The optional ELSE statement allows an alternative statement or block of statements to execute if the Boolean evaluation is false.

There is also a CASE keyword that you can use to return a value based on the value of a variable or column, although strictly speaking this isn't the sort of thing you're looking at in this section. It is incapable of conditionally executing one of a number of blocks of code — unlike the C# equivalent select...case structure, which is far more powerful.

In the remainder of this section you explore WHILE loops and IF...ELSE branching in more detail.

WHILE Loops

Here's the syntax for a WHILE loop:

```
WHILE <condition>
    <statement to execute>
```

Here, `<condition>` is evaluated when the loop starts. If it is true, `<statement to execute>` is executed. If it is false, the statement is not executed. If the statement is executed, the `<condition>` is evaluated again, and the statement may be executed again (and again, and again, and again . . .).

If the statement you want to execute conditionally is a block of code, it must be enclosed in BEGIN and END keywords. For example:

```
DECLARE @Counter int
SET @Counter = 0
WHILE @Counter < 10
BEGIN
    SELECT @Counter AS Counter
    SET @Counter = @Counter + 1
END
```

Although this simple code isn't particularly useful, it illustrates WHILE looping. An @Counter variable of type int is declared and set to the value 0. The evaluation in the WHILE loop is a check to see if @Counter has a value of less than 10. The block of statements that is executed if the condition is true returns a result set consisting of the value of @Counter (as a single value in a single column called Counter), and then increments @Counter. The result of this SQL code is to return ten result sets, where the value of each is a number from 0 to 9.

This kind of processing can be useful in some circumstances, such as adding year on year interest at a fixed percentage to a starting currency amount, but where WHILE loops are really useful is in combination with cursors, to process rows in a result set sequentially, as you will see later in the chapter.

You can use the BREAK keyword to exit a WHILE loop, or the CONTINUE keyword to end processing of the current loop cycle and start the next loop cycle (if the condition still evaluates true, otherwise the loop will be exited).

IF...ELSE Branching

Here's the syntax for using IF:

```
IF <condition>
    <statement to execute if true>
```

And you can add an ELSE block as follows:

```
IF <condition>
    <statement to execute if true>
ELSE
    <statement to execute if false>
```

This structure operates exactly as you might expect — one of the specified statements is executed depending on the evaluation of the condition. As with WHILE loops, you can execute blocks of statements conditionally.

Unlike WHILE, the IF structure is useful regardless of whether you combine it with cursors and other structures. For example, say you have a table called RestrictedTable that includes a bit column called Editable, and you want to restrict modification to rows in the table such that users can only modify data if the value of that column is 1. You could restrict modification of the table to stored procedures rather than to direct table access, and provide the following stored procedures for modification (the update stored procedure assumes the table has a varchar column called ValueColumn):

```
CREATE PROCEDURE [dbo].[RestrictedTableUpdate]
(
    @RestrictedTableId uniqueidentifier,
    @ValueColumn varchar(100)
)
AS
    IF (SELECT Editable FROM RestrictedTable
        WHERE RestrictedTableId = @RestrictedTableId) = 1
        UPDATE RestrictedTable SET ValueColumn = @ValueColumn
        WHERE RestrictedTableId = @RestrictedTableId
    ELSE
        RAISERROR('Unable to edit row.', 0, 1)
GO


CREATE PROCEDURE [dbo].[RestrictedTableDelete]
(
    @RestrictedTableId uniqueidentifier
)
AS
    IF (SELECT Editable FROM RestrictedTable
        WHERE RestrictedTableId = @RestrictedTableId) = 1
        DELETE FROM RestrictedTable WHERE RestrictedTableId = @RestrictedTableId
    ELSE
        RAISERROR('Unable to delete row.', 0, 1)
GO
```

Here, a SELECT statement is used in the condition used for the IF statement. It's fine to do this — and can be a useful technique. The SELECT statement returns a single result that is checked to see if it is the value 1. If it is, the column is editable; if it isn't, the ELSE block of code executes.

The RAISERROR() function is used to generate an error in this code sample. That isn't the only way you could deal with this situation — you could simply return a result code to indicate the success or failure of the edit operation. However, it is a technique that you may find yourself using (and lends itself to SQL error handling, although that is a subject for later in the book). There are a number of ways to call this function. The method used here is to specify an error message followed by a severity and state value. These are intended for use by SQL error-handling code, but you have to specify them to make a valid call to the function. Alternatively, you can generate an error code instead of an error message by passing an integer value as the first parameter.

One technique often used with `IF` statements is to employ the `EXISTS` operator to check for the existence of a row. For example:

```
IF EXISTS (SELECT EndingId FROM Ending WHERE EndingType = 'Sad')
    SELECT 'Yep.' AS Result
ELSE
    SELECT 'Nope.' AS Result
```

In this query, a `SELECT` statement obtains a value from the `Ending` table, based on the value of the `EndingType` column. If the statement returns a value (or more than one value), applying the `EXISTS` operator to it results in the condition evaluating to `true`. Alternatively, if no such row exists, the `SELECT` statement returns a value of `NULL`, and `EXISTS` evaluates this to `false`. You can also use `NOT EXISTS` to invert the value return.

Using EXISTS provides the basis for dealing with a situation you encountered earlier — how to update multiple linked tables simultaneously. By providing updates through a stored procedure, you can test to see if the requested value in the parent table exists, and if necessary, create it. For example:

```
CREATE PROCEDURE InsertStoryWithEnding
(
    @Name varchar(100),
    @Summary text,
    @EndingType varchar(100),
    @ClassificationId uniqueidentifier,
    @SourceId uniqueidentifier
)
AS
BEGIN
    SET NOCOUNT ON

    IF NOT EXISTS (SELECT EndingId FROM Ending WHERE EndingType = @EndingType)
    INSERT INTO Ending (EndingType) VALUES (@EndingType)

    DECLARE @EndingId uniqueidentifier
    SET @EndingId = (SELECT EndingId FROM Ending WHERE EndingType = @EndingType)

    INSERT INTO Story (EndingId, ClassificationId, SourceId, Name, Summary)
        VALUES (@EndingId, @ClassificationId, @SourceId, @Name, @Summary)
END
GO
```

Here a test is made to see if the requested `EndingType` exists in the `EndingTable`. If it does, its `EndingId` value is obtained for use in the new row in the `Story` table. If it doesn't, a new row is added to the `Ending` table, and the new `EndingId` generated for that row is obtained and used in the `Story` table.

In this example, the `ClassificationId` and `SourceId` values for `Story` are passed directly as parameters, but similar code could be used for these to add new values if required.

If identity columns are used for primary keys, you can obtain the identity of the most recently added column using the `SCOPE_IDENTITY()` *function. However, only integer values can be used for identity specification, so this technique cannot be used in the* `FolktaleDB` *sample database, which uses* `GUID` *primary keys.*

Cursors

Cursors provide a way in which SQL code can process individual rows within a result set. As such, they are similar in function to the data reader classes you've used in this book in C# code. The difference is that you can use cursors in SQL scripts, including stored procedures.

The use of cursors is quite an advanced technique, and in most applications you will not need to use them. However, they can achieve things that would otherwise be very difficult to do, so they are by no means redundant. Having said that, this may be a section you want to skip for now, and come back to when you find yourself needing to find out more on the subject.

Using a cursor involves the following stages:

1. Create the cursor.
2. Open the cursor.
3. Use the cursor to retrieve and (possibly) modify data.
4. Close (and de-allocate) the cursor.

In this section you learn the basic syntax of cursor use, cursor options, and how to navigate and modify data using cursors.

Basic Cursor Usage

To create a cursor you must declare it and specify the result set that it is to use. You use the DECLARE keyword as usual with the cursor name (which can't include the @ prefix that is used for variables) and then the FOR keyword to associate the cursor with a result set as follows:

```
DECLARE MyCursor CURSOR FOR <select statement>
```

The `<select statement>` is a SQL SELECT statement that returns the result set that the cursor will act on. There are a number of options that you can specify when you create cursors, and they are discussed a little later.

You can also declare cursor typed variables to which you can assign cursors:

```
DECLARE @MyCursorVariable CURSOR
SET @MyCursorVariable = MyCursor
```

This syntax enables you to pass references to cursors to stored procedures, functions, and so on.

Here's an example of a cursor creation:

```
DECLARE ClassificationCursor CURSOR FOR (SELECT * FROM Classification)
```

Once you have created a cursor, you must open it before you can use it to read row data. This simply means using the OPEN keyword as follows:

```
OPEN MyCursor
```

When a cursor is open, you can use it to fetch and, if the cursor options permit, modify data. Depending on other options that are defined for the cursor, you can navigate results in various ways. You'll look at how to do this shortly.

After you have finished using a cursor, close it using the CLOSE keyword:

```
CLOSE MyCursor
```

Closing a cursor releases any results and row locks that the cursor may have, but the cursor remains available for reopening and reusing if you need to.

If you have completely finished with a cursor, de-allocate it using the DEALLOCATE keyword:

```
DEALLOCATE MyCursor
```

A de-allocated cursor is destroyed completely and cannot then be reopened. However, you can use the name of the cursor again, creating a new cursor with its own select statement using that name. Under certain circumstances, cursors may be de-allocated automatically, but as a rule of thumb it's good to de-allocate cursors manually.

Cursor Options

Depending on the options you choose when you create a cursor, some operations may be unavailable or work in a slightly different way. Options can affect how the cursor is stored in the DBMS, how data is accessed, whether temporary storage is used, whether the data is updateable and if so in what way, and so on. The exact syntax of the options and keywords you use for options vary between DBMSes. This section examines SQL Server-specific syntax.

If you use any options, include the relevant keyword(s) between the CURSOR and FOR keywords, like this:

```
DECLARE MyCursor CURSOR <keyword> <keyword> FOR <select statement>
```

The options are explained in the following list.

❑ **Cursor scope** — There are two choices for defining cursor scope:

    ❑ GLOBAL, meaning it can be accessed by any SQL code anywhere.

    ❑ LOCAL, meaning that the cursor is local to the current context. The "context" of a cursor refers to the batch of SQL statements that contains the declaration of the cursor, which includes the SQL code that defines a stored procedure. If you use a local cursor in a stored procedure, it's automatically de-allocated when the stored procedure terminates and all references to the cursor have gone out of scope. Stored procedures with an output parameter of type CURSOR are permitted when local cursors are used, in which case the cursor remains in existence until the calling code is finished with it.

    If you don't define the cursor scope option, the database default value — GLOBAL, unless you specify otherwise — is used.

    As a general rule, use local cursors in stored procedures because that removes the possibility of the cursor being modified by external code. Note that it is possible for both a local and a global cursor to use the same name.

❑ **Cursor read behavior** — You have two choices for defining cursor read behavior:

    ❑ FORWARD_ONLY, which means that navigation can occur only from one row to the next in a result set, and once a row is passed it cannot be subsequently retrieved.

    ❑ SCROLL, which enables alternative navigation techniques, such as moving the cursor to the first or last row in the result set.

If neither option is specified, the default read behavior for the cursor is FORWARD_ONLY.

❑ **Cursor type** — There are four choices for affecting the way data is accessed:

    ❑ STATIC: A temporary copy of the data accessed by the cursor is created and that's what you see when you read it through the cursor — you won't see any changes made to the underlying data by external sources, and the cursor does not allow modification of data.

    ❑ KEYSET: Data modification is allowed. A list of primary key values is held in temporary storage, so the rows in the result set are fixed. It is possible that the cursor will attempt to access a row that no longer exists in the underlying data storage, such as if the row has been deleted or its primary key value has changed. It's also possible that rows added to the underlying data after the cursor is used will not be visible through the cursor.

    ❑ DYNAMIC: Data modification is allowed, but no temporary data is stored so row order may change as you view it.

For STATIC, KEYSET, and DYNAMIC, the default cursor read behavior is set to SCROLL, although using DYNAMIC does affect the navigation operations that are available as you will see in the next section.

    ❑ FAST_FORWARD: Specifies that the cursor is read-only, and it implicitly uses the FORWARD_ONLY read behavior.

❑ **Cursor data modification behavior** — To affect whether the cursor allows data modification and, if so, how concurrency is handled, choose one of the following keywords:

    ❑ READ_ONLY specifies that data modification is prohibited.

    ❑ SCROLL_LOCKS enables data modification if the row isn't implicitly read-only. This may occur if, for example, the FAST_FORWARD option is used. Assuming that data modification is permitted, SCROLL_LOCKS means that rows loaded into the cursor are locked and cannot be modified externally, so data modifications made through the cursor are guaranteed to succeed.

    ❑ OPTIMISTIC enables data modification just as SCROLL_LOCKS does except rows are not locked and, if they have been modified externally and then updated through the cursor, will fail.

❑ **Conversion warning** — In some advanced circumstances it's possible for a cursor to be converted into a different type — that is, its select statement — and therefore the columns it can return can vary. You can use the TYPE_WARNING keyword to receive a warning message if this occurs. The likelihood of this situation occurring is extremely remote — especially when using your own databases that are only accessed though C# — so in all probability, you can ignore this option.

When you use cursors that can modify data, you can also specify an additional option after the specification of the select statement used by the cursor: FOR UPDATE OF. It's followed by a comma-separated list of columns for which modification is permitted. This option makes it possible to lock certain columns in the result set so that they are unavailable for editing.

Navigating Results with Cursors

Assuming data exists, you will always be able to read data through cursors no matter what options you use. To do so, use the FETCH keyword, specifying the cursor to use. That returns a result set consisting of a single row, and sets the position of the cursor within the result set to the returned row:

```
FETCH FROM MyCursor
```

Alternatively, you can fetch a result into variables by using INTO:

```
FETCH FROM MyCursor INTO @MyVar1, @MyVar2
```

Here the values from each column in the result row are copied to the variables in the order in which they appear. This technique can be useful in stored procedures because you can process data from each row in a result set in turn.

When you specify the name of a cursor, you can precede it with the GLOBAL keyword to specify that a global cursor should be used. Both cursor names and variables of type CURSOR can be used with the FETCH keyword.

Using the preceding syntax enables you to move from one row to the next in the result set. If you are using a cursor with the SCROLL option, you can use a navigation option to move through data in other ways:

```
FETCH <navigation option> FROM MyCursor
```

Here, can be one of the following keywords:

Keyword	Description
NEXT	The default behavior, which means that the cursor moves to the next row in the result set.
PRIOR	Moves the cursor to the previous row.
FIRST	Moves the cursor to the first row in the result set.
LAST	Moves the cursor to the last row in the result set.
ABSOLUTE n	Returns a row that is n rows from the start of the cursor or n rows from the end of the cursor if n is negative. If n is 0, no rows are returned. This option is not available if the DYNAMIC option is used for the cursor.
RELATIVE n	Returns a row that is n rows from the current position of the cursor or n rows before the current position of the cursor if n is negative. If n is 0, the current row is returned, or if no rows have yet been fetched, no rows are returned.

For example, the following operation fetches the previous row in the result set:

```
FETCH PRIOR FROM MyCursor
```

And the following operation fetches the third row in the result set:

```
FETCH ABSOLUTE 3 FROM MyCursor
```

Whichever navigation method you use to fetch data, there will be circumstances in which no row is returned. For instance, if you are using NEXT, no row is returned when the end of the result set is reached, or for KEYSET cursors when a row is encountered that has been moved or deleted, no row is returned.

To detect this occurrence, you can examine the value of the global @@FETCH_STATUS variable. This variable can have one of three values, described in the following table.

Value	Meaning
0	The FETCH operation was successful.
1	Moves the cursor to the previous row. The FETCH operation failed because the requested row is beyond the limits of the result set.
2	The FETCH operation failed because the requested row is missing (only applicable to KEYSET cursors).

One common use of this variable is to move through a complete result set in a WHILE loop as follows:

```
FETCH NEXT FROM MyCursor
WHILE @@FETCH_STATUS = 0
BEGIN
    -- Operate on current row
    FETCH NEXT FROM MyCursor
END
```

In this code, a result set is returned for each row in the cursor data, and an additional, empty result set is also returned. If you are performing operations on the current cursor row you would add code where the comment appears in this code, at which point you are guaranteed to have a row available.

You can also obtain the fetch status by looking in system tables or via the sys.dm_exec_cursors management function. These are advanced techniques, and you should refer to the MSDN documentation if you want more information on them.

The following is an example of a stored procedure that uses a cursor to return a string consisting of all the character names in the Character table in the FolktaleDB database:

```
CREATE PROCEDURE GetCharacterNames
AS
BEGIN
```

```
        DECLARE CharacterCursor CURSOR LOCAL FOR (SELECT Name FROM Character)

        OPEN CharacterCursor

        DECLARE @Name varchar(100)
        DECLARE @Result varchar(8000)
        SET @Result = ''

        FETCH NEXT FROM CharacterCursor INTO @Name
        WHILE @@FETCH_STATUS = 0
        BEGIN
            SET @Result = @Result + ', ' + @Name
            FETCH NEXT FROM CharacterCursor INTO @Name
        END
        SET @Result = SUBSTRING(@Result, 3, LEN(@Result) - 2)

        CLOSE CharacterCursor

        DEALLOCATE CharacterCursor

        SELECT @Result AS Result
    END
    GO
```

Here, a cursor is used to access the Name column for each row in the Character table. Each of these values in turn is placed in the @Name variable and added to a string in the @Result variable. After trimming the leading comma and space from the string using string manipulation functions, the cursor is closed and de-allocated, and the result is returned.

This stored procedure fails if the total length of the names is greater than 8,000 characters. To avoid that, the text data type can be used, but unfortunately you can't use this type for a local variable. To get around this, you have to use a temporary table with a single column of type text and modify the value in this column as you go along.

> *Microsoft now advocates the use of the* varchar(max) *data type rather than* text, *which may be phased out in the future.*

Modifying Data with Cursors

When you navigate through data sets with a cursor, regardless of whether you obtain data in variables or as result sets, you also position the cursor at the row that you navigate to. You can, if you want, use the primary key values returned by the cursor to modify rows in the underlying data table or tables. If you do that, it's possible to use a READ_ONLY cursor, although if you want the changes you make to be reflected in the cursor data, you should use DYNAMIC or KEYSET cursors. In some circumstances, such as when the result consists of more than one table joined in a complex way, using the primary keys you obtain to modify data is your only option.

Alternatively, you can edit data through the cursor by accessing the current row directly. To do so, you cannot use a READ_ONLY cursor, and can only edit columns specified in the FOR UPDATE OF clause of the cursor declaration. Keeping within these rules, you can update or delete rows using the standard

UPDATE and DELETE syntax, but you must include a specific value in the WHERE clause of these statements. That clause is as follows:

```
WHERE CURRENT OF <cursor name or cursor variable>
```

For example:

```
DECLARE ClassificationCursor CURSOR FOR (SELECT * FROM Classification)
OPEN ClassificationCursor

FETCH NEXT FROM ClassificationCursor
IF (@@FETCH_STATUS = 0)
    DELETE FROM Classification WHERE CURRENT OF ClassificationCursor

CLOSE ClassificationCursor
DEALLOCATE ClassificationCursor
```

This SQL code deletes the first row returned by the query SELECT * FROM Classification, and also returns a result set consisting of the deleted row.

This deletion may not be possible if a foreign key reference is held for the row to be deleted, so if you try executing this query against the sample database you may receive the following error: The DELETE statement conflicted with the REFERENCE constraint "FK_Story_Classification". The conflict occurred in database "FolktaleDB", table "dbo.Story", column 'ClassificationId'. *This is behavior by design, not a problem with the query.*

The syntax for UPDATE statements is identical: Simply include the specified WHERE clause and you are editing the fetched row.

By combining this technique with WHILE loops to obtain data sequentially, IF blocks to conditionally operate on rows, and other techniques such as string manipulation and so on, you can create stored procedures that can do pretty much anything.

In the following example, you use some of the more advanced features of stored procedures that you've studied here.

Try It Out   Advanced Stored Procedures

1. Open Visual C# Express and create a new Windows application called Ex0704 - Advanced Sprocs. Save the project in the C:\BegVC#Databases\Chapter07 directory, with the Create Directory For Solution option unchecked.

2. Add the FolktaleDB.mdf database to your project as a local database file. If prompted by the Data Source Configuration Wizard, click Cancel.

3. In the Database Explorer window, expand the database and right-click Stored Procedures. Click Add New Stored Procedure.

4. Add a new stored procedure as follows:

```
CREATE PROCEDURE [dbo].[GetParents]
(
    @CharacterId uniqueidentifier,
```

```
            @MotherId uniqueidentifier OUTPUT,
            @FatherId uniqueidentifier OUTPUT,
            @MotherName varchar(100) OUTPUT,
            @FatherName varchar(100) OUTPUT
    )
    AS
    BEGIN
        SET NOCOUNT ON

        -- Declare parentage cursor
        DECLARE ParentCursor CURSOR LOCAL FOR
        (
            SELECT Character.MotherId, Character.FatherId,
                MotherTable.Name AS MotherName, FatherTable.Name AS FatherName
            FROM Character
            LEFT OUTER JOIN Character AS MotherTable
                ON Character.MotherId = MotherTable.CharacterId
            LEFT OUTER JOIN Character AS FatherTable
                ON Character.FatherId = FatherTable.CharacterId
            WHERE Character.CharacterId = @CharacterId
        )

        -- Get parentage information using cursor
        OPEN ParentCursor
        FETCH NEXT FROM ParentCursor
            INTO @MotherId, @FatherId, @MotherName, @FatherName
        CLOSE ParentCursor
        DEALLOCATE ParentCursor

        -- Return Status
        IF (@MotherId IS NULL AND @FatherId IS NULL)
            RETURN -1
        ELSE
            RETURN 0
    END
```

5. Add another new stored procedure as follows:

```
CREATE PROCEDURE [dbo].[GetLineage]
(
    @CharacterId uniqueidentifier,
    @Lineage varchar(8000) OUTPUT,
    @ReturnResult bit = 1
)
AS
BEGIN
    SET NOCOUNT ON

    -- Local declarations
    DECLARE @RC int
    DECLARE @MotherName varchar(100)
    DECLARE @FatherName varchar(100)
    DECLARE @MotherId uniqueidentifier
    DECLARE @FatherId uniqueidentifier
```

```
                DECLARE @TempResult varchar(8000)

                -- Get initial information using sproc
                EXECUTE @RC = GetParents
                    @CharacterId,
                    @MotherId OUTPUT,
                    @FatherId OUTPUT,
                    @MotherName OUTPUT,
                    @FatherName OUTPUT

            SET @Lineage = ''
            IF (@RC <> -1)
            BEGIN
                IF (@MotherId IS NOT NULL)
                BEGIN
                    -- Add mother's name
                    SET @Lineage = @Lineage + @MotherName

                    -- Add mother's lineage
                    EXEC GetLineage @MotherId, @TempResult OUTPUT, 0
                    IF (@TempResult <> '')
                        SET @Lineage = @Lineage + ' (' + @TempResult + ')'
                END
                IF (@FatherId IS NOT NULL)
                BEGIN
                    -- If mother as well, add comma
                    IF (@MotherId IS NOT NULL)
                        SET @Lineage = @Lineage + ', '

                    -- Add father's name
                    SET @Lineage = @Lineage + @FatherName

                    -- Add father's lineage
                    EXEC GetLineage @FatherId, @TempResult OUTPUT, 0
                    IF (@TempResult <> '')
                        SET @Lineage = @Lineage + ' (' + @TempResult + ')'
                END
            END

            -- Return result
            IF (@ReturnResult = 1)
                SELECT @Lineage AS Lineage
        END
```

6.   Add a new view to the database called `CharacterInfo` that uses the following query:

```
SELECT dbo.Character.CharacterId, dbo.Character.Name, dbo.Character.Gender,
       dbo.Character.Notes, dbo.Character.Email, dbo.Character.Occupation,
       dbo.Character.Age, dbo.Species.Species, dbo.Species.Description,
       dbo.Species.Immortal
FROM   dbo.Character INNER JOIN dbo.Species
ON     dbo.Character.SpeciesId = dbo.Species.SpeciesId
```

7.   Add a new data set called `FolktaleDBDataSet` that returns all columns from the `CharacterInfo` view, and also includes the `GetLineage` stored procedure.

8. In `Form1`, change the `Form1.Text` property to `Character Info`, and then add the `CharacterInfo` table data to the form as a details view, with the `CharacterId` field hidden. Format the layout to achieve an aesthetically pleasing look. Figure 7-16 shows an example.

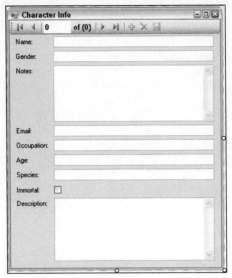

Figure 7-16: Form layout

9. Add a new button to the toolbar called `getLineageButton`, with a `Text` property of `Get Lineage` and a `DisplayStyle` property of `Text`.

10. Add an event handler for the button as follows:

```
private void getLineageButton_Click(object sender, EventArgs e)
{
    try
    {
        // Get current row.
        DataRowView currentRowView =
            characterInfoBindingSource.Current as DataRowView;
        FolktaleDBDataSet.CharacterInfoRow currentRow =
            currentRowView.Row as FolktaleDBDataSet.CharacterInfoRow;
        FolktaleDBDataSetTableAdapters.QueriesTableAdapter queryAdapter =
            new FolktaleDBDataSetTableAdapters.QueriesTableAdapter();

        // Get lineage with stored procedure.
        string lineage = "";
        queryAdapter.GetLineage(currentRow.CharacterId, ref lineage, true);

        // Display result
        MessageBox.Show(lineage == "" ? "Unknown." : lineage,
            "Lineage of " + currentRow.Name,
            MessageBoxButtons.OK, MessageBoxIcon.Information);
    }
```

```
        catch
        {
        }
    }
```

11. Run the application and obtain the lineages for characters using the Get Lineage button. An example is shown in Figure 7-17.

12. Close the application and Visual C# Express.

Figure 7-17: Character lineage

How It Works

This example uses extensive stored procedure code to extract the lineage of a character in the Character table of the database. This is possible because the Character table includes hierarchical linking — each character has a mother and a father, which are foreign key references to other primary keys in the Character table.

To make things easier to understand, and to split the code into reusable parts, two stored procedures are used:

❑ GetParents: Uses a cursor to obtain row information from the Character table based on the specified CharacterId. It returns the IDs and names of the parent characters, if any, and a status code saying whether the character has any known parents.

❑ GetLineage: Obtains the lineage of a character specified by a CharacterId value, in the form of a string. It does this by calling itself recursively, so that as parents are discovered, grandparents are processed, then great-grandparents, and so on.

The rest of the application is fairly simple, and doesn't really use any code you haven't already seen, so this discussion focuses only on the stored procedures.

The GetParents stored procedure starts by defining one input parameter and four output parameters for the parent information to be returned:

```
CREATE PROCEDURE [dbo].[GetParents]
(
    @CharacterId uniqueidentifier,
    @MotherId uniqueidentifier OUTPUT,
    @FatherId uniqueidentifier OUTPUT,
    @MotherName varchar(100) OUTPUT,
    @FatherName varchar(100) OUTPUT
)
```

The body of the stored procedure starts by defining a cursor for a query that can get parent information, which requires outer joins to ensure that data is returned, and table aliases to differentiate between rows in multiple versions of the same table:

```
DECLARE ParentCursor CURSOR LOCAL FOR
(
    SELECT Character.MotherId, Character.FatherId,
        MotherTable.Name AS MotherName, FatherTable.Name AS FatherName
    FROM Character
    LEFT OUTER JOIN Character AS MotherTable
        ON Character.MotherId = MotherTable.CharacterId
    LEFT OUTER JOIN Character AS FatherTable
        ON Character.FatherId = FatherTable.CharacterId
    WHERE Character.CharacterId = @CharacterId
)
```

Then the cursor is used to populate the output parameters. Any information that is missing will result in NULL values for these parameters:

```
OPEN ParentCursor
FETCH NEXT FROM ParentCursor
    INTO @MotherId, @FatherId, @MotherName, @FatherName
CLOSE ParentCursor
DEALLOCATE ParentCursor
```

Finally, the result is checked to see if both CharacterId values returned are NULL, and a result code is returned as appropriate:

```
IF (@MotherId IS NULL AND @FatherId IS NULL)
    RETURN -1
ELSE
    RETURN 0
```

You'll see how this stored procedure is used in GetLineage in a moment.

The GetLineage stored procedure has three parameters as follows:

```
CREATE PROCEDURE [dbo].[GetLineage]
(
    @CharacterId uniqueidentifier,
    @Lineage varchar(8000) OUTPUT,
    @ReturnResult bit = 1
)
```

Here, @CharacterId is the character to extract the lineage information for, @Lineage is an output parameter to return the output (used by the recursive stored procedure calls), and @ReturnResult determines whether a result set is returned. This last parameter is used because although there is no need for this stored procedure to return a result set when called recursively, external applications or script might require it.

In the body of the stored procedure, after local variable declarations have been made, the `GetParents` stored procedure is called and the `@Lineage` return parameter is initialized:

```
-- Get initial information using sproc
EXECUTE @RC = GetParents
    @CharacterId,
    @MotherId OUTPUT,
    @FatherId OUTPUT,
    @MotherName OUTPUT,
    @FatherName OUTPUT

SET @Lineage = ''
```

If the return value of `GetParents` indicates that parents exist, `@Lineage` is constructed. First, if the character has a mother, the mother's name is added:

```
IF (@RC <> -1)
BEGIN
    IF (@MotherId IS NOT NULL)
    BEGIN
        -- Add mother's name
        SET @Lineage = @Lineage + @MotherName
```

The mother's lineage is assembled by a recursive call to `GetLineage`. The output of this stored procedure is stored in the local `@TempResult` variable, and `@ReturnResult` is set to 0 to avoid spurious result sets:

```
EXEC GetLineage @MotherId, @TempResult OUTPUT, 0
```

The result is added to `@Lineage`, with surrounding parentheses to indicate that it is the mother's parents that are being output:

```
IF (@TempResult <> '')
    SET @Lineage = @Lineage + ' (' + @TempResult + ')'
END
```

The process is repeated for the father and father's lineage, with the inclusion of a comma if the character has both a father and mother:

```
IF (@FatherId IS NOT NULL)
BEGIN
    IF (@MotherId IS NOT NULL)
        SET @Lineage = @Lineage + ', '

    SET @Lineage = @Lineage + @FatherName

    EXEC GetLineage @FatherId, @TempResult OUTPUT, 0
    IF (@TempResult <> '')
        SET @Lineage = @Lineage + ' (' + @TempResult + ')'
END
END
```

Finally, the result is returned as a result set if `@ReturnResult` is 1:

```
IF (@ReturnResult = 1)
    SELECT @Lineage AS Lineage
END
```

The interaction between these stored procedures results in a complex operation being performed by SQL Server, and makes the code to retrieve this information in your application simple.

Summary

In this chapter you have looked at how to use views and stored procedures to improve the database access techniques used by your applications. By judicious use of these techniques, you can streamline your applications and shift more of the work needed to process data to SQL Server. That means that less data transfer needs to take place, and less code is required in your applications. SQL Server can also optimize the performance of views and stored procedures, giving your applications a further boost.

However, these bonuses come at the cost of increased complexity of scripts within your database, which (if you are just learning about these techniques) can be tricky to get to grips with. Debugging can also be an issue because you may have to deal with cryptic error messages from SQL Server, rather than stepping through C# code. Finally, data modification issues can arise when you work with data sets obtained in non-conventional ways.

To summarize, there is nothing that you can do in views and stored procedures that you can't do manually from C# code. However, it is often more appropriate to do things in the database, saving you time and effort in your application development if done right. As you learn more about this subject, and gain experience in using views and stored procedures, you will quickly get a feel for what is the best way to achieve your aims.

In this chapter you have looked at:

❑   How to create views graphically using the view editor in Visual C# Express and SQL Server Management Studio Express. This generic query designer tool is used for all sorts of SQL queries, and can be used to quickly and easily create queries joining results from multiple tables. You also can use it to create queries with grouped, sorted, and filtered data.

❑   How to create views from script, including the syntax required to create, modify, and delete views in a database, and how to use the CREATE VIEW, ALTER VIEW, and DROP VIEW commands.

❑   How to view and modify data through views. Querying views uses the same syntax as querying tables, and modifying data through views can be restricted by the structure of the view. You learned that in some circumstances, data modification is not permitted through a view, and in others, the modification you can perform is limited.

❑   Binding data to views, which is the same as binding to a table, but you saw that data modification through bound controls is limited.

❑ How to create stored procedures — both from scratch, using the CREATE PROCEDURE statement, and using templates provided by Visual C# Express and SQL Server Management Studio Express. You learned about the syntax of stored procedures; how return values and parameters can be used to exchange data; and how to modify stored procedures with ALTER PROCEDURE and remove them with DROP PROCEDURE.

❑ How to execute stored procedures using C# code, using a SqlCommand object, and using wizards to include stored procedures in data binding. You also saw how stored procedures can be executed from SQL script. When data binding, you learned how it can be necessary to provide multiple stored procedures to allow for select, insert, update, and delete queries to be made. Updating data through stored procedures can be complicated by the data made visible by stored procedures, but you have greater flexibility in dealing with this because you can write stored procedures to do exactly what you want.

❑ How to use conditional logic and looping structures in stored procedures. You saw how the rich SQL syntax allows for more complicated branching and looping code, enabling you to perform complicated actions inside a database.

❑ How to use cursors in stored procedures, an advanced technique that enables you to write stored procedures that operate on result sets rather than individual row and column values. You saw how different types of cursor can be created, used, and disposed of.

In the next chapter you return to the subject of data binding, and explore in depth how to control its behavior.

Exercises

1. Which of the following are valid reasons for using views in your database?

    a. Restricting access to underlying data

    b. Adding additional functionality

    c. Ease of data access

    d. Data formatting

    e. Increasing performance

    f. Data abstraction

2. Why is it not always possible to modify data through views?

3. Stored procedures are useless without parameters, and so parameters are mandatory. True or false?

4. How would you construct a looping structure in a stored procedure to emulate a C# for loop?

5. Modify the GetLineage stored procedure from Ex0704 - Advanced Sprocs such that the number of generations to search can be specified by GetLineage (1 for parents, 2 for parents and grandparents, and so on). This should be included as an integer parameter, @Generations, which defaults to -1, indicating that there is no limit. (Hint: You will need another parameter, @GenerationCount, to keep track of the current generation for recursive calls.)

Custom Data Objects

This chapter presents some of the more advanced techniques that you can use with data binding and the representation of data in your applications. There are a variety of reasons why you might want to avoid using a `DataSet` or typed data set class in your application, including for situations in which data transferred to other applications is required to be in a different format. For example, transferring data sets via web services (something you explore in more detail in Chapter 10) is something that you might often want to do differently. By creating your own data classes, you will have more flexibility in data transfer, particularly to non-.NET clients if you desire such behavior.

With your own data classes, data binding to your data is still possible using object data sources instead of database data sources. There are some things to consider when doing this, but as you will see, you can use the same powerful techniques that you've already looked at in this book. Because there are some differences between the implementation of binding to object data sources between Windows and web applications, you examine both situations in this chapter.

This chapter focuses on creating custom data objects and binding to object data, including the following topics:

❑   Passing data reader objects

❑   Making use of existing .NET Framework classes

❑   Developing your own data-aware classes

❑   Binding to object data in web applications

❑   Binding to object data in Windows applications

Custom Data Objects

The `DataSet` class, as you know, is not always the ideal way to represent data. In some situations, such as when transferring data between applications, other data storage structures are a better choice. Also, the `DataSet` class is often criticized for being heavyweight — that is, for including far more functionality than you are likely to need in many applications, which can affect performance in your applications. If performance is critical, you'll want to look at alternative avenues for obtaining and updating your data, avoiding the use of data sets (and typed data sets) as well as data adapters. Instead, you can concentrate on efficient usage of command and data reader objects to interact with your database.

Creating your own families of data objects requires varying degrees of complexity, depending on your needs. Simpler solutions require less effort and less time to implement, but may suffer by being less functional and robust. Ranging from simple to more complex, the advantages and disadvantages of some of your options are described briefly in the following table.

Option	Advantages	Disadvantages
Don't use data objects; pass data reader objects to where they are needed.	Quick and easy. Good solution for read-only situations and web applications.	Lack of persistent in-memory data storage. Breaks n-tier design rules. Can be difficult to manage connections.
Use existing .NET classes such as `Hashtable` or `Dictionary`.	Fast to implement. Flexible code can often be reused with multiple data sources.	Convoluted syntax. Limited functionality. Lack of strong typing. Data binding difficult or impossible.
Create your own data structures, and use .NET collections and/or generic collection classes to create lists of data.	Simple syntax when classes designed correctly. Capability to add business logic and additional functionality to classes. Strong typing. Object data binding possible.	More time-consuming to implement.
As above, but include n-tier design principles.	As above, but n-tier design improves robustness and prepares for future development.	Even more time-consuming to implement. Design complexity.
Extend the above to provide data-aware classes.	The ultimate in functionality and flexibility.	More time-consuming and complex. Overkill for many applications.
Use or create an alternative framework for automating the creation of fully functional data-aware classes using n-tier design principles.	The ultimate in functionality and flexibility combined with ease of use.	Lengthy development time, or lengthy period of acclimatization with third-party tools or framework.

That's by no means an exhaustive list, but it should give you some idea of the considerations that you have to contemplate.

Toward the more complex end of the scale, entire books have been published on strong n-tier development. For example, you might want to look at *.NET Enterprise Development in C#: From Design to Deployment* (ISBN 1861005911), which I co-authored with Matthew Reynolds, or *Expert C# 2005 Business Objects* (ISBN 1590596323) by Rockford Lhotka, in which he lays out the principles of his Component-based Scalable Logical Architecture (CSLA) .NET Framework. Once you've learned the techniques involved, both of these books (and numerous others) make it quick and easy for you to create families of data-aware objects. There are also a variety of tools for creating data-aware object families available at www.codegeneration.net.

This book explores the options toward the simpler end of the scale, reaching as far as the basic principles of n-tier data-aware classes, but without getting too bogged down in implementation details. First, however, and to put subsequent discussions into context, you should learn a little about what is meant by n-tier design.

n-Tier Application Design Primer

Many applications, including monolithic applications (which consist of a single executable and few if any external code references), make no distinction between code that accesses databases, code that manipulates the data, and code that presents the data to users and enables them to interact with it. Because there's no logical separation of such code, debugging, streamlining, or upgrading these applications can be difficult, and may require complete reworking of the application. For simple applications, this may not be a particularly serious problem, but for large-scale enterprise applications it is critical.

An alternative approach is to decide at the outset to separate code into a number of categories, known as *tiers*, with the code in each tier responsible for different tasks. There are many ways to divide your applications like this. Depending on the architecture of your applications, code in different tiers may be distributed across local networks — or even across the Internet. Typically, three tiers are used as follows:

❑   **Data tier:** Code responsible for interacting with data sources, such as data stored in databases. Generally, classes in the data tier are designed to be *stateless* — that is, no data is stored in this tier. It is, instead, a tier that contains functional classes and acts as a bridge between data sources and classes in other tiers in the application.

❑   **Business tier:** Contains classes that store in-memory representations of data obtained through the data tier, and classes that can manipulate the data or provide additional functionality. Classes often combine these techniques, enabling you to both store and perform operations on data.

❑   **Presentation tier:** Responsible for providing a user interface for users to interact with. This is likely to involve a combination of classes that are designed solely for display purposes, and classes whose display is controlled by the contents of classes in the business tier.

In practice, the lines between the tiers are often blurred. For example, the way that Windows forms applications work, by allowing you to place code in the class definition of your forms, effectively enables you to have a class that spans both the presentation and business tiers — as well as the data tier in many circumstances. It is also possible for classes to span the data and business tiers if, for example, a data storage class is given the capability to interact with a database directly — this example is not necessarily bad practice because it allows you to separate out the presentation tier, and still encapsulates database data reasonably well.

Again, this is a subject to which entire books are devoted, and no attempt is made here either to enforce the rules and principles of n-tier design practice, or to explore the techniques and consequences in any great depth. However, by simply being aware of what n-tier design means, and knowing enough not to simply place all your code in one place, you will (almost without realizing it) write better applications.

To some extent, as you are using the .NET Framework you are already well positioned to take advantage of n-tier design. Some aspects of .NET (and specifically ADO.NET) that you have already seen are geared toward n-tier design. DataSet objects, for example, make no attempt to format data for display purposes, so they are business tier objects that do not exist in the presentation or data tiers. However, some aspects of the .NET Framework and its implementation in both web and Windows applications do not work well with n-tier design principles, causing many n-tier purists to continually argue for changes. In my mind, this is really a case of "if it ain't broke, don't fix it," and I'm perfectly happy to live with things the way they are. That isn't to say that you should ignore n-tier design, however, and there are many ways that you can use it to your advantage despite these limitations.

Passing Data Reader Objects

In earlier chapters you saw how to read data using data reader objects, specifically instances of the SqlDataReader class, and how you can make use of the CommandBehavior enumeration when you execute a command that obtains a data reader. The CommandBehavior.CloseConnection option allows connections to be closed when a data reader using the connection is closed, which means you can provide methods from which data reader objects can be returned to other code, allowing that code to read data without your having to worry about connecting to databases and such. By placing all of the data access code in the data tier of your application, you also provide basic tier separation. Many people consider data readers passing between tiers to be bad practice, but you can use the technique to great effect, and it's certainly simple to implement.

Basically, the technique involves providing one or more classes whose sole responsibility is to obtain data reader objects for use by other classes, including both presentation and business tier code. For example, you might define a class as follows:

```
public static class DataAccess
{
    public static string connectionString = "<connection string>";

    public static SqlDataReader GetMyTableReader()
    {
        // Get connection and command.
        SqlConnection conn = new SqlConnection(connectionString);
        SqlCommand cmd =
            new SqlCommand("SELECT ColumnA, ColumnB FROM MyTable", conn);

        // Open connection and execute command to return a data reader.
        conn.Open();
        return cmd.ExecuteReader(CommandBehavior.CloseConnection);
    }
}
```

Using this code, code elsewhere can access data in the `MyTable` table with ease. Here's an example:

```
// Get Reader.
SqlDataReader reader = DataAccess.GetMyTableReader();

// Use reader to read data.
...

// Close reader and underlying connection.
reader.Close();
```

This may look simple — even trivial — and yet already you have the advantage of not having the code that actually accesses the data in the code that uses the data.

You can abstract things further by sharing the code that handles connections in the `DataAccess` class, perhaps having a single field of type `SqlConnection` that is used by many methods similar to the `GetMyTableReader()` method shown previously. You can also have parameterized methods that pass parameters to stored procedures that return data readers, for example to filter data.

This technique introduces little extra complexity to your applications, but places your data access code in one place — a definite bonus. However, because `SqlDataReader` objects are still required by code in other tiers, you are not completely separated from DBMS-specific code, and you must remember to close the data readers you obtain so that database connections can be closed.

In the following example you see this in action in a web application.

Try It Out   Data Readers

1. Open Visual Web Developer Express and create a new web site called `Ex0801 - Data Readers` in the `C:\BegVC#Databases\Chapter08` directory, File System option for Location and Visual C# for the Language selection.

2. Add the `FolktaleDB.mdf` database to the `App_Data` directory of your project.

3. Add a `web.config` file to your project and add a connection string setting as follows:

```
<configuration>
  ...
  <connectionStrings>
    <add name="connectionString" connectionString="Data Source=.\SQLEXPRESS;
      AttachDbFilename=|DataDirectory|\FolktaleDB.mdf;Integrated Security=True;
      User Instance=True" />
  </connectionStrings>
  ...
</configuration>
```

4. Add a new class file to your project called `DataAccess.cs`. If prompted, accept the suggestion to place your code in the `App_Code` folder. Add code for this class as follows:

```
...

using System.Data.SqlClient;
```

...

```
public static class DataAccess
{
    public static SqlDataReader GetSpeciesReader()
    {
        // Get connection and command.
        SqlConnection conn = new SqlConnection(
            ConfigurationManager.ConnectionStrings["connectionString"]
            .ConnectionString);
        SqlCommand cmd =
            new SqlCommand(
            "SELECT SpeciesId, Species, Description, Immortal FROM Species"
            + " ORDER BY Species", conn);

        // Open connection and execute command to return a data reader.
        conn.Open();
        return cmd.ExecuteReader(CommandBehavior.CloseConnection);
    }
}
```

5. Open `Default.aspx` in Design view, and add a `PlaceHolder` control to the form.

6. Double-click on the form to add a `Page_Load()` event handler. Add code to this method as follows:

...

```
using System.Data.SqlClient;
```

...

```
public partial class _Default : System.Web.UI.Page
{
    protected void Page_Load(object sender, EventArgs e)
    {
        // Get data reader.
        SqlDataReader reader = DataAccess.GetSpeciesReader();

        // Output HTML.
        while (reader.Read())
        {
            PlaceHolder1.Controls.Add(new LiteralControl(
                "<div style=\"float: left; background-color: #ffffa0; width: 250px;"
                + " height: 140px; border: solid 1px #ff4040; margin: 10px;"
                + " padding: 8px;\"><h3>"));
            if ((bool)reader["Immortal"])
            {
                PlaceHolder1.Controls.Add(new LiteralControl("Immortal: "));
            }
            PlaceHolder1.Controls.Add(
                new LiteralControl(reader["Species"] as string));
            PlaceHolder1.Controls.Add(new LiteralControl("</h3><small><i>("));
            PlaceHolder1.Controls.Add(
                new LiteralControl(reader["SpeciesId"].ToString()));
```

```
                      PlaceHolder1.Controls.Add(new LiteralControl(")</i></small><br />"));
                      PlaceHolder1.Controls.Add(
                          new LiteralControl(reader["Description"] as string));
                      PlaceHolder1.Controls.Add(new LiteralControl("<br /></div>"));
                  }

                  // Close reader.
                  reader.Close();
              }
          }
```

7. Run the application. If prompted, enable debugging in `web.config`. The result is shown in Figure 8-1.

8. Close the application and Visual Web Developer Express.

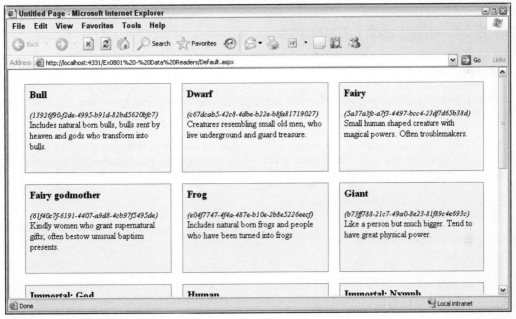

Figure 8-1: Application output

How It Works

This example employs a data layer consisting of a static class with a single public static method that obtains a data reader object that uses the `CommandBehavior.CloseConnection` behavior.

The code for the data access class is exactly as shown earlier, although with the connection string and query relating to the `FolktaleDB` database. In this case, the query obtains information from the `Species` table.

In the code for `Default.aspx.cs`, the `Page_Load()` event handler uses the data tier method to obtain a data reader, reads items for that, and adds literal controls to a `PlaceHolder` control on the form. Look at the generated HTML for the page to see code similar to the following for each item added:

```
<div style="float: left; background-color: #ffffa0; width: 250px; height: 140px;
border: solid 1px #ff4040; margin: 10px; padding: 8px;"><h3>Dwarf</h3><small>
<i>(c67dcab5-42c8-4dbe-b22e-b8fa81719027)</i></small><br />Creatures resembling
small old men, who live underground and guard treasure.<br /></div>
```

Finally, the code closes the data reader, which also closes the underlying connection. Remember that this is important — leaving connections open can cause problems, which is one of the limitations of this technique. In spite of that, code such as this can be used to great effect to obtain results in situations where you want a greater degree of control over the exact HTML output in web applications.

Using Existing .NET Classes

The next step in the process taking you toward data-aware classes is to use existing classes in the .NET Framework that enable you to store data in the form of name/value pairs, and to have collections of data. Once you have a way of storing data, you can persist it, and it doesn't have to be read every time you require it. This is advantageous for web applications because you can store data between HTTP requests, reducing the load on the server — although it does mean that data can become outdated.

The simplest class capable of representing a row of data in a database table is `Hashtable`. This class allows you to store a number of key/value pairs, where both the key and value are of type `object`. You can populate a `Hashtable` object from a data reader (that has a row loaded) as follows:

```
Hashtable item = new Hashtable();
for (int index = 0; index < reader.FieldCount; index++)
{
    item.Add(reader.GetName(index), reader[index]);
}
```

When dealing with multiple rows, you can simply use an array of `Hashtable` objects. However, that means that you would need to find out how many rows were required to initialize the array, and resizing the array for adding or removing rows becomes awkward. Collection classes are a much better option, and with the generic collection types in .NET, you can create a collection of objects easily. You have three classes to choose from to do this:

❑   `System.Collections.ObjectModel.Collection<T>`: Provides a basic implementation of a collection, with strongly typed methods such as `Add()` and `Remove()`, as well as an enumerator and iterator that enable you to navigate the collection in looping structures. For simple situations, or if you want to create your own collection class by deriving from a simple base collection class, this is the best class to use. It implements a number of interfaces used for collection functionality, including `ICollection`, `IList`, and `IEnumerable`, as well as generic equivalents of these interfaces.

❑   `System.Collections.Generic.List<T>`: Implements the same interfaces as `Collection<T>`, and provides all the functionality that `Collection<T>` does, but it includes additional functionality. It allows for sorting and searching of the data it contains, and lets you specify an initial capacity for its items, which enables better performance because its internal data array doesn't have to be resized as data is added.

❑ `System.ComponentModel.BindingList<T>`: Inherits from `Collection<T>`, and includes additional functionality that is specifically tailored for data binding in Windows applications. It implements some additional interfaces to make that possible, and can raise events so that you can keep track of changes to its data. You examine this class a little later in the chapter when you look at how to bind to object data. The class doesn't really give you any additional functionality for web applications.

`Collection<T>` is generally the best choice, particularly when you don't want to get into data-binding situations, unless you have a real need to use the additional functionality of `List<T>`. Alternatively, in more complex situations, you might want to derive your own class from `IList` or `IList<T>`, gaining complete control over how the collection class operates.

Using `Collection<T>` to hold data in the form of `Hashtable` objects simply means supplying the `Hashtable` class as the type to use for the generic class. For example:

```
Collection<Hashtable> data = new Collection<Hashtable>();
while (reader.Read())
{
    Hashtable item = new Hashtable();
    for (int index = 0; index < reader.FieldCount; index++)
    {
        item.Add(reader.GetName(index), reader[index]);
    }
    data.Add(item);
}
```

The code that obtains the data reader used by this code is, again, omitted for simplicity.

There are options besides `Hashtable` at your disposal. You can create your own data classes, as discussed in the next section. Alternatively, you can make use of the fact that database data always consists of a `string` column name and an `object` value, and creates a strongly typed collection accordingly, using the `Dictionary<T>` class:

```
Collection<Dictionary<string, object>> data;
```

When it comes to usage, there really isn't much difference between using `Hashtable` or `Dictionary`, although strongly typing the key to a `string` value may improve performance.

The next example extends the previous web application to use a collection of objects to obtain data and store it in view state.

Try It Out   Collections

1. Copy the web site directory from the last example, `Ex0801 - Data Readers`, to a new directory, `Ex0802 - Collections`.

2. Open Visual Web Developer Express and open the copy of the web site from its new location.

3. Modify `DataAccess.cs` as follows:

   ...

```csharp
using System.Collections.ObjectModel;
using System.Collections.Generic;

...

public static class DataAccess
{
    private static SqlDataReader GetSpeciesReader()
    {
        ...
    }

    public static Collection<Dictionary<string, object>> GetSpeciesData()
    {
        // Get data reader.
        SqlDataReader reader = GetSpeciesReader();

        // Populate data collection.
        Collection<Dictionary<string, object>> data =
            new Collection<Dictionary<string, object>>();
        while (reader.Read())
        {
            Dictionary<string, object> item = new Dictionary<string, object>();
            for (int index = 0; index < reader.FieldCount; index++)
            {
                item.Add(reader.GetName(index), reader[index]);
            }
            data.Add(item);
        }

        // Close reader.
        reader.Close();

        // Return result.
        return data;
    }
}
```

4. Modify `Default.aspx.cs` as follows:

   ...

```csharp
using System.Collections.Generic;
using System.Collections.ObjectModel;

...

public partial class _Default : System.Web.UI.Page
{
    protected Collection<Dictionary<string, object>> Data
    {
```

```
            get
            {
                return ViewState["genericListData"]
                    as Collection<Dictionary<string, object>>;
            }
            set
            {
                ViewState["genericListData"] = value;
            }
        }

        protected void Page_Load(object sender, EventArgs e)
        {
    if (!IsPostBack)
    {
        // Populate data.
        Data = DataAccess.GetSpeciesData();
    }

            // Output HTML.
            foreach (Dictionary<string, object> item in Data)
            {
                PlaceHolder1.Controls.Add(new LiteralControl(
                    "<div style=\"float: left; background-color: #ffffa0; width: 250px;"
                    + " border: solid 1px #ff4040; margin: 10px;"
                    + " padding: 8px;\"><h3>"));
                if ((bool)item["Immortal"])
                {
                    PlaceHolder1.Controls.Add(new LiteralControl("Immortal: "));
                }
                PlaceHolder1.Controls.Add(
                    new LiteralControl(item["Species"] as string));
                PlaceHolder1.Controls.Add(new LiteralControl("</h3><small><i>("));
                PlaceHolder1.Controls.Add(
                    new LiteralControl(item["SpeciesId"].ToString()));
                PlaceHolder1.Controls.Add(new LiteralControl(")</i></small><br />"));
                PlaceHolder1.Controls.Add(
                    new LiteralControl(item["Description"] as string));
                PlaceHolder1.Controls.Add(new LiteralControl("<br /></div>"));
            }
        }
    }
```

5. Open `Default.aspx` in design view and add a `Button` control to the page immediately after the `PlaceHolder` control.

6. Run the application and verify that it functions as in the previous example.

7. Add a breakpoint in the code for the `Page_Load()` event handler, and then click the button on the form. Verify that the data is not loaded from the database, but that it is still displayed on the form.

8. Close the application and Visual Web Developer Express.

How It Works

This example uses the objects of type `Dictionary<string, object>` to store rows of data, and groups those objects in a collection of type `Collection<Dictionary<string, object>>`. By having an intermediate storage object, you can persist database data in the view state of the application so that it remains available between HTTP requests. You tested this by performing a post-back operation, triggered using a `Button` control.

In the static `DataAccess` class definition, a new method is added to get data. It uses the existing `GetSpeciesReader()` method to obtain a reader used to populate the resultant collection. Because this method is no longer required by other code, it's made private. This simple change makes the `DataAccess` class a much better behaved data tier object, because at no point is database access code used directly outside of the class. The class used to hold data, `Collection<Dictionary<string, object>>`, is then effectively used as a business tier object, storing and manipulating data obtained via the data tier. The code used to populate this object is similar to that shown prior to this example, and the code closes the data reader (and the underlying connection) when it has finished with it.

In the code for the form `Default.aspx.cs`, a property called `Data` is added to store data obtained from the data tier in view state, using the `ViewState` property exposed by the base class for the form, `System.Web.UI.Page`:

```
protected Collection<Dictionary<string, object>> Data
{
    get
    {
        return ViewState["genericListData"]
            as Collection<Dictionary<string, object>>;
    }
    set
    {
        ViewState["genericListData"] = value;
    }
}
```

The `Data` property is set in the `Page_Load()` event handler — but only where no post-back operation is in progress:

```
protected void Page_Load(object sender, EventArgs e)
{
    if (!IsPostBack)
    {
        Data = DataAccess.GetSpeciesData();
    }
}
```

Finally, the `Data` property is used to render data using code similar to that in the previous example, but modified to use the data storage class rather than a data reader.

A `Button` control is added to the form to test the behavior of the application when a post-back operation is triggered. This post-back occurs even though the `Button` control has no click event handler. The result is that the data displays as before — but without being obtained from the database. Instead the stored data was used.

As mentioned earlier, doing things this way isn't without its problems — including the fact that data is not refreshed from the database, so changes won't be reflected in the data displayed. Without introducing additional round trips to the database, this is inevitable. Yet, it is a price worth paying for performance, especially where data doesn't change too often, such as when displaying product information in an e-commerce application.

Another disadvantage, which you can see by looking at the source of the page when viewing it in a browser, is that a large amount of data is stored in the view state of the page. In this case that's acceptable, and in most circumstances it won't be a problem because people tend to have Internet connections capable of coping with fairly large amounts of data. When displaying much larger amounts of data, however, it may be worth reducing the amount of view state data, in which case it can be better to obtain data from the database every time the page is loaded, regardless of whether a post-back is in progress.

Basic Data-Aware Class Design

The code in the previous example is a definite step forward, but still has a problem when it comes to n-tier application design — namely that code in the presentation tier (the web form) must access the data tier directly. To improve encapsulation, you could abstract the access into business-tier classes. That means you probably want to create your own business tier classes rather than simply using the generic classes as detailed previously.

There is an additional benefit of doing this — you can strongly type your classes and provide properties and methods that exactly match the data stored in them. The result is much the same as using typed data set classes rather than simply using `DataSet` instances to hold data; the syntax required to use the classes is greatly simplified. However, this behavior comes at a cost because you will have to spend time creating families of classes that are appropriate for all the data in your database that you want to access.

You can use data-aware classes in your presentation and business layers without needing any conception of how data is accessed; it might come from a database or any other source.

There are a number of design decisions to make when implementing data-aware classes. Exactly where to place the boundaries between layers — and how to pass data between tiers — can be complicated. Depending on the architecture of your applications, you may have different tiers in the same application, but you might also separate tiers across process or machine boundaries. In these more advanced cases you have even more to consider — including marshaling and ensuring that your objects are represented consistently in all circumstances, even if, for example, one of the computers involved in the process is inadvertently disconnected. This can mean making use of additional technologies, such as COM+ services, messaging, and so on.

In this book, however, you won't be looking at these advanced situations. Instead, all you need to know at this stage are the basics. It's also worth bearing in mind that for smaller scale applications, the techniques you've already looked at in this chapter may be more than enough to meet your needs. Unless you really need to, then, there is no need to get too embedded in data-aware class design because it's hardly worth introducing complexity for the sake of it.

DataAwareObjects Class Library

The downloadable code for this book includes a class library — DataAwareObjects — that contains a starting point for developing your own data-aware classes. The library contains some basic plumbing and some base classes that you can use to derive your own classes. This section examines the library and shows you how to use it.

> *The code in this class library, and the code used to illustrate it in the Try It Out later in this section, is significantly more complex than most of the code you've seen so far in this book. This is intentional because the class library is intended as a starting point for you to use and develop in real-world applications. Many of the techniques illustrated here are professional, tried and tested techniques. While you may not understand everything the first time you read through this section and experiment with the code, there's a lot to be gained by persevering with it.*

The DataAwareObjects class library has been created with the following design considerations:

❑ Single class library containing data and business tier classes.

❑ Data access code restricted to the data tier.

❑ Generic class definitions used in two of the base classes so that implementation code can be included and there is less work to defining derived classes.

❑ Three base classes for each table:

    ❑ Item class for storing row data, TableItem.

    ❑ Collection class for storing items, TableCollection<T>.

    ❑ Data tier class for data access, TableDataAccess<T, U>.

❑ One extra static class called DataAccess containing code to make database connections, which must be initialized with a connection string by the client before data access is permitted.

❑ Data item class uses new, dirty (modified), and deleted flags to keep track of data modification.

❑ Single-level undo (cancel changes) functionality included.

The DataAwareObjects class library contains full XML documentation. It isn't reproduced in the discussions in this section to save space; you can browse it at your leisure.

The functionality of the library — as well as that of custom libraries and how this fits into overall application function — is shown in Figure 8-2.

DataAccess Class

The code for DataAccess is as follows:

```
public static class DataAccess
{
    public static string ConnectionString;

    public static SqlConnection GetConnection()
    {
        // Check for connection string
```

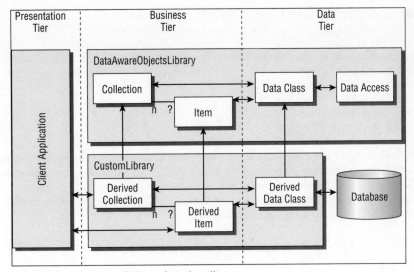

Figure 8-2: DataAwareObjects functionality

```
        if (ConnectionString == null)
        {
            throw new ApplicationException("Please supply a connection string.");
        }

        // Return connection and command.
        return new SqlConnection(ConnectionString);
    }
}
```

A client application must set the `ConnectionString` field before other classes can use this class to obtain a `SqlConnection` object. This is necessary so that the data tier classes for tables can exchange data with the database, as you'll see shortly.

As an alternative, you could make this class attempt to extract a connection string from a configuration file associated with the client application referencing the library. However, because the client application will have access to its own configuration file, this hardly seems necessary, and the small amount of configuration is hardly a problem.

TableItem Class

The next thing to look at is the class that represents a table row. This class, `TableItem`, is an abstract class definition from which you must derive classes to represent table rows. The class is serializable, making it possible to persist items. It contains two `Dictionary<string, object>` collections to store column data as described earlier in the chapter, only here both the original and current states of the item are stored:

```
    [Serializable]
    public abstract class TableItem
    {
```

```
        protected Dictionary<string, object> originalData;
        protected Dictionary<string, object> currentData;
```

Two flags are included to keep track of whether the object is new or deleted, isNew and isDeleted (which have read-only properties — IsNew and IsDeleted, not shown here — to give clients access to this information):

```
        protected bool isNew;
        protected bool isDeleted;
```

Knowing whether an item has been added or deleted enables you to create appropriate SQL statements or construct appropriate stored procedures for data modification. In addition, you need to know if an item has been modified. To check that, a third flag is defined by the property IsDirty. Again, this property is read-only. However, rather than being set internally, it compares the values of the original and current data collections to obtain a value as follows:

```
    public bool IsDirty
    {
        get
        {
            foreach (string key in originalData.Keys)
            {
                if (originalData[key] != currentData[key])
                {
                    return true;
                }
            }
            return false;
        }
    }
```

The constructor for the class initializes the protected fields, including marking the new item as being new:

```
    public TableItem()
    {
        isNew = true;
        isDeleted = false;
        originalData = new Dictionary<string, object>();
        currentData = new Dictionary<string, object>();
    }
```

The remainder of the TableItem class contains three methods that clients can use to manipulate the item. These are Delete(), to flag the item as deleted; AcceptChanges(), which copies the current state to the original state and removes the isNew flag; and RejectChanges(), which copies the original state to the current state and clears the isDeleted flag:

```
    public void Delete()
    {
        isDeleted = true;
    }

    public void AcceptChanges()
```

```
    {
        originalData = new Dictionary<string, object>(currentData);
        isNew = false;
    }

    public void RejectChanges()
    {
        currentData = new Dictionary<string, object>(originalData);
        isDeleted = false;
    }
}
```

These methods are also used by the other classes in the `DataAwareObjects` class library.

To use the `TableItem` class, your derived class needs to do the following:

❑ Add properties that expose column data stored in the `currentData` store in a strongly typed way

❑ Add a parameterized constructor to add column data to the `currentData` store

❑ If desired, add a default constructor that references the parameterized constructor and configures the `currentData` store with default data

For example, you might add a string property as follows:

```
public string MyStringColumn
{
    get
    {
        return currentData["MyStringColumn"] as string;
    }
    set
    {
        currentData["MyStringColumn"] = value;
    }
}
```

The `currentData["MyStringColumn"]` data entry would be initialized in the parameterized constructor.

TableCollection<T> Class

The next class, `TableCollection<T>`, is an abstract generic base class for making collections of `TableItem` objects. It derives from the `Collection<T>` class you've already used, but restricts type `T` to be a class derived from `TableItem`. It also adds additional functionality appropriate for collections of these items.

The class (which is also marked serializable) contains one constructor that you can use to "auto-load" data when an instance of a derived class is created:

```
[Serializable]
public abstract class TableCollection<T> : Collection<T>
    where T : TableItem
{
```

```
public TableCollection(bool loadData)
{
    if (loadData)
    {
        Load();
    }
}
```

Next, there are two abstract methods that you must implement in derived classes to exchange data with the database using the data tier class you'll look at in the next section:

```
public abstract void Load();
protected abstract void SaveData();
```

Note that one is protected. That's because it is called by the following public method:

```
public void Save()
{
    // Save changes.
    SaveData();

    // Accept changes.
    AcceptChanges();
}
```

This forces changes to be accepted when they are committed to the database, through the use of the AcceptChanges() method:

```
public void AcceptChanges()
{
    // Accept changes.
    Collection<T> itemsToDelete = new Collection<T>();
    foreach (T item in this)
    {
        if (item.IsDeleted)
        {
            // Prepare to delete item.
            itemsToDelete.Add(item);
        }
        else
        {
            // Restore to unchanged state.
            item.AcceptChanges();
        }
    }

    // Remove deleted items.
    foreach (T item in itemsToDelete)
    {
        base.RemoveItem(IndexOf(item));
    }
}
```

`AcceptChanges()` accepts changes on each item in the underlying collection, removing any items that have been flagged as deleted.

There is also a `RejectChanges()` method that rejects changes on all items and removes items flagged as new:

```
public void RejectChanges()
{
    // Reject changes.
    Collection<T> itemsToDelete = new Collection<T>();
    foreach (T item in this)
    {
        if (item.IsNew)
        {
            // Prepare to delete item.
            itemsToDelete.Add(item);
        }
        else
        {
            // Restore to unchanged state.
            item.RejectChanges();
        }
    }

    // Remove added items.
    foreach (T item in itemsToDelete)
    {
        base.RemoveItem(IndexOf(item));
    }
}
```

Finally, the internal method used to remove items from the collection is overridden. That prevents items deleted by client applications from being removed. Instead they are flagged as deleted:

```
protected override void RemoveItem(int index)
{
    // Don't remove, just mark as deleted.
    this[index].Delete();
}
```

In `AcceptChanges()` and `RejectChanges()`, the base class version of `RemoveItem()` is used so that items are actually deleted, not just marked as deleted.

In a derived version of this class you would supply a class to use for `T` that is derived from `TableItem`, and implement the `Load()` and `SaveData()` methods. You should also provide a constructor with a single Boolean parameter that calls the base class constructor with the same signature.

TableDataAccess<T, U> Class

The final class to derive from to create a family of objects for your data-aware classes is the most complicated. This class, `TableDataAccess<T, U>`, provides data access code for your classes. Here, `T` is a class derived from `TableItem` as in `TableCollection<T>`, and `U` is a class derived from `TableCollection<T>`. Again, this enables the data access class to be strongly typed to your other data-aware classes.

`TableDataAccess<T, U>` contains no state, only methods, many of which are left for derived classes to implement. In fact, it could be argued that this class should be static, or contain only static methods. However, that would lead to problems because static classes cannot be derived from, and static methods cannot be overridden; so it's defined as a non-static class with instance methods instead.

The first method to be overridden is `GetReader()`:

```
public abstract class TableDataAccess<T, U>
    where T : TableItem
    where U : TableCollection<T>
{

    protected abstract SqlDataReader GetReader();
```

Derived classes can use `GetReader()` to obtain data via a `SqlDataReader` instance. The reader should use the `CommandBehavior.CloseConnection` option as you've seen in previous examples. How this data reader is obtained is up to you — you can use SQL statements or stored procedures as you see fit.

`GetReader()` is used in the `GetData()` method, which fills an object of type `U` with data:

```
public void GetData(U data)
{
    // Clear existing data.
    data.Clear();

    // Get data reader.
    SqlDataReader reader = GetReader();

    // Populate data collection.
    while (reader.Read())
    {
        T item = GetItemFromReader(reader);
        data.Add(item);
    }

    // Accept changes.
    data.AcceptChanges();

    // Close reader.
    reader.Close();
}
```

This method first clears any existing data in the collection, and then uses a reader to call another method, `GetItemFromReader()`, to get items of type `T` and add them to the collection. Finally, changes are accepted for the collection so that the newly added items are not flagged as being new, and the reader (and underlying connection) is closed.

The `GetItemFromReader()` method is left abstract for implementation in derived classes:

```
    protected abstract T GetItemFromReader(SqlDataReader reader);
```

That's so that you can extract named data. Alternatively, you could initialize items in a constructor of the class you have derived from `TableItem`, but this would break the initial design consideration of leaving data access code in the data tier. A more complicated option is to use reflection to match column names to property names and set the data automatically based on that information. For the purposes of this book, however, it is quite enough to leave these details to the derived classes.

The rest of the code in this class concerns data modification, which is achieved with the `SaveData()` method. That method saves the data in a collection of type `U` to the database:

```
public void SaveData(U data)
{
    // Get and open connection.
    SqlConnection conn = DataAccess.GetConnection();
    conn.Open();

    // Process rows.
    foreach (T item in data)
    {
        // Get command for row.
        SqlCommand cmd = null;
        if (item.IsDeleted && !item.IsNew)
        {
            cmd = GetDeleteCommand(item, conn);
        }
        else if (item.IsNew && !item.IsDeleted)
        {
            cmd = GetInsertCommand(item, conn);
        }
        else if (item.IsDirty)
        {
            cmd = GetUpdateCommand(item, conn);
        }

        // Execute command.
        if (cmd != null)
        {
            cmd.ExecuteNonQuery();
        }
    }

    // Close connection.
    conn.Close();
}
```

In this method, the flags for `TableItem` objects are examined, and the procedure to perform for the object inferred. It might be an update, insert, or delete operation. Three abstract methods are provided so that you can create and return `SqlCommand` objects configured according to the state of items:

```
protected abstract SqlCommand GetUpdateCommand(T item, SqlConnection conn);

protected abstract SqlCommand GetInsertCommand(T item, SqlConnection conn);

protected abstract SqlCommand GetDeleteCommand(T item, SqlConnection conn);
}
```

If a command is obtained for an item (and it might not be, if the item's state is unchanged) the appropriate command is executed, and then this is repeated for each item in the collection.

So, there is a little more work to do in derived classes of this type because five methods must be implemented. None of the methods, however, are particularly complicated.

In the following example you use the DataAwareObjects class library to display data from the Species table in a web application.

Try It Out   Data-Aware Objects

1. Copy the web site directory from the last example, Ex0802 - Collections, to a new directory, Ex0803 - Data Aware Objects.

2. Open the new web site in Visual Web Developer Express.

3. Add a reference to the DataAwareObjects class library to the project. To do so, you may first have to compile the class library, which you can do using Visual C# Express. Open the project and compile it; then the compiled .dll file for the class library will be available in the DataAwareObjects\bin\Release (or Debug) directory (depending on whether you compile the project in debug mode). Next, in Visual Web Developer, right-click on the project in Solution Explorer, select Add Reference, and browse to DataAwareObjects.dll to add the reference. The class library is in the downloadable code for this chapter.

4. Remove the existing DataAccess.cs code file from the App_Code directory for the project.

5. Add a new class to the project called SpeciesItem and modify the code as follows:

```
    . . .

    using DataAwareObjects;

    . . .

    [Serializable]
    public class SpeciesItem : TableItem
    {
        public SpeciesItem()
            : this(Guid.NewGuid(), "New Species", null, false)
        {
        }

        public SpeciesItem(Guid speciesId, string species, string description,
            bool immortal)
        {
            currentData.Add("SpeciesId", speciesId);
            currentData.Add("Species", species);
            currentData.Add("Description", description);
            currentData.Add("Immortal", immortal);
        }

        public Guid SpeciesId
        {
            get
```

```
        {
            return (Guid)currentData["SpeciesId"];
        }
    }

    public string Species
    {
        get
        {
            return currentData["Species"] as string;
        }
        set
        {
            currentData["Species"] = value;
        }
    }

    public string Description
    {
        get
        {
            return currentData["Description"] as string;
        }
        set
        {
            currentData["Description"] = value;
        }
    }

    public bool Immortal
    {
        get
        {
            return (bool)currentData["Immortal"];
        }
        set
        {
            currentData["Immortal"] = value;
        }
    }
}
```

6. Add a new class — `SpeciesCollection` — to the project and modify the code as follows:

...

```
using System.Collections.ObjectModel;
using DataAwareObjects;
```

...

```
[Serializable]
public class SpeciesCollection : TableCollection<SpeciesItem>
{
```

```
        public SpeciesCollection(bool loadData) : base(loadData)
        {
        }

        public override void Load()
        {
        }

        protected override void SaveData()
        {
        }
    }
```

7. Add a new class — `SpeciesDataAccess` — to the project and modify the code as follows:

...

```
using System.Data.SqlClient;
using DataAwareObjects;
```

...

```
public class SpeciesDataAccess : TableDataAccess<SpeciesItem, SpeciesCollection>
{
    protected override SqlDataReader GetReader()
    {
        // Get connection and command.
        SqlConnection conn = DataAccess.GetConnection();
        SqlCommand cmd =
            new SqlCommand(
            "SELECT SpeciesId, Species, Description, Immortal FROM Species"
            + " ORDER BY Species", conn);

        // Open connection and execute command to return a data reader.
        conn.Open();
        return cmd.ExecuteReader(CommandBehavior.CloseConnection);
    }

    protected override SpeciesItem GetItemFromReader(SqlDataReader reader)
    {
        try
        {
            // Load values.
            Guid newSpeciesId = (Guid)reader["SpeciesId"];
            string newSpecies = reader["Species"] as string;
            string newDescription = reader["Description"] as string;
            bool newImmortal = (bool)reader["Immortal"];

            // Obtain item.
            SpeciesItem newItem = new SpeciesItem(newSpeciesId, newSpecies,
                newDescription, newImmortal);

            // Return item.
            return newItem;
```

```
    }
    catch (Exception ex)
    {
        // Throw exception.
        throw new ApplicationException(
            "Unable to load species item from data reader.", ex);
    }
}

protected override SqlCommand GetUpdateCommand(SpeciesItem item,
    SqlConnection conn)
{
    // Get command to modify Species row.
    SqlCommand cmd = new SqlCommand("UPDATE Species SET Species = @Species, "
        + "Description = @Description, Immortal = @Immortal "
        + "WHERE SpeciesId = @SpeciesId", conn);
    cmd.Parameters.Add("SpeciesId", SqlDbType.UniqueIdentifier).Value =
        item.SpeciesId;
    cmd.Parameters.Add("Species", SqlDbType.VarChar, 100).Value = item.Species;
    if (item.Description != null)
    {
        cmd.Parameters.Add("Description", SqlDbType.Text).Value =
            item.Description;
    }
    else
    {
        cmd.Parameters.Add("Description", SqlDbType.Text).Value = DBNull.Value;
    }
    cmd.Parameters.Add("Immortal", SqlDbType.Bit).Value = item.Immortal;
    return cmd;
}

protected override SqlCommand GetInsertCommand(SpeciesItem item,
    SqlConnection conn)
{
    // Get command to add Species row.
    SqlCommand cmd = new SqlCommand("INSERT INTO Species (SpeciesId, Species, "
        + "Description, Immortal) VALUES (@SpeciesId, @Species, @Description, "
        + "@Immortal)", conn);
    cmd.Parameters.Add("SpeciesId", SqlDbType.UniqueIdentifier).Value =
        item.SpeciesId;
    cmd.Parameters.Add("Species", SqlDbType.VarChar, 100).Value = item.Species;
    if (item.Description != null)
    {
        cmd.Parameters.Add("Description", SqlDbType.Text).Value =
            item.Description;
    }
    else
    {
        cmd.Parameters.Add("Description", SqlDbType.Text).Value = DBNull.Value;
    }
    cmd.Parameters.Add("Immortal", SqlDbType.Bit).Value = item.Immortal;
    return cmd;
```

```
    }

    protected override SqlCommand GetDeleteCommand(SpeciesItem item,
        SqlConnection conn)
    {
        // Get command to delete Species row.
        SqlCommand cmd = new SqlCommand("DELETE FROM Species WHERE SpeciesId = "
            + "@SpeciesId", conn);
        cmd.Parameters.Add("SpeciesId", SqlDbType.UniqueIdentifier).Value =
            item.SpeciesId;
        return cmd;
    }
}
```

8. Modify the code in `SpeciesCollection` as follows:

```
public class SpeciesCollection : TableCollection<SpeciesItem>
{
    [NonSerialized]
    private SpeciesDataAccess dataAccess = new SpeciesDataAccess();

    ...

    public override void Load()
    {
        // Load data from database.
        dataAccess.GetData(this);
    }

    protected override void SaveData()
    {
        // Save data.
    dataAccess.SaveData(this);
    }
}
```

9. Modify the code in `Default.aspx.cs` as follows:

```
using DataAwareObjects;

public partial class _Default : System.Web.UI.Page
{
    protected SpeciesCollection Data
    {
        get
        {
            return ViewState["genericListData"] as SpeciesCollection;
        }
        set
        {
            ViewState["genericListData"] = value;
        }
    }
```

```
protected void Page_Load(object sender, EventArgs e)
{
    if (!IsPostBack)
    {
        // Configure data access
        DataAccess.ConnectionString = ConfigurationManager
            .ConnectionStrings["connectionString"].ConnectionString;

        // Populate data.
        Data = new SpeciesCollection(true);
    }

    // Output HTML.
    foreach (SpeciesItem item in Data)
    {
        if (!item.IsDeleted)
        {
            PlaceHolder1.Controls.Add(new LiteralControl(
                "<div style=\"float: left; background-color: #ffffa0; width: 250px;"
                + " border: solid 1px #ff4040; margin: 10px;"
                + " padding: 8px;\"><h3>"));
            if (item.Immortal)
            {
                PlaceHolder1.Controls.Add(new LiteralControl("Immortal: "));
            }
            PlaceHolder1.Controls.Add(new LiteralControl(item.Species));
            PlaceHolder1.Controls.Add(new LiteralControl("</h3><small><i>("));
            PlaceHolder1.Controls.Add(
                new LiteralControl(item.SpeciesId.ToString()));
            PlaceHolder1.Controls.Add(
                new LiteralControl(")</i></small><br />"));
            PlaceHolder1.Controls.Add(new LiteralControl(item.Description));
            PlaceHolder1.Controls.Add(new LiteralControl("<br /></div>"));
        }
    }
}
```

10. Run the application and verify that it functions as in the previous examples.

11. Close the application and Visual Web Developer Express.

How It Works

This example uses the base classes defined in the DataAwareObjects class library to quickly assemble some data-aware classes for the Species table in the FolktaleDB database. You created three classes: SpeciesItem and SpeciesCollection for the business tier, and SpeciesDataAccess for the data tier. These were added to the web application, although they could equally exist in a separate class library.

For SpeciesItem, you added four properties for the columns in the Species table, including one read-only column for the GUID ID of the item. You also provided two constructors for items of this type, including a default one that sets initial values for these properties, which meant generating a new GUID for the ID of the item.

For `SpeciesCollection`, you added code that uses the `SpeciesDataAccess` class. You added a private field for the data access class, and made it non-serialized because there's no state stored in it. Then you used it in both the `Load()` and `SaveData()` method overrides.

Finally, the `SpeciesDataAccess` class included several method overrides. In `GetReader()`, you generated a `SqlDataReader` object using the following SQL command and C# code that you've seen before:

```
SELECT SpeciesId, Species, Description, Immortal FROM Species ORDER BY Species
```

The code for `GetItemFromReader()` is quite interesting. A reader that is positioned at a row by the base class is used to extract a `Species` item. First, each column is obtained:

```
protected override SpeciesItem GetItemFromReader(SqlDataReader reader)
{
    try
    {
        // Load values.
        Guid newSpeciesId = (Guid)reader["SpeciesId"];
        string newSpecies = reader["Species"] as string;
        string newDescription = reader["Description"] as string;
        bool newImmortal = (bool)reader["Immortal"];
```

It's possible that some of this data will be nullable, in which case you have to design your item classes slightly differently, either by using nullable data types or by throwing exceptions when null data is accessed. That's not necessary here because the only nullable field is `Description`, which is a string type, so null values are permitted.

The data obtained is passed to the `SpeciesItem` constructor to get an item, and returned to the method caller. There's no need to accept changes on the item because the base class does that for you.

```
        // Obtain item.
        SpeciesItem newItem = new SpeciesItem(newSpeciesId, newSpecies,
            newDescription, newImmortal);

        // Return item.
        return newItem;
    }
```

If an error occurs, an exception is generated with a more user-friendly message:

```
    catch (Exception ex)
    {
        // Throw exception.
        throw new ApplicationException(
            "Unable to load species item from data reader.", ex);
    }
}
```

The rest of the methods in the class generate `SqlCommand` objects. They are all similar, so you need to look closer at only one of them, such as the `GetUpdateCommand()`:

```
protected override SqlCommand GetUpdateCommand(SpeciesItem item,
    SqlConnection conn)
```

```
{
    // Get command to modify Species row.
    SqlCommand cmd = new SqlCommand("UPDATE Species SET Species = @Species, "
        + "Description = @Description, Immortal = @Immortal "
        + "WHERE SpeciesId = @SpeciesId", conn);
    cmd.Parameters.Add("SpeciesId", SqlDbType.UniqueIdentifier).Value =
        item.SpeciesId;
    cmd.Parameters.Add("Species", SqlDbType.VarChar, 100).Value = item.Species;
    if (item.Description != null)
    {
        cmd.Parameters.Add("Description", SqlDbType.Text).Value =
            item.Description;
    }
    else
    {
        cmd.Parameters.Add("Description", SqlDbType.Text).Value = DBNull.Value;
    }
    cmd.Parameters.Add("Immortal", SqlDbType.Bit).Value = item.Immortal;
    return cmd;
}
```

Here, a parameterized SQL command is created, and the properties of the `SpeciesItem` item are used to provide values for these parameters. These could equally be used for parameters of a stored procedure. The `Description` property can be `null`, but to supply a `null`-valued parameter, you must use `DBNull.Value`, as in this code.

Finally, you modified the existing code for the `Default.aspx` form. There were not a lot of changes because accessing the data with these data objects requires much the same techniques as in previous examples. Here are three points to note:

❑   Objects of type `SpeciesCollection` are serializable in session state because they are marked as serializable.

❑   The client application must first set the connection string to be used for data access.

❑   When presenting objects, only those not marked as deleted are displayed.

That last point is an interesting one. Because client applications may still require access to items marked as deleted, they're still included when enumerating the collection. This means that, to prevent the display of these objects, a test is made of the `IsDeleted` property for items. Alternatively, you could provide a second enumerator in the collection class that could be used by client applications to obtain only those items that aren't deleted. That is an exercise for you at the end of the chapter.

You can develop the classes presented here in many ways, and you may want to do so in your own applications. There are some notable omissions:

❑   No sorting/searching functionality is included (apart from what is possible using generic collection base classes).

❑   No capability to navigate relational data is available.

❑   No transactional support or concurrency management (see Chapter 9) is included.

There is nothing to stop you from adding code for these, however.

Binding to Object Data

When you move away from using the .NET types for storing data to using your own objects, whether via generic collection classes or through more complex types, you may still want to bind your data to controls. In both web and Windows applications, this is possible using the existing data-binding framework. In Windows applications you can employ a `DataSource` control that uses an object (such as a collection object) as its data source. In web applications, there's a specialized control called `ObjectDataSource` that enables you to bind to object data.

In this section you see how this is achieved.

Windows Applications

You may remember from when you originally looked at adding data sources to Windows applications that three options are available when choosing a data source type, and that one of them is Object, as shown in Figure 8-3.

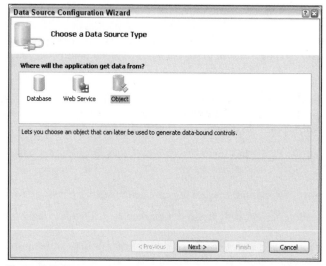

Figure 8-3: Data source type selection

If you select that data source type, you're presented with a list of the namespaces in your solution, and you can navigate through them to find the type that you want to use for data binding. Once you have done so, the binding source is configured according to the definition of that type. This works for pretty much any type you can think of.

This works only for applications and assemblies that have been compiled, so you have to build your project before you can see it in action.

When you reference a type this way, all public properties of the type become available for binding. If the class is not a collection class, then, internally, a collection is created to support the `IBindingList` interface, enabling you to access multiple objects of the selected type via data binding. If the class is a collection, the properties of the items it contains are used for data binding. The `IBindingList` interface is also used here — and if your collection class doesn't support the interface, an intermediate collection class that does support it is created by the binding source and is used to access the objects in your collection.

On adding an object data source, the data source definition is included in your project in the `Properties` folder, in a sub-folder called `DataSources`. You can look at this file if you like, although it doesn't really tell you a lot. It contains the name of the data source, the type that the data source is intended to contain, any customizations to the controls that will be generated if you drag the data source onto a form and generate a detail view, and some other information. In short, you'll probably never need to look at or edit this information directly.

Once you have defined an object-binding source, you can add it to your form just like with data sets, or you can add a `BindingSource` control and set its `DataSource` property to the name of the data source. Either way, a `BindingSource` control is created and you can use it to access a collection of items of the type you specified. You don't need to explicitly assign a value, such as a ready-filled collection, to the control because it instantiates its own collection internally. Instead, you can proceed to add items directly through the control using, for example, its `Add()` method. You can, if you want, assign its `DataSource` property to an existing collection, but if you do so, changes to the collection made externally might not be reflected in the collection stored in the `BindingSource`. If you make changes, you'd have to call the `BindingSource.ResetBindings()` method.

In the following example you create a Windows application and use simple object data-binding techniques to bind to a list of objects.

Try It Out   Windows Application Object Data Binding

1. Open Visual C# Express and create a new Windows application called `Ex0804 - Object Data Binding`. Save the project in the `C:\BegVC#Databases\Chapter08` directory, with the Create Directory For Solution option unchecked.

2. Add a new class to the project called `SimpleObject` with the following code:

```
namespace Ex0804___Object_Data_Binding
{
    public class SimpleObject
    {
        private string stringData;
        private bool boolData;

        public SimpleObject(string newStringData, bool newBoolData)
        {
            stringData = newStringData;
            boolData = newBoolData;
        }

        public string StringData
        {
            get
            {
                return stringData;
            }
        }
```

```
                set
                {
                    stringData = value;
                }
            }

            public bool BoolData
            {
                get
                {
                    return boolData;
                }
                set
                {
                    boolData = value;
                }
            }
        }
    }
```

3. Build the project.

4. In the Data Sources window, click Add New Data Source.

5. In the first page of the Data Source Configuration Wizard, select Object and then click Next.

6. In the next page of the Data Source Configuration Wizard, expand the namespace hierarchy and select the `SimpleObject` class, as shown in Figure 8-4. Click Next and then click Finish to complete the wizard.

7. Open `Form1` and drag the `SimpleObject` data source from the Data Sources window onto the form. Position it as you please.

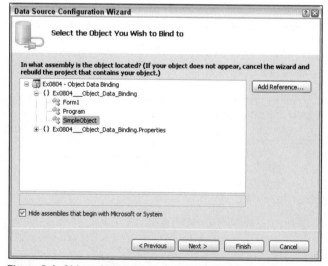

Figure 8-4: Object data source class selection

8. Add a `Form1_Load()` event handler, and add code as follows:

```
private void Form1_Load(object sender, EventArgs e)
{
    simpleObjectBindingSource.Add(new SimpleObject("Extra Strong Mints", true));
    simpleObjectBindingSource.Add(new SimpleObject("Walnut Whips", false));
    simpleObjectBindingSource.Add(new SimpleObject("Mint Imperials", false));
    simpleObjectBindingSource.Add(new SimpleObject("Jelly Beans", true));
    simpleObjectBindingSource.Add(new SimpleObject("Wine Gums", true));
}
```

9. Run the application. The result is shown in Figure 8-5.

10. Close the application and Visual C# Express.

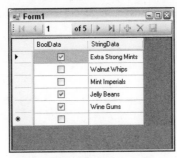

Figure 8-5: Application result

How It Works

This example, which doesn't use any database access, shows how you can bind any data to data-bound controls. The fact that this is possible means that, as far as data binding is concerned, it really doesn't matter what data structures you use to store data in.

Note that two of the buttons in the navigation bar — add item and save data — are unavailable. To enable item addition, you simply need to set the `AllowNew` property of the `BindingSource` to `true` — the navigator will detect this change and allow new items to be added to the collection stored by the data source. Saving is another matter because there's no obvious way that the wizards can guess exactly what you hope to achieve by saving the data. Should it save to a file? A database? This choice is up to you, and you can implement an event handler for this control any way you see fit.

Web Applications

Web applications are also capable of binding to object data, although the method for doing so is somewhat different from the Windows applications technique. For web applications, you can bind to object data by using an `ObjectDataSource` data source object. Unlike in Windows applications, there are two things that the `ObjectDataSource` needs to know about. The first is a class with methods capable of reading and, if required, modifying data — either for singular or multiple objects (which may be static or instance methods). This type is known as the *business object*. The second is a type to use for items in a collection, either complex types or simple ones — for binding to a list of string values, for instance. This second type can usually (but not always) be inferred from the methods of the first class.

When you add an `ObjectDataSource` to a web form and configure it using the tasks window for the object, you must first select a type to use for the business object, as shown in Figure 8-6.

The business object class can be defined in the web application, or in an external assembly that is referenced by the application.

Once you have selected a type, you move on to select methods to use for reading and modifying data, as shown in Figure 8-7.

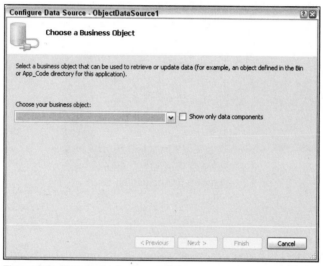

Figure 8-6: Choosing a business object

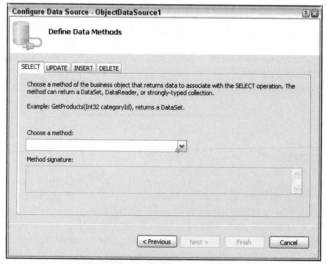

Figure 8-7: Defining data methods

One method should be supplied for each operation that is required. The methods are referred to using database terminology, so at most you can supply select, update, insert, and delete methods. The text in the wizard lets you know exactly what the method should do. If any methods require additional parameters, you can click Next to configure them; otherwise click Finish to complete the data source configuration.

Typically, your business objects (including types such as the data-aware object collection examined earlier in this chapter) will not have methods suitable to do all of this. Even list objects such as objects that inherit from generic lists won't have the right methods. For generic lists, there is no method to return the collection contained within, although that's simple to add because you can just have a method that returns this. Updating objects is also a problem, but again you can add an update method without too much trouble.

One issue to deal with when using the `ObjectDataSource` control is that it does not know what fields, if any, to use for primary key information. This means that you can run into trouble when updating item data because you won't know which item requires updating. The same applies to deleting data. It is the job of the presentation control that binds to the `ObjectDataSource` (a `GridView`, for example) to keep track of this information, so it is extremely important that, once you have set up an `ObjectDataSource` and are binding a control to it, you do one of the following:

❑ Set the `DataKeyNames` property of the bound control to the name of the primary key field or fields for items.

❑ Set the `ConflictDetection` property of the `ObjectDataSource` to `CompareAllValues`.

The first technique ensures that the primary key field is always passed to update methods, and you can use the value in your code to locate the object to be updated or edited. The second technique means that all field values will be passed to data modification methods, regardless of whether they are primary keys, and you can use that information to identify objects.

As with much of this material, the best way to learn about it is to work through an example. Because there isn't much to be gained by binding to simple data (as you did in the Windows example), the following example shows you how to bind to the data-aware objects created earlier in the chapter.

Try It Out Web Application Object Data Binding

1. Copy the web site directory from the earlier example, Ex0803 - Data Aware Objects, to a new directory, Ex0805 - Web Object Binding.

2. Open Visual Web Developer Express and open the copy of the web site from its new location.

3. Remove the `PlaceHolder` and `Button` controls from the `default.aspx` form, and all the code in the `_Default` class definition in the `.aspx.cs` file.

4. Modify the code for `SpeciesItem.cs` as follows:

```
public Guid SpeciesId
{
    get
    {
        return (Guid)currentData["SpeciesId"];
    }
}
```

```
        set
        {
            currentData["SpeciesId"] = value;
        }
    }
```

5. Add a new class in the App_Code directory called SpeciesCollectionInterface, with code as follows:

```
using System;
using System.Configuration;
using System.Web;
using DataAwareObjects;

public static class SpeciesCollectionInterface
{
    private static SpeciesCollection Data
    {
        get
        {
            // Configure data access.
            DataAccess.ConnectionString = ConfigurationManager
                .ConnectionStrings["connectionString"].ConnectionString;

            // Get data from session state (load if necessary).
            if (HttpContext.Current.Session["speciesData"] == null)
            {
                HttpContext.Current.Session.Add("speciesData",
                    new SpeciesCollection(true));
            }
            return HttpContext.Current.Session["speciesData"] as SpeciesCollection;
        }
        set
        {
            HttpContext.Current.Session["genericListData"] = value;
        }
    }

    public static SpeciesCollection Select()
    {
        // Return data.
        return Data;
    }


    private static SpeciesItem GetById(Guid speciesId)
    {
        // Get item by its GUID ID value.
        foreach (SpeciesItem item in Data)
        {
            if (item.SpeciesId == speciesId)
            {
                return item;
            }
```

```
        }
        return null;
    }

    public static void Insert(SpeciesItem item)
    {
        // Add and save item.
        Data.Add(item);
        Data.Save();
    }

    public static void Delete(SpeciesItem item)
    {
        // Get item to delete.
        SpeciesItem itemToDelete = GetById(item.SpeciesId);

        if (itemToDelete != null)
        {
            // Delete item and save data.
            Data.Remove(itemToDelete);
            Data.Save();
        }
    }

    public static void Update(SpeciesItem item)
    {
        // Get item to update.
        SpeciesItem itemToUpdate = GetById(item.SpeciesId);

        if (itemToUpdate != null)
        {
            // Update item and save data.
            itemToUpdate.Species = item.Species;
            itemToUpdate.Description = item.Description;
            itemToUpdate.Immortal = item.Immortal;
            Data.Save();
        }
    }
}
```

6. Save the `SpeciesCollectionInterface.cs` file.

7. Open `default.aspx` and add an `ObjectDataSource` control.

8. Click Configure Data Source to open the Data Source Configuration Wizard.

9. Select `SpeciesCollectionInterface` as the business object, using the drop-down list. Click Next.

10. Select the `Select()`, `Update()`, `Insert()`, and `Delete()` methods for the data access methods to use, one on each tab of the Define Data Methods Wizard page. Click Finish when you are done.

11. Add a `FormView` control to the page, and select `ObjectDataSource1` as its data source.

12. Set the `DataKeyNames` property of the `FormView` control to `SpeciesId` and the `AllowPaging` property to `true`.

13. In Source view, modify the templates for the `FormView` control as follows:

```
<asp:FormView ID="FormView1" runat="server" DataSourceID="ObjectDataSource1"
    AllowPaging="True" DataKeyNames="SpeciesId"
        <EditItemTemplate>
          Species:
          <asp:TextBox ID="SpeciesTextBox" runat="server"
            Text='<%# Bind("Species") %>' /><br />
          Immortal:
          <asp:CheckBox ID="ImmortalCheckBox" runat="server"
            Checked='<%# Bind("Immortal") %>' /><br />
          Description:
          <asp:TextBox ID="DescriptionTextBox" runat="server"
            Text='<%# Bind("Description") %>' /><br />
          <asp:LinkButton ID="UpdateButton" runat="server" CausesValidation="True"
            CommandName="Update" Text="Update" />
          <asp:LinkButton ID="UpdateCancelButton" runat="server" CausesValidation="False"
            CommandName="Cancel" Text="Cancel" />
        </EditItemTemplate>
        <InsertItemTemplate>
          Species:
          <asp:TextBox ID="SpeciesTextBox" runat="server"
            Text='<%# Bind("Species") %>' /><br />
          Immortal:
          <asp:CheckBox ID="ImmortalCheckBox" runat="server"
            Checked='<%# Bind("Immortal") %>' /><br />
          Description:
          <asp:TextBox ID="DescriptionTextBox" runat="server"
            Text='<%# Bind("Description") %>' /><br />
          <asp:LinkButton ID="InsertButton" runat="server" CausesValidation="True"
            CommandName="Insert" Text="Insert" />
          <asp:LinkButton ID="InsertCancelButton" runat="server" CausesValidation="False"
            CommandName="Cancel" Text="Cancel" />
        </InsertItemTemplate>
        <ItemTemplate>
          Species:
          <asp:Label ID="SpeciesLabel" runat="server"
            Text='<%# Bind("Species") %>' /><br />
          Immortal:
          <asp:CheckBox ID="ImmortalCheckBox" runat="server"
            Checked='<%# Bind("Immortal") %>' Enabled="false" /><br />
          Description:
          <asp:Label ID="DescriptionLabel" runat="server"
            Text='<%# Bind("Description") %>' /><br />
          <asp:LinkButton ID="EditButton" runat="server" CausesValidation="False"
            CommandName="Edit" Text="Edit" />
          <asp:LinkButton ID="DeleteButton" runat="server" CausesValidation="False"
            CommandName="Delete" Text="Delete" />
          <asp:LinkButton ID="NewButton" runat="server" CausesValidation="False"
            CommandName="New" Text="Add New Species" />
        </ItemTemplate>
        <EmptyDataTemplate>
```

```
            <asp:LinkButton ID="NewButton" runat="server" CausesValidation="False"
                CommandName="New" Text="Add New Species" />
        </EmptyDataTemplate>
    </asp:FormView>
```

14. In Design view, apply the autoformatting option of your choice to the `FormView` control.

15. Add an event handler for the `ItemInserting` event of the `FormView` control as follows:

```
public partial class _Default : System.Web.UI.Page
{
    protected void FormView1_ItemInserting(object sender,
        FormViewInsertEventArgs e)
    {
        e.Values.Add("SpeciesId", Guid.NewGuid());
    }
}
```

16. Execute the application and experiment with browsing, modifying, adding, and deleting data. The display (with Oceanic autoformatting) is shown in Figure 8-8.

17. Close the application and Visual Web Developer Express.

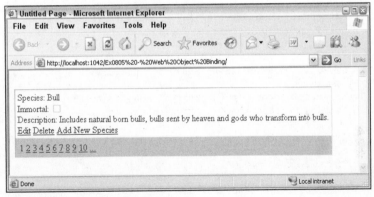

Figure 8-8: Application display

How It Works

This example uses the `ObjectDataSource` control in a web application to view and modify data through the data-aware objects you created earlier in the chapter. A fair amount of the code added in the example concerns presentation, but there are quite a few points to discuss.

First, you modified the `SpeciesId` property of the `SpeciesItem` control to make it read/write rather than read-only. That was necessary because the data-binding controls in ASP.NET aren't designed to work with "intelligent" data-aware objects. As such, behind the scenes, objects are created as the data-binding controls require them and then are destroyed, and state is set via properties (using reflection). If the field is left read-only, an error would be generated when any edit operation was performed on items because the data-bound controls would need to create and load state into a new item, and that would fail for the `SpeciesId` field. This is a minor problem because it does break the design principles by which the data-aware object was created, but in practice it doesn't cause too many headaches. The behavior has been somewhat criticized in the developer community, and greater control may be possible in future updates to ASP.NET.

The most important class to discuss here is the (static) class `SpeciesCollectionInterface`. It is provided as an interface between the `ObjectDataSource` control and the data-aware `SpeciesCollection` class, and makes data binding to this object possible without modifying it. Internally, this class contains an instance of the `SpeciesCollection` class, which is stored in session state between web requests so that if no modification is performed, data reading operations are fast indeed. Alternatively, with appropriate locking and caching code you could store the object in application state — something you look at in more detail in Chapter 10.

The `SpeciesCollection` object is loaded as it is requested, with code in the `get` accessor for the property in which it is held (`Data`). That property also configures the connection string for data access, although this can be performed elsewhere if desired.

```
public static class SpeciesCollectionInterface
{
    private static SpeciesCollection Data
    {
        get
        {
            // Configure data access.
            DataAccess.ConnectionString = ConfigurationManager
                .ConnectionStrings["connectionString"].ConnectionString;

            // Get data from session state (load if necessary).
            if (HttpContext.Current.Session["speciesData"] == null)
            {
                HttpContext.Current.Session.Add("speciesData",
                    new SpeciesCollection(true));
            }
            return HttpContext.Current.Session["speciesData"] as SpeciesCollection;
        }
        set
        {
            HttpContext.Current.Session["genericListData"] = value;
        }
    }
}
```

Once you have provided access to the data this way, the `Select()` method is simplicity itself — it simply returns the stored `SpeciesCollection` object:

```
public static SpeciesCollection Select()
{
    // Return data.
    return Data;
}
```

This is possible because `SpeciesCollection` derives ultimately from a generic collection class, which means that the `ObjectDataSource` control can extract all the type information it needs from the type definition. Look at the Source view for `default.aspx` and you see that not only has the `TypeName` property for the `ObjectDataSource` control been set to `SpeciesCollectionInterface`, but that the `DataObjectTypeName` property has been set to `SpeciesItem`. That information has been extracted from the type definition of `SpeciesCollection`.

Next you have a utility method, `GetById()`, which is used by subsequent code that must obtain a `SpeciesItem` object from a GUID ID value, `SpeciesId`:

```
private static SpeciesItem GetById(Guid speciesId)
{
    // Get item by its GUID ID value.
    foreach (SpeciesItem item in Data)
    {
        if (item.SpeciesId == speciesId)
        {
            return item;
        }
    }
    return null;
}
```

This code can be included in the `SpeciesCollection` class, but it's included here to minimize modification to existing code in this example.

The rest of the code consists of the remaining data access methods. First, `Insert()` allows items to be added by simply adding them to the `SpeciesCollection` object stored in `Data` and using the `Save()` method to save changes to the database:

```
public static void Insert(SpeciesItem item)
{
    // Add and save item.
    Data.Add(item);
    Data.Save();
}
```

Next, `Delete()` uses the `SpeciesId` passed as part of its parameter to obtain an item and remove it:

```
public static void Delete(SpeciesItem item)
{
    // Get item to delete.
    SpeciesItem itemToDelete = GetById(item.SpeciesId);

    if (itemToDelete != null)
    {
        // Delete item and save data.
        Data.Remove(itemToDelete);
        Data.Save();
    }
}
```

If you set the `ConflictDetection` property of the `ObjectDataSource` to `CompareAllValues`, the item passed to `Delete()` will have all its fields populated; otherwise, only the key values specified by the bound control are included — specified through the `DataKeyNames` property as discussed earlier.

Finally, there is the Update() method, which locates the appropriate item in the collection, changes its values, and saves the changes:

```
public static void Update(SpeciesItem item)
{
    // Get item to update.
    SpeciesItem itemToUpdate = GetById(item.SpeciesId);

    if (itemToUpdate != null)
    {
        // Update item and save data.
        itemToUpdate.Species = item.Species;
        itemToUpdate.Description = item.Description;
        itemToUpdate.Immortal = item.Immortal;
        Data.Save();
    }
}
```

The rest of the example is similar to other web data-binding examples you've already seen in this book. You added a data-bound control — in this case, a FormView control — set its data source (and DataKeyNames property), configured its templates, changed its presentation, and made sure that newly added items would have a primary key value using an event handler.

Summary

This chapter explored how to change the way your applications are structured so that they use custom data objects for storing and modifying database data. This enables you to implement a more robust application structure, all the way to complex n-tier applications if desired. There are many advantages to this, including how the logical separation of code improves reusability and modification within a team of developers.

You also examined how, even without using the ADO.NET-supplied classes, you can still provide data-binding functionality in your applications. As you have seen, you can bind to a variety of objects, including objects designed by you. That means that you can take full advantage of the rapid application development and great functionality that this technique provides, at the same time as using the improved structure and functionality gained by using custom data objects.

Specifically, you have learned to:

❑   Use data reader objects to access data in a basic data tier. This technique gives you the advantage of separating data access code from other code, but passing data readers between tiers is not a perfect n-tier strategy. While this is simple and effective, it does mean that the business tier has additional responsibilities, such as closing data readers after using them.

❑   Use existing .NET classes and generic collection to wrap data. You saw a more advanced technique in which generic collection classes are used to hold your database data. That avoids the use of `DataSets`, and in many situations can give you both greater performance and greater control over your data. However, because the data structures you use are "dumb" objects, you often need to do more work to access database data in exactly the way you require.

❑ Use data-aware objects in n-tier design. This technique is advisable in more advanced situations, or where you are creating an enterprise-level application. You saw an example of a class library that you can use as a starting point for your own development. While experimenting with that library, you learned many of the techniques required for building intelligent business objects, such as keeping track of "dirty" data and strongly typing your data structures.

❑ Bind object data to Windows controls. You used the object data source type to bind to object data in Windows applications. That is a powerful technique, enabling you to use your objects — often without additional modification — and display them to users without having to write a lot of plumbing code yourself. Because of the nature of object data binding, however, there are usually tweaks that you have to make, and you may want to implement the `IBindingSource` interface in your classes to make things work as effectively as possible.

❑ Bind object data to web controls. In web applications you saw how to use the `ObjectBindingSource` component to configure a binding source for object data. As with Windows object data binding, there are extra factors to consider here, and perhaps even more tweaking is necessary in web applications. You learned to deal with a number of issues that arise, such as keeping track of primary key fields.

In the next chapter, you look at how to use transactions and deal with concurrency issues in your applications.

Exercises

1. Which of the following are good reasons for using n-tier design in your applications?

    a. Logical separation of code into specialized units.

    b. Capability to load-balance applications for performance improvement.

    c. Ease of data access.

    d. It sounds impressive.

    e. Ease of updateability of individual components.

2. In what situations would you avoid using n-tier design principles?

3. Using data-aware class libraries is much better than using existing ADO.NET classes. Do you agree with this statement?

4. Modify the `TableCollection<T>` class to provide a default enumerator that returns only non-deleted items. Also, provide a second enumerator that client applications can use to enumerate all items.

5. Which interface is required for Windows forms to bind to your objects? Do you have to implement this interface for Windows data binding to occur? How would you implement it?

6. How do you ensure that data-bound controls in web applications are aware of the primary keys that are used in your data objects? Why is this important?

Transactions and Concurrency

As I've hinted throughout this book, there are additional issues to consider when scenarios involve a high level of database access and/or high numbers of database users. If, for example, two users attempt to modify the same data at the same time, you are likely to run into problems. Unless you design your applications with this in mind, there might be no indication that anything untoward has occurred because edits from both users will appear to have been committed to the database successfully. When you look at the data later, however, you might find that only one user's changes have been applied to the database, while the other user's changes have been discarded.

To prevent this from happening, you must include code that manages *concurrency*. Concurrency is a property of computing systems where two or more processes overlap, in that they both attempt to use the same resource at the same time where the resource in question does not permit this sort of operation. It doesn't just apply to database access — it may apply, for example, in accessing file system resources. However, it is of particular importance in the context of databases because DBMSes are designed to be used by multiple applications. As you will see in this chapter, there are a number of techniques that you can use (both in the way you access databases and in the way that the user interfaces of your applications work) to ensure that the effect of concurrency issues is minimized.

You also look at the related subject of *transactions*. Transactions are a way of grouping database operations together, such that if one operation fails, all operations will fail. If an operation that is part of a transaction has resulted in a change to the database prior to the transaction failing, that change must be "rolled back" — that is, the change must be undone so that the database is in the same state as it was before the transaction started. This is an extremely important aspect of database access, and should never be overlooked. One frequent example is where a database is used to record the credit balances of customers, with each row in a table representing the balance of a single customer. Transferring credit from one customer to another, therefore, involves two changes to the database — subtracting an amount from the balance of one customer and adding an amount to the balance of a second customer. Without transactions, it is possible that only one of these operations will succeed, and that credit either disappears or is created from nothing. With transactions in use, you can be 100 percent sure that either the credit is transferred or that it isn't, and that the database is never put into an illegal state.

Both these subjects are covered in this chapter as they are usually used in combination. As part of concurrency management you often use transactions such that operations that fail will not result in database changes — even if some of those changes are unrelated to the change that resulted in a concurrency violation. To summarize, then, this chapter looks at the following:

❑   Concurrency

❑   Transactions

Concurrency

As you briefly saw in Chapter 1, three types of concurrency control are possible with database access, of which two are possible in ADO.NET. To recap, the options are:

❑   **"Last in wins":** Rows are unavailable only while they are being updated, which means that if two users edit a row, the last edit made applies and earlier changes are lost. This is the default behavior in ADO.NET.

❑   **Optimistic concurrency control:** Rows are unavailable while they are being updated, and attempts to update a row after it has already been updated results in an error. Effectively, this could be called "first in wins." It's relatively easy to implement in ADO.NET (it is the default behavior when data binding using the wizard) and is the focus of this chapter.

❑   **Pessimistic concurrency control:** Rows are locked from the moment they are retrieved until the moment they are updated, which may adversely affect performance, but guarantees the protection of data. This is impossible using ADO.NET. There are advanced techniques that you could use to implement it, but they won't be covered in this book.

This section covers the first two options.

Last in Wins

The way that the "last in wins" option works is that rows in database tables are identified only by their primary keys. When you update a row, you simply identify a row with the primary key of a row that you have modified and apply changes to that row. This means that you will not be aware if the row has changed or been deleted since you retrieved it, so one of two things occurs:

❑   The row is be updated, and any changes made since you retrieved it are lost.

❑   No update is made because the row you are attempting to update no longer exists.

Custom Data Access Code Behavior

If you are using custom data access code to perform data updates, you may not be aware of what occurs when you update a row. For example, consider the following code:

```
SqlConnection conn = new SqlConnection(<connection string>);
SqlCommand cmd = new SqlCommand(
    "DELETE FROM Source WHERE SourceId ='" + Guid.NewGuid().ToString() + "'",
    conn);
```

```
conn.Open();
try
{
    cmd.ExecuteNonQuery();
}
finally
{
    conn.Close();
}
```

Here the delete command does not delete a row because no rows have a GUID ID that matches the one used — it is a new one generated for the purposes of illustration. However, executing this code does not result in an error — the command is perfectly legal SQL code, and the fact that the where clause doesn't match an existing row doesn't stop the command from executing.

Instead of relying on errors to detect such a "failed" deletion, you must check the return value of the ExecuteNonQuery() method, which returns the number of rows affected (0 in this example):

```
SqlConnection conn = new SqlConnection(<connection string>);
SqlCommand cmd = new SqlCommand(
    "DELETE FROM Source WHERE SourceId ='" + Guid.NewGuid().ToString() + "'",
    conn);
int rowsAffected = -1;
conn.Open();
try
{
    rowsAffected = cmd.ExecuteNonQuery();
}
finally
{
    conn.Close();
}
```

```
switch (rowsAffected)
{
    case -1:
        MessageBox.Show("Command failed to execute.");
        break;
    case 0:
        MessageBox.Show("Row not deleted as it doesn't exist.");
        break;
    case 1:
        MessageBox.Show("Row deleted.");
        break;
}
```

In this code, the result is used to output a message, although depending on how the code is used in your application, you could throw an exception if the command fails. There's no need to check for other values of rowsAffected in this case because the SourceId column is guaranteed unique.

The same thing applies to updating a row. You can tell by the return value of ExecuteNonQuery() whether a successful update occurs. When using "last in wins" concurrency management, however, it is impossible to tell whether the resultant row contents are as you expected them to be, or if you have over-written changes that may have occurred to the row since you read its contents. Depending on the update you have made, and whether you have updated all (non-primary key) column values or a subset of these columns, you may even end up with a row that contains values merged from multiple updates. For example:

1. Application A obtains a row from the database.

2. Application B modifies ColumnA and ColumnB of the row in the database (application A is unaware of this, and does not refresh its data).

3. Application A modifies ColumnA of the row in the database.

After these steps, the row will contain the ColumnA value set by application A and the ColumnB value set by application B (because the column wasn't modified by Application A). Unless application A refreshes its view of the data, it is still unaware that ColumnB contains a new value.

The upshot of all this is that if you are using "last in wins" concurrency management you should consider including code that does the following:

❑   Checks the return value for ExecuteNonQuery() method calls to see whether data has been successfully modified.

❑   Performs appropriate actions when concurrency violation occurs, such as raising/dealing with exceptions, and/or informing the user that something has gone wrong.

❑   Refreshes data after modifying it to ensure that current data is accurately reflected.

Having said all this, there are reasons to use this form of concurrency management. In many applications there's no need to worry about concurrency issues, particularly where you can be sure that only one application or user will use the database. That's common in Windows applications, or in web applications that have a single administrator for data updates and where external access to the database is restricted.

Data Set/Data-Binding Behavior

When you use a data set or typed data set (such as when you use the wizard for data binding), attempting to update or delete a row that no longer exists with a data adapter results in an exception of type DBConcurrencyException being thrown. You can prevent this from happening by setting the ContinueUpdateOnError property of the data adapter to true if you want, and instead dealing with problems by handling the SqDataAdapter.RowUpdated event.

> *You explore the* DBConcurrencyException *exception and the* RowUpdated *event in detail later in this chapter.*

Updating or deleting an existing row that's been modified after it was retrieved won't generate any exception when you use "last in wins" concurrency management, however. As with custom code, you have to deal with this eventuality yourself. Other than the fact that you don't have to write code to detect concurrency violations, using this method of data access and level of concurrency management still requires you to deal with problems as they arise.

To use "last in wins" concurrency management with data sets, you must change the default behavior used to generate commands so that only primary keys are used to identify rows to be updated. If you are using a typed data set, do this through the DataSet Designer view, by right-clicking on a `TableAdapter` and selecting Configure. The TableAdapter Configuration Wizard includes an Advanced Options button (which you've looked at briefly in previous chapters), as shown in Figure 9-1.

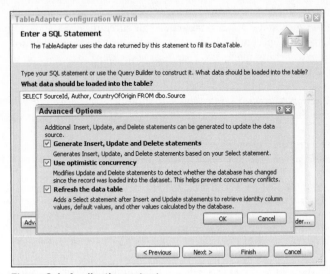

Figure 9-1: Application output

The default option for concurrency management, as shown in Figure 9-1, is to use optimistic concurrency. Unselecting that option results in the use of "last in wins" concurrency.

Note that you can also use this dialog box to choose whether to refresh data after making updates, which can assist you in keeping up-to-date with database contents.

Alternatively, if you are generating commands for a data adapter using a `SqlCommandBuilder` object, you can set the `SqlCommandBuilder.ConflictOption` property to `ConflictOption.OverwriteChanges` to get "last in wins" functionality. This class also includes a Boolean `SetAllValues` property that you can set to `true` to ensure that values are provided for all columns when updating a row. That prevents the "merge changes" functionality discussed in the previous section.

Optimistic Concurrency Management in ADO.NET

Optimistic concurrency can require additional implementation, although (as you have seen in the chapters on data binding) you often receive assistance along the way so it's never too tough to do. You can use optimistic concurrency management in your applications in two ways:

❑   Compare all column values to ensure that updates are made to "current" row versions.

❑   Record the version of a row by a version number or timestamp, and ensure that it matches the current row's version number or timestamp before updating the row.

Comparing All Columns

Optimistic concurrency is the default option when using the wizards to create typed data sets for data binding. That form of optimistic concurrency compares the values of all columns; for example:

```
DELETE FROM [dbo].[Source] WHERE ((([SourceId] = @Original_SourceId) AND ↵
([Author] = @Original_Author) AND ([CountryOfOrigin] = @Original_CountryOfOrigin))
```

Here, if any of the columns in the `Source` table (`Author` or `CountryOfOrigin`) have changed since the row was retrieved, the row will not be deleted. The same type of command can be constructed using `SqlCommandBuilder` by setting the `SqlCommandBuilder.ConflictOption` property to `ConflictOption.CompareAllSearchableValues`.

As with updates to removed rows, updates made to modified rows through a data adapter result in `DBConcurrencyException` (assuming that the `ContinueUpdateOnError` property is `false`).

If you want to use this form of concurrency management in custom code, you have to construct the commands (and command parameters) by hand. Here's an example:

```
SqlCommand cmd = new SqlCommand("DELETE FROM Source WHERE SourceId = @SourceId"
    + " AND Author = @Author AND CountryOfOrigin = @CountryOfOrigin", conn);
cmd.Parameters.Add("SourceId", SqlDbType.UniqueIdentifier).Value = sourceId;
cmd.Parameters.Add("Author", SqlDbType.VarChar, 100).Value = author;
cmd.Parameters.Add("CountryOfOrigin", SqlDbType.VarChar, 100).Value = country;
```

As with the code you saw earlier, you can detect if the command affected your data only by looking at the return value for `ExecuteNonQuery()`, and you should deal with the result in a similar way.

Timestamps and Row Versions

Rather than checking the values of all columns in a row, it is possible to add an additional column to a table whose only purpose is to keep track of the version of the row. By ensuring that this column is updated whenever a row is updated in any way, you can simply check the value of this column to see if you are modifying the correct version of the row.

You can, if you want, achieve this by including a row that contains a version number, which would perhaps start at 0 when a row is added to a table, and would then be incremented whenever the row data changes. However, the implementation of such a system can be problematic. To begin with, you need to ensure that this column is accessed only in the correct way. That means either designing your applications in such a way as to always increment this column when required, or making the DBMS take care of the value of this column. The latter option is preferable because you may not have control over all client applications, and relying on client applications may result in this column being set to an unexpected value, or not incremented properly. To avoid corruption of the version number, you are left with restricting access to your table using views and adding triggers so that you can control what happens when rows in the view are modified. This is a fairly advanced situation that you won't look at in this book, and, frankly, is hardly ideal because it introduces restrictions on database access that you might prefer to avoid.

The advantage of using a version number is that you will be able to see, to some degree, database activity, and in some situations that can be important. You can, if necessary, keep old versions of rows so that any amount of changes can be rolled back if desired. Again, this is an advanced topic that won't be discussed here.

As an extension of this row versioning idea, you can keep track of the last time a row was modified, using a date/time data type, which again would need updating either by carefully designed client applications or database triggers.

A much simpler alternative is to use the SQL Server `timestamp` data type. That effectively achieves much of what was just discussed, but without your having to do anything to enable it. A column of type `timestamp` cannot be updated from a client application. Instead, its value is determined by the DBMS. Every time a row is modified in any way, a new value is assigned to its `timestamp` column. This makes `timestamp` columns great for concurrency management — changes are detected, and client applications can use much simpler SQL statements when using optimistic concurrency.

Despite the name of the data type, this column is not intended to be used to determine the time when a row was last modified. Instead, it contains an 8-byte value that is established by a database-internal counter. You cannot, therefore, expect to get meaningful information in your applications by looking at the value in this column — you can use it only for concurrency management.

Once you've added a column of type `timestamp` to a table, it's automatically detected by the wizards used to create typed data sets for data binding. In the dialog that you saw in the previous section, selecting Use Optimistic Concurrency results in queries such as the following:

```
DELETE FROM [dbo].[Enchantment] WHERE ((([EnchantmentId] = ↵
@Original_EnchantmentId) AND ([LastModified] = @Original_LastModified))
```

Note that, in this example, only the `EnchantmentId` and `LastModified` columns are used to identify the row, not any other columns (such as `Name` for the `Enchantment` table in this case). In general, only primary key and timestamp columns are required for this form of concurrency management.

If you are using your own table adapters and command builders, you can achieve the same result by setting the `SqlCommandBuilder.ConflictOption` property to `ConflictOption.CompareRowVersion`. In custom code, you write SQL statements such as the preceding one, comparing the values of any primary key fields as well as any timestamp fields to uniquely identify rows.

In the following example you investigate optimistic concurrency further, and confirm that it works in the way discussed in this chapter.

Try It Out   Optimistic Concurrency

1. Open Visual C# Express and create a new Windows application called `Ex0901 - Optimistic Concurrency`. Save the project in the `C:\BegVC#Databases\Chapter09` directory, with the Create directory for solution option unchecked.

2. Add the `FolktaleDB.mdf` database to your project as a local database file. When prompted by the Data Source Configuration Wizard, expand tables and select the `Enchantment` table. Click Finish.

3. Open the DataSet Designer for `FolktaleDBDataSet.xsd`, right-click on `EnchantmentTableAdapter`, and select Configure.

4. Click Advanced Options, and verify that optimistic concurrency is selected. Click OK and then click Cancel to cancel configuration changes.

5. With the `EnchantmentTableAdapter` object selected, examine the queries used in the Properties window by expanding the commands and looking at the `CommandText` sub-properties. You should see that `LastModified` is used in the `UpdateCommand` and `DeleteCommand` properties.

6. Open `Form1` in design view, and drag the `Enchantment` table on to the form from the Data Sources window to add a data-bound `DataGridView` control.

7. Right-click on the `DataGridView` control, select Edit Columns, remove the `LastModified` column from the list, and set the `AutoSizeMode` property of the `Name` column to `Fill` before clicking OK to return to the form view.

8. Add a button to the form below the data grid with the text Modify Table Data.

9. Arrange the controls as shown in Figure 9-2, with appropriate `Dock` and `Anchor` properties to allow the form to be resized without affecting the layout.

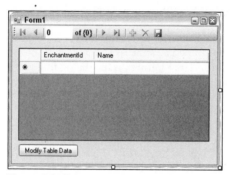

Figure 9-2: Form Layout

10. Double-click the button to add an event handler, and add code as follows:

```
using System.Data.SqlClient;

namespace Ex0901___Optimistic_Concurrency
{
    public partial class Form1 : Form
    {
        ...

        private void button1_Click(object sender, EventArgs e)
        {
            // Get connection.
            SqlConnection conn = new SqlConnection(
                global::Ex0901___Optimistic_Concurrency.Properties.Settings.
                Default.FolktaleDBConnectionString);

            // Get data from 1st row in Enchantment table.
            SqlCommand readCmd = new SqlCommand(
                "SELECT TOP 1 * FROM Enchantment", conn);
            conn.Open();
```

```
        SqlDataReader reader = readCmd.ExecuteReader();
        reader.Read();
        Guid rowId = (Guid)reader["EnchantmentId"];
        string name = reader["Name"] as string;
        reader.Close();

        // Modify row.
        SqlCommand cmd = new SqlCommand(
            "UPDATE Enchantment SET Name = @Name WHERE EnchantmentId = "
            + "@EnchantmentId", conn);
        cmd.Parameters.Add("EnchantmentId", SqlDbType.UniqueIdentifier).Value =
            rowId;
        cmd.Parameters.Add("Name", SqlDbType.VarChar, 300).Value = name
            + " (modified)";
        int rowsModified = cmd.ExecuteNonQuery();
        conn.Close();

        // Notify user.
        if (rowsModified == 1)
        {
            // Success.
            MessageBox.Show("Row with Name value of '" + name + "' modified.",
                "Row modification report", MessageBoxButtons.OK,
                MessageBoxIcon.Information);
        }
        else
        {
            // Failure.
            MessageBox.Show("Row modification failed.",
                "Row modification report", MessageBoxButtons.OK,
                MessageBoxIcon.Error);
        }
    }
  }
}
```

11. Run the application. You should see rows from the Enchantment table displayed in the DataGridView.

12. Click the Modify Table Data button. A message box like the one shown in Figure 9-3 should appear.

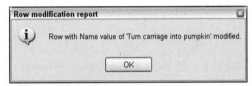

Figure 9-3: Notification dialog box

13. Click OK, and then modify the Name column for the same row indicated by the dialog box (in this case, Turn carriage into pumpkin).

14. Click the Save Data icon on the form. The following error should occur:

```
System.Data.DBConcurrencyException was unhandled
  Message="Concurrency violation: the UpdateCommand affected 0 of the ↵
expected 1 records."
```

15. Stop debugging, and close Visual C# Express.

How It Works

This example shows how to use optimistic concurrency with a timestamp column, and tests it by changing a row in a database table in a concurrent way. One data-bound control retrieves data and a second, concurrent, data access modifies a row; then the original data-bound control attempts to modify the same row. The result is a concurrency violation.

To start with, you verified that the wizards used to generate a typed data set correctly identified the form of optimistic concurrency management that you wanted to use, namely the use of a timestamp column. You checked this by looking at the configuration of the table adapter and at the generated SQL commands.

Adding a DataGridView control to the form to display data from the Enchantment table provided all the infrastructure required to retrieve and bind data, as well as the code necessary to make updates to the data. You removed the timestamp column (LastModified) from the view because this data cannot be displayed using the DataGridView column templates. Because it is interpreted as a byte[] type, the DataGridView attempts to display it as a bitmap, which fails if the application is run at this point. Removing the column solves the problem.

Once the DataGridView is added, the application can be used to modify data in the Enchantment table. To illustrate optimistic concurrency, however, a button was added to make independent modifications to data in this table. The code for it starts by creating a connection using the connection string stored in the application settings (in the same way as the code in the EnchantmentTableAdapter.InitConnection() method):

```csharp
private void button1_Click(object sender, EventArgs e)
{
    // Get connection.
    SqlConnection conn = new SqlConnection(
        global::Ex0901___Optimistic_Concurrency.Properties.Settings.
        Default.FolktaleDBConnectionString);
```

Next, a single row is retrieved from the Enchantment table:

```csharp
    // Get data from 1st row in Enchantment table.
    SqlCommand readCmd = new SqlCommand(
        "SELECT TOP 1 * FROM Enchantment", conn);
    conn.Open();
    SqlDataReader reader = readCmd.ExecuteReader();
```

The primary key and `Name` column are then retrieved from the obtained data reader, and the reader is closed:

```
reader.Read();
Guid rowId = (Guid)reader["EnchantmentId"];
string name = reader["Name"] as string;
reader.Close();
```

Next, a command is created to modify the `Name` column for the retrieved row — the string `" (modified)"` is added. After that, the connection is closed, because no further database access is required:

```
// Modify row.
SqlCommand cmd = new SqlCommand(
    "UPDATE Enchantment SET Name = @Name WHERE EnchantmentId = "
    + "@EnchantmentId", conn);
cmd.Parameters.Add("EnchantmentId", SqlDbType.UniqueIdentifier).Value =
    rowId;
cmd.Parameters.Add("Name", SqlDbType.VarChar, 300).Value = name
    + " (modified)";
int rowsModified = cmd.ExecuteNonQuery();
conn.Close();
```

Finally, a message box is displayed noting the result of the modification:

```
// Notify user.
if (rowsModified == 1)
{
    // Success.
    MessageBox.Show("Row with Name value of '" + name + "' modified.",
        "Row modification report", MessageBoxButtons.OK,
        MessageBoxIcon.Information);
}
else
{
    // Failure.
    MessageBox.Show("Row modification failed.",
        "Row modification report", MessageBoxButtons.OK,
        MessageBoxIcon.Error);
}
}
```

Purely for the purpose of brevity, this code doesn't include a lot of the error checking/exception handling that you would normally incorporate for database access.

When the application is run and the button is clicked, a modification is made to the database. When a change is attempted on the same row using the data-bound `DataGridView` control, the operation fails because optimistic concurrency detects that it would result in a loss of data. A `DBConcurrencyException` exception is thrown, and because it is not handled, the application crashes.

Now that you have seen how to implement optimistic concurrency in database access, it's time to look at how to deal with situations where violations occur, including what to do when you receive a DBConcurrencyException exception.

Concurrency Violations in Client Applications

When a concurrency violation occurs in your application you have two options: ignore it or act on it. Generally speaking, ignoring it isn't really viable. That confuses users, and possibly results in inconsistencies between database data and the data that users see. Taking things to the next level, you can simply report that an error has occurred and reject changes that users have made — either all changes as a block, or just the changes that caused violations. Again, this isn't ideal because changes made by users will be lost.

A much better choice is to provide users with options when violations occur. For example, you might use the decision tree shown in Figure 9-4 to decide what to do next.

In this diagram, diamonds indicate decisions made in your code, namely checking for concurrency violations, checking to see if the external edit resulted in a row being deleted, and checking to see if the requested action is to delete the row. The rounded rectangles indicate the action to take (if any).

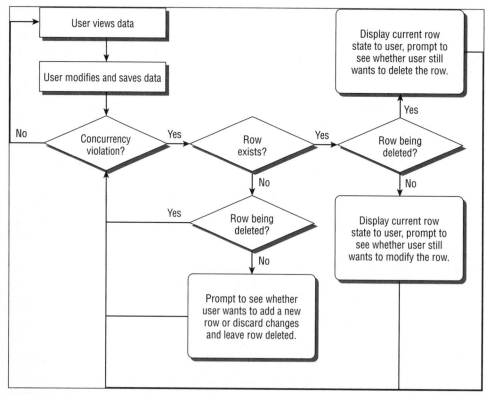

Figure 9-4: Concurrency decisions

Multiple concurrency violations may occur in a single "save data" operation by the user, so you might have to repeat this test/prompt/act cycle several times. That isn't possible when you are dealing with DBConcurrencyExceptions because the exception interrupts subsequent database accesses. Instead, you must use the SqlDataAdapter.RowAdapted event. You look at both of these topics in this section, and see how to implement the system displayed in Figure 9-4 in the next section.

Be aware that the decisions illustrated here are not the only ones possible, and the design of your applications may dictate the implementation of alternative strategies. However, you need to know the techniques described here to achieve them.

Refreshing Disconnected Data

Before looking into what to do when a concurrency violation occurs, it's worth noting a technique for avoiding them in the first place, namely keeping client data as up-to-date as possible by periodic (manual or automatic) data updates. The problem in doing this with data-bound controls is that refreshing the data source results in the data being re-bound to the control, so that any current edits/selections are lost unless you write quite a lot of code to cater for it.

Manual data refreshing is perhaps the preferable option because you can warn users that current unsaved changes will be lost before continuing. A more advanced technique that is possible with SQL Server 2005 is to make use of the service broker to detect changes in the database, and update data automatically if this occurs. Again, with data binding this can lead to loss of changes, and you have to be careful how you implement it. There are classes to help you — SqlDependancy and SqlNotificationRequest — but their use in Windows applications is beyond the scope of this book. In the next chapter, you look in more depth at data dependencies when using cached data in web applications, which is, thankfully, much simpler.

DBConcurrencyException

For individual data updates through custom commands, or where you don't want to continue trying to update database data when a violation occurs, the DBConcurrencyException is your friend. In the earlier example application, you saw a situation in which this exception was thrown. Now you examine that exception in more detail and see how you can use it to resolve concurrency violations.

As well as the normal exception properties, the DBConcurrencyException exception has a property called Row. It can be used to obtain the row that caused an update violation in the form of a DataRow object. When using typed data sets, the object will be an instance of whatever strongly typed row is appropriate, such as EnchantmentRow object in the earlier example. The row stored in this property is a reference to the row in the data set that has caused a violation, and will have a HasErrors property of true and a RowError property matching the Message property of the exception. The row state is available only for update command errors — if you delete a row, no columns in the Row property are available, and you receive an exception if you try to access their values. You can find out if they are available by checking the value of the Row.RowState property, which is DataRowState.Deleted if the row has been deleted.

In itself, having this information isn't enough for you to resolve the concurrency violation because it doesn't include any information concerning the current state of the database. However, it contains enough information (notably the primary key of the row) for you to obtain whatever additional data you need. For example, on receiving this information you could immediately query the database for an up-to-date version of the row in question and act accordingly.

The following code shows a modification that you can apply to the previous example to catch and process the DBConcurrencyException it generates. The behavior here is to reject the change and notify the user — later in this chapter you use a more advanced mechanism to deal with violations.

```
private void enchantmentBindingNavigatorSaveItem_Click(object sender, EventArgs e)
{
    try
    {
        this.Validate();
        this.enchantmentBindingSource.EndEdit();
        this.enchantmentTableAdapter.Update(this.folktaleDBDataSet.Enchantment);
    }
    catch (DBConcurrencyException ex)
    {
        // Alert user.
        MessageBox.Show(
            "Concurrency violation detected, unable to modify row "
            + "as it has been modified or deleted. "
            + "Changes discarded.",
            "Row modification report", MessageBoxButtons.OK,
            MessageBoxIcon.Error);
    }

    // Update bound data.
    this.enchantmentTableAdapter.Fill(this.folktaleDBDataSet.Enchantment);
}
```

This code checks only for concurrency violations. If other database restrictions are violated (a foreign key violation, for instance), the exception will go unhandled. The same applies to other errors, such as a failure to connect to the database. You would need to add additional code to check for these errors, by catching exceptions of type SqlException, and act accordingly.

SqlDataAdapter.RowUpdated Event

Users often make several modifications to data and apply them in one go. Unfortunately, as soon as a DBConcurrencyException exception is thrown, updates cease, making the previous technique unsuitable for multiple simultaneous updates using data adapters. In fact, the exception handling situation is even worse because updates made before the violation are committed, while updates to be made subsequently are not.

To have more control over this, you must configure the SqlDataAdapter object in use to continue attempting updates when errors occur, and examine the results of individual data updates as they occur. This involves the following:

1. Set the SqlDataAdapter.ContinueUpdateOnError property to true.

2. Add an event handler for the SqlDataAdapter.RowUpdated event, which fires when an attempt is made to update data.

3. Add logic in the event handler to notify the user and provide her with options for the row in question.

This is easy enough when using your own data adapters, but it's slightly more difficult when using wizard-created typed data sets. That's because the wizard creates its own table adapter class, which wraps the `SqlDataAdapter` object used to interact with the database. The class created does not expose the `RowUpdated` event or allow you to set the `ContinueUpdateOnError` property.

However, the table adapter class created is a partial class definition, and you can add your own code to deal with this problem. In the following example you add to the table adapter class definition, inserting the code required to deal with multiple concurrency violations, although you leave the resolution of these until the next section.

Try It Out   Optimistic Concurrency

1. Copy the `Ex0901 - Optimistic Concurrency` directory created in the previous example to a new folder called `Ex0902 - RowUpdated Event`. Open the solution file from the new directory in Visual C# Express, and rename the solution and project to match the directory name. Save the project.

2. Right-click on `FolktaleDBDataSet.xsd` and click View Code. Remove the default code added to the new `FolktaleDBDataSet.cs` file, and add the following code:

```
namespace Ex0901___Optimistic_Concurrency.FolktaleDBDataSetTableAdapters
{
    public partial class EnchantmentTableAdapter
    {
        public void SetContinueUpdateOnError()
        {
            _adapter.ContinueUpdateOnError = true;
        }

        public void RegisterRowUpdatedEventHandler(
            System.Data.SqlClient.SqlRowUpdatedEventHandler handler)
        {
            _adapter.RowUpdated += handler;
        }
    }
}
```

This code includes the namespace from the earlier example. You can, if you want, change the namespace to one that includes the title of the current exercise, but if you do, you'll have to change it throughout the project. It's simpler, for the purposes of demonstration, to leave the namespace unchanged because it makes no difference to the function of the application.

3. Open the `Form1.cs` code file and modify the code as follows:

```
private void enchantmentBindingNavigatorSaveItem_Click(object sender, EventArgs e)
{
    this.Validate();
    this.enchantmentBindingSource.EndEdit();
    this.enchantmentTableAdapter.Update(this.folktaleDBDataSet.Enchantment);

    // Refresh data.
    this.enchantmentTableAdapter.Fill(this.folktaleDBDataSet.Enchantment);
```

```
    }

    private void Form1_Load(object sender, EventArgs e)
    {
        // TODO: This line of code loads data into the 'folktaleDBDataSet.Enchantment'
        // table. You can move, or remove it, as needed.
        this.enchantmentTableAdapter.Fill(this.folktaleDBDataSet.Enchantment);

        // Configure for multiple violation detection and continuation.
        this.enchantmentTableAdapter.SetContinueUpdateOnError();
        this.enchantmentTableAdapter.RegisterRowUpdatedEventHandler(
            new SqlRowUpdatedEventHandler(AdapterRowUpdated));
    }

    private void AdapterRowUpdated(object sender,
        System.Data.SqlClient.SqlRowUpdatedEventArgs e)
    {
        // Check for problem.
        if (e.Status == UpdateStatus.ErrorsOccurred)
        {
            // Get details
            Guid rowId = (Guid)e.Command.Parameters["@Original_EnchantmentId"].Value;
            string updateAction =
                (e.Row.RowState == DataRowState.Deleted ? "delete" : "update");

            if (e.Errors is DBConcurrencyException)
            {
                // Alert user.
                MessageBox.Show(
                    "Concurrency violation detected, unable to "
                    + updateAction + " row with ID '"
                    + rowId + "' as the row has been modified or deleted. "
                    + "Changes discarded.",
                    "Row modification report", MessageBoxButtons.OK,
                    MessageBoxIcon.Error);
            }
            else
            {
                // Alert user.
                MessageBox.Show(
                    "Error detected, unable to "
                    + updateAction + " row with ID '"
                    + rowId + "'. Error message: "
                    + e.Errors.Message
                    + " Changes discarded.",
                    "Row modification report", MessageBoxButtons.OK,
                    MessageBoxIcon.Error);
            }
        }
    }
```

4. Run the application, and click the Modify Table Data button. The message box should appear as before. Click OK to accept it.

5. Modify the Name column for the first two rows (the first row should be the one indicated by the dialog box).

6. Click the Save Data icon on the form. A dialog box should appear, as shown in Figure 9-5.

Figure 9-5: Notification dialog box

7. Click OK and note that the display has been refreshed. The first row should include the suffix "(modified)" as set by the button event handler, and the second row should include the modification you made.

8. Delete the first row and then click Save Data. A different error should be reported, as shown in Figure 9-6.

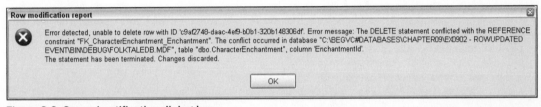

Figure 9-6: Second notification dialog box

9. Click OK, and close the application and Visual C# Express.

How It Works

This example shows how to use the SqlDataAdapter.RowUpdated event to detect errors when updating rows without aborting subsequent updates. The code detects both concurrency errors and other types of errors that may occur.

Because the wizard technique is used to generate a typed data set along with associated utility classes, it is necessary to extend the class definition for the generated table adapter to implement this functionality. The extension added allows the client application to have a greater degree of access to the underlying SqlDataAdapter used to access database data (stored in a private member called _adapter). Specifically, code is added to set the ContinueUpdateOnError property to true:

```
public void SetContinueUpdateOnError()
{
    _adapter.ContinueUpdateOnError = true;
}
```

and to allow client applications to register event handlers for the RowUpdated event by supplying a delegate:

```
public void RegisterRowUpdatedEventHandler(
    System.Data.SqlClient.SqlRowUpdatedEventHandler handler)
{
    _adapter.RowUpdated += handler;
}
```

In the client form, a number of modifications are made. First, code is added to enchantmentBindingNavigatorSaveItem_Click() to refresh data after an update because modifications may not have been committed:

```
this.enchantmentTableAdapter.Fill(this.folktaleDBDataSet.Enchantment);
```

Next, code is added to Form1_Load() to use the new methods added to the table adapter:

```
this.enchantmentTableAdapter.SetContinueUpdateOnError();
this.enchantmentTableAdapter.RegisterRowUpdatedEventHandler(
    new SqlRowUpdatedEventHandler(AdapterRowUpdated));
```

The AdapterRowUpdated event handler is then ready to be called for each row update. The first thing to do in this method is to see if an error has occurred. That's possible using the SqlRowUpdatedEventArgs.Status property, which is of type UpdateStatus:

```
private void AdapterRowUpdated(object sender,
    System.Data.SqlClient.SqlRowUpdatedEventArgs e)
{
    if (e.Status == UpdateStatus.ErrorsOccurred)
    {
```

If this is UpdateStatus.ErrorsOccurred, the next step is to obtain information about the row that caused the error. While the row properties might not be available directly through SqlRowUpdatedEventArgs.Row (because the row might have been deleted, and this property is set according to the same rules as the one in DBConcurrencyException), it is possible to access the command used to update (or delete) the row. Whether it's an update or delete command, it has a parameter called @Original_EnchantmentId that you can use to discover the ID of the row being modified. You can also discover the modification being attempted by using the Row.Rowstate property as discussed earlier in the chapter in the context of DBConcurrencyException:

```
Guid rowId = (Guid)e.Command.Parameters["@Original_EnchantmentId"].Value;
string updateAction =
    (e.Row.RowState == DataRowState.Deleted ? "delete" : "update");
```

The next thing to look at is the error that occurred, which is available in the SqlRowUpdatedEventArgs.Errors property. For concurrency errors, this will be of type DBConcurrencyException — the exception is included here rather than being thrown, as in earlier examples. The code uses this to report an error (although no attempt is made to deal with the error at this stage):

```
if (e.Errors is DBConcurrencyException)
{
```

```
                  // Alert user.
                  MessageBox.Show(
                      "Concurrency violation detected, unable to "
                      + updateAction + " row with ID '"
                      + rowId + "' as the row has been modified or deleted. "
                      + "Changes discarded.",
                      "Row modification report", MessageBoxButtons.OK,
                      MessageBoxIcon.Error);
              }
```

Alternatively, a different error may have occurred — such as the foreign key violation shown in the example. The remaining code in this method deals with alternative exception types stored in `Error`:

```
              else
              {
                  // Alert user.
                  MessageBox.Show(
                      "Error detected, unable to "
                      + updateAction + " row with ID '"
                      + rowId + "'. Error message: "
                      + e.Errors.Message
                      + " Changes discarded.",
                      "Row modification report", MessageBoxButtons.OK,
                      MessageBoxIcon.Error);
              }
          }
      }
```

When the application runs, exceptions are not thrown when update errors occur. Instead, the code in the event handler detects errors, including concurrency violations, and reports them.

Resolving Concurrency Violations

Previous sections have demonstrated how to design your applications to allow for concurrency, and how to detect violations of concurrency when they occur. The next step is to do something about violations when they happen, rather than simply discarding changes. At the beginning of the last section you saw a flow chart detailing the decisions that need to be taken into account and suggesting how you might approach resolutions. In this section you implement that scheme.

Actually, this is more about straight programming than database trickery. The code that you will see in this section doesn't introduce anything earth-shatteringly new, but uses techniques you've already investigated extensively and puts them together in a way that achieves the desired result. For this reason it's best to dive straight in with some sample code.

Try It Out   Resolving Concurrency Violations

1. Copy the `Ex0902 - RowUpdated Event` directory created in the previous example to a new folder called `Ex0903 - Resolving Violations`. Open the solution file from the new directory in Visual C# Express, and rename the solution and project to match the directory name. Save the project.

2. Open `FolktaleDBDataSet.xsd` in DataSet Designer view.

3. Right-click `EnchantmentTableAdapter` and select Add | Query. Use the Use SQL Statements and SELECT Which Returns Rows options, and add the following query:

    ```
    SELECT EnchantmentId, Name, LastModified FROM dbo.Enchantment WHERE ↵
    EnchantmentId = @EnchantmentId
    ```

4. Click Next, uncheck Fill a DataTable, and change the name of the Return a DataTable method to `GetEnchantmentByID`. Click Next and then click Finish.

5. Right-click `EnchantmentTableAdapter` and select Add | Query. Use the Use SQL Statements and DELETE options, and add the following query:

    ```
    DELETE FROM dbo.Enchantment WHERE EnchantmentId = @EnchantmentId
    ```

6. Click Next and change the name of the query to `DeleteEnchantmentById`. Click Next and then click Finish.

7. Right-click `EnchantmentTableAdapter` and select Add | Query. Use the Use SQL Statements and UPDATE options, and add the following query:

    ```
    UPDATE dbo.Enchantment SET Name = @Name WHERE EnchantmentId = @EnchantmentId
    ```

8. Click Next and change the name of the query to `UpdateEnchantmentById`. Click Next and then click Finish.

9. Right-click `EnchantmentTableAdapter` and select Add | Query. Use the Use SQL Statements and INSERT options, and add the following query:

    ```
    INSERT INTO dbo.Enchantment (EnchantmentId, Name) VALUES (@EnchantmentId, @Name)
    ```

10. Click Next and change the name of the query to `InsertEnchantment`. Click Next and then click Finish.

11. Add the following methods to `Form1.cs`:

    ```csharp
    private void ProcessNonConcurrencyError(Exception error, string updateAction,
        Guid rowId)
    {
        // Alert user.
        MessageBox.Show(
            "Error detected, unable to "
            + updateAction + " row with ID '"
            + rowId + "'. Error message: "
            + error.Message
            + " Changes discarded.",
            "Row modification report", MessageBoxButtons.OK,
            MessageBoxIcon.Error);
    }

    private FolktaleDBDataSet.EnchantmentRow GetCurrentRowState(Guid rowId)
    {
        // Use new query to get current row state.
        FolktaleDBDataSet.EnchantmentDataTable currentData =
            enchantmentTableAdapter.GetEnchantmentByID(rowId);
    ```

```
        // Return row or null.
        if (currentData.Rows.Count == 1)
        {
            return currentData[0];
        }
        return null;
    }

    private void DeleteModifiedRow(FolktaleDBDataSet.EnchantmentRow currentRow)
    {
        // Prompt.
        DialogResult userChoice = MessageBox.Show(
            "Attempt to delete modified row detected. "
            + "Row in database has Name of '"
            + currentRow.Name + "'. Confirm deletion?",
            "Concurrency Violation Detected",
            MessageBoxButtons.YesNo,
            MessageBoxIcon.Question);

        // Take action if necessary.
        if (userChoice == DialogResult.Yes)
        {
            enchantmentTableAdapter.DeleteEnchantmentById(currentRow.EnchantmentId);
        }
    }

    private void UpdateDeletedRow(FolktaleDBDataSet.EnchantmentRow newRow)
    {
        // Prompt.
        DialogResult userChoice = MessageBox.Show(
            "Attempt to update deleted row detected. "
            + "Add new row with Name value of '"
            + newRow.Name + "'?",
            "Concurrency Violation Detected",
            MessageBoxButtons.YesNo,
            MessageBoxIcon.Question);

        // Take action if necessary.
        if (userChoice == DialogResult.Yes)
        {
            enchantmentTableAdapter.InsertEnchantment(Guid.NewGuid(), newRow.Name);
        }
    }

    private void UpdateModifiedRow(FolktaleDBDataSet.EnchantmentRow currentRow,
        FolktaleDBDataSet.EnchantmentRow newRow)
    {
        // Prompt.
        DialogResult userChoice = MessageBox.Show(
            "Attempt to update modified row detected. "
            + "Row in database has Name of '"
            + currentRow.Name + "'. Change this value to '"
            + newRow.Name + "'?",
            "Concurrency Violation Detected",
```

```
                    MessageBoxButtons.YesNo,
                    MessageBoxIcon.Question);

            // Take action if necessary.
            if (userChoice == DialogResult.Yes)
            {
                enchantmentTableAdapter.UpdateEnchantmentById(newRow.Name,
                    currentRow.EnchantmentId);
            }
        }
    }
```

12. Modify `AdapterRowUpdated()` as follows:

```
    private void AdapterRowUpdated(object sender,
        System.Data.SqlClient.SqlRowUpdatedEventArgs e)
    {
        // Check for problem.
        if (e.Status == UpdateStatus.ErrorsOccurred)
        {
            // Get details
            Guid rowId = (Guid)e.Command.Parameters["@Original_EnchantmentId"].Value;
            string updateAction =
                (e.Row.RowState == DataRowState.Deleted ? "delete" : "update");

            if (e.Errors is DBConcurrencyException)
            {
                try
                {
                    // Get current row state.
                    FolktaleDBDataSet.EnchantmentRow currentRow =
                        GetCurrentRowState(rowId);

                    // Determine course of action
                    if (e.Row.RowState == DataRowState.Deleted)
                    {
                        // Delete attempt made.
                        if (currentRow == null)
                        {
                            // No action required - row already deleted.
                        }
                        else
                        {
                            // Show modified row data, prompt for deletion.
                            DeleteModifiedRow(currentRow);
                        }
                    }
                    else
                    {
                        // Update attempt made.
                        if (currentRow == null)
                        {
                            // Prompt to add new row or discard changes.
                            UpdateDeletedRow(
                                e.Row as FolktaleDBDataSet.EnchantmentRow);
                        }
```

```
                  else
                  {
                      // Show modified row data, prompt for deletion.
                      UpdateModifiedRow(currentRow,
                          e.Row as FolktaleDBDataSet.EnchantmentRow);
                  }
              }
          }
          catch (Exception ex)
          {
              // Alert user.
              ProcessNonConcurrencyError(e.Errors, updateAction, rowId);
          }
      }
      else
      {
          // Alert user.
          ProcessNonConcurrencyError(e.Errors, updateAction, rowId);
      }
  }
}
```

13. Execute the application and experiment with various concurrency violations. To assist you in this, you might want to open the current version of the database and edit rows of the Enchantment table manually. To do this, view the Solution Explorer window while the application is running (it may be hidden), choose to view all files, expand the bin and Debug folders, and double-click on the current version of the database you find there. You should be able to open the contents of the Enchantment table and modify/delete records to cause concurrency violations that will then be dealt with by the application.

14. When you are satisfied that things are working correctly, close the application and Visual C# Express.

How It Works

In the first part of this example you add four new queries for direct database access, which is necessary for two reasons:

❑ The current database access queries do not provide a way to fetch single rows identified by ID.

❑ To avoid additional concurrency problems, new queries that ignore the LastModified column are required.

As you know from previous chapters, adding queries results in the addition of methods to use those queries, and it is those queries that are used in the form code to read and update data.

The code in AdapterRowUpdated() is modified so that the decision tree presented earlier can be implemented. This involves obtaining the current row values from the database, using the GUID ID for the row obtained in the same way as in the previous example. Depending on whether the requested row exists and whether an attempt is being made to update or delete the row, action could be taken. This action is carried out in one of three methods, DeleteModifiedRow(), UpdateModifiedRow(), and UpdateDeletedRow(). Each of these methods informs the user about the situation, and gives him a choice to override the values in the database or discard changes. This is simplified somewhat by the fact that rows in the Enchantment table use only a single column for data, Name. For other tables you might have to display additional information, and perhaps you would give the option to merge data for updating modified rows, but the principle would be the same.

A separate method is provided for dealing with any other problems that may occur, in the form of other exceptions. It uses the same code employed previously when exceptions occurred, so it could be used in two places.

As noted prior to this example, the exact form of the code used is nothing new, so there's no need to go through it line-by-line.

Transactions

As mentioned at the beginning of the chapter, transactions are a way of grouping operations together such that they either all complete or none of them do. Even if some operations have completed successfully at the time when one of them fails, using a transaction results in the previously performed operations being "rolled back" so that the result is the same as if they had never been performed.

There's no explicit reference to databases in the preceding paragraph because the subject of transactions is larger than that — databases are just one type of resource to which transactions apply. Other resources include files, application state, and so on. Internally, each resource must have an associated resource manager that is responsible for keeping track of changes, committing or rolling them back as required.

It is even possible for transactions to include multiple resources simultaneously. If that's the case, even if the two resource managers are of the same type (for example if two separate databases take part in the transaction), a transaction monitor is required to coordinate resource managers, and the transaction is known as a *distributed* transaction. In .NET scenarios this usually is the job of the Microsoft Distributed Transaction Coordinator (MSDTC) — although this isn't a detail you normally have to worry about.

In this book, however, you won't be looking into transactions as deep as that, and you won't learn about distributed transactions and the tips and tricks associated with the subject. Instead you concentrate on database transactions. It is worth noting, however, that the implementation of database transactions in .NET 2.0 is such that the techniques you learn here are directly transferable to the context of distributed transactions. That's because database transactions are *promotable* transactions, meaning that distributed transactions are created only when they are needed. In practice, that means you can start a transaction using one resource and then add additional resources; the transaction is automatically promoted to a distributed transaction.

This chapter looks at two types of database transactions:

❑   **SQL transactions:** The transaction is created and managed using SQL code in stored procedures.

❑   **.NET transactions:** You create and use transactions in C# code.

As you will see, both types of transactions have their place in application development, although the techniques involved differ dramatically.

SQL Transactions

When you use SQL Server, you are actually performing transactions all of the time because that's the way SQL commands are interpreted. In fact, every command results in a transaction being performed. If the command doesn't result in an error, then its result is committed to the database. If the command results in an error, the transaction containing the command is rolled back. This mode of operation, the default in SQL Server, is known as *autocommit transactions*.

Autocommit transactions apply to individual commands, not batches of commands such as those that make up a stored procedure. For example, consider the following commands:

```
DELETE FROM Enchantment
    WHERE EnchantmentId = 'c9af2748-daac-4ef9-b0b1-320b148306df'
DELETE FROM Enchantment
    WHERE EnchantmentId = '124d8dfb-b48a-4815-a9db-369912de6da9'
```

Here, a transaction is created for each of the two DELETE commands, not one for both of them together, even if they are executed as part of a single batch of commands. This means that even if the first command fails (perhaps because of a foreign key violation), the second will still be performed.

Now consider the following two commands:

```
DELTE FROM Enchantment
    WHERE EnchantmentId = 'c9af2748-daac-4ef9-b0b1-320b148306df'
DELETE FROM Enchantment
    WHERE EnchantmentId = '124d8dfb-b48a-4815-a9db-369912de6da9'
```

Here the first command contains a syntax error — the keyword DELTE is not a SQL keyword. You might think the result would be the same as the preceding example — that the second command would commit. However, there is a difference between semantic (where a command fails as a result of database restrictions, using a non-existent table name, and so forth) and syntax errors. With syntax errors, SQL Server fails to compile the commands internally, and therefore neither command is executed.

This situation is often misinterpreted as being the result of a single transaction failure, where the command that doesn't contain a syntax error has been rolled back. It is important to know that is not the case — SQL Server transactions don't work that way!

To group multiple SQL commands in a single transaction, you must use a different mode of execution. The two of these you'll look at in this book are implicit transactions and explicit transactions. An *implicit transaction* is where a transaction is automatically started when command execution begins, and ends when a command is given to commit or roll back the transaction. When this happens, a new transaction is automatically started, so transactions are continuously being created for all commands. *Explicit transactions* involve SQL Server being told to start transactions, either by ADO.NET or through SQL keywords. There are SQL keywords to begin, end, commit, and roll back transactions. As such, they are perhaps most useful in stored procedures because executing individual commands using (for example) ADO.NET does not provide a lot of scope for handling batches of commands — at least not in a particularly user-friendly way.

To execute a batch of SQL commands as a transaction you must define the start of the transaction using the BEGIN TRANSACTION (or BEGIN TRAN) keywords, and then define the end of the transaction by committing or rolling back the changes. Typically the end of the transaction is defined by committing the transaction, using COMMIT TRANSACTION. In that case, changes are rolled back automatically if an error occurs during the processing of the statements in the transaction. In some circumstances, such as in branching code, you might use the keywords ROLLBACK TRANSACTION to explicitly roll back a transaction. So, the basic structure of a SQL explicit transaction is as follows:

```
BEGIN TRANSACTION

...

COMMIT TRANSACTION
```

The statements that make up the transaction go between these two lines of code.

Optionally, you can provide a name for the transaction, although that's primarily for user friendliness in reading the SQL code and doesn't really afford any additional functionality:

```
BEGIN TRANSACTION MyTransaction

...

COMMIT TRANSACTION MyTransaction
```

You can also nest transactions inside other transactions, although again that does not provide additional functionality. The main reason why it's allowed is so you can call a stored procedure that uses an explicit transaction from within a batch of commands that uses its own explicit transaction.

Nested transactions do not actually commit changes when they complete, even if a COMMIT TRANSAC-TION *statement is encountered. The nested transaction changes are committed only when the outermost transaction is committed. There is no practical limit to the number of transactions that can be nested inside one another.*

Within a SQL transaction, errors result in the transaction being rolled back only if they are of a high enough severity. Many errors, such as adding records with duplicate primary key values (as in the following example), don't result in the entire transaction being rolled back. Instead, only the statement generating the error fails to commit — which is the same behavior illustrated earlier in the autocommit transactions discussion.

There are two ways to modify this behavior. First, you can use SQL exception-handing code to detect errors, and use ROLLBACK TRANSACTION to roll back the entire transaction if desired. If you do that, however, subsequent calls to COMMIT TRANSACTION will result in an error because the transaction is already terminated. To deal with that, check the value of the @@TRANCOUNT variable before calling COMMIT TRANSACTION. This variable stores the current number of active transactions:

```
BEGIN TRANSACTION MyTransaction

...

(code which might call ROLLBACK TRANSACTION)

...
```

```
IF @@TRANCOUNT > 0
    COMMIT TRANSACTION MyTransaction
```

Alternatively, you can set the XACT_ABORT option for the database to ON. Then, any runtime error, including "less severe" ones, will abort the transaction and cause changes to be rolled back. During the processing of SQL transactions, locks are applied to the rows being modified so that other code cannot interfere with the data in the rows while they are being updated.

In the following example, you use this technique to observe transactions both succeeding and failing.

Try It Out   **SQL Transactions**

1. Copy the Ex0903 - Resolving Violations directory created in the previous example to a new folder called Ex0904 - SQL Transactions. Open the solution file from the new directory in Visual C# Express, and rename the solution and project to match the directory name. Save the project.

2. In the Database Explorer window, open the connection to the FolktaleDB database and expand its contents. Right-click on the Stored Procedures folder and select Add Stored Procedure.

3. Add a stored procedure as follows:

```
CREATE PROCEDURE dbo.AddTwoEnchantments
(
    @FirstId uniqueidentifier,
    @FirstName varchar(300),
    @SecondId uniqueidentifier,
    @SecondName varchar(300)
)
AS
SET XACT_ABORT ON
BEGIN TRANSACTION
    INSERT INTO Enchantment (EnchantmentId, Name) VALUES (@FirstId, @FirstName)
    INSERT INTO Enchantment (EnchantmentId, Name) VALUES (@SecondId, @SecondName)
COMMIT TRANSACTION
SET XACT_ABORT OFF
```

4. Save the stored procedure, and open FolktaleDBDataSet.xsd in DataSet Designer view.

5. Right-click on EnchantmentTableAdapter and select Add | Query. Select the Use Existing Stored Procedure option, click Next, and select AddTwoEnchantments from the drop-down selector on the next page. Click Next again and select No Value. Then click Next, Next, and Finish.

6. Open Form1 in design view, and add a new button to the right of the existing button, with the text **SQL Transactions**. Also set the Anchor property of the button to Bottom, Left.

7. Double-click the new button to add an event handler, and then add code as follows:

```
private void button2_Click(object sender, EventArgs e)
{
    // Define parameters.
    Guid firstId = Guid.NewGuid();
    Guid secondId = Guid.NewGuid();
    Guid thirdId = firstId;
```

```
Guid fourthId = Guid.NewGuid();
string firstName = "Ability to fly";
string secondName = "Insomnia";
string thirdName = "Premature baldness";
string fourthName = "Odd smell of lavender";

try
{
    // Execute sproc twice.
    enchantmentTableAdapter.AddTwoEnchantments(
        firstId, firstName, secondId, secondName);
    enchantmentTableAdapter.AddTwoEnchantments(
        thirdId, thirdName, fourthId, fourthName);
}
catch (SqlException ex)
{
    MessageBox.Show(ex.Message, "Transaction error", MessageBoxButtons.OK,
        MessageBoxIcon.Error);
}

// Refresh display.
enchantmentTableAdapter.Fill(folktaleDBDataSet.Enchantment);
}
```

8. Run the application and click the SQL Transactions button.

9. Click OK in the error dialog box that appears, and then check the records in the main form. You should see that only two records from the first transaction are added. The two records from the second transaction are not added because there was an error adding one of them.

10. Close the application and Visual C# Express.

How It Works

In this example you added a new stored procedure to the FolkloreDB database, and then added code to use it to the application that you have been building in this chapter.

The stored procedure itself is one that can be used to add two records to the Enchantment table as part of a single transaction. This is perhaps a little artificial, but it illustrates the techniques and doesn't introduce too much complexity to the example application. The stored procedure sets the XACT_ABORT option for the transaction to be rolled back if even minor errors occur — such as when one record fails to add because of a duplicate primary key, which is what the code in the application triggers.

After adding the stored procedure, the next step's familiar: Add the method to call the stored procedure to the table adapter. It could then be used from the client form, in this case via a button click event handler. The code calls the stored procedure twice — once with IDs and Name values for two new Enchantment rows with fresh, unique ID values, and once using one new row with a new ID value, and one with a duplicate of an existing ID value. The result here is that the transaction for the first call commits, while the second one rolls back so that only two rows are added.

Now that you have seen how to use transactions in SQL code, you might think that this is all you need. Whenever you want to do anything with a database, surely you can just make a stored procedure to do it and gain the benefits of transactions, right? Well, no, you probably will not want to do so. For a start, while this technique is flexible (stored procedures can call other stored procedures, even in other databases), it is far from ideal, and you are limited to using the SQL Server resource manager. You can't, for example, modify file system data easily. Also, complex, nested stored procedures performing multiple operations may require a lot of parameters, and can be difficult to test and debug.

That being said, it's still worth noting that there are situations where SQL transactions are ideal. For example, in the situation described in the introduction to this chapter, where a currency amount is to be transferred from one row to another, this technique would be perfect. You can use a stored procedure with three parameters — the IDs of two rows, and an amount to be transferred. The stored procedure can then update both rows in a single transaction, using two UPDATE commands. That satisfies your requirements — that either both or no rows are modified, and that the total currency amount remains constant. In addition, keeping all the transactional code in the database is efficient, and can result in better performance than writing C# code in many situations.

.NET Transactions

The other option, and probably the one you will use most often, is to manage transactions using .NET code. That means that you can include database access code and code that accesses other resources in the same transaction if desired, and the code is pretty simple. This option also makes things a lot easier to debug and gives you more flexibility in what you can do with database data — all without having to write SQL code, which is often more difficult to do than it looks.

The transaction framework is improved in .NET 2.0, and it is much easier to use transactions — especially distributed transactions — than it was in the past. Using classes from the System.Transactions namespace, you can integrate all your transaction needs, including those in ADO.NET.

There are two ways to deal with transactions in .NET. You can either obtain a SqlTransaction object representing a transaction and perform operations through it, or you can auto-enlist database access code in transactions by using TransactionScope and Transaction objects. In this section you examine both of these objects, and then take a brief look at transaction isolation levels, which are important in multi-user environments.

Using SqlTransaction

SqlTransaction objects represent transactions that can contain database access code. To create a SqlTransaction object, you call the BeginTransaction() method of a SqlConnection object. This can be done only if the connection is open.

```
SqlConnection conn = new SqlConnection(ConnectionString);
conn.Open();
SqlTransaction transaction = conn.BeginTransaction();
```

A SqlTransaction object thus obtained can be used only with a single connection, making it unsuitable for use in distributed transactions.

The SqlTransaction class definition is found in the System.Data.SqlClient namespace so there's no need to add a using statement for any new namespaces if you have already done so for you database access code. There is also no need to add any new references to your application.

The `SqlTransaction` object has two methods that you can use to commit or roll back changes, helpfully named `Commit()` and `Rollback()`. Typically, you would use a `try...catch` block to control the calling of these methods:

```
SqlConnection conn = new SqlConnection(ConnectionString);
conn.Open();
SqlTransaction transaction = conn.BeginTransaction();
try
{
    // Database manipulation code.
    ...

    // Commit transaction.
    transaction.Commit();
}
catch (Exception ex)
{
    // Roll back transaction.
    transaction.Rollback();

    // Process exception.
    ...
}
conn.Close();
```

Depending on what might go wrong during a transaction, it's possible that the `Rollback()` method will also fail — if the connection to the database is lost, for instance. For this reason you may want to wrap the call to this method in a second `try...catch` block to handle such errors.

Any commands that you want to execute as part of the transaction must also be explicitly enrolled in the transaction, which you can achieve by setting the `SqlCommand.Transaction` property to the `SqlTransaction` object. If you don't do so, executing the command generates an exception even though the `SqlConnection` object already has a reference to the transaction. For example:

```
SqlConnection conn = new SqlConnection(ConnectionString);
SqlCommand cmd = new SqlCommand(CommandString, conn);
conn.Open();
SqlTransaction transaction = conn.BeginTransaction();
cmd.Transaction = transaction;
try
{
    // Database manipulation code.
    cmd.ExecuteNonQuery();
    ...
```

This has implications when using data adapters, which use up to four commands. If you want those commands to participate in a transaction, you must set the `SqlCommand.Transaction` property on all of them. If you use `SqlCommandBuilder`, however, it will use the `Transaction` property of the select command to build the other commands, so at least that saves some time. However, using the wizards and creating the strongly typed table adapter for a query does not result in transaction enrollment, or any obvious way to achieve this. The DataSet Designer does not include any transaction functionality. If you want to use a `SqlTransaction` object to manage transactions in a typed data set, you are forced to add code to the partial class definition for the typed table adapter class, much like you did earlier in this chapter. You can, for example, add a `Transaction` property that, when set, results in any commands defined for the wrapped data adapter (as well as any additional commands used) being configured. That could take a form similar to the `Connection` property already used, perhaps as follows:

```
protected System.Data.SqlClient.SqlTransaction _transaction;

internal System.Data.SqlClient.SqlTransaction Transaction
{
    get
    {
        return _transaction;
    }
    set
    {
        _transaction = value;
        if ((Adapter.InsertCommand != null))
        {
            Adapter.InsertCommand.Transaction = value;
        }
        if ((Adapter.DeleteCommand != null))
        {
            Adapter.DeleteCommand.Transaction = value;
        }
        if ((Adapter.UpdateCommand != null))
        {
            Adapter.UpdateCommand.Transaction = value;
        }
        for (int i = 0; (i < CommandCollection.Length); i = (i + 1))
        {
            if ((CommandCollection[i] != null))
            {
                ((System.Data.SqlClient.SqlCommand)(this.CommandCollection[i]))
                    .Transaction = value;
            }
        }
    }
}
```

However, all this is starting to seem like a lot of work, and you may well be asking why it's necessary. In fact, it isn't. While you can take this approach if you want, there is an easier way to implement transactions in .NET, which doesn't require the additional code.

Using TransactionScope and Transaction

The `TransactionScope` and `Transaction` objects provide a generic way of handling transactional code in .NET applications — of whatever type. This transactional code includes but is not limited to database transactions. Using these classes is quite different than using `SqlTransaction`. For a start they require a lot less work. In addition, they cater to more situations, such as distributed transactions; these are the objects that enable promotable transactions as described earlier in this chapter.

Unfortunately, there is quite a lot of theory to get through in this section. Don't worry if it doesn't all make sense the first time you read it — just concentrate on the fact that actually using the TransactionScope *and* Transaction *classes is remarkably simple. Having said that, it's well worth getting a thorough grounding in this subject because it will aid you later.*

Unlike the `SqlTransaction` class, the definition of the `TransactionScope` and `Transaction` classes is found in the `System.Transactions` namespace, and you must add a reference to the `System .Transactions.dll` library to use these classes in your applications. Once you have done this, you can write code as follows:

```
using (TransactionScope transactionScope = new TransactionScope())
{
    // Transactional code, including any database access.
    ...
}
```

When you create a `TransactionScope` instance, a transaction (in the form of a `Transaction` object) becomes available for code to use up until the point where the `TransactionScope` object is disposed. In the preceding code, a `using` block is employed so that the `TransactionScope` object is disposed properly in case of error, and won't consume additional resources. Alternatively, you could use a `try...catch... finally` block to ensure that the object is disposed, depending on your application and your code writing style.

The transaction used can be a new transaction, or it can be an existing transaction (if there is an existing transaction, it is known as the *ambient* transaction), enabling you to nest `TransactionScope` objects in a variety of ways. To control this behavior, you can supply the `TransactionScope` constructor with a `TransactionScopeOption` enumeration value, which allows three possibilities:

❑ `TransactionScopeOption.Required`: If there is an existing (ambient) transaction, it will be used by the `TransactionScope`; otherwise a new transaction is created. This is the default behavior if this parameter is not specified.

❑ `TransactionScopeOption.RequiresNew`: Regardless of whether there is an existing (ambient) transaction, a new transaction is created.

❑ `TransactionScopeOption.Supress`: Within the context of the `TransactionScope`, no code has access to a transaction, and therefore will not run in a transactional way.

Alternatively, if there is a specific `Transaction` object that you want to use, you can supply that object as a parameter to the `TransactionScope` constructor.

There are three other constructor parameters that you can use when instantiating a `TransactionScope` object. First, you can supply a `TimeSpan` object to specify the timeout value for the transaction, after which it will roll back any changes and become unavailable (the default value for this is 1 minute). Second, you can use a `TransactionOptions` structure to specify the requirements for the transaction to use if a new transaction is created. This includes a timeout value, and also the isolation level required for the transaction, which you'll examine in the next section. Finally, you can supply an `EnterpriseServicesInteropOption` value, which enables you to integrate your transactional code with COM+ transactions, or to prevent such integration as you see fit. This is an advanced subject that isn't covered in this book, but which has implications in some applications where COM+ services are used.

To commit changes within the context of a `TransactionScope`, you must call the `TransactionScope .Complete()` method, which you do if all the operations perform correctly. If `TransactionScope` generated a new transaction when it was created, calling the `Complete()` method results in the transaction being committed. If a transaction spans several `TransactionScope` objects, the transaction commits only when all these have called `Complete()`; otherwise the transaction rolls back. Within the `using` block of a `TransactionScope` you typically use exception-handling code, and only call the `Complete()` method if no exceptions occur.

The beauty of using this system for database transactions is that there is no need to explicitly associate database connections or commands with the transaction. If there is an ambient transaction available (as there will be in the using block of a TransactionScope object unless you use TransactionScopeOption .Suppress) and you create a SqlConnection object, the connection automatically enlists in that transaction. To prevent this from happening (for whatever reason), you can include the name/value pair Enlist= false in the connection string used to create the connection. Should you then decide to enlist in the ambient transaction (or to a different transaction object: although that's structurally inadvisable when using TransactionScope), you can pass a Transaction object to the SqlConnection.EnlistTransaction() method.

> The SqlConnection *class also includes an* EnlistDistributedTransaction() *method for enlisting in COM+ transactions, although this is mainly for backward compatibility and you shouldn't ever need to use it.*

To access the current ambient transaction, you can use the static property Transaction.Current, which will get you the current transaction in the form of a Transaction object. This can be useful for several reasons:

❑   You can use the Transaction object to enlist any resources that haven't automatically enlisted (including SqlConnection objects, as described previously).

❑   The Transaction object exposes properties that you can use to retrieve information about the connection: a property called IsolationLevel to get the isolation level, and another called TransactionInformation that contains other information including when the transaction was created. Both of these properties are read-only. Perhaps the most useful piece of information you can obtain in this way is TransactionInformation.Status, which is a value taken from the TransactionStatus enumeration. It can be Aborted for rolled-back transactions, Committed for committed transactions, Active if the transaction has not been committed or rolled back, or InDoubt if unknown.

❑   You can use the Transaction.Rollback() method to roll back the transaction. There is no Commit() method: Committing happens implicitly.

❑   If you want to be notified when the transaction completes, you can add an event handler to the Transaction.TransactionCompleted event. The event handler has a parameter of type TransactionEventArgs, which has a property called Transaction containing the transaction that has completed. From this object you can find out whether the transaction committed or rolled back using the Transaction.TransactionInformation.Status property.

In most simple situations, however, you won't need to access the current transaction in this way. In the following example you see just how simple it can be to use transactions with this system.

Try It Out   Transaction Scope

1.   Copy the Ex0904 - SQL Transactions directory created in the previous example to a new folder called Ex0905 - Automatic Transactions. Open the solution file from the new directory in Visual C# Express, and rename the solution and project to match the directory name. Save the project.

2.   Open Form1 and change the text on the second button to Automatic Transactions (make the button bigger if the text doesn't fit).

3. Add a project reference to the `System.Transactions.dll` library.

4. Open the code for `Form1.cs`, and add the following `using` statement:

```
using System.Transactions;
```

5. Modify the button click handler for the second button as follows:

```csharp
private void button2_Click(object sender, EventArgs e)
{
    // Define parameters.
    Guid firstId = Guid.NewGuid();
    Guid secondId = Guid.NewGuid();
    Guid thirdId = firstId;
    Guid fourthId = Guid.NewGuid();
    string firstName = "Ability to fly";
    string secondName = "Insomnia";
    string thirdName = "Premature baldness";
    string fourthName = "Odd smell of lavender";

    using (TransactionScope transactionScope = new TransactionScope())
    {
        try
        {
            // Add rows.
            enchantmentTableAdapter.Insert(firstId, firstName);
            enchantmentTableAdapter.Insert(secondId, secondName);
            enchantmentTableAdapter.Insert(thirdId, thirdName);
            enchantmentTableAdapter.Insert(fourthId, fourthName);

            // Complete transaction scope.
            transactionScope.Complete();
        }
        catch (SqlException ex)
        {
            MessageBox.Show(ex.Message, "Transaction error", MessageBoxButtons.OK,
                MessageBoxIcon.Error);
        }
    }

    // Refresh display.
    enchantmentTableAdapter.Fill(folktaleDBDataSet.Enchantment);
}
```

6. Run the application. The first time you click the button you may see the error message similar to the one shown in Figure 9-7 (if you don't, continue on to Step 8).

Figure 9-7: Error notification

7. If you received the error, it means that either the MSDTC transaction coordinator service is not started, or that there has been a security error in accessing it. To resolve this, do the following:

   a. Open the Component Services configuration tool, which you will find in Control Panel ⇨ Administrative Tools.

   b. Expand Component Services and then Computers.

   c. Right-click on My Computer and select Properties.

   d. Select the MSDTC tab, and if the service status is shown as Stopped (see Figure 9-8), click Start.

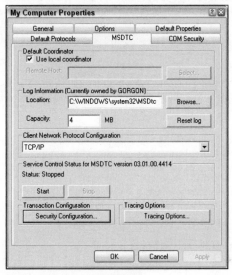

Figure 9-8: Starting MSDTC

   e. Test the application again. If it still doesn't work, click the Security Configuration button on the MSDTC tab, enable Network DTC Access, and select No Authentication Required.

   f. The application should now work.

8. With everything working properly, you should receive the same error message as in the previous example, saying that a primary key duplicate has been detected. When you click OK, you should see that no rows have been added.

9. Stop the application and modify the code as follows:

```
// Define parameters.
Guid firstId = Guid.NewGuid();
Guid secondId = Guid.NewGuid();
Guid thirdId = Guid.NewGuid();
Guid fourthId = Guid.NewGuid();
string firstName = "Ability to fly";
string secondName = "Insomnia";
string thirdName = "Premature baldness";
string fourthName = "Odd smell of lavender";
```

10. Run the application again and click the button. This time you shouldn't receive an error and four rows should be added.

11. Close the application and Visual C# Express.

How It Works

This example uses the classes in the `System.Transactions` namespace to automatically enroll database operations in a transaction. The first step was to reference the `System.Transactions.dll` library, and add a using statement for the namespace to simplify the code.

You modified the existing button click event handler, leaving the parameters (four pairs of `EnchantmentId` and `Name` values) unchanged, and adding a line of code to create a `TransactionScope` object:

```
using (TransactionScope transactionScope = new TransactionScope())
{
```

Within this `using` block, a `Transaction` object becomes available. It's used automatically by database access code, which consists of four calls to the wizard-generated `Insert()` method:

```
try
{
    enchantmentTableAdapter.Insert(firstId, firstName);
    enchantmentTableAdapter.Insert(secondId, secondName);
    enchantmentTableAdapter.Insert(thirdId, thirdName);
    enchantmentTableAdapter.Insert(fourthId, fourthName);
```

This is followed by a line of code to complete the transaction:

```
    transactionScope.Complete();
}
```

Should an error occur in the database access code, an exception-handling block is executed, and the `Complete()` method isn't called:

```
catch (SqlException ex)
{
    MessageBox.Show(ex.Message, "Transaction error", MessageBoxButtons.OK,
        MessageBoxIcon.Error);
}
}
```

Finally, as before, the display is refreshed so that you can see changes:

```
// Refresh display.
enchantmentTableAdapter.Fill(folktaleDBDataSet.Enchantment);
}
```

The first time the code runs, it is possible that the MSDTC is unavailable, and so a distributed transaction cannot be created. This error, if it occurs, happens on the second database access. A distributed transaction is required because of how the generated table adapter executes database actions. Connections are recycled, but are interpreted as separate database accesses, so the transaction is deemed to span multiple resources. This is slightly odd behavior, but is sadly a consequence of using the wizards to generate the database access code. If you hand-code command execution, you can ensure that a single connection is used, and opened and closed only once, avoiding this problem.

The MSDTC may be unavailable if its service is stopped, or for security restrictions. In the example, steps were supplied to solve these problems, if they occur. The solution given (remove security restrictions) is not suitable for an enterprise application spanning multiple computers: in such situations, you need to add more code relating to security and properly authenticate to the MSDTC, but that is beyond the scope of this book.

In testing the code, the first execution resulted in the transaction being rolled back because an attempt was made to add a duplicate primary key value. In that case, no rows were added, even though the error occurred only on the third row insert operation — evidence that the transaction was being properly handled. You removed the code that generated the error by creating a new GUID for use as the primary key of the third row insert. That solved the problem, which resulted in the transaction being committed and four rows being added.

One additional point to discuss here is how this technique can be useful when updating databases from modified typed data sets. Earlier you saw how an error such as a concurrency error can lead to some changes being made to the database, but not others. Specifically, changes made before the error are committed, the operation generating the error fails, and subsequent changes are not committed. You dealt with this by setting the `ContinueUpdateOnError` property of the data adapter and handing the `RowUpdated` event. Using transactions, you have an alternative solution — you can use a transaction for the data update task, and roll back all changes when there is an error (for example, you receive a `DBConcurrencyException` exception). Then you can inform the user that updates are impossible because there are errors, and perhaps display all the errors at once with possible resolutions highlighted, before attempting the (complete) update again. As with the earlier example, this is simply a matter of adding the appropriate logic and user interface elements; there is nothing new to cover here. However, transactions definitely provide you with a new and powerful weapon to use in the struggle against concurrency problems.

Transaction Isolation Levels

When you looked at SQL transactions earlier in this chapter it was noted that during a transaction, locks are placed on rows so that other operations cannot be performed against them. This means that other applications won't accidentally read or modify data that is already being accessed, which is a potential source of problems. However, it also means that applications may be blocked from performing database access while transactions are in progress, which can also be a problem if performance is critical.

As with many things, this is a tradeoff. You can't maximize both robustness and performance simultaneously. For that reason, you can specify what sort of access external operations can have on the data that takes part in .NET transactions. This can be a confusing topic, and is worth explaining as fully as possible. The data that is accessed by a transaction is known as *volatile* data, implying that it is subject to change (although, of course, depending on the result of the transaction, it might not change at all). It is this volatile data that an isolation level places restrictions on. Specifically, the isolation level determines whether other operations can read, modify, or add rows to volatile data. Depending on the isolation level, certain types of errors may occur during a transaction:

❑ **Lost updates:** If two transactions are given unrestricted access to volatile data so that they can both read and modify it, changes made by one transaction can overwrite changes made by the other. Optimistic concurrency management, as you saw earlier in this chapter, is one way to deal with this.

❑   **Non-repeatable read:** If two transactions are both capable of modifying data as part of their operation, a transaction that reads a row more than once may receive two different values for row data during its operation.

❑   **Dirty reads:** Similar to non-repeatable reads, but these are when the inconsistent read (the second read, which obtains a different value from the first) occurs during the processing of another transaction that is subsequently rolled back. That is to say, one transaction reads the value of a row that is never actually committed.

❑   **Phantom reads:** A row is deleted during the operation of one transaction, but is read just before it is deleted by another transaction. This means that if the second transaction attempts to modify the row, there will be an error because the row doesn't exist any more.

The different isolation levels possible are described in the following table. Each possibility is a member of the `IsolationLevel` enumeration.

IsolationLevel Value	Meaning
Serializable	The default level for .NET database transactions, and the most restrictive. Using this isolation level, volatile data can be read by other transactions, but cannot be modified. Also, no new data can be added by other transactions. The result is that your transaction is guaranteed not to receive dirty, non-repeatable, or phantom reads. However, a consequence of this is that other transactions may be blocked until the transaction commits.
RepeatableRead	Almost the same as `Serializable`, but other transactions are allowed to add new data, so phantom reads are possible.
ReadCommitted	Other transactions are not permitted to read volatile data, but can modify it. Dirty reads are prevented, but you may still get non-repeatable and phantom reads.
ReadUncommitted	Other transactions can read and modify volatile data. This is the least restrictive option, resulting in the best performance, but also allowing dirty, non-repeatable, and phantom reads.
Snapshot	Using this level, the transaction doesn't lock data but works with a separate, isolated version of it. When the transaction commits this snapshot, data is committed in one go, with errors being reported if the underlying data has been modified by another transaction. This isolation level cannot be used by distributed transactions.
Chaos	This level is not supported by SQL Server, but would result in an inability to modify data that has been changed by transactions with a higher isolation level.
Unspecified	Any other level of isolation. Using this value results in an exception.

In most cases, especially in simpler applications, `Serializable` is the most sensible option and will prevent most if not all concurrency problems. If you are absolutely certain that only one application will access the database at any time, you can use `ReadUncommitted` and get a slight performance boost, but be prepared to live with the consequences. Should you want to use a different value for the isolation level of the transaction used in your `TransactionScope` block, you must first create a `TransactionOptions` structure with the required level; for example:

```
TransactionOptions tOptions = new TransactionOptions();
tOptions.IsolationLevel = System.Transactions.IsolationLevel.ReadUncommitted;
using (TransactionScope transactionScope =
    new TransactionScope(TransactionScopeOption.RequiresNew, tOptions))
{
    ...
```

Note that there is also a type called `System.Data.IsolationLevel`, so you may need to use the fully qualified name of `System.Transactions.IsolationLevel` to refer to this enumeration.

Summary

In this chapter you learned about two important subjects that will enable you to perform more advanced operations and deal with unforeseen circumstances. First, you saw how to deal with concurrency problems, which can (and will) occur when databases are accessed simultaneously by multiple users and/or applications. You saw ways of detecting problems as they occur, and how to gracefully deal with them without causing users to lose their data and send you hate mail. You implemented a scheme involving a decision tree to make the user experience much smoother.

You also examined transactions, and saw how to implement these using both SQL and .NET code, and you learned the differences between these approaches. When it came to .NET code you saw how to do things "the old fashioned way" using SQL server-specific transactions, and then moved on to look at the way transactions are dealt with in .NET 2.0. You saw how easy it is to create and use transactions, and how effective they can be in your applications.

Specifically, you have learned:

❑ What concurrency violations are, and what forms of concurrency management are possible. The possible concurrency management schemes are "last one in wins," optimistic, and pessimistic — but pessimistic cannot be easily implemented in .NET.

❑ How to use "last in wins" and optimistic concurrency management. You saw how to structure SQL statements in such a way as to either ignore changes (by identifying rows only by their primary key) or to detect changes (by identifying rows using other columns). For optimistic concurrency management, you saw two ways of achieving this: looking at the values of all columns, or using `timestamp` columns.

❑ How to catch and use `DBConcurrencyException` exceptions. You also learned about the `SqlDataAdapter.RowUpdated` event, which you can use to deal with multiple concurrency violations in one go.

❑ How to resolve concurrency violations. You worked through an example that implemented a decision tree to allow users to control what happens when a concurrency violation occurs. For example, if a record has been changed by an external agent, you give the user the option of overwriting this change.

❑ How to implement SQL transactions and how to control transactions using SQL code. You also learned about the different types of SQL Server transactions: autocommit transactions for individual SQL statements, and implicit and explicit transactions for blocks of SQL code.

❑ How to configure the level of error required to cause SQL transactions to roll back, using the XACT_ABORT option.

❑ How .NET transactions work, and how promotable transactions are used to minimize processing where distributed transaction processing isn't necessary. You also explored the role that the MS DTC service plays in transaction processing.

❑ How to use SqlTransaction objects to perform ADO.NET transactions.

❑ How to use TransactionScope and Transaction objects to automatically enroll in transactions with minimum effort.

❑ What isolation levels are, and how to configure the isolation level for a transaction.

In the next chapter, you learn more about disconnected data, and about web service data sources and data caching.

Exercises

1. Which of the following are types of concurrency management that are possible in .NET applications?

    a. Optimistic

    b. Ambiguous

    c. Pessimistic

    d. Last in wins

    e. Last one in buys the drinks

2. What two techniques can you use to detect concurrency violations?

3. When using data adapters and a concurrency violation occurs, how can you prevent the situation where execution ceases, and subsequent changes are not committed to the database? You should have two answers — one where only the specific operations that result in concurrency violations are not committed, and one where, if a concurrency error occurs, no changes are committed.

4. Write the code for a stored procedure called TransferBalance that transfers a currency amount between two rows of a table called CustomerBalance. This table has a primary key column of type uniqueidentifier called CustomerBalanceId and a money type column called Balance. A SQL transaction should be used to guarantee data consistency.

5. To avoid having dirty reads in your transaction, what isolation level should you use?

Working with
Disconnected Data

Throughout this book you have worked with databases that have been local to applications or at least on the same machine. Often, especially in a production environment, that won't be the case. The usual way of doing things is to have a computer dedicated to the sole purpose of running a DBMS, such as SQL Server. It is separated from computers running applications, either across a local area network (LAN) or across the Internet. In either case, it is sometimes possible to have direct connections using connection strings that specify the address of the database server in the form of an IP address. Sometimes, however, that's not possible — firewalls may separate you from a database, or ports may be blocked so that you must choose an alternative access method. In such an environment (often termed a *distributed* environment) you need to use an intermediary to access data.

Perhaps the most well-known (and popular) form of intermediary is the *web service*. Web services are web applications that you can access via the Internet, using a URL just like a web site. Unlike web sites, however, web services aren't concerned with displaying HTML. Instead, they provide a framework for making remote method calls.

The way that .NET implements web services and web method calls is, to be honest, quite remarkable. Once you have designed a web service, you can access and use it from a client application using amazingly simple syntax. At no point (unless you want to start getting advanced) do you have to worry too much about how objects are serialized to XML, sent across the Internet in SOAP packets, de-serialized at the other end, and so on. You simply call methods, receive results, and smile contentedly.

You can use web services to send data in the form of custom objects, data sets, and so on across the Internet with ease. A typical architecture (and the one you'll concentrate on in this chapter) is to have a Windows application communicating with a web service over HTTP, which in turn communicates with a database — either local to the web service, or located on a database server on the same LAN as the web service. In this book, all these components reside on the same computer, but the way things work is essentially the same.

Web services are not the only way to communicate with remote databases. You can also use direct connections over secure channels, remoting, or you can send data to other locations using a motorcycle courier. However, web services are what you'll concentrate on in this chapter.

In this chapter you look at:

❑ Exposing database data through web services

❑ Consuming database data through web services

❑ Data caching in web services

Exposing Web Service Data

In this section, you learn to create web services that allow applications to access data stored in remote databases. Before starting, however, take a little time covering the basics and seeing how to build and use a web service.

Web Service Primer

To create a web service, you must use Visual Web Developer Express (or the full version of Visual Studio), and select File ➪ New Web Site as if you were going to produce an ASP.NET web site. Then select the ASP.NET Web Service template and provide the location for the web service, as shown in Figure 10-1.

When you click OK, an ASP.NET web site is created at the specified location, but instead of adding a web page in an `.aspx` file, a web service is added in an `.asmx` file. You can also add web services to existing ASP.NET projects by right-clicking on the project in the Solution Explorer window, selecting Add New Item, and then selecting Web Service, as shown in Figure 10-2.

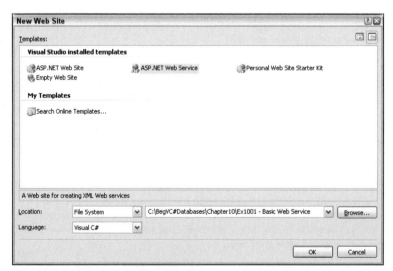

Figure 10-1: Creating a Web service

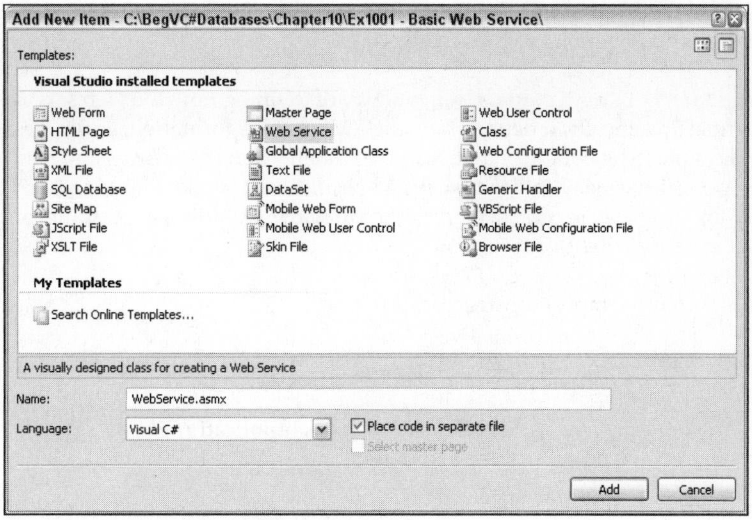

Figure 10-2: Adding a web service

The `.asmx` file for a web service provides a URL for the web service, but the real work is performed using C# code. If you use code behind files (the preferable way of doing things), the `.asmx` page will contain just a single line of code:

```
<%@ WebService Language="C#" CodeBehind="~/App_Code/Service.cs" Class="Service" %>
```

That code defines the file as a web service and links the file to a class, in this case a class called `Service` in the file `/App_Code/Service.cs`.

The file's code begins with some `using` statements for web and web service namespaces:

```
using System;
using System.Web;
using System.Web.Services;
using System.Web.Services.Protocols;
```

Next is the class definition of the web service class, which inherits from the base class `System.Web.Services.WebService`:

```
[WebService(Namespace = "http://tempuri.org/")]
[WebServiceBinding(ConformsTo = WsiProfiles.BasicProfile1_1)]
public class Service : System.Web.Services.WebService
{
```

Two attributes are used here. The first, `WebService`, defines a namespace for the web service. That's used to identify the XML schema used to transfer data across the Internet. It needn't refer to an actual schema file location; it just helps to ensure that the vocabulary used for XML serialization is uniquely defined for the web service. Unless you are using fairly advanced techniques, you generally won't notice much of an effect when you set this attribute, although it is good practice to do so and, as you will see shortly, you are warned if you leave it unchanged.

The second attribute, `WebServiceBinding`, is a way of defining how the web service communicates across the Internet. Specifically, it defines how the XML used is formatted, and it's essential in certain advanced applications. The default code used here declares that the web service conforms to the Web Services Interoperability Basic Profile version 1.1 specification. Again, knowing what this actually means isn't necessary for basic web service design; suffice to know that it is a good thing, and you won't have to worry about messing with it.

Then, there's a (currently empty) constructor:

```
public Service()
{
  //Uncomment the following line if using designed components
  //InitializeComponent();
}
```

And, finally, the most important part — a web method:

```
[WebMethod]
public string HelloWorld()
{
  return "Hello World";
}
}
```

This is a sample web method that illustrates how easy it is to create one. Notice the `WebMethod` attribute used here. It is required to identify the method as a web method, and it has a few properties that you can use to customize how the web method is identified and used, and how it serializes data (which, again, you don't have to worry about too much at this stage). The actual method definition, however, is exactly the same as any other method that you have seen or used. Web methods can contain parameters and return values, and these are exchanged across an Internet connection, using the HTTP protocol.

Client applications need to know how to access the web services you design. They need to know, for example, what methods are available, what the signatures of those methods are, and in what format to exchange XML data. That's the job of the *Web Service Description Language (WSDL)*. WSDL is another XML format that is used to define web services, using a combination of an XML schema to define the types that can be exchanged by web methods and specialized syntax to define web methods and bindings. .NET web services are capable of describing themselves using WSDL, and .NET client applications can define C# interfaces by reading a WSDL file, so that is another thing you don't have to worry about. It is important to note, however, that unlike classes in type libraries, you don't need to add references to DLLs to use web services. Instead, you add web references that enable client applications to build proxy classes to access web services by using the WSDL description of the Web Service.

In the following example you create and use a simple web service.

Try It Out   Basic Web Service

1. Open Visual Web Developer Express.

2. Create a new web site with the ASP.NET Web Service project template, in the directory `C:\BegVC#Databases\Chapter10\Ex1001 - Basic Web Service`, using the File System location and Visual C# language.

3. Open `Service.cs` from the `App_Code` folder, and add the following code:

```csharp
using System.Collections.Generic;

[WebService(Namespace = "http://tempuri.org/")]
[WebServiceBinding(ConformsTo = WsiProfiles.BasicProfile1_1)]
public class Service : System.Web.Services.WebService
{
    ...
```

```csharp
    [WebMethod]
    public List<int> GetPrimes(int maxNumber)
    {
      List<int> primes = new List<int>();
      for (int primeTest = 2; primeTest <= maxNumber; primeTest++)
      {
        bool isPrime = true;
        for (int divisor = 2; divisor <= (int)Math.Sqrt(primeTest); divisor++)
        {
          if (primeTest % divisor == 0)
          {
            isPrime = false;
            break;
          }
        }
        if (isPrime)
        {
          primes.Add(primeTest);
        }
      }
      return primes;
    }
}
```

4. Run the application (which will start the development web server and open a browser pointing at the `.asmx` page). If prompted, click OK to enable debugging in the `web.config` file. When loaded, you should see the page shown in Figure 10-3.

5. Click the Service Description link and review the WSDL shown.

6. Click Back, and then click the GetPrimes link to open the page shown in Figure 10-4.

Figure 10-3: Web service test page

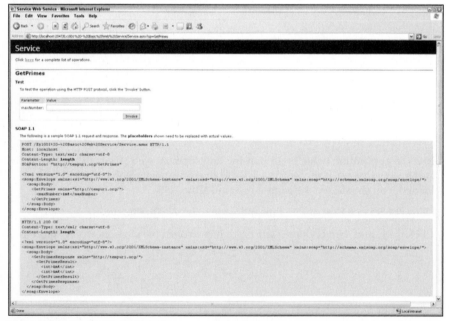

Figure 10-4: Testing GetPrimes()

7. Type the value **100** for `maxNumber`, and click the Invoke button. A new window opens, containing the following XML document:

```xml
<?xml version="1.0" encoding="utf-8"?>
<ArrayOfInt xmlns:xsi="http://www.w3.org/2001/XMLSchema-instance"
xmlns:xsd="http://www.w3.org/2001/XMLSchema" xmlns="http://tempuri.org/">
<int>2</int>
<int>3</int>
<int>5</int>
<int>7</int>
<int>11</int>
<int>13</int>
<int>17</int>
<int>19</int>
<int>23</int>
<int>29</int>
<int>31</int>
<int>37</int>
<int>41</int>
<int>43</int>
<int>47</int>
<int>53</int>
<int>59</int>
<int>61</int>
<int>67</int>
<int>71</int>
<int>73</int>
<int>79</int>
<int>83</int>
<int>89</int>
<int>97</int>
</ArrayOfInt>
```

8. Close the two browser windows, which stops the debugging session.

9. Change the namespace for the web service as follows:

```
[WebService(Namespace = "http://www.wrox.com/BegC#Databases/WebServices")]
```

10. Run the application again, and observe the changes.

11. Close the browser and Visual Web Developer Express.

How It Works

This example adds some simple code to define a web service and tests the result. The added method uses a straightforward mathematical algorithm for finding primes up to a specified maximum, and isn't worth explaining in any great depth. The important thing is the method signature:

```
public List<int> GetPrimes(int maxNumber)
```

The method has a single parameter of type `int` and returns a generic list of `int` values.

When you ran the application the first time, you may have noticed that, without having programmed in any ASP.NET or HTML code, a web page was created for you. That is the default behavior when you create .NET web services — a test page is generated from the web service description to enable you to test web methods using a browser. That's extremely useful, and means that you needn't create a client application to test a web service.

Because the namespace was left with the default value, however, most of the web page is taken up with a message telling you to change the value, and the reasons why you should. What's important on the page are the links at the top, which enable you to examine the WSDL description of the web service and test web methods. Later, when you changed the namespace for the web service, all that extra information disappeared.

You first looked at the WSDL file, which is not a particularly easy thing to read by eye (it's intended for use by application code), although it does contain a lot of information that you can see relatively easily.

After the XML declaration and a whole bunch of namespaces is the schema that should be used to exchange data with the web service, containing element definitions to be used to communicate with each web method. For the GetPrimes() web method, the schema is as follows:

```
<s:element name="GetPrimes">
 <s:complexType>
  <s:sequence>
   <s:element minOccurs="1" maxOccurs="1" name="maxNumber" type="s:int" />
  </s:sequence>
 </s:complexType>
</s:element>
<s:element name="GetPrimesResponse">
 <s:complexType>
  <s:sequence>
   <s:element minOccurs="0" maxOccurs="1" name="GetPrimesResult"
    type="tns:ArrayOfInt" />
  </s:sequence>
 </s:complexType>
</s:element>
<s:complexType name="ArrayOfInt">
 <s:sequence>
  <s:element minOccurs="0" maxOccurs="unbounded" name="int" type="s:int" />
 </s:sequence>
</s:complexType>
</s:schema>
```

Here you can see how the XML should be formatted for both request and response messages involving this method.

Next, the WSDL document describes how these messages are formatted and bound to the web service, using code that you won't look into in any more depth. You saw the end result of this description when you navigated to the web page used to test the GetPrimes() method. That page showed samples of how messages should be formatted to communicate with the web method using various protocols: SOAP 1.1, SOAP 1.2, and HTTP. Behind the scenes, that's what gets sent and received — although in most circumstances the format of the messages won't matter too much to you.

You also saw how the test pages supplied a text box and button so that you could send and receive test data to and from the GetPrimes() method, and you saw the XML result. The XML can be interpreted by a client application and converted back into a List<int> type. If your web methods use complex types for input parameters, you won't always be able to test them this way because the test page isn't designed for advanced usage. Despite that, the page can be useful — particularly when no parameters are required.

There are a number of key points to take away from this simple example:

❑   It is easy to create web services, despite the fact that the underlying communication looks pretty complex.

❑   .NET web services are easy to analyze and/or test using automatically generated test pages.

❑   Communication is not limited to simple types such as int values. Collections and, as you see in the next section, database data can be transmitted just as easily.

Exposing Database Data

It's a surprisingly short step from creating and using simple web services to exchanging data with a database. In fact, without learning an awful lot more, you can take many of the examples you've already seen in this book and simply use a web service in the data tier to provide remote database access.

That is possible because all of the data containing classes you've seen so far in this book — from data sets to custom business objects — can be sent to and from web services. All that remains, then, is to add some C# code that uses ADO.NET to access database data, and a few web methods to access and manipulate this data, and you have a fully functional, database-accessing web service.

One thing you can't do with web services is exchange some of the more "active" objects such as connections and commands. With web services, you exchange objects containing data, not objects that allow you to access a database. You can't, for example, send a data reader to a client and expect the client to be capable of communicating with the database. Even if you could, that's hardly an efficient way of doing things because every time a new row is loaded or data fetched, round trips across the Internet are necessary.

In the following example, you combine what you've learned so far in this chapter with the database access techniques taken from previous chapters to give access to data in a local copy of the FolktaleDB database via a web service.

Try It Out   Web Service Data Access

1.   Open Visual Web Developer Express.

2.   Create a new web service in the directory C:\BegVC#Databases\Chapter10\Ex1002 - WS Data Access, using the File System location and Visual C# language.

3.   Remove the auto-generated Service.cs and Service.asmx files.

4.   Add a new web service item to the project called FolktaleService.asmx, with the Place Code In Separate File option selected.

5. In the Solution Explorer window, right-click `FolktaleService.asmx` and select Set As Start Page.

6. In the Solution Explorer window, right-click the `App_Data` folder and select Add Existing Item. Navigate to the `FolktaleDB.mdf` database file in the downloadable code for this book and click OK.

7. In the Solution Explorer window, right-click the `App_Code` folder and select Add NewItem. Add a new `DataSet` called `FolktaleDBDataSet.xsd`.

8. Click Cancel in the TableAdapter Configuration Wizard dialog box.

9. Open the Database Explorer window, expand `FolktaleDB.mdf` and `Tables`, and drag the tables `Address`, `Character`, `CharacterAddress`, `CharacterStory`, and `Story` to the DataSet Designer.

10. Click on the background of the DataSet Designer, change the `Namespace` property of the data set to the following, and then save the data set.

```
http://www.wrox.com/BegCSharpDatabases/WebServices/FolktaleDBDataSet.xsd
```

11. Modify `FolktaleService.cs` as follows:

```
using FolktaleDBDataSetTableAdapters;
using System.Data;
```

```
[WebService(Namespace = "http://www.wrox.com/BegCSharpDatabases/WebServices")]
[WebServiceBinding(ConformsTo = WsiProfiles.BasicProfile1_1)]
public class FolktaleService : System.Web.Services.WebService
{
  private AddressTableAdapter addressTableAdapter =
    new AddressTableAdapter();
  private CharacterAddressTableAdapter characterAddressTableAdapter =
    new CharacterAddressTableAdapter();
  private CharacterStoryTableAdapter characterStoryTableAdapter =
    new CharacterStoryTableAdapter();
  private CharacterTableAdapter characterTableAdapter =
    new CharacterTableAdapter();
  private StoryTableAdapter storyTableAdapter =
    new StoryTableAdapter();

  public FolktaleService()
  {
  }
```

```
  [WebMethod]
  public FolktaleDBDataSet GetData()
  {
    // Create data set.
    FolktaleDBDataSet data = new FolktaleDBDataSet();

    // Populate data set.
    addressTableAdapter.Fill(data.Address);
```

```
            characterAddressTableAdapter.Fill(data.CharacterAddress);
            characterStoryTableAdapter.Fill(data.CharacterStory);
            characterTableAdapter.Fill(data.Character);
            storyTableAdapter.Fill(data.Story);

            // Return data set.
            return data;
        }

        [WebMethod]
        public void UpdateData(FolktaleDBDataSet data)
        {
            // Split updates.
            FolktaleDBDataSet addedModifiedData =
                data.GetChanges(DataRowState.Added | DataRowState.Modified)
                as FolktaleDBDataSet;
            FolktaleDBDataSet deletedData =
                data.GetChanges(DataRowState.Deleted)
                as FolktaleDBDataSet;

            // Update added and modified data in parent tables.
            if (addedModifiedData != null)
            {
                addressTableAdapter.Update(addedModifiedData);
                storyTableAdapter.Update(addedModifiedData);
                characterTableAdapter.Update(addedModifiedData);
            }

            // Update child tables.
            characterAddressTableAdapter.Update(data);
            characterStoryTableAdapter.Update(data);

            // Update deleted data in parent tables.
            if (deletedData != null)
            {
                addressTableAdapter.Update(deletedData);
                storyTableAdapter.Update(deletedData);
                characterTableAdapter.Update(deletedData);
            }
        }
    }
```

12. Run the application, and examine the WSDL for the web service by clicking the Service Description link.

13. Click Back and then click GetData; click Invoke to examine the result of the GetData() web method of which a portion is shown in Figure 10-5.

14. Close the browser and Visual Web Developer Express.

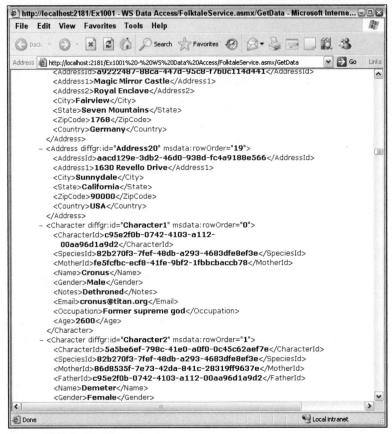

Figure 10-5: Application output

How It Works

This example uses familiar database access techniques to create a web service that can access a database. You added a local database file and a typed data set to the web service project in the same way you have done in the past for both web and Windows applications. You provided two methods: GetData(), to retrieve a populated data set, and Update(), to update data using the typed data set.

You added an instance of each of the table adapters created by the typed data set as fields in the class definition to provide easy access to them from both methods. The GetData() method creates an instance of the typed data set class, fills it with data using the table adapter objects, and returns the result. The Update() method is slightly more complicated because it follows the rules laid out earlier in the book to update multiple related tables without running into problems. Because of this, the data changes must be applied in a specific order, rather than just calling Update() once for each table adapter.

When you ran the code and inspected the WSDL you may have noticed that the schema information is kept in a separate file — namely the .xsd file used to define the typed data set:

```
<s:import namespace=
```

```
    "http://www.wrox.com/BegCSharpDatabases/WebServices/FolktaleDBDataSet.xsd" />
  <s:import schemaLocation=
    "http://localhost:2181/Ex1001%20-%20WS%20Data%20Access/↵
  FolktaleService.asmx?schema=FolktaleDBDataSet"
    namespace=
    "http://www.wrox.com/BegCSharpDatabases/WebServices/FolktaleDBDataSet.xsd" />
```

The URL is provided so that client applications can load the schema and configure types accordingly. This syntax is slightly different, but makes a lot of sense and is more evidence of how closely associated database and XML data is in the .NET Framework.

Finally, you tested the `GetData()` method and saw database data serialized in XML format, according to the schema for the data set.

You didn't test the other method — `Update()` — in this example, but you'll see it in action in the next Try It Out when you use a client application to consume the web service.

Consuming Web Service Data

The next step in using web services is to write a client application to consume them. Again, the .NET Framework is helpful here, and makes using web services easy. As mentioned earlier, all you need to do is to add a web reference to your application, using the URL of the web service. Then the WSDL for the web service will be read and used to create a proxy class that you can use from your application.

The proxy class created can be used just like any other class — you instantiate it and call its methods. All of the Internet communication, data type serialization, and optimization is carried out behind the scenes. In practice you hardly know that you are using a web service rather than a local object — although, of course, performance won't be quite as fast.

In addition to a proxy class, all types used by the web service are also interpreted and re-created on the client, in a namespace matching the name of the web reference. With typed data sets this means that the same typed data set is available on the client as in the web service code. There is no need, for example, to make do with a straight `DataSet` object, or copy schema files manually to re-create a typed data set. That's all done for you, leaving you with the task of using the available types to create your client application.

Through a proxy class you can call web methods and get results, but if that were all you could do, there would still be a lot of work ahead. You'd have to obtain data and bind it to controls by hand. However, you haven't heard everything yet about how web services that provide you with typed data sets work. In fact, as you may recall from screenshots earlier in the book, it is possible to treat a web service as a data source and bind controls to it just as you bind controls to database data.

In practice, things are a little more complicated than that because binding controls to web service data simply uses the schema information to define and instantiate a typed data set that is used to format controls — the columns to use in a `DataGridView`, for example. The actual act of obtaining the data from the web service is still left to you, although the steps required are minimal. You also have to manually add code to accomplish other tasks, such as updating data or calling other web service methods. Again, this is fairly painless.

Now, on to the details. First, to add a web service data source, open the Data Sources window and click Add New Data Source. Then select a data source of type web service, as shown in Figure 10-6.

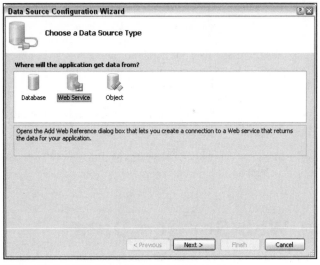

Figure 10-6: Adding a web service data source

On the next page of the wizard, locate the web service you want to use. You can use the links provided to search for local or remote web services, or you can simply type in the URL of the web service and click Go. If the web service you select is usable, you will see a list of the operations it supports, and have the option to add a reference, as shown in Figure 10-7.

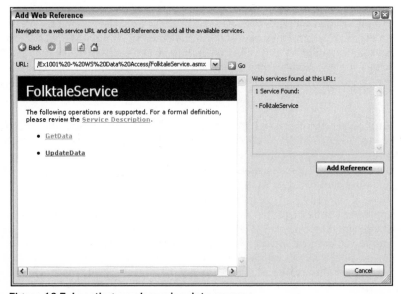

Figure 10-7: Locating a web service data source

The data source you add appears in the Data Sources window just like a database data source. The name of the data source is the domain name where the web service is hosted. An example is shown in Figure 10-8, with the domain name `localhost`.

Figure 10-8: Web service data source

The icon used for web service data sources, a globe with some colored squares, makes it easy to differentiate them from other data sources. When you use remote web services, the domain name also will be easier to recognize — after all, `localhost` is a bit vague.

You can then use the items in the data sources display to add data-bound controls to a form, such as `DataGridView` or detail view controls, just like database data sources. You will also find that you can add components for the typed data set or service to your forms after you compile the application.

In the following example you work through this procedure using the web service created in the previous example, and construct a functioning data-access application for viewing and modifying addresses. Because you've already covered a lot of techniques in this book, this is larger and more complex than most of the examples you've seen so far. The end result is worth it, however.

Try It Out   Consuming Web Service Data

1. Open Visual C# Express and create a new Windows application called `Ex1003 - Consuming Data`. Save the project in the `C:\BegVC#Databases\Chapter10` directory, with the Create Directory For Solution option unchecked.

2. If it is not currently open, open Visual Web Developer Express and open the web application from the last example (`C:\BegVC#Databases\Chapter10\Ex1002 - WS Data Access`).

3. Start the web application. This is necessary because without Visual Web Developer Express open, the development web server stops running, and the web service is unavailable to client applications.

4. Switch back to Visual C# Express, open the Data Sources window, and click Add New Data Source.

5. Add a web service data source, using the URL of the `FolktaleService.asmx` service copied from the browser window. This URL will be on `localhost` and use a (fairly random) port number. The web reference will be added with the name `localhost`.

6. Compile the project.

7. Open `Form1` in design view, and drag instances of `FolktaleDBDataset` and `FolktaleService` from the Toolbox onto the form. Name the components `data` and `service`.

8. Change the `Text` property of the form to **Character Addresses**.

9. Add two `Label` controls, two `ComboBox` controls (called `storyBox` and `characterBox`), a `DataGridView` control (called `addressView`), and a `Button` control (called `saveButton`) to the form, as shown in Figure 10-9. In the figure, the top `ComboBox` is `storyBox`; its `Anchor` property is set to `Top, Left, Right`. Below `storyBox` is `characterBox`, which has the same `Anchor` property value. `addressView` is the next control down; its `Anchor` property is `Top, Bottom, Left, Right`. Finally, the `Button` control at the bottom, `saveButton`, has a `Text` property of `Save Changes` and an `Anchor` property of `Bottom, Left, Right`.

Figure 10-9: Form layout

10. Click on the `storyBox` control and open the `Tasks` window for the control. Select Use Data Bound Items and set the Data Source for the control to Other Data Sources ⇨ Project Data Sources ⇨ localhost ⇨ FolktaleDBDataSet ⇨ Story. Select a Display Member of `Name` and a Value Member of `StoryId`.

11. Do the same for the character box control, but use a Data Source of Other Data Sources ⇨ Project Data Sources ⇨ localhost ⇨ FolktaleDBDataSet ⇨ Character, a Display Member of `Name` and a Value Member of `CharacterId`.

12. Next, use the `Tasks` window for `addressView` to set the Data Source of the `DataGridView` control to Other Data Sources ⇨ Project Data Sources ⇨ localhost ⇨ FolktaleDBDataSet ⇨ Address. Remove the `AddressId` column from the display.

13. Add a `Form1_Load()` event handler by double-clicking on the form. Add code as follows:

```
using Ex1003___Consuming_Data.localhost;

namespace Ex1003___Consuming_Data
{
  public partial class Form1 : Form
  {
    . . .
```

```csharp
private void Form1_Load(object sender, EventArgs e)
{
    // Get web service and load data.
    service = new FolktaleService();
    data = service.GetData();

    // Set data sources.
    storyBindingSource.DataSource = data.Story;
    characterBindingSource.DataSource = data.Character;
    addressBindingSource.DataSource = data.Address;
}
    }
}
```

14. At this point you can, if you want, run the application for a first test. If everything has worked properly, the controls on the form populate with all the stories, characters, and addresses in the database.

15. Add event handlers to the `CurrentChanged` event for each of the three `BindingSource` components on the form, `storyBindingSource`, `characterBindingSource`, and `addressBindingSource`. Add the following code to `Form1.cs`:

```csharp
private void storyBindingSource_CurrentChanged(object sender, EventArgs e)
{
    // Filter characters by story.
    SetCharacterFilter();
}

private void characterBindingSource_CurrentChanged(object sender, EventArgs e)
{
    // Filter addresses by character.
    SetAddressFilter();
}

private void addressBindingSource_CurrentChanged(object sender, EventArgs e)
{
    // Refilter view (to cater for newly added rows).
    SetAddressFilter();
}


private void SetCharacterFilter()
{
    // Clear if no story selected.
    if (storyBindingSource.Current == null)
    {
        characterBindingSource.Filter = "Name = 'None'";
        return;
    }

    // Get CharacterStory Rows.
    FolktaleDBDataSet.CharacterStoryRow[] characterStoryRows =
        ((storyBindingSource.Current as DataRowView).Row
        as localhost.FolktaleDBDataSet.StoryRow).GetCharacterStoryRows();
```

```csharp
      if (characterStoryRows.Length > 0)
      {
        // Build filter string.
        string filterString = "CharacterId IN (CONVERT('{";
        for (int index = 0; index < characterStoryRows.Length; index++)
        {
          if (index != 0)
          {
            filterString += "}', 'System.Guid'), CONVERT('{";
          }
          filterString += characterStoryRows[index].CharacterId.ToString();
        }
        filterString += "}', 'System.Guid'))";

        // Apply filter.
        characterBindingSource.Filter = filterString;
      }
      else
      {
        // Default filter - display nothing.
        characterBindingSource.Filter = "Name = 'None'";
      }
    }

    private void SetAddressFilter()
    {
      // Clear if no character selected.
      if (characterBindingSource.Current == null)
      {
        addressBindingSource.Filter = "AddressId = ''";
        return;
      }

      // Get CharacterAddress rows.
      FolktaleDBDataSet.CharacterAddressRow[] characterAddressRows =
        ((characterBindingSource.Current as DataRowView).Row
        as localhost.FolktaleDBDataSet.CharacterRow).GetCharacterAddressRows();
      if (characterAddressRows.Length > 0)
      {
        // Build filter string.
        string filterString = "AddressId IN (CONVERT('{";
        for (int index = 0; index < characterAddressRows.Length; index++)
        {
          if (index != 0)
          {
            filterString += "}', 'System.Guid'), CONVERT('{";
          }
          filterString += characterAddressRows[index].AddressId.ToString();
        }
        filterString += "}', 'System.Guid'))";

        // Apply filter.
        addressBindingSource.Filter = filterString;
```

```
        }
        else
        {
          // Default filter - display nothing.
          addressBindingSource.Filter = "AddressId = ''";
        }
    }
```

16. Add an event handler to the `AddressBindingSource.AddingNew` event as follows:

```
private void addressBindingSource_AddingNew(object sender, AddingNewEventArgs e)
{
    // Must have character selected.
    if (characterBindingSource.Current == null)
    {
      return;
    }

    // Create new Id.
    Guid addressId = Guid.NewGuid();

    // Get data table view
    DataView dataTableView = addressBindingSource.List as DataView;

    // Create row from view
    DataRowView rowView = dataTableView.AddNew();

    // Configure defaults
    rowView["AddressId"] = addressId;
    rowView["Address1"] = "Unknown";
    rowView["City"] = "Unknown";
    rowView["State"] = "Unknown";
    rowView["ZipCode"] = "Unknown";
    rowView["Country"] = "Unknown";

    // Set new row
    e.NewObject = rowView;
}
```

17. Add an event handler to the `addressView.UserAddedRow` event as follows:

```
private void addressView_UserAddedRow(object sender, DataGridViewRowEventArgs e)
{
    // Add associated characterAddress (only when row actually added,
    // not just requested).
    Guid characterAddressId = Guid.NewGuid();
    data.CharacterAddress.AddCharacterAddressRow(characterAddressId,
      (characterBindingSource.Current as DataRowView).Row
      as FolktaleDBDataSet.CharacterRow,
      (addressBindingSource.Current as DataRowView).Row
      as FolktaleDBDataSet.AddressRow, false);
}
```

18. Add an event handler to the `addressView.UserDeletingRow` event as follows:

```
private void addressView_UserDeletingRow(object sender,
  DataGridViewRowCancelEventArgs e)
{
  // Need to delete row from CharacterAddress, not Address.
  e.Cancel = true;

  // Get row data.
  FolktaleDBDataSet.CharacterRow characterRow =
    (characterBindingSource.Current as DataRowView).Row
    as FolktaleDBDataSet.CharacterRow;
  FolktaleDBDataSet.AddressRow addressRow =
    (e.Row.DataBoundItem as DataRowView).Row as FolktaleDBDataSet.AddressRow;
  FolktaleDBDataSet.CharacterAddressRow[] characterAddressRow =
    data.CharacterAddress.Select(
    "CharacterId = CONVERT('{" + characterRow.CharacterId.ToString()
    + "}', 'System.Guid')"
    + " AND " +
    "AddressId = CONVERT('{" + addressRow.AddressId.ToString()
    + "}', 'System.Guid')")
    as FolktaleDBDataSet.CharacterAddressRow[];

  // Delete CharacterAddress row.
  characterAddressRow[0].Delete();

  // Cancel row deletion if no more references to address.
  characterAddressRow = data.CharacterAddress.Select(
    "AddressId = CONVERT('{" + addressRow.AddressId.ToString()
    + "}', 'System.Guid')")
    as FolktaleDBDataSet.CharacterAddressRow[];
  if (characterAddressRow.Length == 0)
  {
    addressRow.Delete();
  }

  // Refilter view.
  SetAddressFilter();
}
```

19. Finally, add an event handler to the `saveButton.Click` event as follows:

```
private void saveButton_Click(object sender, EventArgs e)
{
  // Save data using Web service.
  FolktaleDBDataSet changes = data.GetChanges() as FolktaleDBDataSet;
  if (changes != null)
  {
    service.UpdateData(changes);
    data.AcceptChanges();
  }
}
```

20. Run the application. You should be able to navigate through the characters in each story and the addresses defined for each character. You should also be able to add, edit, and modify addresses for each character. If you quit the application and restart it, the data modifications persist — in the local database file used by the web service. Figure 10-10 shows sample output.

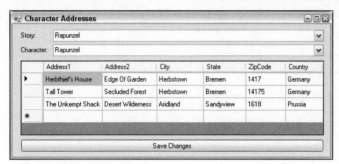

Figure 10-10: Form layout

21. Close the application, the web service browser, Visual C# Express, and Visual Web Developer Express.

How It Works

This example binds a Windows application to a remote data source exposed by a web service. You used many of the techniques that you've learned throughout this book (as well as a few new ones) to make a fully functioning application that you can use to view and modify database data.

Taking things from the top, you ensured that the web service was available by running the example created earlier in this chapter. This step isn't necessary in a production environment where web services are hosted on web servers such as IIS, which is always running. For development, however, it is essential for the web server to be running. It also provides you with a quick and easy way to get the URL of the web service, which you used to create a web service data source.

Next you compiled the application, which enabled you to add components to the form to use from your code behind. The web service component let you access the web service, and the typed data set component gave you a data store to store the data returned by the web service.

With the web service used as a data source, you were able to configure data binding for the controls you added to the form. That meant the data in the data sources could be used to configure the controls — in particular the column layout for the `DataGridView` control. But that isn't enough to actually load data into the controls. To do that, you needed to add some code to the `Form1_Load()` event handler. You used the web service to load data into the data store:

```
service = new FolktaleService();
data = service.GetData();
```

Then you bound the three data-bound controls on the form to tables inside the typed data set:

```
storyBindingSource.DataSource = data.Story;
characterBindingSource.DataSource = data.Character;
addressBindingSource.DataSource = data.Address;
```

That's enough code to load data, but not enough to result in a fully functioning application that does what you want it to do. The next step adds code to filter the controls based on the selected items in other controls. The character selector is filtered according to the selected story, and the address view is filtered by the selected character. The code for the `SetCharacterFilter()` and `SetAddressFilter()` methods is similar, so you need to look at only one here. The code for `SetAddressFilter()` starts by checking if a character is selected; otherwise the `Filter` property of the `addressBindingSource` is simply set to a value that will result in no data being displayed (because no `Address` rows have an `AddressId` value of `''`):

```
private void SetAddressFilter()
{
  if (characterBindingSource.Current == null)
  {
    addressBindingSource.Filter = "AddressId = ''";
    return;
  }
```

As the `Character` and `Address` tables have a many-to-many relationship, filtering is made a little more complicated. You start by obtaining all the rows in the linking table `CharacterAddress` that are linked to the selected `Character` row. To do so, you get the selected character `DataRowView` from the `characterBindingSource.Current` property, use that object to obtain the current row, cast the row to a `CharacterRow`, and finally use `GetCharacterAddressRows()` to obtain an array of `CharacterAddressRow` objects:

```
FolktaleDBDataSet.CharacterAddressRow[] characterAddressRows =
  ((characterBindingSource.Current as DataRowView).Row
  as localhost.FolktaleDBDataSet.CharacterRow).GetCharacterAddressRows();
```

If any rows are found (some characters don't have any addresses), you proceed to build a filter string to filter the address view. You have to use some slightly odd syntax for this. First, the easiest way to filter against a set of values is to use the filter clause `"Value IN (value1, value2, ... valueN)"`. That's simple enough, but to compare GUID values, you must take the additional step of ensuring that GUID values are properly represented in the set of values. If you attempt to compare a GUID column with a string representation of a GUID, you receive an error (along the lines of "unable to compare GUID values with string values"). Instead you have to output GUID values in the form:

```
CONVERT('{xxxxxxxx-xxxx-xxxx-xxxx-xxxxxxxxxxxx}', 'System.Guid')
```

This is unfortunate, and likely to trip you up if you don't know the trick, but it is simple enough to put into practice:

```
if (characterAddressRows.Length > 0)
{
  string filterString = "AddressId IN (CONVERT('{";
  for (int index = 0; index < characterAddressRows.Length; index++)
  {
    if (index != 0)
    {
      filterString += "}', 'System.Guid'), CONVERT('{";
    }
    filterString += characterAddressRows[index].AddressId.ToString();
```

```
        }
        filterString += "}', 'System.Guid'))";

        addressBindingSource.Filter = filterString;
    }
```

If there are no matched `CharacterAddress` rows then the default, `"show none"` filter value is used:

```
    else
    {
        addressBindingSource.Filter = "AddressId = ''";
    }
}
```

With the two filtering methods, you can now filter data by story and address. However, adding and deleting rows will cause problems. There are two things to take into account when adding address rows. First, as you've seen in earlier chapters, you need to add code to ensure that new rows are assigned new GUID IDs. You do so by handling the `AddingNew` event for the `addressBindingSource` component, using code of the form you've already seen. The event handler you added starts by aborting if no character is selected (preventing you from adding rows in this situation):

```
private void addressBindingSource_AddingNew(object sender, AddingNewEventArgs e)
{
    if (characterBindingSource.Current == null)
    {
        return;
    }
```

Next you create a new GUID ID value:

```
    Guid addressId = Guid.NewGuid();
```

The remaining code should look familiar. You obtain the `DataView` that is used by the `BindingSource` to hold data, use it to create a new `DataRowView` object, and add default column values before returning the added object by setting the `NewObject` property in the event arguments:

```
    DataView dataTableView = addressBindingSource.List as DataView;
    DataRowView rowView = dataTableView.AddNew();
    rowView["AddressId"] = addressId;
    rowView["Address1"] = "Unknown";
    rowView["City"] = "Unknown";
    rowView["State"] = "Unknown";
    rowView["ZipCode"] = "Unknown";
    rowView["Country"] = "Unknown";
    e.NewObject = rowView;
}
```

This works for adding rows to the `Address` table, but because of the many-to-many relationship between characters and addresses, you have to do a little more. To make things work properly, that is, ensuring that the address is associated with a character, you handle the `UserAddedRow` event of the `DataGridView` control used to display addresses. The event is raised when the user modifies the default values for a row. If the user doesn't do that, the row is immediately deleted and you don't have to worry about this step.

The code in the event handler must add a row to the `CharacterAddress` table to associate the character with an address. As with other rows, a new GUID ID is required, so the first step is to generate one:

```
private void addressView_UserAddedRow(object sender, DataGridViewRowEventArgs e)
{
  Guid characterAddressId = Guid.NewGuid();
```

Next, the new row is added directly to the typed data set that stores your data — namely the `data` component. The `FolktaleDBDataSet.CharacterAddress.AddCharacter()` method can do this, using an overload that accepts a GUID ID value, a `CharacterRow` object, an `AddressRow` object, and a Boolean value determining whether the address is the primary one for the character. You can get both of the row objects (a `CharacterRow` and an `AddressRow`) from the `Current` properties of the relevant binding sources, using the `DataRowView.Row` property and casting as per usual:

```
  data.CharacterAddress.AddCharacterAddressRow(characterAddressId,
    (characterBindingSource.Current as DataRowView).Row
    as FolktaleDBDataSet.CharacterRow,
    (addressBindingSource.Current as DataRowView).Row
    as FolktaleDBDataSet.AddressRow, false);
}
```

The "primary address" aspect of the database isn't actually used in this example, but it still needs to be set.

Once a new row is added, it's necessary to re-filter the address view to make it display because the GUID ID value of the new address won't be included in the current filter. This cannot be done as part of the preceding event handler — that would result in problems adding data to the new row. Re-filtering data will lose the current cell selection and make users swear. Instead, the re-filtering is performed when the selected row in the address view changes:

```
private void addressBindingSource_CurrentChanged(object sender, EventArgs e)
{
  SetAddressFilter();
}
```

Now that adding rows is possible, it's time to look at deleting rows. Here the problem is that multiple characters may reference a single `Address` row. If you don't deal with it, deleting an address from one character will result in it being deleted for all characters. In addition, there will still be a row in the `CharacterAddress` table that references the deleted row, which results in an error when you save changes to the database (a foreign key violation occurs). So, what you have to do is this:

❑   Delete the row from the `CharacterAddress` table that links the character to the address.

❑   Check to see if there are any remaining rows in the `CharacterAddress` table that reference the address. If there aren't, delete the address to prevent it from being orphaned.

In this application the `UserDeletingRow` event handler for the `DataGridView` control handles these steps. You start by canceling the pending deletion because you are providing your own implementation:

```
private void addressView_UserDeletingRow(object sender,
  DataGridViewRowCancelEventArgs e)
{
  e.Cancel = true;
```

Next, you need to find the row in the `CharacterAddress` table that should be deleted. To do so, you need to find the GUID ID values for the character and address rows. The character row can be found, as in previous code, through the `characterBindingSource.Current` property:

```
FolktaleDBDataSet.CharacterRow characterRow =
   (characterBindingSource.Current as DataRowView).Row
   as FolktaleDBDataSet.CharacterRow;
```

The address row is (indirectly) passed through the event arguments for the event handler. To extract it, you use the `Row` property of the event arguments, and get the `DataRowView` that the row is bound to using the `Row.DataBoundItem` property. This can then be used in the usual way to obtain an `AddressRow` object.

```
FolktaleDBDataSet.AddressRow addressRow =
   (e.Row.DataBoundItem as DataRowView).Row as FolktaleDBDataSet.AddressRow;
```

Now that you have the two rows, you can find the `CharacterAddress` row by using the `Select()` method of the `CharacterAddress` table. As with the filtering code you've already seen, you are comparing GUID values here, so you must use the CONVERT syntax in a search expression, looking for a row that has the required `CharacterId` and `AddressId` values:

```
FolktaleDBDataSet.CharacterAddressRow[] characterAddressRow =
   data.CharacterAddress.Select(
   "CharacterId = CONVERT('{" + characterRow.CharacterId.ToString()
   + "}', 'System.Guid')"
   + " AND " +
   "AddressId = CONVERT('{" + addressRow.AddressId.ToString()
   + "}', 'System.Guid')")
   as FolktaleDBDataSet.CharacterAddressRow[];
```

You delete the row you find by calling its `Delete()` method:

```
characterAddressRow[0].Delete();
```

With the `CharacterAddress` row deleted, the next step is to see whether the `Address` row can be deleted. To do so, you use `CharacterAddress.Select()` again, but this time just look to see if any rows reference the `Address` row:

```
characterAddressRow = data.CharacterAddress.Select(
   "AddressId = CONVERT('{" + addressRow.AddressId.ToString()
   + "}', 'System.Guid')")
   as FolktaleDBDataSet.CharacterAddressRow[];
```

If no rows are obtained, the address can be deleted:

```
if (characterAddressRow.Length == 0)
{
   addressRow.Delete();
}
```

Finally, the address view is refreshed to take into account the deleted entry:

```
// Refilter view.
SetAddressFilter();
}
```

The other method you added is the event handler for the Save Changes button. It uses the
`FolktaleDBDataSet.GetChanges()` method to obtain a data set containing just the changes that have
been made, if any, or a `null` value. Any changes are updated to the database through the web service
`Update()` web method.

```
private void saveButton_Click(object sender, EventArgs e)
{
  FolktaleDBDataSet changes = data.GetChanges() as FolktaleDBDataSet;
  if (changes != null)
  {
    service.UpdateData(changes);
    data.AcceptChanges();
  }
}
```

Doing the update this way minimizes the amount of data that is sent to the web service — there's no
need to send the entire data set.

You have looked through quite a lot of code in this example, but the end result is a fluid, responsive
application that allows easy data access in a distributed environment. It is well worth learning these
techniques because they're all common ones that you will more than likely find yourself using.

One final point is that the application doesn't take concurrency issues into account. As users of the client
application are likely to spend some time modifying data before saving changes, it is possible that changes
will fail to commit on the server. If that's the case, the web service will raise a `DBConcurrencyException`
as you saw in the previous chapter, and you can deal with it the same way. Because you're using bulk
updates here, it's probably a better idea to record all of the failed updates before raising an exception that
the client can handle, to avoid excessive round trips to the server. That modification, however, is left as an
exercise for you.

Caching Web Service Data

One of the main differences between Windows applications and web applications is that, as discussed in
Chapter 5, web applications tend to deal with multiple users simultaneously. This applies to web service
applications as much as it does web site applications.

In both cases, particularly when clients use the web application primarily to read data, you have the
opportunity to improve performance by *caching* data in the web application. That means the web application keeps a local copy of database data in memory, which is shared by all users, so that, in most cases,
user requests can be handled without the web application having to read data from the database. This
reduces network traffic and the load on the database server, as well as making things faster for clients.

There are, however, certain things of which you must be aware when implementing caching in a web application. First, and perhaps most important, is that the database may be modified by other applications, and those modifications will not be reflected in the web application's cached data unless the cache is refreshed. That means that you either have to refresh the cached data periodically, or include a mechanism for detecting database changes and refresh the data accordingly. Lucky for us, both of these techniques are relatively easy to implement.

Another point to bear in mind is that changes to the cached data should be committed to the database as soon as possible to avoid data inconsistency and concurrency errors. In many situations, the web application is only used to read data, or perhaps read much more often than modified, so this won't be a huge problem. Sometimes, however, you have to use the concurrency and transaction techniques you learned in Chapter 9 in combination with frequent commits of cached data to the database. If that becomes an issue, you can always use the simpler technique of not worrying about caching. The choice, as ever, is up to you and the requirements of your application.

This section explains how you can cache data, where you can store cached data, and how you can ensure that your cached data stays as up-to-date as possible.

Web Method Output Caching

The simplest method of caching data is to use output caching. In a web application you can use output caching so that a web page returns the same HTML for a given period of time. That means the first time the page is accessed, the code is processed in the usual way and the output HTML is generated. The HTML is returned to the client, and it is also cached (stored). Subsequent requests bypass ASP.NET processing and simply obtain the cached HTML for the page, greatly improving performance. This happens until the cache expires, at which point the next request causes the page to be re-processed, and cached again.

The same thing is possible for web methods. You can set an output cache to store the result of a web method, and subsequent requests (which use matching parameters, if the web method has any parameters) receive the cached result.

Configuring web method caching is the work of moments. Simply set the CacheDuration property of the WebMethod attribute used in the method declaration to the number of seconds to cache output for (the default value is 0). For example:

```
[WebMethod(CacheDuration=60)]
public FolktaleDBDataSet GetData()
{
    ...
}
```

This causes the GetData() web method to cache its output for 60 seconds at a time.

The problem is that modifications to the database are not reflected in the cached data until it refreshes. This means that a client could get data, modify it, get it again, and not see the modifications that it made seconds before. Eventually changes are reflected, but this can lead to concurrency problems.

Still, if you are prepared to deal with the consequences, this is a highly efficient way of doing things because much of the time no code execution is required to obtain web method results.

Caching Data in Application State

When a web application is first accessed, it's compiled and loaded into the ASP.NET process. This happens only once — subsequent accesses use the already compiled application, and there's only one application that serves all subsequent requests. That is the case until the application is unloaded in one of the following ways:

❑ Manually

❑ Automatically as a result of code file changes

❑ When the hosting server restarts

❑ When the application times out (if a timeout setting has been applied)

During the lifetime of the web application you can, if you want, store shared data in what is known as *application state*. That state is accessible from all requests for all users, making it the ideal place to store database data and other shared information.

You use the `HttpApplication` object, which is generated when an ASP.NET application is loaded, to access web application state. That object is accessible using the `Page.Application`, `WebService.Application`, and `HttpContext.Current.Application` properties, to name but a few. Generally, whenever you are writing code for a web application, the `HttpApplication` object is easily accessible.

You can use the `HttpApplication.Add()` method to add information to application state. It takes a string key and an object value as its parameters, meaning that you can store any serializable object this way, with a string identifier. Once stored, you can access and manipulate the data using standard collection syntax. To obtain a value stored with the key `MyData`, for example, you can just use the syntax `Application["MyData"]`. The `HttpApplication` class also includes a `Remove()` method to remove data, a `Count` property to see how many items are stored, and so on.

Crucially, the `HttpApplication` class defines `Lock()` and `Unlock()` methods. If you call `Lock()`, no requests other than the current one can read or modify application data until you call `Unlock()`. If you are modifying application state, place your modification code between `Lock()` and `Unlock()` calls to prevent concurrency problems (yes, they exist here, too). That allows you to control how cached data is refreshed — if a client updates data through a web service, you can manually update the cached data, ensuring that subsequent requests for data have an up-to-date version of the data. This is an improvement over output caching, described in the previous section, although performance is not so good.

The best time to cache data in application state is when the application loads. That does not — repeat, not — mean that you should do this in the web form constructor. There is a much better place: the global application class for the application. This class isn't included in web applications by default, but you can add it by right-clicking on your project, selecting New Item, and then selecting it from the list of Visual Studio Installed Templates, as shown in Figure 10-11.

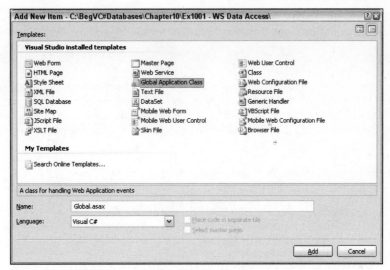

Figure 10-11: Adding a global application class to a web application

The generated file, `global.asax`, contains code as follows:

```
<%@ Application Language="C#" %>

<script runat="server">

  void Application_Start(object sender, EventArgs e)
  {
    // Code that runs on application startup
  }

  void Application_End(object sender, EventArgs e)
  {
    // Code that runs on application shutdown
  }

  void Application_Error(object sender, EventArgs e)
  {
    // Code that runs when an unhandled error occurs
  }

  void Session_Start(object sender, EventArgs e)
  {
    // Code that runs when a new session is started
  }

  void Session_End(object sender, EventArgs e)
  {
    // Code that runs when a session ends.
    // Note: The Session_End event is raised only when the sessionstate mode
    // is set to InProc in the Web.config file. If session mode is set to
```

```
    // StateServer or SQLServer, the event is not raised.
  }

</script>
```

The comments here are fairly self-explanatory. The purpose of the file is to enable you to execute code at various points in the lifecycle of a web application, and the important thing for the purposes of this discussion is the `Application_Start()` method. It is executed only once — when the web application starts — which means that it's the ideal place to load database data into application storage. Here's an example:

```
void Application_Start(object sender, EventArgs e)
{
  // Load data.
  FolktaleDBDataSet data = new FolktaleDBDataSet();
  FolktaleDBDataSetTableAdapters.CharacterTableAdapter adapter =
   new FolktaleDBDataSetTableAdapters.CharacterTableAdapter();
  adapter.Fill(data.Character);

  // Store data
  Application.Add("cachedData", data);
}
```

Then, code elsewhere in the application can get the data as follows:

```
FolktaleDBDataSet data = Application["cachedData"] as FolktaleDBDataSet;
```

Remember to have your code lock and unlock application state when modifying this cached store.

Caching Data in the Application Cache

Application state may appear to be ideal for storing database data, but in fact there is something even better: the application cache. Using the application cache is similar to using application state, but the storage is more specialized. The major difference is that objects stored in the application cache are volatile, meaning that they are not stored for the lifetime of the application. Instead, you can configure items to expire after a set period of time, which can be a great advantage in streamlining the resource usage of your applications. However, the fact that this storage is volatile means that you should always check for the presence of a saved object before attempting to retrieve it, and re-create it if necessary.

Another advantage of the application cache is that you can configure items to expire on other conditions, including database changes. That's extremely useful because rather than polling the database periodically to check for changes, you can find out automatically. You can configure dependencies on any number of tables so that any changes to them result in the cache item expiring.

You can access the application cache programmatically in a similar way to application state, using `HttpContext.Current.Cache` from web service code, or the `Page.Cache` property in web site applications. Sometimes in web site applications, as you will see shortly, you can configure data caching in the application cache without needing to do this. For web services, however, you will need to manipulate the application cache manually.

Let's take a look at how you can configure and use the application cache for database data.

Enabling Database Dependency

To respond to database changes, you must first configure the database to supply notifications to you. You must also configure any tables for which you want to be notified of changes. There are two ways to do so:

- ❏ Using the `aspnet_regsql.exe` command line tool
- ❏ Programmatically

The command line tool is located in the following directory:

```
<WindowsDirectory>\Microsoft.NET\Framework\<Version>\aspnet_regsql.exe
```

Run it with the command line parameter `-?` to find instructions on how to use the tool. You can connect to a database either by supplying a connection string as the `-C` parameter, or by providing the server name using `-S`, authentication details using `-U` and `-P` for username and password, or `-E` for integrated security. Then you give the database name using `-d` and enable SQL cache dependency using `-ed`. You then need to run the tool again, specifying that you want to enable a database table using `-et`, and specifying the table name using `-t`. The following two commands enable the `Wish` table in the `FolktaleDB` database for SQL cache dependency:

```
aspnet_regsql -S .\SQLEXPRESS -d FolktaleDB -E -ed
aspnet_regsql -S .\SQLEXPRESS -et -t Wish -d FolktaleDB -E
```

You can also run the tool with the `-W` parameter, or with no parameters, and configure a database using the ASP.NET SQL Server Setup Wizard, shown in Figure 10-12.

Unfortunately, the command line tool doesn't give you access to all the options, such as configuring individual tables. Also, the tool (in command line or wizard mode) cannot configure local database files.

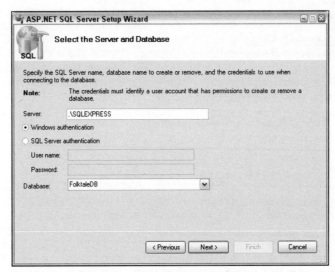

Figure 10-12: Using the aspnet_regsql.exe wizard

Programmatic configuration is often the easier option — and works with local database files. You use the `SqlCacheDependencyAdmin` class, which is located in the `System.Web.Caching` namespace. This class includes two static methods that you can use to configure a database. The first, `EnableNotifications()`, enables a database for notifications. You supply it with a connection string for a database, which you can take from the connection strings stored in `web.config` if you want:

```
string connectionString =
    ConfigurationManager.ConnectionStrings["ConnectionString"].ConnectionString;
SqlCacheDependencyAdmin.EnableNotifications(connectionString);
```

The other method is `EnableTableForNotifications()`. It enables individual tables and requires a connection string and a table name as follows:

```
SqlCacheDependencyAdmin.EnableTableForNotifications(connectionString, "Wish");
```

You can also check to see if a specific table is enabled by getting a list of enabled tables using the `GetTablesEnabledForNotifications()` method. If you try this and the database isn't enabled for notifications, you receive a `DatabaseNotEnabledForNotificationException` exception.

Attempting to enable a database or table more than once won't cause an error, but you can use the following code to test whether a database and table are enabled, and then you can enable them if not:

```
string connectionString =
    ConfigurationManager.ConnectionStrings["ConnectionString"].ConnectionString;
try
{
  string[] tables =
    SqlCacheDependencyAdmin.GetTablesEnabledForNotifications(connectionString);
  bool tableEnabled = false;
  foreach (string table in tables)
  {
    if (table == "Wish")
    {
      tableEnabled = true;
      break;
    }
  }
  if (!tableEnabled)
  {
    SqlCacheDependencyAdmin.EnableTableForNotifications(connectionString,
      "Wish");
  }
}
catch (DatabaseNotEnabledForNotificationException)
{
  SqlCacheDependencyAdmin.EnableNotifications(connectionString);
  SqlCacheDependencyAdmin.EnableTableForNotifications(connectionString, "Wish");
}
```

You can disable these notifications from databases and tables by using two other methods of the `SqlCacheDependencyAdmin` class, `DisableNotifications()` and `DisableTableForNotifications()`, should you want to.

SQL Dependency Configuration

The next step in configuring SQL dependencies for the application cache is to add a small amount of configuration code to the `web.config` file. In it you can configure a few specifics for use in cache dependency checking, and in many cases that's enough to configure data access without using any additional code in your applications. Once configured, you can reference the configuration using declarative syntax in your ASP.NET pages, as you will see in the next section.

Caching settings are configured in the `<caching>` element in `web.config` files, which is a child of the `<system.web>` element. This element isn't added by default, so you need to add it yourself:

```
<system.web>
 ...
 <caching>
  ...
 </caching>
</system.web>
```

You can add several settings here, including SQL dependency, which is the only one you'll look at here. It is configured using the `<sqlCacheDependency>` element. This element has two attributes:

❑   `enabled`: Set to `true` to enable dependency checking.

❑   `pollTime`: Time, specified in milliseconds, that determines how often the database should be polled for changes. The default value is 1 minute, and you cannot set it to a value of less than 500 milliseconds. This attribute is optional.

Here's an example of setting these attributes:

```
<caching>
 <sqlCacheDependency enabled="true" pollTime="1000">
  ...
 </sqlCacheDependency>
</caching>
```

Within the `<sqlCacheDependency>` element, you must include a `<databases>` element (which has no attributes). It defines one or more databases to poll for changes using child `<add>` elements. Each `<add>` element has a name defined by a `name` attribute, which is used to identify the SQL dependency in declarative and programmatic code. `<add>` elements also require a connection string identifying the database to poll, specified using the `connectionStringName` attribute. This attribute refers to a connection string defined elsewhere in the `web.config` file. Here's an example:

```
<caching>
 <sqlCacheDependency enabled="true" pollTime="1000">
  <databases>
   <add name="FolktaleDB" connectionStringName="ConnectionString" />
  </databases>
 </sqlCacheDependency>
</caching>
```

This configuration does not include table names, which are specified in your code depending on what tables you need to access.

Optionally, you can include a pollTime attribute for the database so that different databases can be polled with different frequencies.

Web Site SQL Dependency

In web applications you can configure SQL cache dependency when you add SqlDataSource controls to pages. To do so, you simply configure the SqlCacheDependency property on the control. The property is a semicolon-separated list identifying database tables to poll for changes. It uses the database configuration in the web.config file. Each database table is identified by a database and a table name, separated by a colon, in the following way:

```
<databaseName>:<tableName>
```

Here, <databaseName> refers to the name property of an <add> element in the web.config configuration file, as described in the previous section. For example:

```
SqlCacheDependency="FolktaleDB:Wish"
```

This simple configuration is all that's required to use a SQL dependency for a SqlDataSource control. There are, however, some other properties to further customize things. They are required because the control needs to know how long to cache data for. As discussed in the introduction to this section, cached data can expire after a period of time or be invalidated by database changes. The amount of time that data is cached by a SqlDataSource control is defined by the CacheDuration property, in seconds. The time period can be absolute (the data expires so many seconds after it is retrieved) or sliding (every time the data is used in a web request, the caching duration is renewed). With enough frequent web requests, a sliding expiration policy can mean that the cached data won't expire — unless, of course, it is made to expire by a SQL dependency. The expiration policy is defined using the CacheExpirationPolicy property, which can be Absolute or Sliding. Finally, you can make one cached item depend on another, so that if a specified item expires, the cached data will expire, too. To do this, you supply the name of the cached item to depend on, using the CacheKeyDependency property. You can use this property to group together cached items that depend on each other.

The following is the code for a SqlDataSource control that uses the SQL cache dependency shown in the previous section, with a 10-second sliding expiration policy:

```
<asp:SqlDataSource ID="SqlDataSource1" runat="server" CacheDuration="10"
  CacheExpirationPolicy="Sliding"
  ConnectionString="<%$ ConnectionStrings:ConnectionString %>"
  EnableCaching="True"
  SelectCommand="SELECT [WishId], [Name] FROM [Wish] ORDER BY [Name]"
  SqlCacheDependency="FolktaleDB:Wish">
</asp:SqlDataSource>
```

Note that the same connection string is used for both this control and the SQL cache dependency in web.config.

Also, you never have to worry about the control not exposing any data. It fetches data as and when required — which probably won't be every time a web request is received for the page. When cached data expires, it is refreshed automatically the next time the control is required to supply data for data binding or from your C# code.

Because `SqlDataSource` controls won't be used in web service code, and in some situations in web pages, you also need to know how to use cache dependencies and the application cache programmatically.

Programmatic SQL Dependency

You've already seen many of the techniques you need to use the application cache programmatically. You must configure the database and tables for SQL dependency notifications and you must add configuration code to `web.config` to define the dependency and its polling time. However, you must also add data to the application cache manually, and check whenever you access that data in case it has expired.

To add an item to the application cache, you use the `Cache.Add()` or `Cache.Insert()` method. `Insert()` doesn't need as many parameters as `Add()`, and overwrites a value with the same name if one exists. Using `Add()` means defining all of the associated properties for the cached data, while `Insert()` allows you to skip a few. The simplest way to use `Insert()` involves just an identifying name for the added item and the item itself:

```
Cache.Insert("MyCachedItem", item);
```

Once added, you can access the item using the indexer of the `Cache` object, as `Cache["MyCachedItem"]`. As discussed earlier, you must always check to see if the item exists — application cache state is volatile, and items may have expired or been removed for other reasons. At times, cached items are automatically removed by the .NET runtime to free resources. You can also use `Remove()` to remove a named item:

```
Cache.Remove("MyCachedItem");
```

The next version of `Insert()` requires a third parameter, of type `CacheDependency`. To add a SQL dependency, use the `SqlCacheDependancy` class, which is created by specifying a database (as with the code in the previous section, this is the `Name` attribute of a database defined in `web.config`) and a table name:

```
SqlCacheDependency myDependency = new SqlCacheDependency("FolktaleDB", "Wish");
Cache.Insert("MyCachedItem", item, myDependency);
```

A `SqlCacheDependency` object can only place a dependency on a single table. To add dependencies for multiple tables, you must use an `AggregateCacheDependency` object, which has an `Add()` method for adding multiple dependencies. You can then use the `AggregateCacheDependency` object in the `Insert()` method. You'll see this in action in the next Try It Out.

You can also specify the caching time in the `Insert()` method using two more parameters. The first of these is a `DateTime` value that you can use to define an absolute expiration time, or `DateTime.MaxValue` if you want to use a sliding expiration policy. The second is a `TimeSpan` value that is used for a sliding expiration policy, and is the amount of time by which to extend the lifetime of the cached object each time it is used:

```
Cache.Insert("MyCachedItem", item, myDependency, DateTime.MaxValue,
    TimeSpan.FromHours(1));
```

Finally, there are two additional parameters that you can use in `Insert()`. You can specify a priority for the cached data, of type `CacheItemPriority`, which determines how likely the cached item is to be removed if .NET decides to clean up resources. You can use `CacheItemPriority.NotRemovable` if you'd rather the .NET Framework didn't remove the data — although the item will still be removed when it expires. The other parameter can be used to supply a callback method, of type `CacheItemRemovedCallback`.

In the following example, you configure the earlier web service application to cache data in the application cache, and test the functionality.

Try It Out   Cached Web Service Data

1. Copy the web service application directory created earlier in the chapter (`C:\BegVC#Databases\Chapter10\Ex1002 - WS Data Access`) to a new directory, `C:\BegVC#Databases\Chapter10\Ex1004 - Caching Data`. Open Visual Web Developer and open the application from its new location.

2. Add a Global Application Class, `Global.asax`, to the project.

3. Add code to `Application_Start()` in `Global.asax` as follows:

```
void Application_Start(object sender, EventArgs e)
{
    // Get connection string.
    string connectionString =
      ConfigurationManager.ConnectionStrings["FolktaleDBConnectionString"]
      .ConnectionString;
    try
    {
        // Get configured tables and check for required tables.
        string[] tables =
          SqlCacheDependencyAdmin.GetTablesEnabledForNotifications(
          connectionString);
        int tablesConfigured = 0;
        foreach (string table in tables)
        {
            if (table == "Address" || table == "CharacterAddress"
              || table == "CharacterStory" || table == "Character"
              || table == "Story")
            {
                tablesConfigured++;
            }
        }

        // If necessary, configure tables.
        if (tablesConfigured < 5)
        {
            SqlCacheDependencyAdmin.EnableTableForNotifications(
              connectionString, "Address");
            SqlCacheDependencyAdmin.EnableTableForNotifications(
              connectionString, "CharacterAddress");
            SqlCacheDependencyAdmin.EnableTableForNotifications(
              connectionString, "CharacterStory");
            SqlCacheDependencyAdmin.EnableTableForNotifications(
              connectionString, "Character");
            SqlCacheDependencyAdmin.EnableTableForNotifications(
              connectionString, "Story");
```

```
        }
      }
      catch (DatabaseNotEnabledForNotificationException)
      {
        // Configure database and tables.
        SqlCacheDependencyAdmin.EnableNotifications(connectionString);
        SqlCacheDependencyAdmin.EnableTableForNotifications(connectionString,
          "Address");
        SqlCacheDependencyAdmin.EnableTableForNotifications(connectionString,
          "CharacterAddress");
        SqlCacheDependencyAdmin.EnableTableForNotifications(connectionString,
          "CharacterStory");
        SqlCacheDependencyAdmin.EnableTableForNotifications(connectionString,
          "Character");
        SqlCacheDependencyAdmin.EnableTableForNotifications(connectionString,
          "Story");
      }
    }
```

4. Add the following cache definition to `web.config`:

```
<configuration>
  ...
  <connectionStrings>
   <add name="FolktaleDBConnectionString" connectionString="..."/>
  </connectionStrings>
  <system.web>
   <caching>
    <sqlCacheDependency enabled="true" pollTime="5000">
     <databases>
      <add name="FolktaleDB"
          connectionStringName="FolktaleDBConnectionString" />
     </databases>
    </sqlCacheDependency>
   </caching>
   ...
  </system.web>
</configuration>
```

5. Open the `FolktaleService.cs` code and add the following using statements:

```
using System.Configuration;
using System.Web.Caching;
```

6. Add the following method to the `FolktaleService` class:

```
private void RefreshData()
{
  // Create data set.
  FolktaleDBDataSet data = new FolktaleDBDataSet();

  // Populate data set.
  addressTableAdapter.Fill(data.Address);
  characterAddressTableAdapter.Fill(data.CharacterAddress);
  characterStoryTableAdapter.Fill(data.CharacterStory);
  characterTableAdapter.Fill(data.Character);
```

```
storyTableAdapter.Fill(data.Story);

// Define dependencies.
SqlCacheDependency addressDependency =
  new SqlCacheDependency("FolktaleDB", "Address");
SqlCacheDependency characterAddressDependency =
  new SqlCacheDependency("FolktaleDB", "CharacterAddress");
SqlCacheDependency characterStoryDependency =
  new SqlCacheDependency("FolktaleDB", "CharacterStory");
SqlCacheDependency characterDependency =
  new SqlCacheDependency("FolktaleDB", "Character");
SqlCacheDependency storyDependency = new
  SqlCacheDependency("FolktaleDB", "Story");
AggregateCacheDependency dependency = new AggregateCacheDependency();
dependency.Add(addressDependency, characterAddressDependency,
  characterStoryDependency, characterDependency, storyDependency);

// Save data.
HttpContext.Current.Cache.Insert("data", data, dependency, DateTime.MaxValue,
  TimeSpan.FromSeconds(5));
}
```

7. Modify `GetData()` as follows:

```
public FolktaleDBDataSet GetData()
{
    // Check for data.
    if (HttpContext.Current.Cache["data"] == null)
    {
      // Refresh data.
      RefreshData();
    }

    // Return data set.
    return HttpContext.Current.Cache["data"] as FolktaleDBDataSet;
}
```

8. Place a breakpoint on the first line of the `RefreshData()` method.

9. Run the application (you may need to set `FolktaleService.asmx` as the start page of the project again because adding `global.asax` and/or copying a project to a new location sometimes interferes with this).

10. Invoke the `GetData()` method through the web interface. Note that the code pauses on the breakpoint, and then resumes application execution.

11. Close the `GetData()` results window and execute `GetData()` again. This time, the breakpoint is not hit. This indicates that a cached copy of the data is being used, so there is no need for `RefreshData()` to be called.

12. Wait 5 seconds, and invoke `GetData()` again. This time the breakpoint is hit. The cached data has expired, and so it must be refreshed from the database.

13. Stop debugging, and close any open browser windows for the application and Visual Web Developer Express.

How It Works

This example modifies the earlier web service application to enable application cache storage of the FolktaleDBDataSet data. The first modification adds code to be run when the web application is loaded to ensure that the database is enabled for dependency notifications. You saw this code earlier in the chapter, although this version is modified slightly to check for the required tables. It uses simplified code, just counting the enabled databases and if the required number isn't enabled, it enables them. When multiple applications use the same database, you'd probably want to check each table individually, but here this is fine. You also added caching configuration to web.config, using code you've seen in previous sections.

You added a new method to refresh the cached data, RefreshData(). It starts by retrieving data in the same way as the old version of GetData():

```
private void RefreshData()
{
  FolktaleDBDataSet data = new FolktaleDBDataSet();
  addressTableAdapter.Fill(data.Address);
  characterAddressTableAdapter.Fill(data.CharacterAddress);
  characterStoryTableAdapter.Fill(data.CharacterStory);
  characterTableAdapter.Fill(data.Character);
  storyTableAdapter.Fill(data.Story);
```

Next, dependencies are defined — one for each table in the data set:

```
  SqlCacheDependency addressDependency =
    new SqlCacheDependency("FolktaleDB", "Address");
  SqlCacheDependency characterAddressDependency =
    new SqlCacheDependency("FolktaleDB", "CharacterAddress");
  SqlCacheDependency characterStoryDependency =
    new SqlCacheDependency("FolktaleDB", "CharacterStory");
  SqlCacheDependency characterDependency =
    new SqlCacheDependency("FolktaleDB", "Character");
  SqlCacheDependency storyDependency = new
    SqlCacheDependency("FolktaleDB", "Story");
```

The dependencies are then added to a single AggregateCacheDependency object:

```
  AggregateCacheDependency dependency = new AggregateCacheDependency();
  dependency.Add(addressDependency, characterAddressDependency,
    characterStoryDependency, characterDependency, storyDependency);
```

Finally, the Cache.Insert() method is used to add the cached item, overwriting any additional item with the same name if one exists. The name data is used to identify the item:

```
  HttpContext.Current.Cache.Insert("data", data, dependency, DateTime.MaxValue,
    TimeSpan.FromSeconds(5));
}
```

You then modified the GetData() method to use the cached data. The first step checks whether any cached data exists and calls RefreshData() if it doesn't:

```
public FolktaleDBDataSet GetData()
{
  if (HttpContext.Current.Cache["data"] == null)
  {
    // Refresh data.
    RefreshData();
  }
```

After that, you know you have some data stored, so you return it:

```
  return HttpContext.Current.Cache["data"] as FolktaleDBDataSet;
}
```

These changes are all quite simple and, if there were a lot of users, would definitely improve performance.

One additional modification that you could make if you wanted to use a long poll time would be to call RefreshData() at the end of the UpdateData() method so that the refreshed data is updated. This isn't necessary for short poll times, however, because updating the data causes the cached item to be removed, and it's refreshed the next time it is requested.

Summary

This chapter explained how to deal with data in a distributed environment. You looked at using web services to expose data so that it can be consumed by remote applications via an Internet connection. You have seen how this is possible in Windows applications, but there is nothing stopping you from using web services from web applications — in fact, that's common.

Specifically, you learned to:

❑ Create basic web services and web methods.

❑ Use a web service to expose database data. You saw how a typed data set can be used as the return value of a web method, and how that data is serialized.

❑ Consume web services from a Windows application, including how to define web service data sources, how to bind to web service data, and how to update data through a web service.

❑ Improve the performance of web applications by using data caching.

❑ Use web method output caching to cache the responses of web services.

❑ Store data in application state in web applications.

❑ Cache data in the ASP.NET application cache.

❑ Configure databases and database tables for SQL dependency notifications.

❑ Cache database data that will update when database data changes using SQL dependency notifications.

The next chapter — the final chapter in this book — shows you how to write managed code to run inside SQL Server.

Exercises

1. Which of the following types of applications can use web services?

    a. Windows application

    b. Windows services

    c. Web applications

    d. Web services

2. What are the steps required to call a web method from a Windows application?

3. What is the simplest method of caching web service responses? Why is this sometimes inadvisable?

4. Give the code that you would need to add to the `web.config` file for a web application to define two SQL dependencies for connection strings called `ConnectionString1` and `ConnectionString2`. These should have poll times of 1 second and 10 seconds, respectively.

5. How would you determine if a database was enabled for SQL dependency notifications?

6. How do you set dependencies on multiple tables for `SqlDataSource` controls, and how would you do it programmatically?

SQL Server CLR Integration

Integrating CLR (Common Language Runtime) code in SQL Server, a functionality that was introduced with .NET 2.0 and SQL Server 2005, enables you to write .NET code that runs inside SQL Server (or SQL Server Express). You can write stored procedures and functions, provide user-defined types to be used as column types in database tables, and write your own triggers. The motivation for doing this is primarily so that the code can perform many tasks that would be difficult or impossible to perform using SQL code. For example, your code can access external resources such as files and network resources in the same way it can from within .NET applications.

This development technique has another major advantage: You use a common code base for both your applications and SQL Server access. That means that you won't need to learn so much about the SQL language because you can bypass its more advanced features, creating them in .NET code instead. As a .NET developer, you're likely to be much more comfortable with this method, and performing more advanced tasks will be much easier.

There are, however, limitations of which you should be aware. For example, certain namespaces in the .NET Framework are not available for use by code running inside SQL Server. These limitations are sensible, however, and leave you with more than enough scope to create really useful applications.

Also, it is worth remembering that the fact that you can use CLR code in SQL Server doesn't mean you will never use SQL code again. In many circumstances, particularly in circumstances in which you need only simple functionality, writing stored procedures in SQL code, for example, is still a good idea. For more complex functionality, however, there is no substitute for CLR code.

In this chapter, then, you look at writing .NET code for CLR integration with SQL server, and learn what you have to do to enable the use of managed C# code in SQL Server, as well as how to actually place code there and use it. You'll also look at creating and using functions and stored procedures written in C#, including scalar, table-valued, and aggregate functions.

Briefly, you will learn:

- ❑   To enable CLR integration
- ❑   To add assemblies to SQL Server

❑   To register CLR code

❑   About the common features of CLR integrated code

❑   To write and use managed functions and stored procedures

Before starting this chapter, note that Visual C# Express is not the ideal tool for working with CLR integration code. It's one area in which the full version of Visual Studio supplies you with many more tools and facilities. You are perfectly capable of writing code — including the full range of CLR functionality — with Visual C# Express, but you won't have wizards to help you along the way, the capability to automatically deploy code to SQL Server, and the capability to debug code running in SQL Server. None of that is a problem in the context of this chapter because you still can learn the techniques required, and having to do more things manually will give you greater insight into what is required to make CLR integration work.

Overview of CLR Integration

Exactly when is it a good idea to integrate CLR with SQL Server? What benefits can you expect? As you will see, there are many situations where CLR integration is not the best option, and you should use SQL code instead.

The most obvious advantage of using .NET code is that it is far more powerful and versatile than SQL code. C# code has more and better structures for processing data, such as arrays, collections, `foreach` loops, and so on. With its object-oriented approach to programming, C# code also allows you to make use of inheritance, polymorphism, and more. None of this is easy to implement in SQL code. It is possible to emulate those features, but that can be time-consuming and lead to nightmarish SQL code. Put simply, there are some things that you simply can't achieve with any degree of fluency using SQL code.

In addition, .NET Framework contains a wealth of classes in various namespaces for dealing with all sorts of situations. Direct access to file system data, system configuration and registry information, web resources, and more can be achieved with .NET code using syntax you've either used before or could find out about easily enough.

Because .NET code is compiled to native code prior to execution, processor-intensive operations can also receive a marked performance boost when written in C# rather than SQL. However, that leads to an important decision — exactly how much processing should your database server do? After all, the role of a database server is primarily to store and give access to data. In many cases it's better to perform processor-intensive tasks on client computers, especially in an environment where the database server is best suited to "playing dumb" and simply responding to huge numbers of client requests as quickly and efficiently as possible. That decision is likely to be influenced by your enterprise architecture as much as anything else. The actual operations will be achieved with .NET code in either case, meaning that you will most likely use the same techniques to actually code them, and where the code actually ends up may not be that important from your perspective.

As mentioned earlier, some namespaces in the .NET Framework are not available to code running in SQL Server. By default, only types found in the following assemblies are available:

❑   `System`

❑   `System.Configuration`

- ❑ System.Data
- ❑ System.Data.OracleClient
- ❑ System.Data.SqlXml
- ❑ System.Deployment
- ❑ System.Security
- ❑ System.Transactions
- ❑ System.Web.Services
- ❑ System.Xml
- ❑ Anything in the mscorlib.dll library (covers most commonly used types, including collection, IO, and security classes)
- ❑ Classes in the CustomMarshallers.dll library (includes classes used for COM interoperability in the System.Runtime.InteropServices.CustomMarshalers namespace)
- ❑ Classes in the Microsoft.VisualBasic.dll and Microsoft.VisualC.dll libraries (which include runtime libraries for Visual Basic and C# as well as code generation classes)

This is actually a list of namespaces and type libraries that have been fully tested for CLR integration, found to be safe to use, and made available to the SQL Server process. If you use code from any of these, no further configuration is necessary. They are loaded from the GAC as required. If you want to use other .NET libraries, you have to import them into SQL Server, and may have to test them for compliance along the way. For that reason, this book only looks at the libraries that are allowed by default, as in the preceding list.

Enabling CLR Integration

The CLR integration features of SQL Server (and SQL Server Express) are disabled by default. To enable them, you must make a small configuration change, which is achieved using the clr enabled option. Change the value of the option from 0 (meaning disabled) to 1 (meaning enabled), using the sp_configure stored procedure. Here's the SQL code:

```
EXEC sp_configure 'clr enabled', 1
RECONFIGURE
```

The first line sets the clr enabled option to 1, and the second line commits the change and applies it to the running instance of the server. For some configuration changes to take effect, the server must be restarted, but that's not the case for this option.

You can also check the current state of this option by using the sp_configure stored procedure with no parameters:

```
EXEC sp_configure
```

This returns a result set showing the available configuration options and their settings, as shown in Figure 11-1.

	name	minimum	maximum	config_value	run_value
1	allow updates	0	1	0	0
2	clr enabled	0	1	1	1
3	cross db ownership chaining	0	1	0	0
4	default language	0	9999	0	0
5	max text repl size (B)	0	2147483647	65536	65536
6	nested triggers	0	1	1	1
7	remote access	0	1	1	1
8	remote admin connections	0	1	0	0
9	remote login timeout (s)	0	2147483647	20	20
10	remote proc trans	0	1	0	0
11	remote query timeout (s)	0	2147483647	600	600
12	server trigger recursion	0	1	1	1
13	show advanced options	0	1	0	0
14	user instances enabled	0	1	1	1
15	user options	0	32767	0	0

Figure 11-1: Viewing database option settings

Figure 11-1 shows the `clr enabled` option set to `1`.

Adding Assemblies to SQL Server

To execute .NET code in SQL Server, you must write it in a certain way using attributes and types found in the `System.Data` namespace, as you will see later in this chapter. Then you compile your code into an assembly (DLL file), and load that assembly into SQL Server. That's another task that you achieve using SQL code, namely the `CREATE ASSEMBLY` statement.

> *The full version of Visual Studio enables you to create database projects that simplify this procedure. You can create projects using the Database Project template, which gives you the option to deploy assemblies directly into a SQL Server database. Unfortunately this feature is not available in Visual C# Express, and because that is the product you're using in this book, you'll see alternative ways of doing things.*

The `CREATE ASSEMBLY` statement is used as follows:

```
CREATE ASSEMBLY <assembly name> FROM <path to dll file>
WITH PERMISSION_SET = <permission set>
```

Here you can use a local or network path to the DLL file to load, and you can use either SAFE, EXTER-NAL_ACCESS, or UNSAFE for the permission set. The permission set defines the permissions assigned to the assembly. SAFE is the most restrictive option, and should be used wherever possible. It means that the code will not have access to any resources outside the SQL Server process, such as files and the system registry. EXTERNAL_ACCESS permits code access to these resources. UNSAFE allows code to access both these resources and additional resources inside the SQL Server process. UNSAFE code can use unmanaged code, which is potentially dangerous because it may interfere with the functionality of SQL Server and lead to all sorts of trouble. Only highly trusted assemblies should be loaded with the UNSAFE option, and the account you use to execute the CREATE ASSEMBLY statement must be a member of the sysadmin role in SQL Server.

Assemblies loaded this way can be seen in the Assemblies folder in the Database Explorer window in Visual C# Express, as shown in Figure 11-2.

Figure 11-2: Viewing loaded assemblies in Visual C# Express

In SQL Server Management Studio Express, the assembly is found in the Programmability ⇨ Assemblies folder, as shown in Figure 11-3.

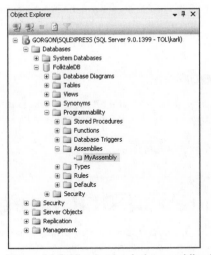

Figure 11-3: Viewing loaded assemblies in SQL Server Management Studio Express

As with other database objects, CREATE ASSEMBLY has an associated DROP ASSEMBLY statement that you can use to remove assemblies from SQL Server. You can do this only if there are no database objects, such as stored procedures, that depend on the assembly. To locate such dependencies in SQL Server Management Studio Express, right-click on the assembly and select View Dependencies.

You can also use the ALTER ASSEMBLY statement to refresh the assembly stored in SQL Server to the latest version, which is handy when you make changes to your code and recompile it.

Requirements of CLR Integration Code

When you load an assembly using the CREATE ASSEMBLY statement, various checks are made to ensure that the libraries it requires are available, and that it conforms to the code requirements. Many of these are enforced automatically simply by the act of compiling code in Visual C# Express, such as creating a valid .NET assembly with the required metadata and so forth. A check is also made for the assemblies referenced by your code; as you have already seen, not all .NET Framework assemblies are available for code running in SQL Server.

Checks are also made for some other aspects of the classes you provide, at least for assemblies imported using the SAFE or EXTERNAL_ACCESS permission sets. You are not allowed to have static class members unless they are read-only, and you cannot use finalizer (destructor) methods in your classes. You should use the various attributes provided to mark methods and classes appropriately, as you will see later in this chapter.

If your code fails any of these checks, an error is raised informing you of the problem and helping you to solve it, and the assembly is not loaded into SQL Server.

Additional checks are also made when CLR integrated code is executed. For example, code running in an assembly using the SAFE permissions set is unable to access external resources, and attempting to do so results in an error. EXTERNAL_ACCESS and UNSAFE assemblies must either be signed and granted the appropriate level of access, or the database owner must have the required permission and the database should be marked using the TRUSTWORTHY option. You'll see this in action later in the chapter, as well, when you create a table-valued function.

Registering CLR Code

To actually use CLR code, you need to do a little bit more work. Loading an assembly into SQL Server makes it available for you to use, but does not, for example, create stored procedures for your methods, or add your classes as user-defined types. There are additional SQL commands required to achieve this, which you'll explore later in this chapter.

Common Features of CLR Integrated Code

All the code you will be writing in this chapter will be in the form of class library projects, with an output of a DLL assembly file that you can load into SQL Server using the techniques you saw in the previous section. Specifically, you will use Visual C# Express to create assemblies for CLR integration, and use SQL Management Studio Express to load and test the assemblies. SQL Server Management Studio Express makes it easier to write and save the queries that you will require. Should you want to test your modified databases from client applications, you may have to detach/reattach databases (as described in Appendix B), but that's simple and quick enough not to be a problem.

You'll want to examine some fundamentals before you start getting into the specifics, however. The topics in this section cover the basic code that you will use for the rest of the chapter. They are common to all types of CLR integrated code, and you will use the techniques shown here extensively. Don't panic — there is nothing too complicated here, and when you see the code in action later, you'll quickly pick up anything you miss the first time around.

Code Structure

You'll be using types defined in the `Microsoft.SqlServer.Server` namespace, which is part of the `System.Data.dll` assembly. In fact, this assembly is automatically added as a reference to class library projects when you create them, which saves you the effort of adding it.

One slightly odd thing about writing code for CLR integration is that you should never include a namespace for your code. When you register your code in SQL Server, classes are referred to in `<assemblyName>.<className>` format, and if the class isn't in the global namespace, you will not be able to access it. In practice, the assembly name is used as the namespace, and because you are unlikely to add assemblies with the same name to a database, this shouldn't cause any naming conflict problems.

Whichever type of code you are creating, you will use attributes from the `Microsoft.SqlServer.Server` namespace to configure your code, as follows:

- ❑ For functions and stored procedures:
  - ❑ `SqlFunction`
  - ❑ `SqlUserDefinedAggregate`
  - ❑ `SqlProcedure`
- ❑ For user-defined types:
  - ❑ `SqlUserDefinedType`
  - ❑ `SqlFacet`
- ❑ For triggers:
  - ❑ `SqlTrigger`

These attributes have various properties that you can use to customize the behavior of your code, as you will see later in this chapter. In most cases, the attributes are optional, and if they are not supplied, default values are assumed. Some of the attribute properties are actually not used by `SqlServer`, but are instead intended to customize the behavior of Visual Studio when it deploys code to SQL Server. Those are not applicable to Visual C# Express, but will be noted in any case because if you use Visual Studio to write CLR integration code in the future they can be useful.

Data Access

You'll use the ADO.NET classes to work with database data. The only real difference in the code you write is how you handle the connection to the database. Because the code is already running inside the database, there's usually no need to supply all the parameters that you would normally include in a connection string. Instead, you simply use the connection string `"context connection=true"`:

```
SqlConnection conn = new SqlConnection("context connection=true");
```

This is known as a *context connection*. It's easy to use although it behaves a little differently than an ordinary `SqlConnection` object. This connection bypasses many of the protocols that are typically used because it exists within the SQL Server process. Performance improves for the same reason. Some functionality is not available with context connections; most of that is advanced functionality such as receiving update notifications and bulk operations. Also, the `SqlConnection.DataSource` property is `null` rather than the SQL Server instance name, and you can have only one context connection for each database connection being used.

You can, if you want to, use connection strings of the same type as in client code — in fact, you must if you want to use the functionality not supported by context connections, or if you want to connect to a remote database from your code. In general, however, use context connections wherever possible.

Call Context

When your code is executed in SQL Server, it's normally initiated by a client. (The exception to that rule is when a trigger is executed, although triggers are not detailed in this chapter.) From CLR integrated code you can gain access to the context of the caller, which enables you to send information to client code and discover the caller's Windows identity. Knowing the Windows identity of the user can be important because it enables you to impersonate the user for external resource access, such as accessing file system data. Without it, you would be forced to use the Windows identity under which the SQL Server process runs, which is likely to have different security permissions.

The call context is made available to your code by means of the `SqlContext` class. Its properties are described in the following table.

Property	Usage
IsAvailable	A Boolean value that tells you if there is a call context for you to use. This is `true` if the code is running in SQL Server, and `false` for client code.
WindowsIdentity	Gives you a `System.Security.Principal.WindowsIdentity` object representing the Windows identity of the current user. If the user accessed the database using SQL Server authentication, this property will be `null`.
Pipe	An instance of the `SqlPipe` class used to communicate with the client, if one is available, as described in the next section.
TriggerContext	Alternative context information for use in CLR integrated trigger definitions.

The property you'll use most often is `SqlContext.Pipe`.

SqlPipe

Depending on the CLR code you are writing, the value of `SqlContext.Pipe` is not always available. For example, the property is `null` in functions because functions cannot return messages. It is, however, available in stored procedures. If in doubt, try using it. The worst that can happen is that you receive an error when SQL Server tries to access it.

After obtaining a `SqlPipe` object through the call context, you can use its `Send()` method to return data to the client. There are three overloads to this method. The first requires a string parameter, and you can use it to send text messages to the client, such as status reports. The second requires a `SqlDataReader` object, and allows you to send a result set consisting of multiple rows to the client. Finally, there is an overload that enables you to send a single row to the client. This version uses another class in the `Microsoft.SqlServer.Server` namespace: `SqlDataRecord`.

The `SqlDataRecord` class represents a single row. The class's constructor requires one or more `SqlMetaData` objects, which define the column names and data types for the row. The `SqlMetaData` class is similar to the `SqlParameter` class you've seen in previous chapters for use with `SqlCommand` objects, and it has similar constructors. To instantiate a `SqlMetaData` object, you supply the column name, column data type (in the form of a `SqlDataType` value), and additional information if required, such as the size of the data.

For example, you could create columns for a row as follows:

```
SqlMetaData column1 = new SqlMetaData("TableId", SqlDbType.UniqueIdentifier);
SqlMetaData column2 = new SqlMetaData("StringColumn", SqlDbType.VarChar, 100);
SqlMetaData column3 = new SqlMetaData("BoolColumn", SqlDbType.Bit);
```

Once you have defined columns, you can create a `SqlDataRecord` object:

```
SqlDataRecord row = new SqlDataRecord(column1, column2, column3);
```

Next you must set the column values for the row, which you can do using the various Set*XXX*() methods that the object exposes. Here's an example:

```
row.SetSqlGuid(0, new SqlGuid(Guid.NewGuid()));
row.SetSqlString(1, new SqlString("A string!"));
row.SetSqlBoolean(2, new SqlBoolean(true));
```

This is, in many ways, similar to accessing data rows through a `SqlDataReader` object (although you cannot set row data through a `SqlDataReader` object). As with `SqlDataReader`, you can access column data through a `SqlDataRecord` object using the indexer for the object or by using one of the various Get*XXX*() methods, such as `GetSqlGuid()` and `GetSqlInt32()`, which get data from the column with the specified index. For example:

```
SqlGuid column1Value = row.GetSqlGuid(0);
```

Finally, if you are creating a row to return it to the client, you use the `SqlPipe.Send()` method:

```
SqlContext.Pipe.Send(row);
```

The `SqlPipe` class also includes the `ExecuteAndSend()` method, which is a useful shortcut for executing SQL commands. It takes a parameter of type `SqlCommand()`, and executes that command, returning any messages and results to the client. For example:

```
using (SqlConnection conn = new SqlConnection("context connection=true"))
{
    conn.Open();
```

```
        SqlContext.Pipe.ExecuteAndSend(new SqlCommand("SELECT * FROM Enchantment",
            conn));
    }
```

Note that the connection used by the command must be open when you call `ExecuteAndSend()`. In the preceding code sample, the `using` code block results in the connection being closed automatically.

Managed Functions and Stored Procedures

The first type of CLR integration assembly you look at in this chapter is where you provide methods that can be used to implement functions and stored procedures in SQL Server. This includes all types of function — scalar functions, table-valued functions, and aggregate functions. As you learn how to do this you'll also see a lot of the basic techniques that are required for all types of CLR integration.

You won't look at triggers or user-defined types in depth, although many of the techniques explained in this chapter apply as much to them as they do to functions and stored procedures. Should you want to learn more about writing managed triggers and user-defined types you should have no trouble finding out more — and you'll have a head start from what you will already know.

Scalar Functions

Scalar functions, as you saw earlier in this book, are functions that return a single scalar value, such as a single integer or string. They can also have parameters, although they can't be output parameters. In addition, scalar functions cannot modify the state of a database. You can't, for example, add, update, or delete rows from tables.

Typically, scalar functions are used to perform simple mathematical tasks on numerical data, or string manipulations. There are many scalar functions defined for you in SQL Server, including `SQRT()` to obtain the square root of a number, `ABS()` to return the absolute value of a number, and `RAND()` to return a random number. Sometimes, however, you will want to add your own functions. You might want to use the .NET Framework to do such things as encrypting data, obtaining hash codes for data, and more advanced string manipulation such as concatenating strings.

Starting with scalar functions is a good way to be introduced to CLR integration because you can concentrate on the CLR integration code without having to worry about data manipulation using ADO.NET code. You can, of course, include ADO.NET code in scalar functions, but to keep things simple here you'll leave that side of things until a little later.

To use .NET code to define a scalar function, you must supply a static method to be used for the function. The function you create must have a return type that is compatible with a SQL scalar data type, such as an `int` or `string`, and scalar functions cannot be declared `void`.

You can also use the `SqlFunction` attribute from the `Microsoft.SqlServer.Server` namespace to further configure function behavior. `SqlFunction` has several properties, and the ones you will use for scalar functions are described in the following table.

Property	Usage
IsDeterministic	A Boolean property that says whether the function is deterministic; that is, it returns the same result every time with a given set of parameters and database state. Most functions in SQL Server are deterministic, but occasionally you find one that isn't. For example, the RAND() function is non-deterministic if no seed is supplied because the value it returns is, by definition, random. It is important that you do not set this property to true for a function that is non-deterministic because that can affect how data is indexed and may lead to problems.
IsPrecise	A Boolean property that says whether the function returns a precise value. Use this property when your function doesn't use floating-point operations — if it does, then the result won't be precise (although it may be accurate to a large number of significant figures). Again, it is important to specify this property accurately because it can cause indexing problems and corrupted data.
DataAccess	Can either be DataAccessKind.Read, meaning that the function accesses database data, or DataAccessKind.None, meaning that it doesn't. If the function does not access database data, setting this property to DataAccessKind.None can improve performance. However, if you use this value and then attempt to access database data, an error occurs and the function fails to operate.
SystemDataAccess	Similar to DataAccess, but says whether the function accesses system data — such as the system catalog or virtual system tables — in SQL Server. It can be set to SystemDataAccessKind.Read or SystemDataAccessKind.None.

There is also a Name property for the SqlFunction attribute, but it isn't used by SQL Server. Instead it is used by Visual Studio if you develop CLR integration code in that environment, determining the name of the function that is created in the database when the code is deployed.

For example, you would define a method to return a random integer between a specified minimum and maximum value as follows:

```
[SqlFunction(IsDeterministic = false, IsPrecise = true,
    DataAccess = DataAccessKind.None,
    SystemDataAccess = SystemDataAccessKind.None)]
public static int RandomIntegerBetween(int minValue, int maxValue)
```

This method is non-deterministic (because it returns a random value), doesn't need database access, and returns a precise value because no floating-point numbers are involved.

If, however, the method included a third value to be used as the seed for the random number generation, then it would be deterministic, and you could alter the IsDeterministic property value accordingly.

After you have created an assembly containing a static method that you want to use for a scalar function and have loaded it into SQL Server, the next step is to create a scalar function in SQL Server and specify that your .NET code should be used for the implementation of the function. To do this, you use the CRE-ATE FUNCTION command as usual, but instead of a SQL implementation, you use the EXTERNAL NAME keywords to specify the name of a method to use. You must also ensure that the parameters and return value type of the method match the signature of the method you have created.

For example, the RandomIntegerBetween() method shown earlier can be linked to a scalar function called CustomRand() as follows (here the assembly name is defined as MyAssembly, and the class containing the method is called MyFunctions):

```
CREATE FUNCTION dbo.CustomRand(@minValue int, @maxValue int) RETURNS int
AS EXTERNAL NAME MyAssembly.MyFunctions.RandomIntegerBetween
```

You can then use the function from SQL code, like this:

```
SELECT dbo.CustomRand(5, 10) AS 'RandomValue'
```

In the following example, you work though the steps required to create, import, and use a simple scalar function with a C# implementation.

Try It Out   Creating a CLR Integrated Scalar Function

1. Open SQL Server Management Studio Express and connect to your local SQL Server Express instance.

2. Expand the Databases folder in the Object Explorer window, and verify that the FolktaleDB database exists. If it doesn't, attach it (see Appendix B for details).

3. Right-click the FolktaleDB database and select New Query. Add the following SQL code:

```
EXEC sp_configure 'clr enabled', 1
RECONFIGURE
```

4. Execute the SQL statement.

5. Close the SQL Query and discard changes.

6. Open Visual C# Express and create a new class library project called Ex1101 - Scalar Functions. Save the project in the C:\BegVC#Databases\Chapter11 directory, with the Create Directory For Solution option unchecked.

7. Remove the auto-generated Class1.cs file, add a new class called Functions, and modify its code as follows (note that this code goes in the global namespace):

```
...

using Microsoft.SqlServer.Server;
using System.Security.Cryptography;

...

public class Functions
{
```

```
        [SqlFunction(IsDeterministic = true, IsPrecise = true,
            DataAccess = DataAccessKind.None,
            SystemDataAccess = SystemDataAccessKind.None)]
    public static string GetHash(string input)
    {
        // Convert input string to byte array.
        UnicodeEncoding encoding = new UnicodeEncoding();
        Byte[] inputBytes = encoding.GetBytes(input);

        // Create hash bytes using SHA1 algorithm.
        SHA1Managed algorithm = new SHA1Managed();
        Byte[] outputBytes = algorithm.ComputeHash(inputBytes);

        // Create output string
        StringBuilder sb = new StringBuilder();
        foreach (Byte outputByte in outputBytes)
        {
            sb.Append(outputByte);
            sb.Append(",");
        }
        string output = sb.ToString();
        output = output.Substring(0, output.Length - 1);

        // Return output bytes as string.
        return output;
    }
}
```

8. Compile the project.

9. Return to SQL Server Management Studio and create another new query for the FolktaleDB
database. Add SQL code as follows:

```
USE FolktaleDB
GO

CREATE ASSEMBLY Ex1101 FROM
  'C:\BegVC#Databases\Chapter11\Ex1101 - Scalar Functions\bin\Release\
Ex1101 - Scalar Functions.dll'
WITH PERMISSION_SET = SAFE
GO

CREATE FUNCTION dbo.GetHash(@input nvarchar(1000)) RETURNS nvarchar(1000)
AS
EXTERNAL NAME Ex1101.Functions.GetHash
GO

SELECT dbo.GetHash('Extremely sensitive information.') AS Hash
GO

DROP FUNCTION dbo.GetHash
DROP ASSEMBLY Ex1101
GO
```

10. Save the query as `CallFunction.sql` in the `C:\BegVC#Databases\Chapter11\Ex1101 - Scalar Functions` directory.

11. Execute the query. The result is shown in Figure 11-4.

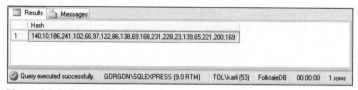

Figure 11-4: Query result

12. Close SQL Server Management Studio Express and Visual C# Express.

How It Works

In this example, you create and use a CLR integrated function. The function, which you created using C#, is one that computes the hash value of a string and returns it as a list of comma-separated byte values.

You started by enabling CLR integration using the SQL code described earlier in this chapter:

```
EXEC sp_configure 'clr enabled', 1
RECONFIGURE
```

Once configured, a SQL Server instance stays configured, so there's no need to store this query for later, unless of course you intend to run it against a different instance of SQL Server.

Next you created the function in Visual C# Express. The class containing your function code, `Functions`, is placed in the global namespace:

```
public class Functions
{
```

You added a static method called `GetHash()`. It always returns the same hash for a given string, so it is marked as deterministic. It also doesn't involve any floating-point operations, so it is precise and doesn't need any database access:

```
[SqlFunction(IsDeterministic = true, IsPrecise = true,
    DataAccess = DataAccessKind.None,
    SystemDataAccess = SystemDataAccessKind.None)]
public static string GetHash(string input)
{
```

The implementation of `GetHash()` uses fairly standard cryptographic code for hash generation. You get the bytes from the input (Unicode) string:

```
UnicodeEncoding encoding = new UnicodeEncoding();
Byte[] inputBytes = encoding.GetBytes(input);
```

You create an algorithm for hashing (an SHA1 algorithm, in this example) and obtain a hashed byte array:

```
SHA1Managed algorithm = new SHA1Managed();
Byte[] outputBytes = algorithm.ComputeHash(inputBytes);
```

And finally, the byte array is converted into a comma-separated list of integer values and returned:

```
StringBuilder sb = new StringBuilder();
foreach (Byte outputByte in outputBytes)
{
    sb.Append(outputByte);
    sb.Append(",");
}
string output = sb.ToString();
output = output.Substring(0, output.Length - 1);

return output;
    }
}
```

Once the assembly is compiled, the next step is to load it into SQL Server:

```
CREATE ASSEMBLY Ex1101 FROM
  'C:\BegVC#Databases\Chapter11\Ex1101 - Scalar Functions\bin\Release\Ex1101 -
Scalar Functions.dll'
WITH PERMISSION_SET = SAFE
GO
```

The SAFE permission set is used because the code requires no external access.

After loading the assembly, you create a scalar function to execute your code, using a CREATE FUNCTION statement (the nvarchar data type is used here because Unicode strings are required):

```
CREATE FUNCTION dbo.GetHash(@input nvarchar(1000)) RETURNS nvarchar(1000)
AS
EXTERNAL NAME Ex1101.Functions.GetHash
GO
```

Then you execute the function. Here it is executed with a simple SELECT statement:

```
SELECT dbo.GetHash('Extremely sensitive information.') AS Hash
GO
```

Finally, the function and assembly are dropped:

```
DROP FUNCTION dbo.GetHash
DROP ASSEMBLY Ex1101
GO
```

This is done so you can execute the SQL script repeatedly without needing separate SQL scripts for the various actions performed. Obviously, you wouldn't do this if you wanted to use the new function from a client application.

Again, the method implementation itself contains only basic code, but isn't something that you could perform easily using SQL code. As you have seen, none of the procedure for adding a CLR integrated scalar function is particularly complex, and the results are well worth it. Writing code this way enables you to create scalar functions that are far more powerful than those written in SQL code.

Table-Valued Functions

The table-valued function returns rows of information rather than single values. The rows returned don't have to match the column specification of an existing table; you can instead create a new row and column specification and return that. The only restriction is that columns cannot use the timestamp or any of the non-Unicode data types (char, varchar, text, and so on). Effectively, table-valued functions are much like views, although you have more capability to customize the data returned, especially when you write a table-valued function in C#.

Unlike scalar functions, defining a table-valued function in .NET code requires two static methods. The first initializes a collection of objects and returns the collection in the form of an IEnumerable interface. That method is referred to as the initializing method. It gives you plenty of flexibility because a lot of collection classes support the interface, including all arrays, generic collections, and so on. The collection itself, however, doesn't provide quite enough information for SQL Server to package items as row data, so you must provide a second method, referred to as the *row-filling method*, which takes information from an item and uses it to populate columns. The columns are then used by SQL Server to create and return a row.

The initializing method uses a SqlFunction attribute, as in scalar method implementation, and an additional property called FillRowMethodName that provides the name of the row-filling method (as a string). You can also use the properties you discussed in the preceding section. An additional property, TableDefinition, specifies the schema for the table as a series of <columnName> <columnType> pairs, although it's another of the properties (like Name) that is used only in the full version of Visual Studio.

You could, therefore, define an initializing method as follows:

```
[SqlFunction(IsDeterministic = true, IsPrecise = true,
    DataAccess = DataAccessKind.Read, SystemDataAccess = SystemDataAccessKind.None,
    FillRowMethodName = "FillRow")]
public static IEnumerable Initialize(int anIntegerParameter,
    string aStringParameter)
```

This code references a row-filling method called FillRow(). Row-filling methods must include an object type parameter as their first parameter. The parameter is passed the value of an item from the collection. You must also include additional out parameters, one for each column you want to appear in the resultant row. These parameters are used to return data, rather than using a method return value. In fact, row-filling methods should be declared as void as well as static.

The code you use in a row-filling method should use the value of the first parameter to extract values for the other parameters. For example:

```
public static void FillRow(object sourceItem, out Guid itemId,
    out string itemCategory)
```

```
{
    itemId = (sourceItem as MyItemClass).Id;
    itemCategory = (sourceItem as MyItemClass).Category;
}
```

The restrictions on the data types that can be returned discussed at the beginning of this section apply to the data types of these parameters. No attribute is required for the FillRow() method.

Once you have created the two methods, you can use them from SQL Server in a similar way to scalar functions — you specify the initializing method in a CREATE FUNCTION definition. The only difference is that the return value of the function is specified using a TABLE (...) specification. Here's an example:

```
CREATE FUNCTION dbo.GetTabularData(@IntParam int, @StringParam nvarchar(250))
RETURNS TABLE (ItemId uniqueidentifier, Category nvarchar(1000))
AS
EXTERNAL NAME MyAssembly.MyFunctions.Initialize
```

You can then use the function in a SELECT statement, like this:

```
SELECT * FROM dbo.GetTabularData(42, "Fish")
```

In the following example, you create and use a table-valued function. The function requires the UNSAFE permission set, so you'll see a way to enable that.

Try It Out   Creating a CLR Integrated Table Function

1. Open SQL Server Management Studio Express and connect to your local SQL Server Express instance.

2. Expand the Databases folder, right-click the FolktaleDB database, and then select New Query. Add the following SQL code:

    ```
    ALTER DATABASE FolktaleDB SET TRUSTWORTHY ON
    EXEC sp_changedbowner 'sa'
    ```

3. Execute the SQL statement.

4. Close the SQL Query and discard changes.

5. Open Visual C# Express and create a new class library project called Ex1102 - Table Functions. Save the project in the C:\BegVC#Databases\Chapter11 directory, with the Create Directory For Solution option unchecked.

6. Remove the auto-generated Class1.cs file and add a new class called Functions with code as follows (the code goes in the global namespace):

    ...

    ```
    using Microsoft.SqlServer.Server;
    using System.Collections;
    using System.Diagnostics;
    ```

    ...

```csharp
public class Functions
{
    [SqlFunction(IsDeterministic = false, IsPrecise = false,
        DataAccess = DataAccessKind.None,
        SystemDataAccess = SystemDataAccessKind.None,
        FillRowMethodName = "FillRow")]
    public static IEnumerable Initialize(string categoryName)
    {
        // Check if category exists.
        if (!PerformanceCounterCategory.Exists(categoryName))
        {
            return null;
        }

        // Get category.
        PerformanceCounterCategory category =
            new PerformanceCounterCategory(categoryName);

        // Check for multi-instance property.
        if (category.CategoryType == PerformanceCounterCategoryType.MultiInstance)
        {
            return null;
        }

        // Return counters.
        return category.GetCounters();
    }

    public static void FillRow(object counter, out string counterName,
        out double categoryValue)
    {
        // Obtain column information from counter.
        counterName = (counter as PerformanceCounter).CounterName;
        categoryValue = (counter as PerformanceCounter).NextValue();
    }
}
```

7. Compile the project.

8. Return to SQL Server Management Studio and create another new query for the `FolktaleDB` database. Add SQL code as follows:

```sql
USE FolktaleDB
GO

CREATE ASSEMBLY Ex1102 FROM
  'C:\BegVC#Databases\Chapter11\Ex1102 - Table Functions\bin\Release\
Ex1102 - Table Functions.dll'
WITH PERMISSION_SET = UNSAFE
GO

CREATE FUNCTION dbo.GetCounters(@CategoryName nvarchar(250))
RETURNS TABLE (CounterName nvarchar(1000),CounterValue float)
AS
```

```
        EXTERNAL NAME Ex1102.Functions.Initialize
        GO

        SELECT * FROM dbo.GetCounters('Server')
        GO

        DROP FUNCTION dbo.GetCounters
        DROP ASSEMBLY Ex1102
        GO
```

9. Save the query as `CallFunction.sql` in the `C:\BegVC#Databases\Chapter11\Ex1102 - Table Functions` directory.

10. Execute the query. A portion of the result is shown in Figure 11-5.

11. Close SQL Server Management Studio Express and Visual C# Express.

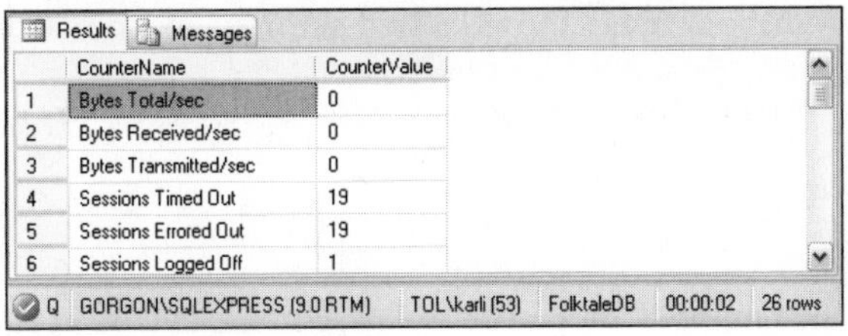

Figure 11-5: Query result

How It Works

This example uses code from the `System.Diagnostics` namespace to create a function that returns the performance counters in a specified category. Because of the nature of this operation, the assembly must use the `UNSAFE` permission set, and the first part of the example configures the database to allow it. Rather than signing the assembly and assigning it the rights required (which is more complicated and beyond the scope of this book), you configure the database to allow the code to execute (using the `TRUSTWORTHY` database setting), and the owner of the database is set to an account with the required privileges — in this case, the `sa` (system administrator) account. In a production environment, you probably wouldn't want to take this approach because without being 100 percent sure about to the functionality of the .NET assembly, you could risk data corruption and/or server crashes. For illustrating an `UNSAFE` assembly, however, this is fine.

These database changes require SQL code to change the database setting, and the `sp_changedbowner` system stored procedure to change the database owner:

```
ALTER DATABASE FolktaleDB SET TRUSTWORTHY ON
EXEC sp_changedbowner 'sa'
```

As with the modification in the previous example, these changes persist, so there's no need to save the SQL script.

Next, you created the code for the assembly, starting with the initializing method, `Initialize()`:

```
[SqlFunction(IsDeterministic = false, IsPrecise = false,
    DataAccess = DataAccessKind.None,
    SystemDataAccess = SystemDataAccessKind.None,
    FillRowMethodName = "FillRow")]
public static IEnumerable Initialize(string categoryName)
{
```

This method is linked to the row filling method, `FillRow()`, using the `FillRowMethodName` property as described earlier. It is also marked as not accessing database data, not precise (because floating-point values are returned), and non-deterministic because results may change even if the parameters and database state stay the same.

You may not be familiar with some of the code for examining performance counters, and it is not the job of this book to describe it fully. However, it is fairly self-descriptive and relatively easy to understand. The method starts by checking whether the requested performance counter category exists:

```
if (!PerformanceCounterCategory.Exists(categoryName))
{
    return null;
}
```

If it doesn't, no results are returned. If it does, a `PerformanceCounterCategory` object is created to access the category:

```
PerformanceCounterCategory category =
    new PerformanceCounterCategory(categoryName);
```

To simplify things, `FillRow()` ignores performance categories having multiple instances (for example, instances for each user session in some cases):

```
if (category.CategoryType == PerformanceCounterCategoryType.MultiInstance)
{
    return null;
}
```

Finally, the counters in the category are obtained in the form of an array of `PerformanceCounter` objects. Arrays support the `IEnumerable` interface, so that's a valid object to return:

```
    return category.GetCounters();
}
```

Each `PerformanceCounter` object has a string name and floating-point value, and it is the job of the `FillRow()` method to extract that information and return it. The method signature of this method defines output parameters of the required types:

```
public static void FillRow(object counter, out string counterName,
    out double categoryValue)
{
```

The method implementation is simple — it just uses the `CounterName` and `NextValue()` members of the `PerformanceCounter` class to extract and return the required information:

```
counterName = (counter as PerformanceCounter).CounterName;
categoryValue = (counter as PerformanceCounter).NextValue();
}
```

The SQL code to load, use, and unload this code is similar to that used in the previous example, although the assembly name and path are different, as well as the `CREATE FUNCTION` specification:

```
CREATE FUNCTION dbo.GetCounters(@CategoryName nvarchar(250))
RETURNS TABLE (CounterName nvarchar(1000),CounterValue float)
AS
EXTERNAL NAME Ex1102.Functions.Initialize
```

Here, a table specification matching the output parameters of the `FillRow()` method is required. Note that, although the second column type is `double` in the C# code, the equivalent type in SQL Server is `float` due to differences in the type definitions. The SQL Server documentation contains a complete list of equivalent types , so it's easy enough to find out which type to use if you are unsure.

The result of the function call is to obtain a table with performance counter names and values. That is yet another thing that would be practically impossible to achieve in other ways, and yet surprisingly simple C# code is all that is needed.

Aggregate Functions

Aggregate functions, as you have seen in previous chapters, are those that operate on multiple values and return a single value. For example, you can use the `COUNT()` aggregate function to count rows, and the `SUM()` aggregate function to obtain the sum of multiple values. You can create aggregate functions with CLR integration code, although the process required is rather more complex than for scalar or table-valued functions.

To create an aggregate function means creating a class definition that contains four instance (that is, non-static) methods. When you register your code in SQL Server, you supply the name of the class, as you will see a little later, and SQL Server implements the aggregate function using the methods you have supplied.

The reason that a class is required is that individual calls are made to your methods at certain times, including each time a new value is found to be included in the function call. This means that, between calls, an object of the class you supply is persisted. That has two important implications. The first is that you can use class members to store state between method calls. The second is that the class must be serializable. When you define your class, you may have to add additional code to provide for that.

To define a class for use as an aggregate function, you must use the `SqlUserDefinedAggregate` attribute, which has the properties described in the following table.

Property	Usage
Format	Determines how the class should be serialized. If your class has only value type members, you can set this property to `Format.Native`, and SQL Server takes care of serialization for you. Alternatively, you can use `Format.UserDefined` and handle serialization by implementing the `IBinarySerialize` interface. This is a common option because of the prevalence of reference types such as `string`. The property is mandatory, and should be specified first, before the named attribute property list.
IsInvariantToDuplicates	A Boolean that states whether the result of the aggregate function can be affected if duplicate values are passed to the function. For example, the `COUNT()` aggregate function would use a value of `false` for this attribute because duplicate values would be counted, while `MAX()` would use `true` because only a single input value is used to generate the result.
IsInvariantToNulls	A Boolean that says whether `null` input values will affect the result (compared to the same input without the `null` values). Again, `COUNT()` still counts `null` values, so would use `false`, while `MAX()` would use `true`.
IsInvariantToOrder	Not currently used by SQL Server because there's no guarantee of the order of values passed to the aggregate function.
IsNullIfEmpty	Set to `true` if the aggregate function returns a `null` value if no input values are passed to the function.
MaxByteSize	This `int` property specifies the maximum amount of storage that the class will use to store its serialized data in bytes. It depends on the processing required. For instance, if you are storing only a single `int` field, you need only a few bytes, but strings might need a lot more. The maximum value is `8000` bytes.

As with `SqlFunction`, *the* `SqlUserDefinedAggregate` *attribute also has a* `Name` *property, but it isn't used in Visual C# Express.*

For example, you might define a class for use as an aggregate function as follows:

```
[SqlUserDefinedAggregate(Format.UserDefined,
    IsInvariantToDuplicates = true, IsInvariantToNulls = true,
    IsNullIfEmpty = true, MaxByteSize = 8000)]
public class MyAggregateFunction : IBinarySerialize
```

Here the `Format.UserDefined` serialization is used — hence the class must implement the `IBinarySerialize` interface, which means implementing the two `IBinarySerialize` methods `Read()` and `Write()`. You'll see how to do this in the Try It Out at the end of this section.

The definition of an aggregate function involves two data types. One is the data type of the input values, and the other is the data type of the result of the aggregate function — these may, of course, both be the same. The four methods that you have to implement to define an aggregate function are described in the following table, where the input and result data types are shown as `InputType` and `ResultType` in the function signatures. As with other function types, these types should have SQL Server data type equivalents to be used in SQL code. The class name of the aggregate function definition is shown as `AggregateClass`. All the functions must be public.

Function Signature	Usage
`void Init();`	Called once when the aggregate function is about to process data; use it to initialize any internal storage, clear stored values, and so on. The same aggregate object instance may be used more than once by SQL Server, so this method should take that into account and clear any existing state if necessary.
`void Accumulate(InputType val);`	Called after `Init()`, once for each value being processed (if any).
`void Merge(AggregateClass source);`	SQL Server may process aggregate functions in sections, each of which will use a separate instance of the aggregate function class. To obtain a complete result, these instances must be combined using this method. For that reason, you may need to provide access to internal state in your class definition so you can use it here.
`ResultType Terminate();`	Called after all values have been processed and (if necessary) all partial results combined. It completes the processing of internal state and returns a result.

For example, consider the `SUM()` aggregate function, and think about how you would mimic it using these four methods for, say, integer values. First, you would define an integer field to store a running total. The field would be set to 0 in the `Init()` method. Each call to `Accumulate()` would pass an integer parameter, which you would add to the running total. The `Merge()` function would take the running total from one instance of the aggregate function class and add it to the current running total. Finally, `Terminate()` would simply return the current running total.

While having to implement all of these methods does complicate things, the structure is logical — and flexible. Often the hardest thing to do is to decide how you will go about serializing your aggregate function objects, which will be illustrated shortly.

Once you have created, compiled, and loaded your assembly into SQL Server, the next step as always is to use the code in an aggregate function. To do so, you use a CREATE AGGREGATE statement as follows:

```
CREATE AGGREGATE dbo.MyAggregate(@ParameterName sqlInputType)
RETURNS sqlResultType
EXTERNAL NAME MyAssembly.MyClass
```

There are also associate ALTER AGGREGATE and DROP AGGREGATE functions.

Try It Out   Creating a CLR Integrated Aggregate Function

1. Open Visual C# Express and create a new class library project called Ex1103 - Aggregate Functions. Save the project in the C:\BegVC#Databases\Chapter11 directory, with the Create Directory For Solution option unchecked.

2. Remove the auto-generated Class1.cs file and add a new class called FirstLetters with code modifications as follows (note that this code goes in the global namespace):

    . . .

```
using Microsoft.SqlServer.Server;
using System.IO;
```

    . . .

```
[SqlUserDefinedAggregate(Format.UserDefined,
    IsInvariantToDuplicates = true, IsInvariantToNulls = true,
    IsNullIfEmpty = true, MaxByteSize = 54)]
public class FirstLetters : IBinarySerialize
{
    // Internal storage.
    private List<char> currentState;

    public List<char> CurrentState
    {
        get
        {
            return currentState;
        }
    }

    public void Init()
    {
        // Create fresh state.
        currentState = new List<char>();
    }

    public void Accumulate(string val)
    {
        // Chack val, add new letter if necessary.
        if (val != null && val.Length > 0 && char.IsLetter(val[0])
            && !currentState.Contains(val.ToUpper()[0]))
        {
            currentState.Add(val.ToUpper()[0]);
```

```
            }
        }

        public void Merge(FirstLetters source)
        {
            // Add letters from source to current letters.
            foreach (char sourceChar in source.CurrentState)
            {
                if (!currentState.Contains(sourceChar))
                {
                    currentState.Add(sourceChar);
                }
            }
        }

        public string Terminate()
        {
            // Sort data.
            currentState.Sort();

            // Make string from data.
            StringBuilder sb = new StringBuilder();
            foreach (char letter in currentState)
            {
                sb.Append(letter);
                sb.Append(",");
            }
            string result = sb.ToString();

            // Trim trailing comma and return string.
            result = result.Substring(0, result.Length - 1);
            return result;
        }

        public void Read(BinaryReader r)
        {
            // Get stored string and build List<char> from it.
            string serializedState = r.ReadString();
            currentState = new List<char>(serializedState.ToCharArray());
        }

        public void Write(BinaryWriter w)
        {
            // Get storage string as concatenated list of letters.
            string serializedState = new string(currentState.ToArray());
            w.Write(serializedState);
        }
    }
}
```

3. Compile the project.

4. Open SQL Server Management Studio Express and connect to your local SQL Server Express instance.

5. Return to SQL Server Management Studio and create a new query for the `FolktaleDB` database. Add SQL code as follows:

```
USE FolktaleDB
GO

CREATE ASSEMBLY Ex1103 FROM
   'C:\BegVC#Databases\Chapter11\Ex1103 - Aggregate Functions\bin\Release\
Ex1103 - Aggregate Functions.dll'
WITH PERMISSION_SET = SAFE
GO

CREATE AGGREGATE dbo.GetFirstLetters(@input nvarchar(1000)) RETURNS
nvarchar(51)
EXTERNAL NAME Ex1103.FirstLetters
GO

SELECT dbo.GetFirstLetters(Name) AS FirstLetters FROM Character
GO

DROP AGGREGATE dbo.GetFirstLetters
DROP ASSEMBLY Ex1103
GO
```

6. Save the query as `CallFunction.sql` in the `C:\BegVC#Databases\Chapter11\Ex1103 - Aggregate Functions` directory.

7. Execute the query. The result is shown in Figure 11-6.

Figure 11-6: Query result

8. Close SQL Server Management Studio Express and Visual C# Express.

How It Works

This example creates an aggregate function using CLR integrated .NET code. The function takes a collection of string values and makes a list of all the first letters of those string values, in the form of a list of uppercase letters separated by commas.

The code for the `FirstLetters` class, which defines the aggregate function, uses a reference as its internal storage, so you must use the `Format.UserDefined` formatting option and implement the `IBinarySerialize` interface. Also, you can say that duplicate or `null` values won't make a difference to the result, that a `null` value will be returned for no data, and that the maximum storage size is 54 bytes. That last fact is something you examine in more depth when you look at the serialization methods, `Read()` and `Write()`, for the class. This leads to the following class definition:

```
[SqlUserDefinedAggregate(Format.UserDefined,
    IsInvariantToDuplicates = true, IsInvariantToNulls = true,
```

```
        IsNullIfEmpty = true, MaxByteSize = 54)]
    public class FirstLetters : IBinarySerialize
    {
```

Next, the code defines a store for the letters found, in the form of a generic List<char> class:

```
        private List<char> currentState;
```

To merge results, this storage is exposed as a public, read-only property:

```
        public List<char> CurrentState
        {
            get
            {
                return currentState;
            }
        }
```

The Init() method for this class simply needs to set the state field, currentState, to a new instance of List<char>:

```
        public void Init()
        {
            currentState = new List<char>();
        }
```

In Accumulate(), you must make several checks before adding letters to the currentState collection. You need to check whether the input string is null, whether it is an empty string, whether the first character is a letter, and whether the first character already exists in the currentState collection. If any of these are the case, the value is ignored; otherwise the letter is added to the collection:

```
        public void Accumulate(string val)
        {
            if (val != null && val.Length > 0 && char.IsLetter(val[0])
                && !currentState.Contains(val.ToUpper()[0]))
            {
                currentState.Add(val.ToUpper()[0]);
            }
        }
```

The string.ToUpper() method is used so that only uppercase letters are stored.

To merge data in the Merge() method, the CurrentState property of the source FirstLetters object is interrogated, and any letters it contains that don't already exist in currentState are added:

```
        public void Merge(FirstLetters source)
        {
            foreach (char sourceChar in source.CurrentState)
            {
                if (!currentState.Contains(sourceChar))
                {
```

```
            currentState.Add(sourceChar);
        }
    }
}
```

The last of the four aggregate functions is `Terminate()`, which returns a string value based on the data stored. First, the characters are sorted alphabetically (using the default comparer):

```
public string Terminate()
{
    currentState.Sort();
```

Then the characters are assembled into a comma-separated string and the result returned:

```
    StringBuilder sb = new StringBuilder();
    foreach (char letter in currentState)
    {
        sb.Append(letter);
        sb.Append(",");
    }
    string result = sb.ToString();
    result = result.Substring(0, result.Length - 1);
    return result;
}
```

Next you have the serialization methods. Here, the data stored in `currentState` is converted into a string — not a comma-separated string in this case, to save memory. That means the maximum string length for serialized data is 26 characters — the number of letters in the alphabet. Allowing 2 bytes for each character, plus a further two for overhead, makes a total of 54 bytes, which is why the maximum amount of storage defined earlier is 54 bytes. Note that an assumption is made here that the English alphabet is used — if you want to include accented letters and so on, you need to increase this value.

With this storage scheme, all you have to do to read data is read a string from the `BinaryReader` object passed to the `Read()` method and use it to initialize a `List<char>` object:

```
public void Read(BinaryReader r)
{
    string serializedState = r.ReadString();
    currentState = new List<char>(serializedState.ToCharArray());
}
```

Similarly, to write data in the `Write()` method, you obtain the contents of `currentState` as a `char[]` object, use that to initialize a string, and write the result to the supplied `BinaryWriter()`:

```
public void Write(BinaryWriter w)
{
    string serializedState = new string(currentState.ToArray());
    w.Write(serializedState);
}
}
```

As with earlier examples, all this code is fairly simple.

In SQL Server Management Studio Express you add the assembly in the standard way (using the SAFE permission set, so no additional configuration is required). Next a CREATE AGGREGATE function is used to define an aggregate function called GetFirstLetters() using your code:

```
CREATE AGGREGATE dbo.GetFirstLetters(@input nvarchar(1000)) RETURNS nvarchar(51)
EXTERNAL NAME Ex1103.FirstLetters
GO
```

Note that the nvarchar data type is used as in previous examples. Also, the return type maximum length is 51 characters. That's one for each letter plus one for each comma that goes between the letters.

Once added, it's simple to use the new aggregate function to obtain the first letters used in the Name field in the Character table:

```
SELECT dbo.GetFirstLetters(Name) AS FirstLetters FROM Character
GO
```

While aggregate functions require a little more work to set up, they are capable of powerful statistical analysis. The existing set of aggregate functions is useful already, but there is scope for plenty more — especially in string manipulation, as in this example.

Stored Procedures

Writing CLR stored procedures is a lot like writing functions; the main difference is that you can do a lot more with the stored procedures, including modifying database data. Stored procedures perform quite a lot of database access, and generally make the task of database access much simpler. When you write them in C#, you have even more flexibility because you can combine their functionality with other areas of the .NET Framework, similar to the function examples earlier in this chapter.

Writing a stored procedure means supplying a single static method, much like a scalar function. You use the attribute SqlProcedure, which has the single property Name. As with the SqlFunction attribute, this property is really used only by Visual Studio, so when developing in Visual C# Express, you can omit it. In fact, you can omit the attribute altogether if you want — default values are assumed, and the attribute is not mandatory.

Many stored procedures use a return value to indicate a return status. If you want to do that, you can make the method you define have an int return value. If you use a void method instead, a status code of 0 is returned automatically.

Stored procedures can also have output parameters. All you have to do to enable that in your C# code is to use an out parameter. Note, however, that SQL types are all nullable, while .NET value types are not. That means that you may have to use types in the System.Data.SqlTypes namespace, and you may also want to use generic nullable types in your code.

Other than that, you already know about all the building blocks required for a stored procedure. So, without further ado, here's an example to work through illustrating all of the preceding.

445

Creating a CLR Stored Procedure

1. Open Visual C# Express and create a new class library project called Ex1104 - Stored
    Procedures. Save the project in the C:\BegVC#Databases\Chapter11 directory, with the
    Create Directory For Solution option unchecked.

2. Remove the auto-generated Class1.cs file and add a new class called Sprocs with code modifi-
    cations as follows (note that this code goes in the global namespace):

    . . .

```csharp
using Microsoft.SqlServer.Server;
using System.Data;
using System.Data.SqlTypes;
using System.Data.SqlClient;
```

    . . .

```csharp
public enum ReturnValue
{
    OK = 0,
    NoStory,
    LocationExists,
    UnknownError
}
```

```csharp
public class Sprocs
{
    [SqlProcedure]
    public static int AddStoryLocation(Guid storyId, string location,
        out SqlGuid locationId)
    {
        // Init locationId to null value before processing.
        locationId = SqlGuid.Null;

        try
        {
            // Check data and process addition.
            using (SqlConnection conn =
                new SqlConnection("context connection=true"))
            {
                // Verify that story exists.
                SqlCommand getStoryCmd = new SqlCommand(
                    "SELECT Name FROM Story WHERE StoryId = @StoryId", conn);
                getStoryCmd.Parameters.Add(new SqlParameter("@StoryId",
                    SqlDbType.UniqueIdentifier)).Value = storyId;
                conn.Open();
                string storyName = getStoryCmd.ExecuteScalar() as string;
                conn.Close();

                // If no story exists, return message and exit.
                if (storyName == null)
                {
                    SqlContext.Pipe.Send("No story with an ID of "
                        + storyId.ToString() + " exists. Unable to add location.");
```

```
        return (int)ReturnValue.NoStory;
}

// Look for existing location.
SqlCommand getLocationCmd = new SqlCommand(
    "SELECT LocationId FROM Location WHERE Location = @Location",
    conn);
getLocationCmd.Parameters.Add(new SqlParameter("@Location",
    SqlDbType.VarChar, 100)).Value = location;
conn.Open();
Guid? existingLocationId = getLocationCmd.ExecuteScalar() as Guid?;
conn.Close();

if (existingLocationId.HasValue)
{
    // Set locationId
    locationId = existingLocationId.Value;

    // If location exists, check for existing story location.
    SqlCommand getStoryLocationCmd = new SqlCommand(
        "SELECT StoryLocationId FROM StoryLocation "
        + "WHERE StoryId = @StoryId AND LocationId = @LocationId",
        conn);
    getStoryLocationCmd.Parameters.Add(new SqlParameter("@StoryId",
        SqlDbType.UniqueIdentifier)).Value = storyId;
    getStoryLocationCmd.Parameters.Add(new SqlParameter(
        "@LocationId", SqlDbType.UniqueIdentifier)).Value =
        locationId.Value;
    conn.Open();
    Guid? existingStoryLocationId =
        getStoryLocationCmd.ExecuteScalar() as Guid?;
    conn.Close();

    // If story location exists, return message and exit.
    if (existingStoryLocationId.HasValue)
    {
        SqlContext.Pipe.Send("Story already has the " + location
            + " location.");
        return (int)ReturnValue.LocationExists;
    }
}
else
{
    // If location doesn't exist, add it and get its ID.
    SqlCommand insertLocationCmd = new SqlCommand(
        "INSERT INTO Location (Location) VALUES (@Location)",
        conn);
    insertLocationCmd.Parameters.Add(new SqlParameter("@Location",
        SqlDbType.VarChar, 100)).Value = location;
    conn.Open();
    insertLocationCmd.ExecuteNonQuery();
    existingLocationId = getLocationCmd.ExecuteScalar() as Guid?;
    conn.Close();
```

```
                                    // Set locationId
                                    locationId = existingLocationId.Value;

                                    // Report addition.
                                    SqlContext.Pipe.Send("The " + location
                                        + " location did not exist, it has been added.");
                                }

                                // Add StoryLocation.
                                SqlCommand insertStoryLocationCmd = new SqlCommand(
                                    "INSERT INTO StoryLocation (StoryId, LocationId) "
                                    + "VALUES (@StoryId, @LocationId)", conn);
                                insertStoryLocationCmd.Parameters.Add(new SqlParameter("@StoryId",
                                    SqlDbType.UniqueIdentifier)).Value = storyId;
                                insertStoryLocationCmd.Parameters.Add(new SqlParameter(
                                    "@LocationId", SqlDbType.UniqueIdentifier)).Value =
                                    locationId.Value;
                                conn.Open();
                                insertStoryLocationCmd.ExecuteNonQuery();
                                conn.Close();

                                // Report addition.
                                SqlContext.Pipe.Send("Story location added.");
                            }
                        }
                        catch (Exception ex)
                        {
                            // Return error and status.
                            SqlContext.Pipe.Send("An exception occurred. Message: " + ex.Message);
                            return (int)ReturnValue.UnknownError;
                        }

                        // Return status of OK.
                        return (int)ReturnValue.OK;
                    }
                }
```

3. Compile the project.

4. Open SQL Server Management Studio Express and connect to your local SQL Server Express instance.

5. Return to SQL Server Management Studio and create a new query for the FolktaleDB database. Add SQL code as follows:

```
USE FolktaleDB
GO

CREATE ASSEMBLY Ex1104 FROM
    'C:\BegVC#Databases\Chapter11\Ex1104 - Stored Procedures\bin\Release\
Ex1104 - Stored Procedures.dll'
WITH PERMISSION_SET = SAFE
GO

CREATE PROCEDURE dbo.AddStoryLocation
```

```
(
    @storyId uniqueidentifier,
    @location nvarchar(100),
    @locationId uniqueidentifier OUTPUT
)
AS EXTERNAL NAME Ex1104.Sprocs.AddStoryLocation
GO

DECLARE @storyId uniqueidentifier
DECLARE @location nvarchar(100)
DECLARE @locationId uniqueidentifier
DECLARE @result int

SET @storyId = 'da47837d-c6a5-490b-96cf-808137d0e760'
SET @location = 'Jungle'

EXEC @result = dbo.AddStoryLocation @storyId, @location, @locationId OUTPUT

SELECT @result AS StatusCode, @locationId AS LocationId
GO

DROP PROCEDURE dbo.AddStoryLocation
DROP ASSEMBLY Ex1104
GO
```

6. Save the query as `CallSproc.sql` in the `C:\BegVC#Databases\Chapter11\Ex1104 - Stored Procedures` directory.

7. Execute the query. The result is shown in Figure 11-7.

Figure 11-7: Query result

8. Click the Messages tab, and note the messages, as shown in Figure 11-8.

Figure 11-8: Query output messages

9. Execute the query again, and note the changes in both the output and the messages you receive. These are shown in Figures 11-9 and 11-10.

Figure 11-9: Second query result

Figure 11-10: Second query output messages

10. Close SQL Server Management Studio Express and Visual C# Express.

How It Works

This example creates a stored procedure that adds a location to a story by adding data to the
`StoryLocation` table. The story is specified by ID and the location by name. Additional logic provides
for the following situations that may arise:

❑ Attempting to add a location to a non-existent story

❑ Attempting to add a non-existent location to a story

❑ Attempting to add a location to a story that already has that location

You see how these are handled as you work through the code.

The code starts with a definition for an enumeration, `ReturnValue`:

```
public enum ReturnValue
{
    OK = 0,
    NoStory,
    LocationExists,
    UnknownError
}
```

The enumeration records the status values that the stored procedure can return. They map to the integer
values 0–3, and you can return the associated `int` value simply by casting a value of that type to an `int`.
That makes it easier to keep track of your return values in the rest of your code.

The stored procedure itself — `AddStoryLocation()` — is a method of a class called `Sprocs`. The
method has an `int` return type and three parameters. The first is a `Guid` value used to identify the story
to add a location for. The second is a `string` value giving the location name. The third is an output
parameter that's used to pass the ID of the location used back to the client. The ID is either the ID of an

existing location or the ID of a newly added location if the location name doesn't already exist. Because this property might not get set, either deliberately or because of errors, you must be able to give it a null value, so the Guid value type is not suitable here. Guid? is also not appropriate because it won't be recognized in SQL Server. Instead, you use the SqlGuid class from the System.Data.SqlTypes namespace:

```
public class Sprocs
{
    [SqlProcedure]
    public static int AddStoryLocation(Guid storyId, string location,
        out SqlGuid locationId)
    {
```

The code starts by setting the output parameter to a null value (SqlGuid.Null) in case of error:

```
locationId = SqlGuid.Null;
```

The remaining code is placed in a try...catch structure to accommodate errors. First, a context connection is created, along with an associated using block:

```
try
{
    using (SqlConnection conn =
        new SqlConnection("context connection=true"))
    {
```

The context connection and story ID are then used to check if the specified story ID refers to an existing row in the Story table. The code attempts to obtain the name of the story as a simple test, and executes the generated command using the ExecuteScalar() method to retrieve the name:

```
SqlCommand getStoryCmd = new SqlCommand(
    "SELECT Name FROM Story WHERE StoryId = @StoryId", conn);
getStoryCmd.Parameters.Add(new SqlParameter("@StoryId",
    SqlDbType.UniqueIdentifier)).Value = storyId;
conn.Open();
string storyName = getStoryCmd.ExecuteScalar() as string;
conn.Close();
```

The connection remains open only for the minimum time — just while the command executes. That's common to all the code in this method, and ensures that the context connection is used as efficiently as possible.

If there is no story, a name won't be returned. If that happens, it's reported using the SqlContext.Pipe.Send() method that you saw earlier in the chapter, and the method terminates with the appropriate status report, ReturnValue.NoStory:

```
if (storyName == null)
{
    SqlContext.Pipe.Send("No story with an ID of "
        + storyId.ToString() + " exists. Unable to add location.");
    return (int)ReturnValue.NoStory;
}
```

If the story exists, the next step is to check whether the specified location exists in the Location table. That uses similar code, but retrieves a GUID ID rather than a string value. Again, the query may return null, and because you can't use a Guid variable to store a null value, you use the generic nullable type Guid? to store the query result:

```
SqlCommand getLocationCmd = new SqlCommand(
    "SELECT LocationId FROM Location WHERE Location = @Location",
    conn);
getLocationCmd.Parameters.Add(new SqlParameter("@Location",
    SqlDbType.VarChar, 100)).Value = location;
conn.Open();
Guid? existingLocationId = getLocationCmd.ExecuteScalar() as Guid?;
conn.Close();
```

Generic nullable types have a HasValue property to check for null values. You use it to see if there is an existing location, and if there is, you set the output locationId parameter using the Guid?.Value property:

```
if (existingLocationId.HasValue)
{
    locationId = existingLocationId.Value;
```

If both the story and location exist, it's possible that there is already a row in the StoryLocation table that links these records. To avoid duplication, the next step checks for such a row by filtering the data by the IDs of the story and location. Again, a Guid? variable is used to obtain the result:

```
SqlCommand getStoryLocationCmd = new SqlCommand(
    "SELECT StoryLocationId FROM StoryLocation "
    + "WHERE StoryId = @StoryId AND LocationId = @LocationId",
    conn);
getStoryLocationCmd.Parameters.Add(new SqlParameter("@StoryId",
    SqlDbType.UniqueIdentifier)).Value = storyId;
getStoryLocationCmd.Parameters.Add(new SqlParameter(
    "@LocationId", SqlDbType.UniqueIdentifier)).Value =
    locationId.Value;
conn.Open();
Guid? existingStoryLocationId =
    getStoryLocationCmd.ExecuteScalar() as Guid?;
conn.Close();
```

If the StoryLocation table already contains an entry, there's nothing more to do. That being the case, the code reports the result and exits, returning the ReturnValue.LocationExists status code:

```
if (existingStoryLocationId.HasValue)
{
    SqlContext.Pipe.Send("Story already has the " + location
        + " location.");
    return (int)ReturnValue.LocationExists;
}
}
```

Alternatively, it's possible that the story exists but the location doesn't. In that case, you add a new row to the `Location` table and then retrieve the ID of the new row. The second part, retrieving the row ID, can use the command you created earlier because the location names will match:

```
else
{
    SqlCommand insertLocationCmd = new SqlCommand(
        "INSERT INTO Location (Location) VALUES (@Location)",
        conn);
    insertLocationCmd.Parameters.Add(new SqlParameter("@Location",
        SqlDbType.VarChar, 100)).Value = location;
    conn.Open();
    insertLocationCmd.ExecuteNonQuery();
    existingLocationId = getLocationCmd.ExecuteScalar() as Guid?;
    conn.Close();
```

Now that you know the location ID, you can set the output parameter:

```
    locationId = existingLocationId.Value;
```

The code then sends the client a message to say that a new location has been added. That isn't essential, but provides useful feedback. A client receiving the message might want to update cached data from the `Location` table. For example:

```
    SqlContext.Pipe.Send("The " + location
        + " location did not exist, it has been added.");
}
```

Regardless of whether the location already exists, or whether the location was added, the final database operation is to add a row to the `StoryLocation` table to link the `Story` and `Location` table rows. That uses familiar code:

```
    SqlCommand insertStoryLocationCmd = new SqlCommand(
        "INSERT INTO StoryLocation (StoryId, LocationId) "
        + "VALUES (@StoryId, @LocationId)", conn);
    insertStoryLocationCmd.Parameters.Add(new SqlParameter("@StoryId",
        SqlDbType.UniqueIdentifier)).Value = storyId;
    insertStoryLocationCmd.Parameters.Add(new SqlParameter(
        "@LocationId", SqlDbType.UniqueIdentifier)).Value =
        locationId.Value;
    conn.Open();
    insertStoryLocationCmd.ExecuteNonQuery();
    conn.Close();
```

A message is also sent to confirm the addition of the story location:

```
    SqlContext.Pipe.Send("Story location added.");
    }
}
```

If an exception occurs at any point in the code, the method includes simple exception-handling code to report the problem and terminate with a status code of `ReturnValue.UnknownError`. You could, of course, include much more error-checking code here to analyze the exception and report in a more specific way — or perhaps even deal with the error and try accessing the database again. That code isn't included here, purely for brevity:

```
catch (Exception ex)
{
    // Return error and status.
    SqlContext.Pipe.Send("An exception occurred. Message: " + ex.Message);
    return (int)ReturnValue.UnknownError;
}
```

Finally, knowing that everything has gone as planned and that no errors occurred, you can terminate the method by returning the status code `ReturnValue.OK` (which has the integer value 0):

```
        return (int)ReturnValue.OK;
    }
}
```

Okay, so that was quite a lot of code to get through, but again, this method provides a lot of functionality. You could write the same stored procedure in SQL — there is nothing .NET-specific here. However, the SQL version of the stored procedure would surely be harder to construct because it's much easier to write .NET code. .NET code is also relatively easy to debug because you can test it in a client application first and place it in an assembly for CLR integration only when you are 100 percent sure that it does what you want it to. Debugging SQL code is notoriously difficult by comparison.

Anyway, having created the assembly, you loaded it into SQL Server and define a stored procedure. You've seen how to define SQL stored procedures in some depth already in this book; the only new thing here is the use of the AS EXTERNAL NAME clause to link the stored procedure to your code:

```
CREATE PROCEDURE dbo.AddStoryLocation
(
    @storyId uniqueidentifier,
    @location nvarchar(100),
    @locationId uniqueidentifier OUTPUT
)
AS EXTERNAL NAME Ex1104.Sprocs.AddStoryLocation
```

Calling the stored procedure from SQL code also uses familiar syntax. For ease of use, variables are first declared for the parameters and return value:

```
DECLARE @storyId uniqueidentifier
DECLARE @location nvarchar(100)
DECLARE @locationId uniqueidentifier
DECLARE @result int
```

Next, the two input parameters are assigned values:

```
SET @storyId = 'da47837d-c6a5-490b-96cf-808137d0e760'
SET @location = 'Jungle'
```

And then the stored procedure is executed:

```
EXEC @result = dbo.AddStoryLocation @storyId, @location, @locationId OUTPUT
```

To report the results, a SELECT query is used to display both the status code and output parameter:

```
SELECT @result AS StatusCode, @locationId AS LocationId
```

To view the messages returned, you had to use the alternate result view by clicking the Messages tab.

I hope you'll agree that this is a nice programming model, and probably one that you'll use frequently. You may even decide that this way of creating stored procedures is preferable to writing them in SQL code in all situations, and that wouldn't be a bad decision. There are so many advantages, from additional capabilities, through simpler syntax, to easier debugging, that it's difficult not to get a little bit excited about this technique. The simpler coding is offset slightly by the additional steps required to deploy CLR integration assemblies, but then those steps are hardly difficult. It takes only a few SQL commands to get up and running, and the results are fantastic.

Summary

This chapter looked at CLR integration, which is a way to write .NET code that runs inside SQL Server. You learned the basics, and moved on to experiment with .NET code to implement functions and stored procedures. To summarize, you learned how:

❑   .NET features can extend the functionality available in SQL Server, and how writing various database object in C# can simplify your development.

❑   CLR integration works, including how to enable CLR integration in SQL Server, and how to load and remove .NET assemblies to and from a database. You also looked at the requirements of CLR code, including what .NET assemblies are available to you by default, and what C# programming elements to avoid (such as destructors).

❑   To register .NET types and methods for use in SQL Server.

❑   To use context connections to access the local database, and how to use the SqlPipe class to send data to the client. You also explored common features available to you from CLR integrated code.

❑   To create scalar, table-valued, and aggregate functions. You looked at the code structures required to implement the various function types and the attributes to control them, and you learned how to register each function type and use it within SQL Server.

❑   To create stored procedures. You saw how to combine the power and flexibility of .NET code with SQL stored procedures. This illustrated how complicated operations involving extensive data access and logic are much easier to create with C# than with SQL.

This is the last chapter in this book, and now you are equipped with all the tools you need to create powerful database applications using C# and SQL Server. Although you have been using Express products, everything you have learned applies equally to the full versions of Visual Studio and SQL Server.

Many subjects in this book, including CLR integration, have been presented as starting points for you. You'll find a wealth of information, both online and in other books, that will enable you to expand your knowledge further. Getting a solid foundation in the fundamentals, and having at least basic exposure to more complicated subjects such as CLR integration, will stand you in good stead and make it much easier for you to progress further.

I wish you all the best in your quest to write perfect database applications. Thank you for reading!

Exercises

1. Which of the following can you create using CLR integrated .NET code?

    a. Views

    b. Aggregate functions

    c. User-defined types

    d. Table types

    e. Stored procedures

2. Outline the steps required to get .NET code running inside SQL Server.

3. How would you access data from CLR integrated code?

4. How would you send row data for a single row to client applications using `SqlContext`? Give the code to send a row consisting of a GUID ID column called `MyTableId` and an integer column called `MyAmount` to the client (with any column values you wish).

5. What attribute would you use to define a class for use as an aggregate function? What property of this attribute is mandatory, and how will it affect the code required for an aggregate function?

Installation

This appendix provides detailed, step-by-step instructions for installing all the programs you need to try out the examples in this book:

❑ Microsoft .NET Framework 2.0

❑ Visual C# 2005 Express Edition

❑ SQL Server 2005 Express Edition

❑ SQL Server Management Studio Express

❑ Visual Web Developer 2005 Express Edition

If you've never installed a program, this might seem quite daunting but don't worry — the process is simple, especially because you'll use default options so you won't have to do any configuration. And there's more good news — all of these programs are free to use.

This appendix contains a separate section for each program. However, you won't necessarily have to install each program individually. If you install Visual C# 2005 Express Edition, .NET Framework 2.0 is installed automatically, and you can also choose to install SQL Server 2005 Express Edition (as detailed later in the Visual C# section). If you already have Visual C# 2005 Express Edition installed without SQL Server 2005 Express Edition, you can install SQL Server separately

There are two very important points to note before you begin:

❑ If you have any previous versions of SQL Server, Visual Studio, or the .NET Framework 2.0 installed on your computer, you must uninstall them first. To avoid problems, the uninstallations must be performed in a specific order. See `http://msdn.microsoft.com/vstudio/express/support/uninstall` for details.

❑ You must have the current version of the .NET Framework 2.0 installed before you can install SQL Server 2005 Express Edition. To ensure that you have the correct version of the .NET Framework 2.0 installed, follow the subset of instructions you need in the order that they are listed in this appendix. If you already have the .NET Framework installed, you can check which version it is by going to Control Panel and using the Add or Remove Programs feature to examine the details of your installation.

.NET Framework 2.0

For the purposes of this book, the easiest way to install .NET Framework 2.0 is to install Visual C# 2005 Express Edition. However, should you ever need to install the .NET Framework independently, go to `http://msdn.microsoft.com/netframework/` and follow the instructions you find there.

Visual C# 2005 Express Edition

To install Visual C# 2005 Express Edition, follow these steps:

1. Go to `http://msdn.microsoft.com/vstudio/express` and click the link for Visual C# 2005 Express Edition. You'll find a product overview and a feature tour as well as a Download Now link.

2. Click Download Now. You're reminded about uninstallation, and receive information about registration and a download link for the installation file, `vcssetup.exe`.

3. Download the file and run it, or run it when prompted after you click the download link. You may see a security warning — if you do, click Run. The files extract to a temporary folder and then a dialog box appears, telling you that Setup is installing components. After the components are installed, the setup wizard opens, as shown in Figure A-1.

4. Click Next. Accept the license agreement (see Figure A-2) to continue installation, and click Next again.

5. Choose optional products: Microsoft MSDN 2005 Express Edition and SQL Server 2005 Express Edition. Obviously SQL Server is required for this book, but it's a good idea to select MSDN 2005 as well. (MSDN is Microsoft's documentation for all its technologies. In this instance you install only the relevant Visual C# and SQL Server information. You can access this information online, but you'll have faster access if you install it.) Click Next.

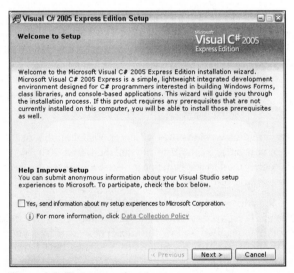

Figure A-1: The setup wizard

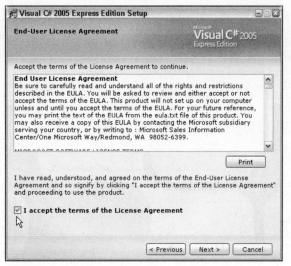

Figure A-2: The license agreement

6. The Destination Folder page (see Figure A-3) asks you to select an install location. Select the folder you want and click Install. (Figure A-3 shows a D:\ drive installation.)

7. The Download and Install Progress page (see Figure A-4) keeps you posted on the process. As you can see, the current version of the .NET Framework is installed automatically.

Figure A-3: The Destination Folder page

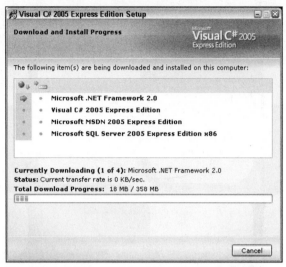

Figure A-4: The Download and Install Progress page

8. When the setup completes, you're notified that installation was successful and that you must register the software. The instructions onscreen tell you how to do this.

   If you decide to register later (you have to register within 30 days), you can use the Register Product option on the Help menu.

SQL Server Express

To download and install SQL Server 2005 Express Edition, follow these steps:

1. Go to `http://msdn.microsoft.com/vstudio/express` and click the link for SQL Server 2005 Express Edition.

2. Click Download Now. You're given a reminder about uninstallation, information about registration, and a selection of download options for SQL Server 2005 products. Under the Install SQL Server 2005 Express Edition heading, click the Download link.

3. When the download completes, open `sqlexpr.exe`. You may see a security warning — if you do, click Run. You have to accept the license agreement before you can proceed. Click Next.

4. The Installing Prerequisites page tells you what components have to be installed prior to SQL Server setup. An example is shown in Figure A-5.

   Follow the instructions onscreen. You're informed when the install has been successful.

5. Click Next to run a system configuration check. The results of the system check display, as shown in Figure A-6.

Figure A-5: The Installing Prerequisites page

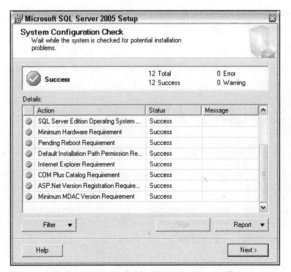

Figure A-6: System configuration check results

6. Click Next. The installation continues. When installation is complete, a registration information box automatically appears. (You don't have to put in your full name if you don't want to; a single word will do.)

7. Click Next to go to the Feature Selection page (see Figure A-7). You can leave the default features selected, but you may need to change the installation path according to the space on your hard drive. Use the Disk Cost button to see how much space you have available. Click Next.

8. The authentication mode is automatically set to Windows Authentication, and you can leave it as it is. Click Next.

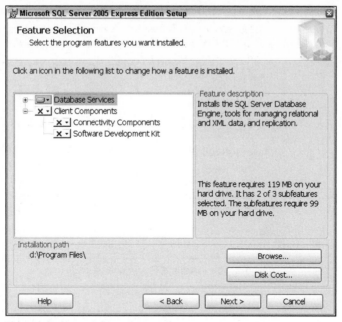

Figure A-7: Feature Selection page

9. All of the settings on the Error and Report Settings page are optional; you might decide you want them but you don't need them for this book. You're ready to install SQL Server. Click Next.

10. The Ready to Install page shows you details of the components that will be installed. Click Install. The Setup Progress page displays, as shown in Figure A-8.

Figure A-8: Setup Progress page

11. When the installation is complete, click Next. The following page contains information about Analysis Services, Reporting Services, Integration Services, Notification Services, and Documentation and Samples. There is also a link to a summary log for the installation, and a link to a Surface Area Configuration Tool that you can use to reduce the server surface area of SQL. However, you can just click Finish and you're done!

SQL Server Management Studio Express

To download and install SQL Server Management Studio Express, follow these steps:

1. Go to `http://msdn.microsoft.com/vstudio/express` and click the link for SQL Server 2005 Express Edition. A product overview displays; scroll down the page to Free Management Tool, and click the Download SQL Server Management Studio Express link.

2. Under the Install SQL Server Management Studio Express heading, click the Download link. When the download is complete, open `SQLServer2005_SSMSEE.msi`. You may see a security warning — if you do, click Run. The Install Wizard appears, as shown in Figure A-9. Click Next.

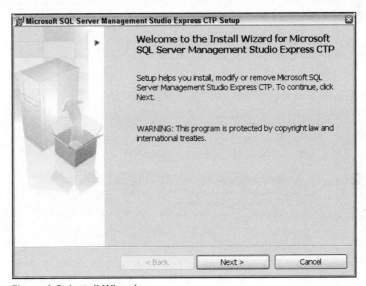

Figure A-9: Install Wizard

3. The next page contains a license agreement, which you must accept to continue. Click Next. Complete the registration information (you don't have to put in your full name if you don't want to; a single word will do) and click Next. The Feature Selection page (see Figure A-10) opens.

4. You don't have to make any changes to how the feature is installed. However, you can use the Disk Cost button in the Installation Path section to check that you have enough disk space for installation. Click Next.

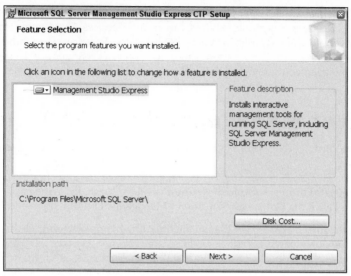

Figure A-10: Feature Selection page

5. The Install the Program page opens. Click Install. It may take a couple of minutes but you will see the progress of the installation, as shown in Figure A-11.

6. When the installation is complete, click Finish to exit.

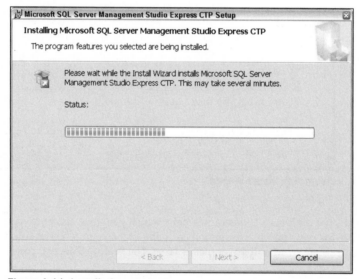

Figure A-11: Installation progress

Visual Web Developer 2005 Express Edition

To download and Install Visual Web Developer 2005 Express Edition, follow these steps:

1. Go to `http://msdn.microsoft.com/vstudio/express` and click the link for Visual Web Developer 2005 Express Edition. A product overview displays along with a feature tour and a Download Now link. Click Download Now; you're given a reminder about uninstallation, information about registration, and a download link. Click the link.

2. When the download completes, run `vwdsetup.exe`. You may see a security warning — if you do, click Run. A page appears telling you that the components are installing. Afterward, you have to accept the license agreement to continue. Then, click Next.

3. The Destination Folder page (see Figure A-12) opens.

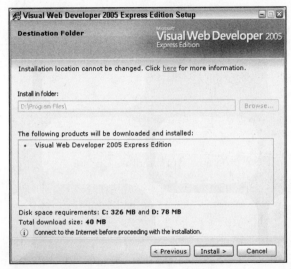

Figure A-12: The Destination Folder page

> Note the message saying that you can't change the destination folder. This is because Visual Web Developer has a dependency on C# Express so they must be installed in the same location. If you don't have enough space for Visual Web Developer in the same location as C# Express, you'll have to uninstall C# Express and reinstall it in a location that has enough space for both.

4. Click Install. The Download and Install Progress page, shown in Figure A-13, opens.

5. When the setup completes, you're informed that the installation was successful and that you must register the software. The instructions onscreen tell you how to do this.

   If you decide to register later (you have to register within 30 days), you can use the Register Product option on the Help menu.

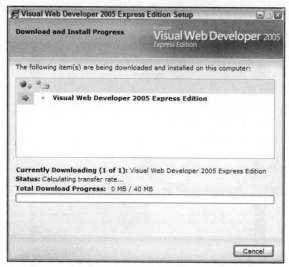

Figure A-13: Download and Install Progress page

To Finish

When you've installed all four programs, run Windows Update.

Help

I hope the installation process has gone smoothly and you now have all the programs you need. However, sometimes installations do fail on the first attempt. This appendix does not offer advice about possible problems because they are likely to be specific to the configuration of your computer. If you have any problems, use the error messages you receive to look for advice on the Microsoft web site.

B

Database Installation

This appendix contains instructions for downloading and installing the sample database used in this book. You can choose between two methods of installation:

❏   Installing database files

❏   Executing a SQL script

Both methods are easy, and the main difference between them is that you can use the SQL script to install the database on a remote server. However, there is one important point to note about using the SQL script method — if you already have the sample database installed, executing this script will overwrite it. This means that the database is returned to its original state and any changes you've made are lost.

If you want to restore the database to its default state you can either execute the SQL script or you can remove (or detach) your version of the database and reinstall the original version. You'll find information about how to detach the database at the end of the installation instructions.

Installing Database Files

1.   In the downloadable code for this book are two files called `FolktaleDB.mdf` and `FolktaleDB_log.ldf`. Copy these files to the default location for SQL Server databases. If you didn't change the default file path when you were installing SQL Server, the path should be `C\Program Files\Microsoft SQL Server\MSSQL.1\MSSQL\Data`.

2.   Open SQL Server Management Studio Express. Connect to your database server when prompted. Right-click Databases in the Object Explorer window and select Attach, as shown in Figure B-1.

3.   On the Add Databases page, click Add. Navigate to the `FolktaleDB.mdf` file, and select it, as shown in Figure B-2. (You don't need to find or select the `FolktaleDB_log.ldf` file because that will be copied automatically with the `.mdf` file.) Click OK.

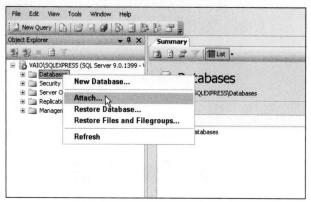

Figure B-1: Attaching a database file

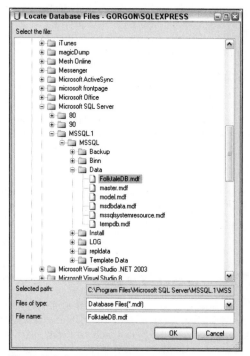

Figure B-2: Locating database files

4. The Attach Databases page displays the name and details of the FolktaleDB database, as illustrated in Figure B-3. Click OK.

The database is attached and ready to use.

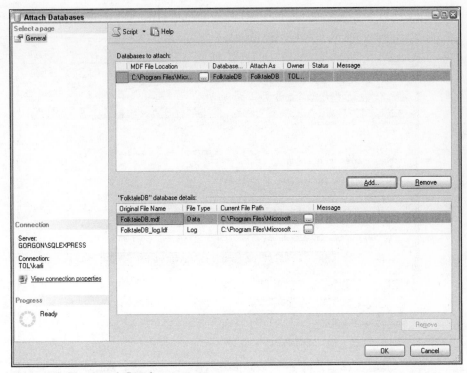

Figure B-3: The Attach Databases page

Executing a SQL Script

1. In the downloadable code for this book is a file called CreateFolktaleDB.sql. You can download it to any location on your computer and then simply double-click it.

2. The file opens in SQL Server Management Studio Express. Connect to your database server when prompted. (Note that the Object Explorer window doesn't open by default when you open a script file using this method.)

3. If you haven't installed SQL Server in the default location, change the file path in the SQL code. The file path information is highlighted in the following code:

```
CREATE DATABASE [FolktaleDB] ON PRIMARY
( NAME = N'FolktaleDB', FILENAME = N'C:\Program Files\Microsoft SQL Server\
MSSQL.1\MSSQL\Data\FolktaleDB.mdf' , SIZE = 3072KB , MAXSIZE = UNLIMITED,
FILEGROWTH = 1024KB )
 LOG ON
( NAME = N'FolktaleDB_log', FILENAME = N'C:\Program Files\Microsoft SQL
Server\MSSQL.1\MSSQL\Data\FolktaleDB_log.ldf' , SIZE = 1024KB , MAXSIZE =
2048GB , FILEGROWTH = 10%)
 COLLATE Latin1_General_CI_AS
GO
```

4. Click Execute on the toolbar. This may take a few moments. The results are shown in Figure B-4. The database is installed and ready to use.

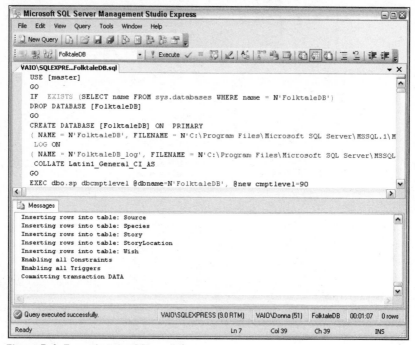

Figure B-4: Executing the SQL script

Detaching a Database

1. In the Object Explorer window, right-click the name of the database you want to detach. Select Tasks ⇨ Detach.

2. The Detach Databases page has the name of the database you've selected, as shown in Figure B-5. Click OK.

3. The database is now detached. Note that this doesn't delete the database files; they still exist in the same location but they are no longer loaded into SQL Server.

This is all straightforward, so let's hope you don't run into any problems. However, if you do, look in the MSDN documentation or go to http://p2p.wrox.com/ *for assistance.*

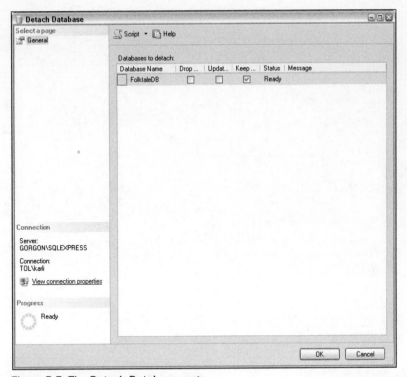

Figure B-5: The Detach Database page

Answers to Exercises

Chapter 1

Exercise 1 Solution

False. Primary keys are a useful aspect of database tables, but it is not mandatory to have them.

Exercise 2 Solution

Answers *a* and *d* are actual joins. Answers *b* and *c* are made up, and *e* occurs only in carpentry.

Exercise 3 Solution

Transactions.

Exercise 4 Solution

a. Nothing — although it will delete every row in the `MyTable` table, which might not be exactly what you intended.

b. This is a mix of insert statement syntax and update statement syntax. A correct insert statement of this form would be:

```
INSERT INTO MyTable (Title, Amount) VALUES ('Oysters', 17)
```

While a correct update statement would be:

```
UPDATE MyTable SET Title = 'Oysters', Amount = 17 WHERE ItemId = 3
```

Exercise 5 Solution

False. To make up a set of rows, the data in an XML document would have to be formatted in a way that mapped with table data, which might not always be the case. However, it is true that any XML document could be added to a SQL database table, although this is only the case if the entire document were added as a single column of a single row. It is also feasible that some process or transformation could be applied to an XML document to extract row data from it and place it into a table.

Chapter 2

Exercise 1 Solution

DbConnection and SqlConnection.

Exercise 2 Solution

False. It is possible to access data, both to read and modify it, using just command and data reader objects. In many circumstances, when performance is an issue and when you don't need the full power of the DataSet class, this is the preferred way to do things.

Exercise 3 Solution

Answers *b*, *c*, and *f* are ADO.NET objects. Data joining and deleting is achieved by command objects, and primary keys are represented by constraints.

Exercise 4 Solution

Because Visual C# Express is designed to work only with local database files. You might, however, use SSMSE to configure more general DBMS features such as security.

Exercise 5 Solution

I hope not. A lot of controls are available for data binding — you can bind data to just about any property of any control if you try hard enough. Yes, these controls are full of useful features, but at times they won't do what you want them to. You can, however, bind data to custom controls that you create using the data-binding framework supplied by ADO.NET.

Exercise 6 Solution

They are stored in the web.config file. This centralized storage is good news — if you want to change the connection for all the data-bound controls in a project, you have to change things in only one place, rather than having to search for hard-coded connection strings throughout your code. It is also easy to access this information from your applications — both in ASP.NET and C# code.

Chapter 3

Exercise 1 Solution

A connection string is a string that contains all the necessary information for a database, including the location of the DBMS, the database to connect to, and authentication credentials.

Exercise 2 Solution

You can add only those queries that return no result or a single result, not queries that return row sets. This applies to stored procedures that you might want to execute as well as SQL queries.

Exercise 3 Solution

Answer in downloadable chapter code.

Exercise 4 Solution

To some extent, yes, although the result you get won't always be what you want. Some types of data, in particular long text fields, are unsuitable for display in small spaces such as the cells provided by columns in a `DataGridView`. It is possible to improve things here, but at times this can require fairly extensive modifications to the functionality of the display, and quite a lot of custom code. This is not really a problem for day-to-day use, however, and the fact that you can make these modifications is a good thing — because it makes the control extremely flexible.

Chapter 4

Exercise 1 Solution

You can initialize data sources using either SQL statements or stored procedures.

Exercise 2 Solution

You should use the Copy If Newer option because you can quit the application and restart it to see if changes have persisted.

Exercise 3 Solution

You would make changes in the following order:

1. Add new rows and update existing rows to `TableA` — but don't delete any rows.
2. Add new rows and update existing rows to `TableB` — but don't delete any rows.
3. Add new rows and update existing rows to `TableC` — but don't delete any rows.
4. Make changes to `TableD` — additions, modifications, and deletions.
5. Delete rows from `TableC`.
6. Delete rows from `TableB`.
7. Delete rows from `TableA`.

Exercise 4 Solution

Answer in downloadable chapter code.

Exercise 5 Solution

You would handle the `Form.FormClosing` event.

Chapter 5

Exercise 1 Solution

Answers *a* and *e* are the only real reasons — security because the web and data servers can be secured separately, and flexibility because it's easy to move the database, change the database, and so on. Answer b counts in favor of local database files. Answer c is irrelevant — performance will be more or less the same in both situations, and is more likely to be affected by other factors. Answers d and f are meaningless — they will work exactly the same in both scenarios.

Exercise 2 Solution

There are two approaches to this: You can store filter settings either in a user's profile or in a cookie. The former has the advantage of working for whatever browser a user connects to your web application in, but does introduce additional complexity because site membership will have to be implemented. Using a cookie is simpler, but works only for a single browser — if the user connects from someone else's computer, the filter settings will be lost. Using session state is not an option here — that remembers settings for a single session only.

Exercise 3 Solution

Answers *a*, *d*, and *f* are real controls.

Exercise 4 Solution

Answer in downloadable chapter code.

Chapter 6

Exercise 1 Solution

False. The .NET Framework uses connection pooling to optimize data access. When you dispose of a connection it remains in the pool, and subsequent code that creates and opens connections may be handed a reference to the existing connection, thus reducing memory usage and increasing performance.

Exercise 2 Solution

You could use either the `SqlDataReader.GetSchemaTable()` method or the `SqlDataAdapter.FillSchema()` method, or you could create a typed `DataSet` graphically and inspect it.

Exercise 3 Solution

The most efficient way is to use a data reader, which doesn't involve populating a `DataSet`. Therefore, *a*, *c*, and *d* are the only classes you'd need.

Exercise 4 Solution

You would use a table mapping. Specifically, you would add a `TableMapping` object for the table to the data adapter, and then a `ColumnMapping` object specifying the source and desired column names.

Chapter 7

Exercise 1 Solution

All of them are valid reasons. Answer *b* (adding additional functionality) is perhaps debatable because you could add the same functionality in C# code, but I think it deserves a mention.

Exercise 2 Solution

Reasons include security settings applied to underlying data tables, use of joins restricting modification to one table in a join, calculated columns, aggregate functions, and use of the `DISTINCT` or `UNION` keywords.

Exercise 3 Solution

False. In fact, there are many situations in which parameterless stored procedures are useful indeed, and you can have anywhere between 0 and 2,100 parameters for a stored procedure.

Exercise 4 Solution

The following code creates a looping structure that emulates a C# `for` loop:

```
DECLARE @Counter int
DECLARE @MaxValue int

SET @Counter = 0
SET @MaxValue = 100

WHILE @Counter < @MaxValue
BEGIN
    -- Operation code
    SET @Counter = @Counter + 1
END
```

Exercise 5 Solution

The code for the sproc is as follows:

```
ALTER PROCEDURE [dbo].[GetLineage]
(
    @CharacterId uniqueidentifier,
    @Lineage varchar(8000) OUTPUT,
    @ReturnResult bit = 1,
    @Generations int = -1,
    @GenerationCount int = 0
)
AS
BEGIN
    SET NOCOUNT ON

    -- Local declarations
    DECLARE @RC int
    DECLARE @MotherName varchar(100)
    DECLARE @FatherName varchar(100)
    DECLARE @MotherId uniqueidentifier
    DECLARE @FatherId uniqueidentifier
    DECLARE @TempResult varchar(8000)
    DECLARE @NextGenerationCount int

    IF (@Generations = -1 OR @GenerationCount < @Generations)
    BEGIN

    -- Get initial information using sproc
    EXECUTE @RC = GetParents
        @CharacterId,
        @MotherId OUTPUT,
        @FatherId OUTPUT,
        @MotherName OUTPUT,
```

```
        @FatherName OUTPUT

    SET @Lineage = ''
    IF (@RC <> -1)
    BEGIN
        SET @NextGenerationCount = @GenerationCount + 1
        IF (@MotherId IS NOT NULL)
        BEGIN
            -- Add mother's name
            SET @Lineage = @Lineage + @MotherName

            -- Add mother's lineage
            EXEC GetLineage @MotherId, @TempResult OUTPUT, 0, @Generations,
                @NextGenerationCount
            IF (@TempResult <> '')
                SET @Lineage = @Lineage + ' (' + @TempResult + ')'
        END
        IF (@FatherId IS NOT NULL)
        BEGIN
            -- If mother as well, add comma
            IF (@MotherId IS NOT NULL)
                SET @Lineage = @Lineage + ', '

            -- Add father's name
            SET @Lineage = @Lineage + @FatherName

            -- Add father's lineage
            EXEC GetLineage @FatherId, @TempResult OUTPUT, 0, @Generations,
                @NextGenerationCount
            IF (@TempResult <> '')
                SET @Lineage = @Lineage + ' (' + @TempResult + ')'
        END
    END

    END

    -- Return result
    IF (@ReturnResult = 1)
        SELECT @Lineage AS Lineage
END
```

Chapter 8

Exercise 1 Solution

Answers *a*, *b*, and *e* are good reasons. Answer *c* isn't really an issue because database access must still occur somewhere along the line. However, you could argue the point here and say that data access is easier — but only for client applications or classes in the presentation tier. Answer *d* is silly, but might apply for résumés.

Exercise 2 Solution

When it is unnecessary, such as in small-scale applications. You should only implement a solution that is as complex as the task prescribes — there is no need to overcomplicate things.

Exercise 3 Solution

The short answer is: It depends. In many applications, ADO.NET classes and typed data sets will meet all of your requirements. However, for ultimate flexibility, you can't beat data-aware classes. In addition, data-aware classes are better for n-tier applications for many reasons, such as the capability to shield database access from client applications.

Exercise 4 Solution

Answer in Q0804 - Modified DataAwareObjects project in the downloadable code for this chapter. The following methods have been added:

```
public new IEnumerator<T> GetEnumerator()
{
    // Return only undeleted items.
    foreach (T item in this.AllItems())
    {
        if (!item.IsDeleted)
        {
            yield return item;
        }
    }
}

public IEnumerable<T> AllItems()
{
    // Return all items.
    return this;
}
```

Also, wherever code enumerates items, in TableCollection.AcceptChanges(), TableCollection.RejectChanges(), and TableDataAccess.SaveData(), code is modified to use the this.AllItems() enumerator.

Exercise 5 Solution

The IBindingList interface. No, you don't have to implement it — if you don't, it's used internally to provide a view of your data to data-binding controls. However, it is advisable to implement it because that gives you greater functionality including some useful events. The easiest way to implement it is to derive a class from the BindingList<T> generic collection class.

Exercise 6 Solution

By setting the DataKeyNames property of data-bound controls. This is necessary because otherwise it would be difficult or impossible for changes made to items in data-bound controls to be applied to your data.

Chapter 9

Exercise 1 Solution

Answers *a* and *d* are supported by ADO.NET. Answer *c* is possible using advanced techniques not covered in this book. Answer *e* is useful if your friends are habitually late for social events.

Exercise 2 Solution

You can either catch DBConcurrencyException exceptions or handle the
SqlDataAdapter.RowUpdated event.

Exercise 3 Solution

There are two ways of doing this:

❑   Use the RowUpdated event and set the ContinueUpdateOnError property of the data adapter
    to true, handling concurrency errors as they arise.

❑   Perform data adapter updates using a transaction, so that either all or no changes are made.

Exercise 4 Solution

```
CREATE PROCEDURE dbo.TransferBalance
(
    @SourceId uniqueidentifier,
    @TargetId uniqueidentifier,
    @Amount money
)
AS
BEGIN TRANSACTION

UPDATE CustomerBalance SET Balance = Balance - @Amount
    WHERE CustomerBalanceId = @SourceId
UPDATE CustomerBalance SET Balance = Balance + @Amount
    WHERE CustomerBalanceId = @TargetId

COMMIT TRANSACTION
```

Exercise 5 Solution

You can use Serializable, RepeatableRead, ReadCommitted, or Snapshot.

Chapter 10

Exercise 1 Solution

Answers *a, b, c,* and *d.* This is a trick question because they can all use web services if they have access to
the hosting location of the web service in question. The point is that web services can be extremely useful in all manner of applications.

Exercise 2 Solution

First you add a web reference to the application, which generates a proxy class; then you instantiate the
proxy class and call its methods. Additionally, you can (if you really want to) use lower level access and
send and receive SOAP messages to and from the web service endpoints. This is an advanced technique,
however, and not covered in this book.

Exercise 3 Solution

The simplest way to cache web method responses is to set the `CacheDuration` property when defining the web method — using the `WebMethod` attribute. However, this can lead to problems as changes to the database will not be reflected in the web method response.

Exercise 4 Solution

```
<caching>
 <sqlCacheDependency enabled="true">
  <databases>
    <add name="Dep1" connectionStringName="ConnectionString1" pollTime="1000" />
    <add name="Dep2" connectionStringName="ConnectionString2" pollTime="10000" />
  </databases>
 </sqlCacheDependency>
</caching>
```

Exercise 5 Solution

You would detect the `DatabaseNotEnabledForNotificationException` exception when attempting to do anything with SQL dependencies with that database. One way of forcing it to happen is to use the `GetTablesEnabledForNotifications()` method, which also allows you to detect whether individual tables are enabled for SQL dependency notifications.

Exercise 6 Solution

In `SqlDataSource` objects you could separate database/table pairs by semicolons. Programmatically, you would use a `AggregateCacheDependency` object containing multiple `SqlCacheDependency` objects.

Chapter 11

Exercise 1 Solution

Answers *b*, *c*, and *e* are correct. Views can be emulated using table-valued functions or stored procedures, but because views are really just stored SELECT statements there is no real justification for being able to create them in C#. Table types don't exist, so you can't create them in C# either.

Exercise 2 Solution

The steps are as follows:

1. Enable SQL Server for CLR integration, and for running non-SAFE code if necessary.
2. Create an assembly containing the code you want to integrate.
3. Load the assembly into SQL Server.
4. Register the classes and/or methods you want to use as appropriate.

If you use Visual Studio, Steps 3 and 4 can be replaced with the alternative step "Deploy the assembly into SQL Server."

Exercise 3 Solution

You would use ADO.NET, just like other .NET applications. There are some differences, however, and you have the opportunity to use context connections to use in-process, direct access to database data.

Exercise 4 Solution

You would use the `SqlContext.Pipe.Send()` method with a `SqlDataRecord` parameter. The code required to send the requested row is as follows:

```
SqlMetaData column1 = new SqlMetaData("MyTableId", SqlDbType.UniqueIdentifier);
SqlMetaData column2 = new SqlMetaData("MyAmount", SqlDbType.Int);
SqlDataRecord row = new SqlDataRecord(column1, column2);
row.SetSqlGuid(0, new SqlGuid(Guid.NewGuid()));
row.SetSqlInt32(1, new SqlInt32(42));
SqlContext.Pipe.Send(row);
```

Exercise 5 Solution

The attribute to use is `SqlUserDefinedAggregate`, and the mandatory property is `Format`. If the value of this property is `Format.UserDefined`, you will have to implement the `IBinarySerialize` interface; if it is `Format.Native`, you can use only value types to store state.

Index